# 'A
# GLORIOUS
# ACCIDENT'

# 'A GLORIOUS ACCIDENT'

## Understanding Our Place in the Cosmic Puzzle

FEATURING

**Oliver Sacks • Stephen Jay Gould**

**Daniel C. Dennett • Freeman Dyson**

**Rupert Sheldrake • Stephen Toulmin**

WIM KAYZER

W. H. FREEMAN AND COMPANY
*New York*

Cover Design: Michael Minchillo
Text Designer: Blake Logan


Dit boek kwam tot stand in samenwerking met de VPRO, die de gelijknamige
televisieserie in januari 1993 uitzond.
©1995 Uitgeverij Contact
©1995 Nederlandse vertaling Uitgeverij Contact
D/1993/0108/540
ISBN 90 254 0725 0
NUGI 6II
CIP

ISBN 0-7167-3144-4
Published in the United States in 1997 by W. H. Freeman and Company,
41 Madison Avenue, New York, NY 10010. First published in The Netherlands by
Uitgeverij Contact, 1995.

Printed in the United States of America

First U.S. printing, 1997

# CONTENTS

# PREFACE

## Too Many, Too Deep,
## Too Unanswerable Questions?

This book deals with more issues than one person could think of in seven lifetimes, but the idea behind it is of breathtaking simplicity.

One languid summer night, I wrote down some questions on the back of an old hotel bill, for no reason except to kill a little time.

Why do some bamboos flower only once every 120 years, and how do they count the passing of the years?

Why do we call grass green?

How can someone love Rilke and Beethoven with all his heart, and at the same time butcher people as methodically as if he were stamping forms?

How does a homing pigeon, released hundreds of miles from its loft, find its way back to those few square inches?

Was the appearance of our consciousness in an insignificant group of monkeys swinging through the trees intentional, pure chance, or an accident?

Will there really be a time when we can download our consciousness in a computer and achieve immortality?

Why is it that, to quote my beloved Immanuel Kant, at one and the same time our existence can seem as majestic as it seems ridiculous.

On the back of the cigar box that was next to the hotel bill, I then wrote down six names out of five billion, names that seemed to flow automatically out of the random list of questions.

There appeared the name of Stephen Jay Gould, the humorous and intriguing paleontologist and evolutionary theorist, the inexhaustible science popularizer, who keeps insisting and proving that evolution has no direction, that it knows no improvement, only change, and that our consciousness is little more than an evolutionary accident.

I put down the name of Freeman Dyson, the almost otherworldly physicist, "the eclectic mathematician-physicist-idea-factory," as the *New York Times* has described him; a man fascinated by space travel, by the prospect of humankind spreading throughout the universe; a man who, after a glittering career, appears to embrace only one adage: "It is as Haldane says: the universe is not only weirder than we have ever imagined it, it is even weirder than we *can* imagine."

Next on the cigar box appeared the name of Oliver Sacks, the hesitant, intriguing psychiatrist and neurologist who is fascinated by the workings of our brain and particularly by its defects; a man who views the brain as a self-ordering world that is largely beyond our control: "The brain is not a computer, it is an orchestra of a thousand musicians; it is a work of art."

Below these names appeared that of Stephen Toulmin, the erudite but shy historian and philosopher of science, who emphasizes at every turn that after three centuries of modern scientific endeavor we have run aground like a ship on the shore, particularly with respect to explanations of our consciousness. "We know a great deal, that much is true, but that is not the same as understanding."

Next up was the name of the philosopher Daniel C. Dennett, who insists on a materialist view of life, and who is convinced that eventually we will unravel the mechanics of our consciousness. After that, we will be able to put our consciousness into computers, "which then we will obviously have to give human rights."

The sixth name to appear on the cigar box, as if inextricably tied to the others, was that of Rupert Sheldrake, the kind biochemist who has devised the theory of morphic resonance, which, if correct, would make him the next Darwin and Einstein rolled into one, or if not, a scientific charlatan of the New Age generation. One thing is sure: he can expect a skeptical reception from the others.

One evening in my mind's eye I saw these six men sitting together. Yes, I saw others in my mind's eye, some already deceased, some still alive, but my thoughts kept returning to these six.

It was one of those empty summer nights; nothing particular to do or to think about, an evening when the mind is blown in every direction. I heard their voices, I imagined their arguments. Which one would be a smoker? I saw them gesticulate. Who would be taciturn? Who would be nostalgic? Who a dreamer? Who would be dogged? Who would unexpectedly win the argument?

One question above all occupied my mind. The differences of opinion were clear, but what would these six men agree upon, if anything?

That was the question with which I embarked upon 'A Glorious Accident.'

In hindsight it is tempting to offer profound reasons, but the entire glorious accident sprang forth from one thing: a daydream on a languid summer night.

It was a preposterous idea. Perhaps I could persuade some of them to be interviewed, but the idea that they could be brought together at one moment in time was ridiculous. Some of them, such as Gould and Sacks, were almost neighbors and had written about each other but had never met face to face. Could one letter from an unknown Dutchman change that?

"This is an exquisite occasion to meet some people I have long wanted to talk to," Freeman Dyson wrote back.

"Whatever happens, it will be a wonderful adventure," wrote Oliver Sacks. "You are approaching some very exciting people who can come at fundamental questions from all angles."

"What a company!" Stephen Toulmin wrote. "I would always regret it if I said no."

"I desperately want to meet Oliver Sacks," Gould wrote. "I see him as a brother, but we've never met. If all your invitees agreed, I would be strongly tempted. That is quite a lineup."

"The idea behind this roundtable is so obvious that no one so far has thought of it," Daniel Dennett responded. "I will certainly come."

Rupert Sheldrake, too, was eagerly looking forward to the roundtable, if only to see if he could convince one of the five scientific hardliners of his theory of morphic resonance.

(Afterward he wrote to me: "After the extraordinary meeting I spent a fairly sleepless night with my mind racing, thinking of things I would like to have said but didn't—especially in relation to Dan Dennett's theory of the mind."

Why did I choose these people above others? Was there not a profound consideration behind my choice, even if the names seemed to have come to be at random?

In hindsight one can always offer elegant explanations for one's actions; with hindsight one might even agree with the critic who wrote that "this company was an intriguing reflection of three centuries of Western scientific thought, with a tuft of New Age on top."

In hindsight it is easy to endorse Oliver Sacks's words: "It was quite an extraordinary meeting for the seven of us, a wild, strange and significant experience. And even if 'the meaning of life' didn't come out, at least we covered, explored, a great range of topics. All of us emerged changed from our exchange, and perhaps we will have some impact on watchers and readers, if only in giving a sense of how vast and how mysterious everything still is."

In hindsight one might endorse the views of the *New York Times*: "The scientists bring to it a good measure of thought and imagination, telling stories, avoiding jargon, and on occasion dangling from fragile branches with very little scientific evidence to back up their delightful speculations."

In hindsight one might also agree with John Leonard of *New York* magazine, whose description of the entire glorious accident was downright euphoric:

> What a splendid time the scientists have—kicking around everything from memory to free will, from consciousness to vegetarianism, from natural selection to artificial intelligence, from the Big Bang to the Holocaust. . . . Not since the gods and mortals last had dinner together, at the marriage of Cadmus and Harmony—after which they had to invent an alphabet to write the history of grief—has there been such a highbrow confab, nor such an adjournment of minds. . . . I'm not about to synopsize here their contentious bickerings about Descartes, Wittgenstein, and Stephen Hawking, visual cortex "dreaming," immortality by database, and "morphic resonance"; astrochickens and Martian potatoes and biological electronics; contingency and morality, culture and progress, baseball and homing pigeons, robots and snails. They know so much and agree on so little and all cite poets. It is an orgy of talking heads that is almost Wagnerian. . . . Snap, crackle, pop: On '*A Glorious Accident,*' the elevator goes all the way to the top floor, where all the lights are on.

In hindsight, everything is true.

In hindsight, again, Daniel Dennett's question seems obvious. "Why did it surprise you so much that our scientific careers are extensions of our childhood questions that have still not been resolved?"

But in the beginning? In the beginning only one thing was clear.

*We are such stuff as dreams are made on, and our little lives are rounded with a sleep.*

Seemingly at random, I took that quote from Shakespeare as the motto for the invitation that I began to write to the men because on that summer night I had nothing else to do. From their replies I gleaned that the letter was somewhat irrelevant: they agreed to participate largely because they wanted to meet each other. Yet in hindsight it did play a role, if only because the questions that I posed in it were later answered in often unexpected ways. As an illustration, let me quote from it:

> Dear Sir:
>
> The guiding principle for '*A Glorious Accident*' is briefly one question: What are the concepts that our consciousness has so far developed about our curious existence in space and in time, and what will we derive most from them, knowledge or understanding? All right, with cheerful determinism we have blown reality to smithereens. Certainly we have let loose innumerable axioms and ideas on the question of what our apparently unique consciousness is, exactly. Yes, in all animals, neurosynapses, genes, formulas, and daydreams we try to dissect ourselves to this end in order to exchange views with each of these phenomena patiently and wholeheartedly.

But to what understanding has this dizzying analysis brought us in the long run at the end of our fascinating but equally sinister twentieth century?

Does every answer we find or construct always and with discouraging regularity extend into the quadrature of the question that was its origin, or are we on the threshold of an era in which we may finally end the currently so mysterious dichotomy between "content" and "process"?

This is not the place to anticipate the questions (which each of you may add to or rephrase to his heart's content). The theme of '*A Glorious Accident,*' however, may also be defined more directly and more personally. "To the question about the meaning of life everybody answers with the story of his own life," wrote the Hungarian author Konrád.

Well, then. What were the questions that fascinated you when you were growing up? Which of those questions have been left intact by time? What questions keep you spellbound today? Are they not—partly at least—the same fascinations of your early days?

The discussion among you is both the backbone of the narrative and its precondition. I am well aware of the time that this will take, but without that discussion, which at this point I would like to describe as an attempt at symbiosis, the enterprise seems rather pointless.

"We sit together and talk and become enthusiastic, and our eyes light up and our voices are raised; just like this, others talked a thousand years ago. The subjects were the same and the players were the same. It will be like this again in another thousand years. The mechanism that prevents us from realizing this is time," wrote Arthur Schopenhauer. The roundtable may prove or disprove his statement.

The first to write back, almost immediately, was Stephen Jay Gould: "I think that you're asking too many, too deep, too unanswerable questions. There's such a thing as too direct an assault upon eternity—and it is not mere paltriness of spirit to point this out."

Too many? Too deep? Too unanswerable?

In hindsight, was Gould's reaction the true motto for the entire enterprise? I doubt it, but I leave you to decide.

WIM KAYZER

# ACKNOWLEDGEMENTS

'A Glorious Accident' could not have been realized without the inspiration and the efforts of Daniel C. Dennett, Freeman Dyson, Stephen Jay Gould, Oliver Sacks, Rupert Sheldrake, and Stephen Toulmin. I provided them with the opportunity, but they took the best possible advantage of it. I thank them for their scientific discourse, but perhaps even more for not hiding their personal motives behind their quest for truth. Giants though they may be in their various scientific disciplines, they proved modest indeed about their personal motivations. It was most refreshing.

'A Glorious Accident' would not have been realized either without the inspiration from my dearest friend Roelof Kiers, now sadly deceased, former director of programs at VPRO television, under whose authority this project was produced for television in Holland. I also thank Gertjan Wallinga, who originally edited the interviews and the forum into book form. He was also my guardian angel on my journeys, and who coupled friendship with humor. When I could see no way forward, he was always convinced that we were on the right track. And vice versa. I must not omit Nellie Kamer. I dearly love people who arrange the impossible and then, when you want to thank them, just respond: "That was nothing special. Why don't you find me something hard to do?"

I thank Elizabeth Knoll for her excellent work on the final edition of this book; and Holly Hodder for her inspiring commitment to its realization.

"Why are you so surprised that our work is an extension of the children's questions which remain unanswered?" Daniel Dennett asked me after completion of the project. Of course I should been reminded of the questions that fascinated me when I was young. In fact, I was reminded of my four children, Eva, Marieta, Károly and Merlijn. Their questions probably were a more important source of inspiration for 'A Glorious

*Accident'* than I would like to believe. It takes time and effort to admit that the best upbringing—often harsh, but sometimes unexpectedly kind—comes not from one's parents, but from one's successors. I know that at least four of the six gentlemen in '*A Glorious Accident'* will agree with me on that.

# PART I

# THE

# INTERVIEWS

# CHAPTER 1

# MIGRAINE

## Oliver Sacks

Thus these patients, some of whom had been thrust into
the remotest or strangest extremities of human possibility,
experienced their states with unsparing perspicacity, and
retained the power to remember, to compare, to dissect
and to testify. Their fate, so to speak, was to become
unique witnesses to a unique catastrophe.

We will talk for hours, on the twelfth floor of a New York building with a vague and misty view of the harbor. Sacks, with a mild case of claustrophobia and the ever-present danger of migraine, wants the window open. Every now and then the psychiatrist and neurologist gets up and scurries confusedly through the room, sometimes mumbling to himself as if continuing the conversation on his own.

Do we find ourselves in New York? That is far from certain.

Just before our meeting, Oliver Sacks has learned that a friend of his youth, a man who was like a twin brother to him, has died. Tomorrow he will have to hurry back to England, where he was born and where he roamed the stunningly charming Hampstead Heath with that friend, to bury not only his friend but, so he claims, also part of himself.

As I drive to his house on Sunday morning through New York, ever fascinating, pompous, and threatening, I feel apprehensive. Dozens of subjects are on my list of questions: the stupefying tricks and unexpected possibilities of consciousness; Sacks's childhood; *Awakenings*, that unsurpassed book about the victims of the "sleeping disease" (encephalitis lethargica), which emerged in Vienna in 1916 and soon spread throughout the world, that staggering account of a group of patients who were stuck for forty years in a state of pathological lethargy, speechless, motionless, and catatonic, but who were brought back to life when Sacks gave them L-dopa. I want to talk at length about these things and about the unique world of the deaf and deaf-mute, about language, about the curious and the unpredictable, which influence our consciousness more deeply than Sacks ever thought.

But his friend has died. I expect that he won't feel like an extended verbal excursion along the outer edges of our consciousness.

That apprehension proves unfounded. Sacks talks almost eagerly about his youth in Hampstead. The memories and the images are at the ready, activated by the death of his friend. "Can I say a word about death?" he asks unexpectedly. Without prompting he starts talking about his friend. About mortality, that ridiculous flip side of our otherwise so majestic life.

4

*Do you always use a typewriter?*

Either that or I write by hand. Never computers. I'm computer illiterate. I'm afraid I might just erase everything I do. I like the mechanical heaviness of this typewriter, but most of all I like to write by hand.

*To feel the stream of consciousness going through your fingers.*

Yeah. You see, I often do little pictures as well, and I write in different colors. Sometimes little diagrams like this. Basically I travel everywhere with pen and paper. All my books were written like this. In my house you'd, see a whole roomful of these. I have my notebook with me now for a study of a patient of mine, a gifted Parkinsonian mathematician/artist who feels that his consciousness has altered from having Parkinson's, in a way that has driven him into art. It's a highly abstract and conceptual art. He also designs furniture of a complex and eccentric sort, which looks sort of both stable and unstable, the way he feels. His condition makes him see space and time, as well as the relations of things and their weight and their balance, so differently that the world can no longer be taken for granted. He feels he is in an unstable world, which demands exact algebraic and geometrical analysis, both in his own person and in whatever he represents. So it is a much more analyzed world, and a much more precarious and much more defended world, both in himself and in his art.

*Immanuel Kant once wrote that this universe is as majestic as it is ridiculous. Do you feel any kinship with this approach to reality?*

I think I often find one, and often the other. Often both. Kant was also divided between a sense of the majesty of cosmic law and the majesty of the moral law inside us. I think the kinship I feel most, and which has probably been most important in the history of science, is Kant's notion that our perceptions are all constituted according to psychic laws. He took these laws to be a priori laws of space and time. I don't agree with that, but there is certainly no raw perception. I think that everything is structured from within.

*You once had a crisis like Hume, which drove you toward Kant. What kind of crisis was that, and to what extent did Kant solve your problems?*

Well, I think that sometimes neurological problems can become philosophical problems, and that one can have a kind of neurophilosophical emergency. I felt I had been thrown into such an emergency after I'd had an accident some years ago. I was climbing in Norway and I injured the nerves and muscles of one leg. I lost the use of the leg, and I lost the sense that the leg was mine. It seemed alien to me. It was also difficult to recollect its normality. There seemed to be a sort of discontinuity between the self who had the accident, who ran and jumped and climbed, and this object I had with me now. It seemed to me in a sense that the leg had disappeared, taking its memory, its time, and also its space with it. This sort of thing can occur in other circumstances. Sometimes if one has a spinal anaesthetic, you not only lose feeling and movement—say below the waist—but you lose yourself. You end at the waist, and what lies below is nothing. And although you know the anaesthetic will wear off in a few hours, yet in some sense you cannot believe it. Similarly for me the leg disappeared, taking its time and space with it, which made me think that time and space must therefore be essential for perceiving one's own body, and that one's own body is constructed in terms of a personal time and space. It was precisely this that Kant, I think, was the first to talk about. The empiricists like Locke and Hume simply talk about impressions, as if those were complete in themselves, whereas here it was clear that the impressions had to be organized in time and space, and also organized in reference to myself. And therefore the notion of self and inner time and space became central, and I turned to Kant to look for some sense.

*But you had seen these kinds of experiences before. What was the difference when you experienced it yourself?*

I had never known what it was like for the patient. I would be sympathetic and intelligent, and yet at some level the experience was unintelligible to me. Similarly, I feel that my own experience, which I describe in the leg book [*A Leg to Stand On*], will be unintelligible to readers, and in an afterword I do in fact suggest that the readers read the book under spinal anaesthesia themselves, so they'll know what I'm talking about. But things like that throw one back on the limits of the imagination, and how far imagination itself is constrained by the body.

*Dennett says; "We are all faced with the baffling phenomenon: how could anything be more familiar but at the same time more weird than the mind?" Did your missing leg give you a feeling comparable to that "baffling phenomenon"?*

A good friend of mine, Jonathan Miller, wrote a book called *The Body in Question*, and if he hadn't already used that title, I might have used it myself instead of *A Leg to Stand On*. Normally the body is not in question. It is transparent and obedient, the instrument of one's desires, one's will, one's perceptions. The body does not present itself as an object, opaque. Here part of my body was presenting itself to me as a thing. Certainly if one experiences one's body as this heavy, clayey, doughy, lumpy, lumpish thing, one would have to think in terms of a dualism. What I was seeing here was the body without mind. Here was a leg without its nerve supply, not under control of the will. This is not how one ever encounters the body normally. So the leg had to be reconstituted as a psychic construct. Before that was possible, it had to have recovered sufficiently neurologically and neurally. It seemed to me that there were two stages in its neural and psychic return. When I first put some weight on the leg, it seemed to me to be of all different sizes and to jump around. The ground seemed very far away and then very close. I had to walk by vision, by keeping an eye on the leg. At that point I was really still treating it as an object, and not as part of myself. Later I felt oddly starved of music. I felt I had lost the music, the kinetic melody of my own movement and walking. And then it came back to me. When Kant speaks about time as the inner form of sense, I found myself equating this with music. It was as if I needed some sort of exterior measurement to get the spatial dimensions, and then a temporal one.

*I would like to talk particularly about memory. Perhaps you will allow me to go back to your own childhood in Hampstead, London. What kind of fantasies did you have in your childhood, what kind of questions did you ask yourself?*

I loved to play as a child—I think I like to play now—and Hampstead Heath was a marvelous place to climb trees, to hide, to play games with others. It's a marvelous place for someone who likes plants and for its historical associations. From Hampstead Heath you can look out on a vista that was there in Roman London.

Many of my uncles and cousins were mathematicians and geologists and physical scientists, and I imagined that at one time I might be something like that myself. I think it was a place where I had sort of scientific fantasies. Once when I was on Hampstead Heath, I went and knocked on the door of Julian Huxley, who lived just by Hampstead Heath. I think he was very surprised. I was ushered in, and this rather precocious dirty little twelve-year-old boy said; "Professor Huxley, I have some questions about evolution." I said I didn't see how man could have evolved so quickly by natural selection. And he said, "Yes, that's not just nature, there's culture as well." That was pretty much the sum of the conversation.

*Did his answer satisfy you? That is to say, culture generating a range of genetically inheritable behaviors?*

Well, I think it was mystifying. Probably at that time I was interested in botany and zoology, and not terribly much with being human. I have probably been facing the real meaning of his answer only relatively recently, when I've thought of the power of language and the development of language, which has only been in the last forty or fifty thousand years.

My first love in science was not biology, I think, but chemistry. I remember going to the science museum when I was ten, and seeing the periodic table up there with the families of elements. I had an overwhelming feeling of this being eternally and necessarily true. I thought that further knowledge would simply serve to deepen the propriety of this tabulation; that this was not an artificial human tabulation, it was actually the way things were. I had a little laboratory at home, and I used to collect the elements, amongst other things. I had a strange collection of bus tickets. At that time bus tickets used to have letters and numbers, and I would try to get the symbol for the element plus a reasonable atomic number, so if I got Hg 210, this was the isotope of mercury, with an atomic number of 210. But there had been a period of great disorder and distress in the war, when I was evacuated, along with many of my generation, and I became uncertain of everything. Science, and the periodic table in particular, seemed to me to stand for stability and order. Now, all these years later, this sense of order is coming back to me in a different form, and perhaps with new questions—or not so much new questions, but maybe new answers or new formulations that couldn't have imagined. I think some of the most exciting discoveries now have to do with the way the universe orders itself at every level, from the cosmic to the biological. So I do partly feel I am the same as that ten-year-old. I am still looking for some sort of order, but an order that's created autonomously and spontaneously in the universe, not one that has a sort of external, divine or Platonic archetype.

*If you were me, at this moment, asking Oliver Sacks questions about his childhood and wanting to evoke that strongest memory all at once, where would you start? Smells, words, images?*

Smells. I suspect some of one's first memories are smells. I think one might also be able to locate them in time. I always have an aching resonance when I go to France. I think it may be because when I was twelve months old and again when I was twenty-four months old the family spent a month on a farm. Somehow the smells of the farm seem to me to be home in a very deep sense, they seem to ground me. What else? I grew up in a house that was very full of music. My parents and my brothers all played the piano. Especially Bach. There was an Italian teacher, Ticciatti. The air was full of two-part inventions and three-part inventions, and I would hear Ticciatti shouting: "No, no, no!" He was sort of like Toscanini. Both of my parents loved Schubert songs, although neither of them really had a voice.

*Do you still remember the Schubert songs?*

Yes, very much so. I got converted to Schubert songs in 1968, when Dietrich Fischer-Dieskau was in New York. I went every night and I simultaneously feel in love with him, with his voice, with Schubert. . . . I couldn't distinguish one from the other. It was only later that I remembered how important Schubert had been in my childhood. A lot of those things come back now. I have a passion for ferns. But then at home in London, the garden was full of ferns. Ferns were important. In a way, it's both surprising and not surprising that those things that were so important in childhood are important still.

Yes, for instance smells. I remember you quoted a poem: "They haven't got no noses, the fallen sons of Eve. Oh, for the happy smell of water, the brave smell of a stone." I think smells have more power of resonance, evocation, and association than anything else. Interestingly—this is something I'm looking at at the moment and I have written about—even in people who have amnesia and lose everything else, I think the memories of smells escape the amnesia. The memories of smells are robust neurologically; they cannot be deleted. I think one loses visual and auditory images relatively easily. But smells go through a very archaic part of the brain. What interested me, for example, is that when I took out an amnesiac patient of mine one evening, the only things that remained in his mind were the smell of pretzels, and, when we got to the Grateful Dead concert, the smell of hash. So I think smells are immensely powerful. Sometimes in the aftermath of a migraine or an epileptic seizure, there is a powerful smell. I've sometimes had such an olfactory aura myself with a migraine. There was an overwhelming smell of hot buttered toast. Now, the first time this happened, I was at the hospital, and I went everywhere looking for that hot buttered toast. The second time it happened, I was out on the freeway, a hundred miles from nowhere. And it was associated with an image of myself as a two-year-old child, about to be put on a high chair for tea. The smell of hot buttered toast goes far back.

I think also that the memory of music is robust neurologically. You can see this often in old people, or demented people perhaps, who may have lost the use of language and much of their conceptual ability, but music is still there. An old song will bring back the time it was performed and the whole world and the identity of its performers.

*But you write that smell is more important even than music.*

One of the pieces I wrote in the hat book [*The Man Who Mistook His Wife for a Hat*] is about a young man who in an abnormal, probably drug-induced state had a sudden enormous heightening, enhancement, of his sense of smell. He could recognize people by smell. He could locate where he was in the streets by smell. And he felt himself to be in a smell world, like a dog. He found the world extremely vivid and full of emotion, very intense and commanding. At the same time he found abstract thought rather difficult. And when after three weeks he returned to his human state and lost this tremendous heightening of sense and above all the heightening of smell, he felt that as both a loss and a relief. But in general this seems to be a sort of allegory of some of the deep biological things which I think we are in danger of forgetting or renouncing in being human.

*Sometimes a lullaby or a certain play of light or a fragrance comes to your mind and suddenly in a split second your entire childhood comes back to you. My question is: Where is this all stored?*

First, I don't think anything is stored in that sort of way. And I'm not sure that the notion of a store is the right one.

*The brain is not a library.*

No, it's not a library, it's not a granary, it's not a computer. Anything that happens comes into the mind again always in a different context, in a different construction. So memory is close to imagination. And I think memories are constructions and not Xeroxes, not facsimiles, not reproductions. Whatever comes into the mind always comes in a new context, and in some sense colored by the present. One sees this very clearly in court, for example. Every witness will give you a different account. Every account is constructed. We have no way of saying what the objective situation is.

*So memory is not a dead book in a library, it is alive along with us throughout our lives, and it grows up with us.*

Yes. Although perhaps when we talk about "cherishing memories," that may be something very different. When Goethe was eighty, someone got up and made a toast to memory. And the old man got very angry and he said, "I don't recognize memory as you put it. One is not allowed to pine for the past. Everything significant that has happened is incorporated into oneself and with this one grows." So memory is part of this growing, of identity. But sometimes this doesn't occur. I have recently been seeing an artist, born in a little village in Italy, who is obsessed with images of his village as it was before he was nine years old. When he was nine, the Germans came and a lot of the village was destroyed. I want to show you something. He hasn't seen that village in forty years. This is a memory painting of a scene in the village, and this is a photograph of it taken forty years later. Now, I think something like this is both prodigious and pathological. Because here it is as though the unfaded memories of childhood are still very, very active in him, dominating. In a strange way, this man is divided. He hasn't quite grown into a normal, integrated being. One part of him is still a child in that little village.

Of course he brings to the reproduction of that memory the technical powers and fluency of an adult, an artist. And yet I think this is the child's vision. But I'm not sure. I'm not sure whether he is a genius or a strange sort of casualty. Perhaps he is both. Perhaps unintegrated memories of this vividness are necessary for art in some ways. For someone like Joyce or Proust, the memories of childhood are woven into a theory of life and a theory of the world. Joyce always goes back to Dublin, but Dublin becomes the Dublin of Bloom's day and finally becomes the cosmic backdrop of *Finnegans Wake*. Whereas here, this little village is somehow fossilized by memory, idealized, eternalized, and protected, as it were, from the processes of growth and becoming. It is not quite alive. Or it is no longer alive, or it is alive only in a strange sort of cherished way.

*That reminds me of your writing that we have a basic feeling that we once were healthy and in harmony with the world. We once found ourselves in an arcadian state. At some moment we lost that primeval state of innocence and bliss, and since then each of us will spend his lifetime trying to recapture that lost arcadia. I wondered, is that just a metaphor? What is this lost arcadia?*

That is a very good association. I hadn't made it myself when I saw this man. Perhaps we all have fantasies of paradise, of a place without sin, without lapse, without tension, possibly even without sexuality. And a place where one is loved. This artist is at pains to say that what he draws is partly a fantasy of the village as it was in childhood, not entirely a memory. And that some of the untidiness and the distress and the dirt of reality have been removed. But of course we would not have survived— not any of us—biologically had we not been deeply loved and cared for in the first years of life. And I think part of this idyllic world has to do with being loved and cared for. One seeks to reproduce it one way or another. You see this with Peer Gynt, who's with Ase and his mother for so long, but then in Solvejg he sort of finds his mother again. Though I think the human figures may undergo a sublimation or whatever the word is, so that one in fact tries to reconstitute an ideal universe.

I was a little distressed this morning when a friend and colleague of mine was talking about the jealousy and the rivalries and the commercialism at a large scientific institute. He said to his companion; "Oliver doesn't want to hear this." And it was true, I didn't want to hear it, because I like to imagine that in science and in the scientific life there can be some regaining of that imagined idyllic purity and transparency of childhood.

*Is this the dualism you wrote about? On the one hand you are a scientist and on the other there is the romantic Sacks. How do you manage to live with the two of them?*

Well, I think there is a proper romantic science. But what I refer to there is probably not romantic but sentimental, which is different. It's sentiment, for example, that made me want—at one time, when I first wrote some of the case histories of *Awakenings*, in 1969—to give them happy endings. That would have been sentimental. But I think the romantic impulse and the scientific impulse can very often go together.

The romantic impulse is some feeling for the whole, for the aesthetic unity and dramatic unity and perhaps a vision of nature which can include oneself. Once at Mount Carmel I was being observed by a young man through this object like a little telescope. On the one hand, it seemed as if a scientific observation of some sort was being made through a theodolite. On the other hand, it also seemed to be a pleasant, affectionate look. I felt I was being beheld and at the same time inspected, in a way that seemed to me very romantic and scientific.

But to say that they can come together . . . There is a very interesting passage in Darwin's autobiography, where he says that as a young man he loved music, painting, and poetry very much. But then he laments that it seems to him that with the practice of science his mind has become a sort of machine for extracting general laws from large volumes of data, and that with this he has lost his love of poetry and painting and music. One might say that in a way he is lamenting the loss of a romantic dimension in himself through the scientific habit. But I don't think that's fair, because in fact one sees, especially in the late Darwin, his love of phenomena and his love of his subjects, in great measure, for example, in his book on orchids. It's the most exquisite scientific study of the fertilization of orchids, but the book is close to poetry. His book about worms is another wonderful example. Interestingly, this partly goes with the science. I think that his pre-evolution books, such as his four volumes on barnacles, to some extent represent a sort of relatively dull scientific catalog. The great unifying theory that made sense of it all has not yet come. But I think both the unifying theory and some sort of love that could hold everything together came together. So I think that the post-1859 books are richer, much more unified.

*Let's come back to memory again. Where does memory start? In childhood? In the womb? Before? Or even before conception? Freud talked about little children possessing phylogenetic information—that is, their memories dated from far back in history. You have seen people with phylogenetic memories. Where do our first memories really come from?*

One is certainly not born as a blank slate. We're little demons, organisms, animals, creatures. We're full of instincts and impulses. We are strongly primate and anthropoid and hominid, right from day one, and probably in utero as well. And clearly, whatever part experience plays in our life, it plays in relation to what is already innate.

*How much of us in innate?*

Something I have seen in some of my patients has to do with the appearance of behaviors that would seem not to have been learned in the course of life in the ordinary way—indeed, they sometimes appear not to be human. Some of my post-encephalitic patients, when they'd been put on L-dopa, instead of taking a cup and drinking or even slurping like this, they would lap from a saucer. I was astonished when I saw that. And the people who showed that behavior were astonished and somewhat mortified. They felt that something primitive had taken over. Sometimes in multiple sclerosis a lesion in the brain stem very low down will cause a movement of the palate or sometimes of the stapedes in the inner ear, sometimes of these long muscles in the neck. One can't make sense of these strange symptoms until one sees that these three areas are the remnants of the gill arches, and what one is seeing is therefore like a gill movement. But phylogenetically we haven't had gill movements since the Jurassic. It's the strangest feeling. When one sees the so-called branchiomyoclonus, you feel that the fish are still there within us. Sometimes in Tourette's syndrome one sees sudden, convulsive movements, and things that resemble an upsurging of very primitive behaviors. Things like this make me a Darwinian, make me feel that not only are we not blanks at birth, we really are a billion years old.

*When you treated those postencephalitic patients with L-dopa at Mount Carmel, you talk about the dark side of existence you saw when you looked into their phylogenetic memories. What did you see, or is language just not capable of describing it?*

I think I felt dark more in the way of mysterious, not evil.

*This is what you called: 'A very mixed landscape, partly familiar, partly uncanny, with sunlit uplands, bottomless chasms, volcanoes, geysers, meadows, marshes. Something like Yellowstone.'*

And I also quote Freud, who said somewhere in his notebooks that he things that neurosis is somewhat like a prehistoric landscape. I think he says like a Jurassic landscape and I said: Well, perhaps, but I have this feeling much more strongly with some of these patients of mine. In a way that may be romantic or scientific or both, I'm very attracted to the primitive and the primal. It's one of the reasons I go to Australia and New Zealand, and why I want to go to Madagascar and the Galápagos. I like to see those primitive landscapes, so full of ferns and cycads and things that the dinosaurs might have eaten. I slightly disapprove of flowering plants and modern inventions of that sort. But I think that one of the interesting things about pathology and some clinical disorders is that they at least sometimes strip off the more recent accretions, so that one sees some of the primitive more clearly.

*Darwin wrote "What a book a devil's chaplain could write about the clumsy, wasteful, blundering, low, cruel works of nature." Is that also what you're heading for?*

In the Darwinian vision of nature, of course, nature gropes and blunders and performs the cruelest acts. There is no steady advance upward, there is no design. This is a vision of nature that I certainly feel myself, and as a neurologist and a clinician I see it in human beings. We are full of all sorts of things—appendixes without a function, pineals that have changed function. We are not very elegantly designed. We've been improvised, yet this turns out itself to be very efficient, though not elegant.

*So you don't agree with Dennett, who says that "conscious human minds are more or less serial virtual machines implemented inefficiently on the parallel hardware that evolution has provided for us."*

I partly disagree, because I don't think we are any sort of machine. I think that any mechanical metaphor is misleading and that one has to think much more along the lines of creaturehood, including mental creaturehood. But certainly nature is amoral. I confess that's one of the reasons why I sometimes like nature, because it exempts me from the moral consciousness that is sometimes such a burden.

*Gould says, "Since nature is amoral, we have to seek for morality within ourselves." Is that what you mean by going back to Darwin? Being free of this morality?*

Well, in a way, although I would also say—I don't know whether Stephen would feel this as well—one sees some things that are like behavioral precursors of morality. In maternal love and in family units, for example. Care is a principle that one sees very deep in nature.

*Morality cannot exist without the fiction of free will. Do you agree? We must be able to choose between good and evil. How free are we when we are born into this world?*

I just met a biologist who was—as it were—investigating the psychology of frogs, and he feels he sees something almost like free will in frogs. As behavior becomes richer and richer, we are faced with more forks and more decisions. An interesting thought about some of the new theories of consciousness is that in a way they might also become theories of conscience. For example, with Gerard Edelman's new theory in *Neural Darwinism*, one is not seen as fated or programmed, but life is very much a question of adventures, hazards, choices, and responsibilities.

We do have to act as though we had free will and could make responsible choices and as though other people could do so. Whether in reality these are pure assertions of the will or the spirit, or whether they are the solutions an organism will arrive at after an enormously complex equation, I am not sure. But certainly life has to be full of what one might call acts of will. It's interesting to see what happens to a life if it's not marked by acts of will.

In *The Mnemonist* Luria describes a man whose powers of imagery and memory were so prodigious that he could visualize with such hallucinatory intensity and such a sense of reality that he could not embark on it. Luria describes his entire life as waiting for something to happen. There can be a similar sort of suspense or will-lessness in people with Tourette's syndrome. In the imagination of such a patient, one idea gives rise to another and another and another and another. Instantly an infinite field of ideas emerges in which the person himself has not been individuated and has somehow been lost. Renouncing certain possibilities may be an integral part of the human will. Now on nature/nurture . . .

*Do you, too, find this nature/nurture debate a tedious blind alley? How far have we come in understanding what we are really all about?*

We are no longer children of nature in the same way as most animals. We have this complex double origin. But clearly nurture can only act on what is already there. However, one can go round and round with nature and nurture. One also needs concepts outside both, concepts that have to do with creation and innovation, and with something that is neither implicit in the person nor given by culture. One sees the appearance of the new throughout the whole universe, from physical systems right up to the mind. Perhaps this was implicit in the etymology of the words "nature" and "growth," but the traditional physical models view nature either as a sort of Newtonian clockwork or as a sort of thermodynamic machine, which is dying. We need a new model of nature which will permit the notion of innovation, creation, the appearance of complexity and indeed evolution at every level. There is always the unexpected.

*The experiences with L-dopa in sleeping disease patients were a tremendous influence in your own life. You wrote that your patients became your friends and tutors. You didn't want to sleep because so much was happening. How did your outlook on life change after all you had seen with the patients at Mount Carmel? How did it affect your views on how the brain works, on how human beings work?*

What it told me more strongly than anything else is that you can never look at an illness or a symptom or a phenomenon in isolation. You always have to see it in a wider context, as part of the person, part of the pattern of life, part of the social context. The problems these patients faced were not just a chemical or a physiological matter, even though chemical and physiological changes lay at the center. I had this really strong feeling of reciprocity everywhere.

For example, in September of 1969 I returned from being away to find the patients were all in tremendous trouble. Some of them had tics, some were shaking, some were in a trance. . . . My first thought was that they had been given the wrong dose of L-dopa. What turned out to be the case was that in my absence the patient community had been disbanded, visiting had been forbidden, and many of the patients were in a state of great distress, of helpless rage and mortification. And this was driving them into symptoms made possible by their damaged nervous systems. So here a moral event was directly expressing itself in physical events.

Sometimes I think one can see the opposite. What one might call the moral tone of Parkinsonism and of chorea is somewhat different. I think the rigidity of Parkinsonism can sometimes produce a certain moral and intellectual rigidity, and the soft, indulgent quality of chorea has, I suppose, a sort of moral equivalent. But above all I have realized how robust identity is.

*Even in the worst circumstances, the deep suffering of people who have lived in nowhere land for thirty or forty years?*

Indeed, in nowhere land, suffering from a disease that tends to undermine identity. . . . And yet there is a robustness about identity, if it is fully formed by the time of the insult. The resilience of these patients astonished me, as well as the fact that most of them were not soul-murdered, as can happen in circumstances such as concentration camps, where indignity rather than nature has been the enemy. I was astonished by the strength of identity of these patients, but also by the way their personality and character would become reorganized, though not distorted, to include their diseases and situations. This constantly astonishes me with all of my patients.

*You also mention "a new kind of tenderness" you discovered. What do you mean by that, in respect to the postencephalitic patients? Because you write about them with so much tenderness.*

As you say, they became friends and teachers, they became my children, my parents. I hope I didn't sacrifice objectivity and detachment, yet I felt empathy and imagined myself into their worlds. This may be partly my romantic impulse, but it may partly be what science has to be when it is at a human level. Or perhaps not just at the human level. Barbara McClintock, the geneticist, likes to talk about "a feeling for the organism"—in her case, maize plants. Einstein liked to speak of an *Einfühlung*, an intellectual love for the phenomena. Certainly I think with a living organism and a person you can't just look at one part. You must simultaneously have a feeling for what the life is like.

*If you would go back to Mount Carmel for a few minutes—can you think of one patient who was perhaps most fascinating, who would be emblematic of the problems you encountered?*

One patient whom I found deeply bewildering and strange but was also very fond of is the patient whom I called Rose in the book. Now this woman had had a very acute attack of encephalitis in 1926. In fact, on the night of the attack she dreamed that she had turned to stone, that she was alive but not alive. In the morning she was found rigid and catatonic. A mirror was put in front of her, and she saw that her dream had come true. She was kept at home for some years and then in 1935 she came to Mount Carmel. I saw her in 1966. Like many of the patients, she looked much younger.

*What happened between 1935 and 1966?*

Nothing, and it's the nature of the nothing that we have to look at. She remained immobile with her head and her gaze averted. She could be walked a little, she could be fed. It was unclear how much she took in of anything around her, as with many of the patients until they became able to talk after being given L-dopa.

I hesitated very much with this particular patient. In *Awakenings* I say that I hesitated because she seemed so elsewhere and so out of the world, and I was rather haunted by something Joyce had written about his mad daughter: "Fervently as I desire her cure, I wonder what then will happen if she comes out of this, as they say, as battered characters face the world."

I hesitated with giving L-dopa to these patients for more than two years, partly because I did not know what might happen in them physiologically. Many of these patients had been extremely impulsive and excited. In the early days of the epidemic, before the slow wave of lethargy and trance came over them, von Economo, who originally described them, spoke of them as extinct volcanoes. I thought they might be dormant volcanoes. I didn't know what would happen. I didn't know what might be there. I thought of Pandora's box. These people had been out of the world for so long that it wasn't just a medical decision, it was also a very complex ethical and existential one. What would it mean to bring them back? What then?

I might have stayed forever in a state of doubt—I'm somewhat given to states of doubt—had not some of the patients died in 1968 and had not others become sicker. I thought I can't spend forever doubting. I must give them the choice. And so, after consulting with their families, I gave some of them L-dopa in 1969. When Rose came to, she became full of animation. She walked around and said, "Fabulous, it's gorgeous." She had an intense delight in movement and life. And yet her manner and her mannerisms were from a different age, were those of a much younger woman. She spoke of Gershwin and others as if they were still alive. She had the vocabulary of the twenties. I wondered very much: Where is she? Is she disoriented? What's happened to her? I asked her some questions, the sort of questions doctors ask. And she was a very quick woman. She said; "I can tell you the dates, I can tell you the date of Pearl Harbor, I can tell you the date of Kennedy's assassination. These things have been registered, but none of them seem real." She said she had been a spectator for the last forty-three years. "I know I'm sixty-four, but I feel like twenty-one. I know it's 1969, I feel as if it's 1926." Nothing had seemed real since that night of the illness. And in some sense I think nothing had been perceived in the normal way. There hadn't been the streaming of consciousness, there had been no change, no growth, no learning. In some sense there was no memory. She only knew a few isolated things, big political events, the war and so forth, like flashbulbs. She had a formal knowledge that things had changed, but there had not in her been the slow evolution of growth and memory which there is— or should be at least—in all of us. She had been fossilized or marooned in the past.

*What did you feel when Rose got L-dopa, and you saw the first symptoms emerge? You didn't know at that time whether she had really recovered or not.*

I came to see this differently after awhile. When I first wrote about Rose in 1970, I spoke of the L-dopa as producing an attack of nostalgia, of remote memories, as some epilepsies can do. Later I came to view it as though I had brought her alive but she had not moved on. Initially I was amazed at the detail of her memories—everything was so vivid and so clear. And at that time I thought: Everything is there! She knew hundreds of songs from the 1920s. She was full of anecdotes. Suddenly the 1920s were there, and her life was there. It was all suddenly revealed. Nothing was lost, nothing was hidden. At first I marveled at a miraculous revelation of the wondrous complexity of memory and human nature. After that I got a sense of fear. What seemed so marvelous to begin with, now by the very freshness of its detail seemed to me to be some sort of terrible casualty of not being updated. As with some of the other patients—but maybe most clearly with her—I got this terrible feeling that she was lost in time, that her world had disappeared, and that bringing her to, to our world, maybe was not the right thing to have done. And she partly said that. She said, "I don't like your world."

*What didn't she like?*

Television. She didn't like television. She said; "Why aren't people reading?" She also objected to the plastic knives and forks in the hospital. She objected to the bad printing of the newspapers. There were a lot of shoddy things she didn't like about the present. But most important, whatever had meaning for her had gone. Her family had abandoned her or grown old or moved away or died. And she said, "What is there for me now?"

And after ten days of wondering this, she suddenly went back into the sort of trancelike, catanonic, rigid, Parkinsonian state she had been in for more than forty years. And after that, neither giving her L-dopa nor anything else would have worked. I'm not quite sure that I would use a word like "willful" here; I don't think such things are within the power of the will. But there was a challenge to create a new identity for a new world, which was, or seemed, impossible for her. Many of the patients were faced with this challenge, but the bewilderment of the anachronism and this tragic marooning were probably strongest with Rose. Other patients were faced with bewilderments of a different sort. Some showed physiological and sometimes psychological behaviors and perceptions of the prehuman, primitive sort that we talked about earlier, which I would not have thought possible.

There was another patient, for example, whom I called Hester, who sometimes would not see movement continuously, but would see a series of stills. She described how once she had seen her brother lighting his pipe. She had seen the match flaring up, the successive position of the match and the tobacco taking fire in the bowl, but only then the match approaching the bowl; that is, she had seen the lighting of the pipe a bit too soon, or else she had seen one of the approaching stages a bit too late. I didn't know how to explain that, but it made me feel that time must be a very complex construct.

I saw more strangeness with these patients and more suddenly than I have ever seen in a few weeks before or since. It was a revelation to me, and even now, twenty-three years later, my mind goes back to this richness of phenomena that I feel may illuminate all sorts of things.

*In this context you have quoted Goethe: "Everything factual is in a sense theory. There is no sense in looking for something behind phenomena, they are theory." Daniel Dennett wrote, "The idea that the self or the soul is really just an abstraction strikes many people as simply a negative idea; a denial rather than anything positive. But in fact it has a lot going for it, including a somewhat more robustly conceived version of potential immortality than anything to be found in the traditional ideas of the soul." What is abstraction, what is fantasy, and how fantastic is reality?*

Let me start at a more elementary level. At first when one gave L-dopa to these patients, there was a response that seemed commensurate with the dose. Things were predictable. And then something happened. The patients' reactions and behaviors ceased to be predictable. Patients would start to oscillate between states of excitement and states of standstill. Sometimes these oscillations were not clearly related to the time of giving the drug. I did everything I could to try to control these oscillations, and I couldn't do so, nor could I predict them. I became bewildered and frightened, because something unpredictable was happening; something more and more complex was emerging which I couldn't stop. I thought I had a rather simple physiological system pinned and fixed, and it was escaping from me. All sorts of strange new phenomena and behaviors appeared which led me in a direction I now turn away from, though I see why I took it—to search for extravagant concepts outside the usual physiological ones. I saw sudden total changes in the complexion of the organism, which would happen in a hundredth of a second or less, from a state of Parkinsonism to a state of normality, or from a state of standstill to a state of movement. I was reminded of what I had read about quantum theory. I wondered if what I had seen with these patients were macro-quantum events. I found myself wondering whether the physiologist should bring in quantum theory and relativity theory to understand what was happening. *Awakenings* and, for that matter, the patients themselves were full of metaphors.

One sophisticated patient spoke of himself as having become a Möbius strip in which his inside became his outside. Another said, "If only I could find the eye of my hurricane." In other words, he felt that he had become a sort of storm, unpredictable. This notion of a storm was often in my own mind. I think in retrospect that what I was seeing probably had a great deal to do with what we now call the concept of chaos, of deterministic chaos, its self-organization, and the way nature itself is creative and brings out new forms. But these concepts were not available in the 1960s.

*Do you also mean that the brain or the mind does not repair itself, but sometimes is transformed into something different, independently of what we call "will"?*

It is not repaired; there is a sudden transformation. I would suddenly, for example, see a great wave of Parkinsonism convert itself into a thing called chorea, little tiny movements. I could not understand in the classical physiological terms—which have to do with localization, and which deal with processes that take time and are mediated by chemicals—how such sudden kaleidoscopic changes in the complexion of the nervous system were possible. I sometimes thought of the drug and the disease and the circumstances between them playing the nervous system like an organ, pulling out stops to produce almost unimaginable physiological and psychological states and forms of consciousness. It gave me the richest feeling of neurological possibility and of the immense delicacy of the nervous system . . . how in a sense everything could be generated from within. Although equally it gave me a sense of people's worlds and people's identities. In a situation like this, so much is visible of the present situation and the present physiology, but also so much of the past became known. In a way it was like a . . . I don't know how to say it. I wanted to say like an experiment with human nature, except that sounds callous, and I think it wasn't.

*You talked about chaos theory—a butterfly flapping its wings in Tokyo and causing a hurricane in New York three days later. What is the connection with your experiences in Mount Carmel?*

Sometimes an infinitesimal difference in starting conditions in a dose would get amplified and lead to some enormous change. One could no longer predict what would happen, just as one can't predict the weather.

This "far-from-equilibrium" state was unpredictable but at the same time very rich: new patterns and new forms would evolve.

*In your childhood you wanted to order the world, to have certainty about reality. Then suddenly in this Mount Carmel hospital, reality metamorphosed into a dizzying sequence of unpredictable circumstances. For you personally, wasn't it frightening?*

Indeed it was, both frightening and liberating. But frightening first to my colleagues and myself. I wrote a letter, which was published in the medical literature in 1970, in which I said that at first things seemed predictable. Then beyond a critical point they started fluctuating and new phenomena appeared and it became impossible to predict or control this. I said that I thought we had to seek an explanation and understanding at a much deeper level. This letter greatly annoyed several of my colleagues—an entire issue of the journal was devoted to anger. Basically I think it was the anger of doctors who were being told: You can't control things, you can't predict them. And beyond this, the anger of reason and will at things that apparently were escaping from reason and will.

I have said this was a liberation as well. Somehow it seemed to me that I was looking at something like evolution in fast-forward and perhaps seeing something of the adventurousness of the universe. What was on the one hand an insult to traditional reason and will was on the other a revelation of what might be the innovative quality of nature itself.

*Would you say that these moments were the most decisive in your life?*

They certainly shook me a great deal. I remember seeing a patient with Tourette's syndrome soon after this. In the excited state of Tourette's syndrome one can see a far-from-equilibrium state with some similarities to the critical state of these postencephalitic patients on L-dopa. I constantly saw things I couldn't predict. I remember writing an essay on "the odd." I wondered if the odd was a principle of nature. Previously the odd was always the exceptional, but then I wondered whether the odd, whether variation might in fact be crucial—the basis, as it were, of a different form of nature. Prigogine likes to talk about "order through fluctuation." But I didn't read Prigogine until '78 or so. When I did, it was with a sense of great excitement. I thought: This is what I have been seeing in some of my patients. I don't know how much this Prigogine-level will extend to mental evolution. Prigogine himself likes to say that the universe is like a giant brain. Arthur Eddington used to say that the more one looks at the universe, the less and less it is like a mechanism, and the more it is like giant thought. At some primitive level in physiology, I think that once simplicity and linearity go, one sees these wonderful and unpredictable and sometimes terrifying things which you can also see in some physical systems. I got this deep sense of newness coming up.

*I am reminded of what Roger Penrose once wrote: "Without consciousness the universe would be impossible." That is, the universe only started to exist when our consciousness appeared in evolution.*

I suspect that evolution would sooner or later produce conscious beings. I think one may have had to wait, say, five billion years for it. During those five billion years there was no consciousness watching or formulating the universe, and yet it may have had some sense of its own. But in a Darwinian sense, not in a Platonic one.

*When I hear you talk, I think the confrontation with Daniel Dennett will be tremendous. Dennett says things like "A virtual machine is a tempting analogy for consciousness." What do you think of such an instrumental approach to the brain?*

In 1948 I was a teenager and very interested in engineering. I visited Grey Walter in Bristol, who had constructed a robot tortoise that was able to charge itself and to wander around. When I first came to the United States in 1960 I called on Marvin Minsky, who is the father of artificial intelligence. Initially I was greatly excited by the AI enterprise and by the intriguing affinities between computation and thinking.

Let's suppose I have a kind of computer in my head. There is the hardware and the software, but then there is also me. Where do I come in? And this, of course, is a sort of dualism. I am now convinced that there is no computer in my head, that natural intelligence is not like artificial intelligence, and that thinking is not like computation. We do not have hardware or software in the usual sense, nor do we have a memory store, or information processing in the mechanical sense. Our brain is altogether more of a biological nature, in some ways much more powerful than computation, in other ways less powerful. I think it's fascinating to see a chess grand master playing against a computer. The performances may be about equal, but the approaches are unimaginably different. A robot seems to have a repertoire that it cannot leave, whereas creatures seem to be above all nonprogrammatic, to change with experience and deal with events.

*Then Daniel Dennett comes in and says, "You can give the computer the option not to be programmatic."*

You can certainly give a computer a sort of decision tree, but I suspect this is not the way we act when we actually arrive at judgments. I should say that there is a tendency to substitute decision trees and mechanical thinking for genuine thinking. For example, a British medical journal publishes what they are pleased to call "clinical algorithms" every week. Let's say a patient comes in complaining of breathlessness. Then one might say that's due to this or that, and this in turn might be due to this or that. A diagnostic computer would behave that way. But I don't think that's how an astute clinician works. I'm worried about the reduction of thought to algorithms. An algorithm is a mechanical procedure to solve a problem. I think one should ask: Is human thought, or for that matter animal thought, algorithmic?

I want to come back to my old vision of an animal. After all, I was brought up with animals and not robots, and I think I am an animal and not a robot. Although I might possibly be a robot to the extent that I am neurotic, since I think that fixed and invariant stereotyped and highly programmed behaviors always appear more mechanical and less alive. Incidentally, some of my Parkinsonian patients would feel that their walking and other behaviors had become somewhat robotic. They would contrast this passive, robotic, instructed, programmed sort of behavior with the feeling of being an agent, alive and autonomous, which they had when they were well. I think "robotic" may be an interesting metaphor for some forms of pathology, but not for health.

*You write "The final form of cerebral representation must allow art, the art for scenery and molding of experience and action." What do you mean by the idea that our brain and our consciousness are a form of art?*

I often don't agree with things I have written in the past. However, I do think that our consciousness and for that matter the responses of many animals, at least higher animals, depend on constructing a scene or a scenario. I think this scene may consist of, if not an infinite, at least a very large number of details, arranged in some sort of organic and dramatic unity, and also a sort of resilience, so that things can be slightly wrong or slightly distorted. This strikes me as being very different from the poverty in the rigor of the instructions one must issue to a computer. As human beings or as organic beings, we approximate all the while. We have none of the inhuman and indeed inorganic accuracy of computers, but we do have a great deal of resilience.

A point I want to bring out is that I cannot in my mind isolate movement from consciousness. Animals are constantly moving and exploring the world. If movement is halted, it does something to consciousness. I saw that myself in the clearest way when I had an immobilized leg. Movement and exploring, building up maps, comparing maps, reflecting on maps and categorizing them at higher and higher levels seem to be characteristic of animals and quite unlike the way any robot goes about things. It's astonishingly difficult to program a computer to recognize a category, such as trees. Part of the reason is that you can't specify in sufficient detail what is needed. But for an animal it's extremely easy to learn a category. If I were to use a mixed metaphor, I might call animal brains categorical machines. Animals are especially expert at the extraction or the construction of categories, perceptual categories, and then higher and higher categories.

The circuitry of a computer has to be extremely accurate; a few small problems and you get grossly distorted results or the computer is down. Now the circuitry of every single nervous system, even in identical twins, is unique at birth. Even in genetically identical people, various epigenetic influences such as cell migration and cell death ensure that by the time of birth every nervous system is unique. It would not be possible, given such diversity of nervous systems, to run algorithms and programs. The hardware is too variable to allow computation. In a computer any variation is an error, but in life variation is of the essence. Variation is of the essence for Darwin in natural selection and also for what Edelman likes to call "neural Darwinsim": the way the nervous system evolves with experience in the life of the organism. Given certain genetic determinants and constraints and what Edelman likes to call "values," an infant will be disposed to respond in particular ways and will build up certain maps of perceptions. These maps will talk to one another. Edelman likes to use the term "reentrant signaling." Basically the nervous system is individual from the start, continues to be individual, and becomes more and more richly individuated throughout the life of the person or the animal. So the tormenting dichotomy between the computer and the person doesn't arise, because your brain is molded by your experience even as it molds your experience. Genetically and phenotypically speaking, your heart is your heart and your kidneys are your kidneys, but your brain contains you, contains your experience, your desires, your hopes, your lusts, your theories, your everything. This notion of the brain as continually teaching and being taught, of the brain as being ourselves and as using a form of integration and categorization and reflection, is quite different from a computer.

All this seems to me theoretically economical and elegant, because it has one dimension of explanation and not two, with an irreconcilable gulf between the instrument and the self. But it also gives me a sense of delight, because it somehow places human life, human will and consciousness, in nature, in animality and creaturehood, and indeed at the apex of the creative and self-organizing processes of the universe. It puts us back at home in the universe and makes us the voice of the universe, as it were, instead of some peculiar sort of disembodied computational principle that has been added to the universe.

*You mentioned Edelman's "neural Darwinism." What have you discovered about neural Darwinism in the field of language, particularly the sign language that deaf-mutes use?*

One form of programmatic thinking has sometimes asserted that each area of the cell of the cortex is prededicated, predetermined for a given function. What is remarkable with children who are born deaf and who use a visual rather than an auditory language is that it produces an immense heightening of visual perception and sensibility of language and memory and physiology. The auditory parts of the brain are reallocated, are turned over to visual processing. I wouldn't have thought such an incredible degree of plasticity was possible, that the brain could adapt so radically to a different demand and different vicissitude in life. When this came to me, I called up a friend and said, "I can't make sense of this in any terms but those of neural evolution." This seemed to me a striking example of neural Darwinism or neuronal group selection at work. Since then there have been countless other examples. But yes, since you bring it up, my experience with deaf children was the point at which I thought there is something in this. It is very difficult to explain this sort of thing in terms of fixed circuitry, even in terms of circuitry with options. What you're seeing is a quite radical change even in the microanatomy of the brain.

*What was your most fascinating encounter with the deaf people? You described sign language as a complete alternative, evolutionary language. How did you feel at Gallaudet [an American college for the deaf] and what was the atmosphere like?*

I had already gathered a theoretical notion of the elaborate spatial syntax and abstract powers of sign language, but until I went to Gallaudet in 1968 I had never really seen this for myself in a whole community. I went to lectures. There was a lecture on Spinoza in American Sign Language. If you can translate or explicate Spinoza in sign, you can do anything. And I attended sign poetry readings, which, with their use of the body and the physical pun and metaphor and simile, have no exact equivalent in spoken poetry.

*How important is language for the development of consciousness?*

It's crucially important for certain forms of consciousness, though I think the development of consciousness and higher mental functions and the development of language have separate biological origins. All of us acquire language almost automatically in the third and fourth years of life, from speaking with our parents. The only people who do not have ready access to language are deaf children. Paradoxically, the deaf children of deaf parents don't have any problems, since they acquire a native sign language from the start. But one of the things that saddened me—and it's a central theme of my book *Seeing Voices*—was seeing deaf children who through mishap of one sort or another had missed the critical period at which they might have acquired language. They had got to adolescence with no language, no sign language, no speech, nothing. One could see that this had a severe effect on thinking and on powers of telling stories, answering questions, and making reference. I once described an eleven-year-old boy, Joseph, who seemed to be confined to a perceptual world, to the here and now. He couldn't refer to things outside the room, or to things that had happened last week. He couldn't

25

refer to abstractions, and his power of imagination was very limited. He had really been severely restricted intellectually through not having access to language.

Now, I'm not saying that all thinking and all of consciousness depend on language, but it is probably crucial in the development. And one needs it early. It is sometimes said that a deaf child of five or six may play normally without language. But I think that if he hasn't had language since the age of two or three, something is missing which may have permanent effects. Clearly, however, there are many kinds of thought that occur in infancy, before language, and there are many kinds of thought that occur without language, especially in the higher apes, and there are many forms of human thought that do not depend on language, although they may have other representation systems. What do we know about Beethoven's consciousness, or for that matter about a mathematician's consciousness? What is the language of the brain? I am even surprised the brain has a language.

This almost leads us back to Kant, where we started. It may be that the brain has to have—if not to have innately, then to construct—representational systems in time and space, in logic, reference, and self-reference, in order to matrix thoughts or feelings, connect them properly with one another, and to focus. A framework of this kind, syntax or syntactics, is crucial. One of the interesting things which Chomsky talks about, and which one can reexamine in deaf children, has to do with grammar. Interestingly, if the hearing parents of a deaf child learn some sign language, this will enable their deaf child to sign. Even if the grammar of the parents is rudimentary, the grammar of the child will be perfect. The child's nervous system apparently has the ability to construct a grammar, or discover a grammar, from what Chomsky would call "meager and degenerate data"—what may often be the rather ungrammatical, poorly grammaticized data of the parents' discourse.

How does a child's nervous system do this? Chomsky thinks in terms of innate mechanisms, of a built-in set of perhaps seven or eight hundred grammatical rules, which are somehow released at a critical age. But an alternative explanation would be that the child's brain is able to construct grammatical categories in the same way it constructs categories of other sorts. The Chomskian explanation demands an almost miraculous sort of hardware and software in the brain—a kind of programming. But one might also view this as a possible example of neural evolution. This might be a nice way to test the theories.

All of this was rather theoretical for me until I went to Gallaudet in 1968 and was able to see sign language at every level. I saw people chatting in corridors and in the bar. There were a couple of thousand often highly gifted students, obviously communicating fully in sign language. Language always has this double use: not just for communication, but also for organizing your thoughts. In intelligence and achievement, these natively signing deaf students were the equals of any students anywhere. And one saw that it is possible to have a complete visual language and a complete visual organization of the brain.

*You wrote that the atmosphere at Gallaudet seemed almost arcadian.*

Congenital deafness is relatively rare, only one person in a thousand. So these people can be very isolated. And there was a wonderful sort of fraternity or community, with a sharing of language, of sensibility, of perspectives, of forms of art, culture, and humor. There are forms of humor, theater, and poetry that are unique to sign language, since they depend on the full use of the body. One can have disembodied speech in a way, but not disembodied sign language. The whole fullness of the body, its emotional expression, and its intellectual possibilities are built into it.

Now, this arcadian community might be seen as a sort of ghetto, but I feel that deaf people don't want an official separation. They do want and need an identity and a language of their own. I think it is very necessary to have this culture within a culture.

*When you talk about "inner speech," what exactly do you mean?*

That refers to something Lev Vygotsky said in the 1920s—that inner speech is unknown to science. Vygotsky also says, "Words die as they give up meaning." For Vygotsky inner thought is thinking in pure meanings. Vygotsky is a genius and a kind of poet. This phrase and this notion of thinking in pure meanings appealed to me, although I am not sure how to understand it. I mentioned it to a friend of mine who is a translator, and she said, "When I'm translating from one language into another, I extract the meaning and I put it in another word, or another phrase. There is an intermediate stage in which the meaning is not in either language, while I'm searching for the appropriate vehicle for it." I don't know what thinking in pure meanings could mean, but perhaps that's what inner speech is.

*You have used the expression "Proustian remembrance." What do you mean by that? What kind of mental process is remembering, and is language at all involved?*

Certainly remembering has to do with looking for meaning, looking for the largest context and for different contexts. Talking about meaning makes me want to come back to robots and animals. It's the nature of human nature, and maybe of animal nature, to search for meaning.

*Is that to say also that if we found the meaning of life, life would become meaningless?*

No, I wouldn't say that. First, I'm not sure what could possibly be meant by the meaning of life. But one form of the search for meaning is making theories. Then the question arises as to whether there is an end to theorizing. Now I think Stephen Hawking, for example, will suggest that there is an end to theorizing, that sooner or later we will arrive at a T.O.E., a theory of everything, and the scientific enterprise will come to an end. I prefer not to think that this is so. Certainly in my own minor way, whenever any solution has become apparent to me, it in turn has opened a new realm of questions which was broader than anything I could have asked before. So it seems to me that the realm of questioning and theorizing and inquiry gets larger and larger. It might be argued that the physical universe is finite and there is a limit to theorizing about it. But not to the biological or the mental universe, which is continually evolving. The very form of theories about the brain may have to be quite different from physical theories. Edelman likes to say that as we had the Galilean revolution four hundred years ago, we may now need a comparable new revolution to produce a science of the subjective, of the unique and individual, and a science of consciousness. I go along with that. One of the reasons I am against mechanical models is that they are too physicalistic, too inductive, too impoverished, and too boring. They break down hopelessly, finally, before the sheer creativity of the brain.

*Mechanical models are inherent in the Cartesian theater.*

Exactly. I am increasingly intrigued by the appearance of the new, with the emergence of apparently unexpected thoughts, images, or patterns into consciousness, for which there is no precedent and no program. I'm not entirely at home talking about language and consciousness. I always want to bring things down to a simpler or more elemental level. Among the things that have fascinated me for many years are visual hallucinations, and specifically the geometrical hallucinations that one may experience preceding an attack of migraines, the so-called migraine aura. I don't know if you have had such attacks yourself.

*Yes, only too often.*

What do you see?

*A quarter-circle that slowly grows into a semicircle.*

And the semicircle itself may have some sort of internal structure?

*Yes, flickering shapes and lines and zigzags and all kinds of things.*

Now beyond these rather fixed forms of the expanding circle with flickering zigzags one can have very complex, unpredictable things. Sometimes half the image may contain strange whirls or spirals, radial figures. Sometimes you may get lattices that constantly fluctuate in shape and size.

I bring these things up because, although the fixed scintillating semicircle is rather predictable—it takes about twenty minutes to develop and always has the same form—these later things never have the same form. They are different in every person and in every attack, although certain features like the lattices and the spirals can come up again and again. In the 1850s the astronomer John Frederick Herschel described these things in himself, wondering what produced these "geometrical specters," as he called them. He wondered if they were due to a "thought" or an "intelligence," as distinct from the personality. Or he wondered if, on the other hand, it could be called "a kind of kaleidoscope or kaleidoscopic power in the brain." Already here you have a sort of dualism. He asked, "Are these produced by an agent, a thought, a spirit, or by a device?" In fact, I don't think they are produced by either. I think these patterns are spontaneously generated, that they develop through the cortex; I think there is self-organization going on. Interestingly, one can mimic this somewhat. With a colleague of mine, Ralph Segal, I have been doing some work with nerve nets. If a nerve net is pushed past the critical point, it develops a migraine so to speak. It starts to develop strange structures. So, once more—this comes back to nature and nurture—things don't have to be built in, nor do they have to come from the outside. To me, the power of the autonomous, the spontaneous, and the creative is the most striking thing in the human brain, not only at the level of what we usually call "creativity" but even at the level of the primary visual cortex.

What comes out for me, even in this very elementary example of the migraine aura, is that the brain is always active. In the past, one had rather mechanical physiologies and psychologies, a stimulus–response model. But the nervous system stimulates itself constantly. New patterns are being generated all the while and at every level, from these very simple geometrical patterns in the primary cortex up to the complex patterns that are thoughts, which Sherrington talks about in a lovely metaphor when he compares the brain to an enchanted loom which is continually weaving patterns that dissolve into one another. The patterns are patterns of meaning. When we're awake, this autonomous activity of the mind and the brain is held in check by our perceptions and by reality, by social constraints. When we're asleep, it's not; then we have the freedom and license to dream. It could reasonably be said that we're dreaming all the while, except that when we're awake, the dreams are constrained by reality. I take those strange geometrical patterns as the dreaming of the visual cortex. I think Parkinsonism is like a dream of the midbrain.

We see autonomous activity everywhere in nature, as if the world itself is dreaming. Machinery is inert. You have to press a button or pull a lever to start it. The world is not inert. There is nothing inert in the world, except some of the devices we make in it. Aristotle said that activity is built into the world. Aristotle also thought that no matter how much delight human beings took in proposing and solving problems, the real delight of the mind was in its own activity. To me, the nature of activity seems to be inexplicable in mechanical terms and to demand creatural terms, the terms of animals. Many years ago I got very excited by Leibniz and his equating existence with activity. In the Leibnizian view of the world, everything is active and autonomous. This is different from the Newtonian or the Galilean view of the world, in which objects stay in a state of rest unless they are impressed by an impulse, and they roll inertly down an inclined plane. There is a continual transfer of energy and a reorganizational energy and activity in living creatures, especially in human brains and at the highest level. It's going on all the time, it never stops.

*"We are such stuff as dreams are made on, and our little lives are rounded with a sleep." That quotation from Shakespeare is the motto for these interviews. What are your views on the dream from a neurological perspective?*

I think we dream nonstop until we come to the sleep at the end. . . .

*What about Freud? What do we do with him at the end of the twentieth century?*

It's right and exciting that Freud's greatest book was about the interpretation of dreams. Freud appears at his full majesty and perhaps ridiculousness in that book. I think the mechanisms which Freud perceives in dreams of condensation and displacement and overdetermination perhaps apply potentially to all thinking, if it's not curtailed one way or another, or restrained by what we like to call reality. Whatever may be questionable in Freud, he protrayed the shape of mental activity and inaugurated a science of what mental activity is actually like in a way that can never be extinguished.

Ten years before Freud, Eddinghouse investigated memory by seeing how people remember nonsense syllables. This is important and it needs to be done. But one might say that Freud's actual task was dealing with remembering as it occurs in vivo, in the living creature that is making its way through the world. I think that there will be some very close rapprochement between the best of psychoanalysis and neuroscience, which at this point I think is moving up to deal with the biology of remembering and dreaming and consciousness. Freud himself wanted to have this neurology project back in the 1890s, but at that time neurology and physiology really could concern themselves only with single neurons and single reflexes in the spinal cord. If Freud were alive now, I think he would be tremendously excited by the state of neuroscience, which is beginning to reach up toward the levels where a sophisticated, analytical psychologist could say, "Yes, that's what I'm talking about." I think that the subjective, interpretive, empathic linguistic and artistic discussion of consciousness will always be necessary, but that it's beginning to meet the approach from below. And this seems to me very exciting. I'm glad to be alive to see the beginnings of this.

*What do you think may be discovered in this field?*

We are just at the beginnings of the biology of consciousness. Within twenty years, if we don't blow ourselves up we may have a radically deeper view of human nature. Some of the computational and artificial intelligence notions may recede in perspective to quaint aberrations of the middle of the century. Since this becomes a neuroscience of the individual, it may also increase our respect for the individual mind and nervous system and for art, which is so unmachinelike and so unreproducible by nature. . . .

*If we don't blow ourselves up, you said. A simple childish question: 'Daddy, why are we organizing a nuclear winter?'*

We are greedy and egocentric. We cut down trees, we use fluorocarbons, we spoil the atmosphere. We think the earth has infinite resource. It doesn't. We are really running into the limited resources of the earth now. The other thing which horrifies me is that human nature's fanaticism and terrorism are so dangerous. When people are filled with fanatical anger, they treat themselves and others as non-human, as not even creatures. No animal behaves as badly as we do. This is the other side of our majestic science. . . .

*Why are you silent?*

Can I say a word about death?

*Yes.*

I want to say that the other side and the tragic side to this wonderful uniqueness of each human being is that we are all mortal. I'm going tomorrow to the funeral of an old friend. Now he is gone, his place in the universe will never be filled. There was never a creature quite like him before, there will never be one quite like him again. Occasionally I lose or break a watch, or the computer goes down, but clearly that doesn't affect me in the same way. I want to say that the other side of this living uniqueness is death and the unfillable gap that follows people's deaths.

*On the one hand, we seem to be the gems of evolution, but on the other, we die just as clumsily, wastefully, cruelly, and horribly as the bees and horses.*

Well, perhaps so. Kierkegaard's last words were "Sweep me up." Yet we have all of us at some level found meaning and created meaning in our lives, and we hand this on. Even at the biological level. Animals become loam, they enrich the earth, and we certainly do so. It may be the only form of immortality we know.

*Do you remember what it meant for you to wander around on
Hampstead Heath when you were twelve? Did you feel immortal
then?*

Hampstead Heath meant a playground. And yes, I think I did feel
immortal when I was twelve, and for that matter, probably through my
twenties and thirties.

*When did you get intimations of mortality?*

I think it was after I almost died on the mountain in Norway. After I had
fallen and badly injured my leg I was at five thousand feet, I was alone,
no one knew where I was, I had no way of giving a signal. I was above
the Arctic Circle and would not have survived the night. I thought it
unlikely that I would be found.

*Can you remember how you felt as night fell?*

There were many different sort of moods. One of them was a vivid,
involuntary recollection of scenes from childhood, and happy scenes
from gardens, Hampstead Heath, the family, friends. It was in fact only
when I thought of a line from one of Auden's last poems—"Let your last
thinks all be thanks"—that I realized at some deep level I was preparing
for dying. I had a sense of the transfer from one generation to another. I
thought how much I had been given, and for myself I thought: Well,
perhaps I have given something to students and patients, and perhaps I
have written a couple of books that are worthwhile.

Now, clearly there were other feelings. And there was sheer animal
fear, there were physical misery and agony, and beyond that, the
unimaginable metaphysical fear of not being. Not so much of dying, but
of not being here. And along with this I was bothered by a feeling of
work that hadn't been done. I don't know whether there is any
appropriate time to die, but I'm glad I didn't die then.

*Can you imagine a time when you might say: This is enough? Because
immortality is the real punishment, the real hell.*

When my mother died of a heart attack, I'm afraid my immediate
thought was: Fucking plumbing. I got annoyed at the notion of a
blocked artery putting an end to human existence. It seemed outrageous.
I have many patients in their nineties, sometimes in their hundreds,
many of them religious, who sometimes say: "My life has been full. Lord,
I'm ready. Nunc dimittis." I can't quite imagine that. I'm not ready yet,
though I don't know what would happen to me if I became ill. This poor
friend of mine—who is a sort of twin, we were born on the same day—
was in the middle of his best work ever, he was a geneticist. He got
cancer of the stomach, and that was it.

I don't know how reconciled he was. He seemed deeply sad all the
way through, although I think there was also a sort of resignation. The

sort of death I like the idea of most is Pavlov's. Pavlov used to have these sudden tremendous bursts, these hurricanes of energy and creativity, when he would get the whole lab going. Everyone was full of creative excitement and the world seemed to be created anew for him and for them when it happened. When he was very ill and tossing and turning in a final pneumonia delirium, his face suddenly changed and he cried, "To work!" with this wonderful creative look. Then he fell back dead.

*Is that the way you would like to pass away?*

I think that would be nice. If I'd had to think of life without that sense of creativity and excitement ever again, I'd feel that maybe it wasn't worth it.

*When you are in England the day after tomorrow, what tricks will time play on you regarding your decreased friend?*

We met when we were eleven and a half, nearly forty-six years ago. It's very difficult to carry a steady sense of duration in one's mind. But I want to try to recover for him and his family the sense of a history, of what it means to have lived a life.

*How do you view these forty-six years?*

They certainly don't have a consistent duration to me. Sometimes it seems immensely long and sometimes no time at all. Like my patient Rose, whom I spoke of earlier, I find it difficult to get used to the disappearance of the familiar and the past. On the whole, I'm excited by the new. Once someone asked me in an interview, "If you were asleep or out of it for thirty years, like one of your patients, and then came to in the 2020s, what's the first thing you would want to do?' And I said, "I'd want to see the *Scientific American.*" I should probably have said my near and dear ones, but somehow . . . I'm especially excited by what's new in science. And neuroscience and physiology are much more exciting than they were thirty years ago. I have a sense of things opening there. When I first came to New York, one saw all the steamships there in their berths. I wish I had paid more attention; I didn't realize those were the last days of the steam era. Sometimes I describe the first car I had or the first motorbike and people say, "But that was a museum piece." And then you say, "Am I a museum piece?" Of course we are not museum pieces so long as we are being updated. Rose's tragedy was that she had become a museum piece. One of the strange things about the death of friends and about the dead generally is that the image can no longer be updated. The friends and relatives who died when I was young are eternally youthful, fossilized in my mind.

It's interesting that one form of consciousness can come to a halt while the rest of consciousness goes on. You see this very clearly in those who go blind, because if you go blind, the images of people are no longer being updated and become progressively more obsolete.

Obviously their voices continue to be updated, but visual consciousness has ceased. Very strange.

*What is the paradox you are concerned with most deeply?*

I've just been reading a book with a strange title, *Tell Me I'm Here*, which deals with the question of who one is, or who anyone is, and with the question of the who as distinct from the what. This is a what, but I'm a who. How does a who arise from a what? How is a what transformed into a who? Of course, when one dies, the who vanishes, leaving us with a what. I don't know where I would begin to answer that question.

It seems to me that the question of personal identity needs to be central at our roundtable. This is the paradox that Hume wrestled with, since his philosophy of empiricism—which has found a descendant in Daniel Dennett and in positivism and mechanism—implies a denial or a nonrecognition of personal identity. Hume said that this drove him into a philosophical melancholy. He felt shipwrecked. He felt at sea, he didn't know what to do. But then he dined with his friends, played backgammon, and went for a walk. After that he felt alive again and recovered his sense of who he was and of the warmth of life. I find that very candid and beautiful. . . .

I wonder if Daniel Dennett has a dog, if he has children. Rosenstock Huessy has written a very nice piece on Descartes as a lover. If one maintains a mechanical view of the world and human beings, what does one do with feeling and love and relationships? Would you put these in a separate compartment or would one say they don't exist?

Sometimes in periods of severe depression, people appear to me to be automata. I can no longer imagine intention or vitality or autonomy. Similarly, in this mood, if I look at poetry, I see a sort of mosaic of words, but no meaning. The poem doesn't let me in, because I don't let it in. Even at our most cognitive and intellectual we have to be informed by passion, by all sorts of passion, whether a personal passion or the *Einfühlung* of which Einstein speaks. Basically I think we all need to be zoologists. After all, we are all forms of life.

# CHAPTER 2

# CONSCIOUSNESS

# EXPLAINED

## Daniel C. Dennett

If the concept of consciousness were to fall to science, what would happen to our sense of moral agency and free will? If conscious experience were reduced somehow to mere matter in motion, what would happen to our appreciation of love and pain and dreams and joy? If conscious human beings were just animated material objects, how could anything we do to them be right or wrong?

"Does Daniel Dennett have children, or a dog?" Oliver Sacks asked in New York, wondering what feelings mean to a man who has such a materialist and intellectualist worldview as Dennett.

Yes, Dennett has children, I have not seen dogs in or around his house, but he professes to like the bears and coyotes that live in the woods surrounding his farm in Maine. "I rarely see them. I only see the signs that betray their presence, but it's simply a positive thing to discover that they are there, and I would be sad if they disappeared."

"How unfair creation is that it blesses one man with such a torrent of stimulating thoughts," writes the British biologist Richard Dawkins. "Each chapter in his new book contains so many wonderful new ideas that the average philosopher would make an entire book of it."

Dennett is the most pronounced materialist of our group of scientists. In fact, he fears he is the only one. He is a fervent opponent of René Descartes's philosophy, as he emphasizes at every opportunity. "Many theorists still presuppose that somewhere, conveniently hidden in the obscure 'center' of the mind/brain, there is a Cartesian theater, a place where it all 'comes together' and consciousness happens. This may seem like a good idea, an inevitable idea, but until we see, in some detail, why it is not, the Cartesian theater will continue to attract crowds of theorists transfixed by an illusion." (*Consciousness Explained*, p. 39) His five colleagues in '*A Glorious Accident*' however insist that however intelligent, funny, and quick-witted he may be, he makes one colossal error: while he thinks he has left the Cartesian theater, he remains a key player on its stage. He believes we will ultimately be able to transfer our consciousness to computers, for instance, because it will not be long before we have unraveled all the tricks of our consciousness. Complicated tricks, but very cheap ones just the same.

During the abundant lunch his wife has made, Dennett holds forth about magic tricks, blind spots, and rooms full of identical Marilyn Monroes.

"Do you really think that during the roundtable you can rein in our differences? It will turn into a madhouse. What will you do to control us?"

Dennett's wife stays upstairs all through the interview, so as not to disturb us. I didn't realize that until afterward. I apologize to her even now.

In his book *Consciousness Explained*, her husband calls himself an optimist. He is a confident and prolific speaker, obsessed by the computer model of the brain and fully convinced that human consciousness will one day be unraveled.

"As some people regard the demystification of consciousness as sacrilege, they will presumably interpret my thoughts as intellectual vandalism, an attack on the last refuge of humanity. But if anything should be lost, there will be abundant compensation in the insights—both scientific and social, both theoretical and moral—that a good theory of consciousness will provide."

Is he the most important philosopher of consciousness at the end of the twentieth century, or a failed Descartes who falls into the same trap as the man whose theories he claims to have left behind him, and who links his ideas to a view of physics that has been outdated for centuries, as Sheldrake and Toulmin claim?

In any case, he makes calvados of very reasonable quality.

■

*You have written, "We are all faced with a baffling phenomenon: how could anything be more familiar and at the same time more weird than a mind?"*

Well, I think that's the problem. On the one hand, we seem to know our minds better than anything else. What could we be more intimately associated with than our own minds? And then when we try to figure out how our minds exist in the world—how, for instance they could be a function of what's going on in our brains—it seems utterly mysterious. When you look for minds in the world, there don't seem to be any. And yet we have the sense at the same time that each one of us has a mind. And that's why it has been so hard to come up with a good theory of consciousness, a good theory of the mind. Because that just seemingly undeniable intuition is in some degree false. We are fooled about our own minds. Descartes famously said, "The one thing I cannot be wrong about is the content of my own conscious thought. Whether it is true or false, that is another matter. But I cannot be wrong about what my thoughts are, nor of the fact that they are my thoughts." I'm claiming that he is wrong about that, the one thing he said he was most certain of.

*What are the main paradoxes concerning the mind and the brain that you are working on now?*

The question is whether those are paradoxes or whether they are just apparent paradoxes. There are certainly some wonderful puzzles, some phenomena where things seem to be one way and then you have very good evidence that they are not the way they seem to be. What makes it fascinating to me is that there is a good rule of thumb, a good strategy to adopt whenever there is stagnation in science: Find the thing that everybody agrees on; deny that and you probably break through the self-evident truth that turns out to be false, however self-evident. One should always look for paradoxes, because they tend to be breakthroughs.

*The motto of this project is a quotation from Shakespeare: "We are such stuff as dreams are made on, and our little lives are rounded with a sleep." I chose this motto before I read* Consciousness Explained. *And suddenly the same quotation crops up early in your book. Why is this quotation so intriguing?*

There are so many different ways of reading that line. One thing that puzzles me and also delights me in some ways is that I eventually put together a theory of the mind, which says that our minds are—if you like—just as real as our dreams. But that is not real enough for some people. They say I'm denying that consciousness exists because I'm saying that there are illusory features to it. But illusions exist. What's wrong with the existence of illusions? Yes, I'm saying that the mind is as real as the illusions that we know to be real. In a way the mind is a sort of illusion itself. To some people that seems just absurd. They say, "An illusion to whom? Who is the subject, who is the victim of this illusion? There has got to be a self there to be fooled, so aren't we right back to Descartes?" My answer is no. We have to build up to this idea gradually, but we can make sense of the idea that a mind is "the brain's user illusion of itself." That looks like a trick with mirrors, but that's what we should expect from a breakthrough here.

*So Shakespeare . . . ?*

I would interpret Shakespeare's line so that it came out to be true. What I am, what you are, most important, is not just a body, because the cells in your body are changed many times over. You can lose and replace really any part of your body in principle. Even parts of your brain.

But if we are going to replace the parts of your brain, we will have to do it in such a way that we preserve what the physicist Richard Feynman once called "the dance of the molecules." They always dance the same dance. That's what makes you you. So what we are really is the information contained in our brains. And as long as that information is preserved, it doesn't make any difference what the physical substrate is. And just as a dream could be recorded in some way, I could be recorded. Put on huge tape banks somewhere, and brought back to life at some later time. However, though this is possible in principle, it's impossible in practice. And that is always important. Philosophers tend to ignore that. But it is also important that it's possible in principle.

*When Stephen Jay Gould was about five years old, his father took him to see the skeleton of a tyrannosaur at the Museum of Natural History in New York. A man next to them sneezed and little Stephen silently started to pray, so that the tyrannosaur wouldn't collapse from the man's sneeze. Later he explained that that was the moment he decided to become a paleontologist. Whether true or not, it's a wonderful story. Have you had similar experiences in your childhood?*

When I was a child, I thought, like many children, that I was unique in that I kept stumbling across philosophical ideas. I invented solipsism. It was lovely to think that I was the only real self in the universe, and all the rest was just a big cinema set for my benefit—that when I went home, the school and the teachers and the rest just disappeared, or they were put away for the night.

I have since discovered that many, many children have this idea. I routinely now ask my students, "How many of you dreamed this up when you were little children?" And half the hands in the room will go up. Always with sort of embarrassed looks on their faces. Ideas of that sort fascinated me, but I didn't know what a philosopher was, so I had no way of saying, "That's what I want to be." I didn't know you could actually do this for a living. So it wasn't until I was in college and read Descartes's *Meditations* that I saw that there was something wonderful that I wanted to do.

*You wrote that at eleven or twelve, you were fascinated by the idea of a knight in the age of chivalry wanting to sacrifice his life for the honor of a princess he had never so much as spoken to. Do you remember that period? What were the odors, the colors, the songs, the music of your childhood?*

My earliest childhood memories are of living in Beirut. My father was a historian, but during the war he was in the OSS, and we lived the life of a diplomatic family in Beirut. I remember the wonderful smells of the food that was sold by people on the street—in particular the sesame seeds that were put on the outside of some the loaves of bread. That was one of my first loves. Also there was a kind of—to my taste today—disgustingly sweet toffee. At the time I rather liked it. As I recall, it was wrapped in a piece of waxed paper that had on it a photograph of King Farouk of Egypt. I have this vivid memory of unwrapping King Farouk from around this brown toffee and popping it into my mouth.

*What are the first colors that come to your mind from those days?*

I suppose all the lush greens. We had a nice garden around our house, and for awhile we had a tame gazelle that lived in our garden. A gazelle that I had named Babar, not caring too much about species at that point.

It seemed a perfectly good name for a gazelle. At that time, if I was a philosopher at all, it was just the way every child is a philosopher, full of wonder and discovering amazing things at every turn.

I remember being transfixed, watching a magician who performed on the pier. We had taken a ship to go to Lebanon, and when we stopped— I think it was at Port Said—there was a magician performing on the pier, way down below the deck of this steamship. Little naked boys were standing on the edge of the pier, and if you threw coins into the water, they dove off into the dirty water and somehow found those coins and brought them to the magician. And he was doing amazing things. And I have actually been fascinated by magic ever since that night. I'm rather a good magician.

*There is a strong connection: brains, mind, and . . .*

Magic. In fact, magic is one of my favorite analogies, because there are lots of cheap tricks in nature that work. Every stage magician knows you can do a rather small trick which is almost instantly blown up in the minds and memories of the audience into something it never was. And then they have a much harder thing to explain than they actually need to. I think this happens again and again and again with our minds. We think the phenomena that need to be explained are much more stupendous than they are. It takes ruthless, skeptical probing to figure out how the magician does the tricks, to uncover the reality and demonstrate how the audience was fooled. And of course this goes hand in hand with an interest in how things work. Magicians are sort of the engineers of the soul. They are very clever at devising cute, clever mechanisms that trick our beliefs and our perceptual systems. I'm fascinated by them because I see so much natural magic, you might say, built into the way our brains work.

*Perhaps that magician in Port Said played a role for you similar to the one the tyrannosaur at the museum in New York played for Stephen Gould.*

I never thought of that before. But it might be. Certainly I remember vividly an intense curiosity about how these effects were done, and as best I recall, never for a moment did I think it was really magic. I think I was a born skeptic about things like that. I've always wanted to figure out how things work and why.

*How does memory work? When you remember those colors and fragrances, do you really remember them, or is it a kind of backward projection? Who is fooling whom, although it's your own experience and your own past?*

Well, people have different ways of thinking about memory. One that is very attractive, and for good reason, is that memories are a sort of storehouse or a library. As you experience things, you put copies of them in this storehouse, and then when you recall something, you bring it out of storage as if it were a videotape and display it on the mind's screen again. That has got to be wrong. There isn't any screen in there to display it on. And yet, undeniably, there is a process that happens. When you asked me to recollect an experience from my early childhood, I had to make something happen in my brain, which provoked my brain to do something it hadn't done for a long time, but which was a sort of faint habit trail, set down by that experience on the ship back in Port Said many years ago. What happened then assaulted my eyes and ears and other senses, and it seems that all that really survives is the visual memory. I don't recall any particular sounds or smells from that experience. The visual memory is quite vivid and has a fair amount of detail.

*Is the visual memory the most important memory? What about smells, music, words . . .*

Music and smells, of course, are famously evocative. Because the olfactory system, the sense of smell, is really the most ancient part of our brains and in some respects the most fundamental, the most tightly tied to our emotional state. And we all have the experience that when we hear a song that comes from an emotionally important moment or period in our lives, it instantly recalls not just the events, but also to some degree the emotional tone of that moment.

*That is what Sacks talks about, the tremendous importance of music as opposed to words or visual images.*

Certainly. And there are many phenomena that underline this. For instance, if you want to remember something, it's useful to make a rhyme out of it; rhyme is very close to music. Maybe it's better still to turn it into a song, because songs stick in the memory in a way that mere spoken words don't. Poetry sticks much more readily than prose. And the more rhythmic and the more rhymed the poetry is, the easier it is. It provides you with more hooks. And if you have lots of vivid imagery to go with it, that too helps. The mnemonic technique of building up your memory by using a visual scene and placing things in that visual scene has been known for centuries. It works because every connection you make engages more of the brain, exploits more of the brains's resources.

*Before we enter the Cartesian theater, just one more question about remembering. What is happening at this moment? You are talking to me. Your words and your image arrive in my brain. How are they stored? Will I be able to bring them back in twenty years? What is happening inside now?*

A philosopher would be foolish to try to answer that question in detail. For that we need neuroscientific research. But I can tell you a few things that aren't happening in your brain right now. What isn't happening is that all of these features, the sights and the sounds—I hope no smells—are arriving in different parts of your brain and are having short-term effects, lasting fractions of seconds, maybe in some cases more than a second or two.

Everything that is coming in through your eyes and ears is being interpreted by specialized parts of your brain. For instance, the parts that are interpreting the words are not the same parts that would interpret music or other sounds. As you are listening to the words, you may also be forming some mental imagery, even though you are looking at me. For instance, if I start telling you about going to a theater, even though there is no theater right here, you may immediately have some sort of quasi-visual picture of a particular theater you know, with the seats or the stage or something like that. So as you're hearing words, your brain is engaged in comprehending those words in many different ways. The outcome will be that you're going to forget most of the words and remember only what they were about. You almost certainly couldn't report back verbatim what I've just been saying to you, but you could give the gist of it very well. The actual words are already lost, probably lost forever in your brain, and replaced by something else. There are indeed some long-term effects that are going to be set down, but not in any one place. For a long time now, brain scientists have known that there is no one part of the brain where memory resides. It's distributed somehow. Only in the last few years have scientists developed models that could actually demonstrate the power of a distributed system of this sort to hold large amounts of information. There's still a great deal that nobody understands. But the process of recollection isn't simply getting the can off the shelf, opening it, and depositing its contents back into the world. It's always a process of reinterpretation. Even when you seem to be reliving an event most vividly and recalling it in all its details, it's not like a film running in a theater.

Time has been twisted around in various ways, and only the essentials are left. Maybe filmmakers would love to able to make a film that could leave out so much detail and still be so vivid. But you can't do it, it's an entirely different medium. I wonder if before motion pictures, it was so obvious to people that when they closed their eyes and recalled an event from their past, it seemed like moving pictures.

*But moving pictures appeared, and then what happened?*

Then the appeal of the metaphor was just overpowering. Of course, we've been through this many times. There was a time back in the seventeenth century when clockwork seemed like a good analogy for the way the brain worked, or the way the mind worked. Later it was the telephone switchboard, and now it's the computer. People have toyed with the idea that it's holograms and lasers. With each new bit of technology that comes along, people try to use it as a metaphor for what the brain is. Of course, some people say these metaphors are all wrong because the brain can't be analogized to anything. That's nonsense. Anything can be usefully analogized. The heart can be analogized to a pump. It isn't exactly a pump, but it's a sort of pump. And the brain is a sort of computer. There is a very real sense in which what brains do is computation. And the brain is much better modelled as a computer than as a telephone switchboard, because the trouble with the telephone switchboard was that there were still human operators in there who answered and who knew what the message was. The great beauty of the computer metaphor—and the reason it's not really a metaphor—is that the computer is the first technology that eliminates the middleman. The computer does the actual information processing, for which in the past you needed a little man in the box.

*You said in a television interview, "It will be a long time before computers become capable of crying, but this is not simply a metaphor." What about all this artificial intelligence?*

Well, I think that a robot could definitely be conscious in exactly, unmetaphorically the same way we are. We are a sort of robot. We are organic robots created by a research-and-development process called natural selection, and also, of course, by a learning process in our own lifetimes. So, as a matter of principle, I am completely confident that there could be consciousness in an artificial device, a robot that lived its life, learned its experiences, and was made of entirely different material, say of silicon. I don't think we're likely to actually see that, for the same reason I don't think we're going to see anybody make a gall bladder out of atoms. I don't think anybody doubts that a gall bladder is just a fancy collection of atoms, but that's not the way to understand gall bladders, and it would be a pointless stunt to try to do it. In the same way, it would be a pointless stunt to try to make an artificial, conscious robot.

We can understand consciousness. We can solve the mysteries and the puzzles theoretically, without actually creating the real thing. If we are only interested in the utility of such a robot, the answer is that there are already plenty of people to do those jobs. The robots that are useful aren't conscious. Robots are useful as mindless automatons, as artificial servants in factories and dangerous places. The last thing you want is for such a robot to be susceptible to boredom or anxiety or fear or hatred. So for practical purposes we shouldn't make a conscious robot. And if we did, it would have the same rights that you and I have, and it would be immoral of us to demand that it go into some dangerous or frustrating or boring place. We shouldn't put a conscious robot anyplace where we wouldn't put a human being. It would have all the rights that we do.

*We will meet this whole computer—not as fantasy, but as science— again later on during our conversation. Let's just go back briefly before we finally enter the Cartesian theater. You were a freshman when you first read Descartes's* Meditations. *At that time you were hooked on the mind-body problem. What exactly was that all about? About duality in the Cartesian theater?*

Descartes says "Even if there is an evil demon deceiving me about everything it is possible to deceive somebody about, I still have got to be there to be the victim, to be deceived. I exist simply in virtue of thinking my thoughts. Cogito ergo sum." At first I thought: Well, that's undeniable, I see that. But then I realized that his discussion of the relationship between the I who thinks, who exists, and the body was completely unsatisfactory. You could tell somehow that Descartes himself was uncomfortable with this account. It hit me right then, at the age of seventeen or eighteen, that that was a worthy project. I checked with my professor to make sure nobody had solved it in the meantime, and he said no, it was a live issue. I thought Okay, that means philosophy is something worth doing, and I began to study logic very assiduously. It turns out that I'm not a very good logician, but it got me going in a big way.

I remember writing a paper for a course on perception in my second year in college, and coming up with an argument about how what we saw couldn't be like a picture at all; how the end product of a perceptual process like vision had to have an entirely different set of properties— nonvisual, nonspatial properties. Ultimately it had to have functional properties. It had to—so to speak—prepare one for a whole variety of different sorts of actions, and whatever the state was that was brought about by this process, it wasn't at all what we took it to be; it wasn't what it seemed to be. I remember thinking that I was onto something, and I remember in my sophomoric way I was so confident of this that when I didn't get a good grade on the paper, I just said; "The professor just isn't ready for this." So I suppose my hubris as a philosopher was born at that moment.

*What was the final or most important decision for you to leave this whole Cartesian theater? Or was it gradual?*

It seems to me it was gradual. As I look back over what I've written about it over the years, I see some embarrassing fossil traces of the Cartesian theater in *Brainstorms*, my first book, where I make exactly the error that I chastise people for so much in *Consciousness Explained*. Suppose there had to be this line you could draw—it might be squiggled or spread out all through the brain, but there had to be a line—so you could put all the preconscious processes on one side and all the postconscious processes on the other side. I called it the awareness line. Big mistake, So, certainly at that point I wasn't clear about it, although shortly thereafter I did a notorious paper about dreaming called "Are Dreams Experiences?" in which I argued from a number of cases that you had to give up a familiar notion of what a dream could be in order to preserve coherence, in order not to contradict yourself.

*Was that the moment at which you got the idea that the dream is an illusion without an illusionist?*

That idea came in several portions. One of the ideas came about not thinking about consciousness at all, but thinking about understanding or interpretation. The British empiricists of the eighteenth century, people like Hume and Locke, have these marvelous theories that are both plausible and very wrong. That's what makes them so interesting—how can a theory so false be so plausible? For Hume, first you have impressions, or sensations, which then sort of fade into ideas. Then we get all those ideas milling about and they get dragged across the stage in a certain order, there's a certain succession. Hume tries to invent a sort of chemistry of locking one idea to the next to create this sort of chain of consciousness. This is the birth of associationism. Associationism has a bad reputation these days because it was a simpleminded theory. But Hume was right about one thing: a librarian or a drillmaster or a master of ceremonies who puts the ideas together is no good. It's the homunculus that creates an infinite regress. Once a student of mine blurted out, "Hume's problem is to get the ideas to think for themselves." And I thought, yes, that's it. That's what Hume's task is. You've got to get rid of the middleman.

At the time I was looking at artificial intelligence, and it was becoming clear to me that that was just what the artificial intelligence scientists were working on. They had these elaborate schemes for creating apparent homunculi, apparent inner agents, which, if you looked at them closely, were composed of smaller, stupider little agents. Finally you got down to agents that were so dumb that all they had to do was remember zero or one. And that is an agent that can be replaced by a machine. Then you realize that the whole thing can be replaced by a machine. Not in one step, but in a finite number of steps. So the old argument looked like an infinite regress. The trouble with the little man in the head is that the little man has got a brain and a mind. What goes on in his brain? He has got a smaller man in the head. And so forth ad infinitum.

The mistake is thinking that it has got to be ad infinitum. You can break the regress by saying that there's not one little man in your head that's all powerful, there's a whole bunch of little men in your head who are partly powerful. You can go inside their heads and break them into smaller ones, stupider ones, but not forever. It's a finite regress, and after some step it's pretty clear that the components at this point are just mechanisms.

*Like the metaphor of the ant colony?*

That's right. Say you discharge the homunculi one at a time. You posit a sort of intelligence in there, an agent, until you can deal with some other part of the theory. Then you tackle that agent. You say, "Now I'm going to discharge this one," and you break that agent down into some simple parts, and then you break those simple parts down. Maybe after two or three steps, you've got a mechanical account, you're home, you've done it.

*You've written, "Should we suppress an investigation for fear of opening Pandora's box? It might be justified if we could convince ourselves that our current belief environment, myth-ridden or not, was clearly a morally acceptable, benign environment. But I submit that it is clear that it is not. Those who are worried about the costs threatened by this unasked-for enlightenment should take a hard look at the costs of the current myths." What are the current myths concerning consciousness and what are the costs?*

The current myths about consciousness include the idea of a distinguishable separate thing that some people call the self, others the soul. This is a very powerful idea, even among people who are not religious. Among people who are religious, of course, it's an idea they have a tremendous emotional attachment to, because they think that immortality—life after death—depends on the truth of this concept. They also think that it's the having of a soul that makes us have moral worth.

*Compared to all the other animals . . .*

This is where one gets into controversy. Do other animals have souls? It's interesting that killing a dog is a bad thing, certainly, but it's not murder anywhere in any country. It's murder only if you kill a human being. We distinguish the human species from all others. I think this is right, but I don't think it's right to say, as Descartes said, that the reason we distinguish the human species from others is that the human species have souls and no other animal does. That creates the illusion of a sharp edge, when in fact there is nowhere near such a sharp edge. There is a tremendous gulf between us and even chimpanzees, and it's a morally important gulf. But it's not one that is well described in terms of a soul or even in terms of the presence or absence of some one feature of consciousness. It's practically an obscenity that the very important debates about abortion are cast by so many people in terms of "At what instant does the fetus acquire a soul?" That's a very dangerous myth, and I think it's time to say that this is not a conceptualization of the issues that stands up to scrutiny. There are better ways of settling these issues.

*The definition of "soul" as we have had it for the last three or four hundred years is nonsense?*

Certainly, yes. The traditional religious doctrine of the soul is nonsense. If some version of this is going to survive in the future, it's going to go all on its own. It's not going to get any help from scientists or from philosophy. Now, there is a doctrine that's a close relative of that, perhaps, which is not nonsense and of which I myself am certain, and that is that what a person is, in fact, is information.

I talk about what I call the "self" as the "center of narrative gravity." The center of gravity of an object is not an atom, it is not a pearl, it is not a bit of stuff. It is a very important abstraction, but it is an abstraction. So a "self" is an abstract object that is definable in terms of a certain set of information. It follows, marvelously, that in principle you and I could be immortal if the information could be preserved. This is scientifically respectable. If immorality is what you crave, then you are much better off with the conception of yourself as fundamentally defined by information, rather than as a sort of immutable mind pearl, a soul of some sort. That is an incoherent idea. And it is also incoherent that it could matter. I mean, people are terribly concerned about, "Will anything matter anymore? Will there be any moral right or wrong if we have a materialistic, physical view of the mind and the brain?"

It's preposterous to think that the way to defend against this is to declare that there is a little bit of intrinsically mattering stuff that by definition matters. That's just playing games. If what we are matters— and it does—it's not because there is this immaterial or material atom which makes all the difference and which is the sort of ultimate locus of all the mattering.

*Why are people so afraid of opening Pandora's box?*

They haven't imagined the consequences in detail, and maybe they think they're not capable of imagining the consequences in detail. We're conservative—better the devil you know than the devil you don't. But when you replace the traditional notion of the soul with a more scientifically respectable idea, you explain the complexity. You actually explain what makes it wonderful. You explain why there is meaning there. In the same way, I suppose, people used to be terribly afraid that biologists were going to explain what life is. And they did! And it turns out much better than we ever thought. Élan vital is boring compared to what we have learned about what makes things living. Now there's a much better story. The kind of life we now understand, thanks to modern biology, is a kind of life you can really revere, you can really stand in awe of.

*For years I thought that if I knew the final goal of my consciousness, everything would come to a standstill. End of story. I would know why I had existed, why I would exist in the future, and the moment itself would lose all its appeal.*

Nobody wants the story to end. But the story doesn't end. Suppose there's a book of your life in the library of all possible books, which tells the truest tale that can be told of your life from the moment of your birth to the moment of your death. But there are also countless books in that library which tell a perfectly true story of your life up to this moment and then diverge billions of ways for each future moment. One of those books is the book of your life. Which one? Who knows? It's impossible to tell until afterward which one tells the truest story of your life. Not because our lives are strictly undetermined—that's an open question. But even if they are determined, we have an epistemic horizon, and we can't—in principle, not just in practice—we can't see over that epistemic horizon. So that is why the future will always be open to us. That is a deep feature of the way the world is. I can appreciate the offensiveness of the idea of somebody being able to demonstrate what our future is going to be right down to the last syllable we utter. On the other hand, we're not terribly upset by the fact that science can now say to a moral certainty that you are not going to live to be a 150 years old. You are also not going to win the Olympic pole vault. That is just physically impossible for you at your age, as it is for me at my age. We don't mind that science tells us about many things that are strictly not in the cards for us, that are quite beyond the realm of physical possibility. There's still plenty of elbow room for awe, plenty of room for striving, for trying. There's plenty of reason to go out there and have big projects. There is absolutely no reason why one should think that this vision of the mind and of human agency implies that it becomes pointless to try to do anything.

*Shall we start from the beginning? That is to say, before humans appeared in evolution. What we see in the Darwinian approach is that there is no striving upward, there is just adaptation to a local environment. The point of the story is: evolution serves no purpose. Isn't that Darwin's Dangerous Idea: Evolution and the Meaning of Life?*

Yes. Let's look at two prehistories—one before humans, and one even further, back, before there were any sentient creatures at all. Let's suppose this is the only planet that has ever known life. And let's go back to the time, the first billion years or so of this planet's existence, before there was any life at all. At that point, there were no purposes anywhere. Things just happened. Nothing happened for good or for bad, it just was. But different things happened.

*Roger Penrose postulates that a universe which is controlled by laws which do not make consciousness possible is not a universe at all. Therefore, in fact, the universe exists by the craving of our consciousness. That means that there wouldn't have been any such universe or earth if not for our eyes and our consciousness. . . .*

I'm glad you raise that question. I don't agree with Penrose—actually with John Archibald Wheeler, whose view that is most particularly. So far I have a much more conservative view. I suppose the universe existed for several billion years before there was any life in the universe, and at that time one can say only in the most metaphorical and retrospective sense that anything mattered at all. We can be glad that the universe had some of the features it did, because eventually it made life on earth possible. But there was no foresight, no planning, no striving.

Then what happened was that replicators, large molecules that were capable of replication, just happened to get sifted out of all the events that were going on. Eventually they became the precursors of DNA, so that eventually you have single-celled organisms. As soon you have replication of this sort going on, and since the conditions for replication are stringent—there are better conditions and worse conditions—one can begin to make a partial division of world states into those that are good and those that are bad for something, specifically for the replicative success of a particular group of molecules. You might say; "That's no big deal. One could also have talked about the conditions conducive to rusting of iron. What's the difference?" Is it a big difference? No. That's very important. The difference is tiny. Don't look for any great cliff anywhere in this story. But once this replication gets going, it creates more and more complex systems, which are self-replicating and which begin to take steps to preserve themselves. They begin to fend off their own deaths in very simple ways. Once they start distinguishing on their own—because, like little automatons, they have been designed to do this—between the beneficent and the maleficent states of their environment, we have the birth of purpose. Now we can begin to say things matter at least a little bit, because we can chart the fortunes of these beings. That's the birth of reasons, and we are simply the most recent entities that have reasons. We are different from just about all other entities in that we represent our reasons to ourselves.

*Yes, but we are not different as far as the genes are concerned.*

No. There is no difference as far as our origins are concerned. We are simply continuous with everything from the flowers in the field to the clams, to the reptiles, to the birds, to the mammals. And we are equally descendants of the same earliest replicators. But it happens that one species has developed enormous talents for self-representation, for representing our reasons to ourselves, and for investigating those reasons. We are reflective in a way no other species, not even a chimpanzee, is reflective.

*Why did such a characteristic evolve in a group of tree-dwelling mammals? Was this, as Gould put it, a glorious evolutionary accident? Or even an evolutionary mistake?*

Well, in one sense everything that happens in evolution is an accident, so that's not saying very much. Every creature is here and has the particular features it has as a result of an amazing series of accidents. But they are accidents that have been filtered through natural selection, and that puts a different cast on them. So we can say: Oh, yes, in one sense it's just an accident that one lineage of hominids or one lineage of primates became the hominid lineage and then eventually arrived at *Homo sapiens*. If there had been a certain mass extinction, which might have happened at any moment in the past, then we would not be here.

*If the dinosaurs had not died as a result of the impact of an asteroid on earth, man would not exist. That asteroid is the sine qua non of our existence.*

Well, at least the sine qua non of our existence is that we weren't wiped out by a second asteroid a million years ago, which could well have happened. In that sense, it is an accident. But I don't agree with Steve Gould that it's unlikely there should be our sort of intelligent life elsewhere in the universe, that it's that kind of accident. I think that intelligence is one of the good solutions to problems, though only one of many.

*Is that how you define "intelligence"—a good solution for a certain problem?*

I think there's a lot to be said for that. Let's look at how a weaverbird builds her nest. It requires a tremendously complicated routine of getting just the right materials, weaving them together, poking the twigs in and out to make this beautiful nest. Now imagine watching a child doing the same thing. Perhaps imagine a child who watches a weaverbird and then copies the weaverbird as it makes a nest. It looks like the same process, as it has the same product. But it is in fact a very different process. The child is thinking about what she is doing in a way that the weaverbird doesn't have to. There are sometimes two different ways for Mother Nature to solve a problem. One is a sort of mindless automatic way and the other requires real reflection. It may be to some degree an accident that our ancestors were tipped in the direction of intelligent, conscious solutions to problems, rather than operating like the weaverbird. This is a topic that interests me a great deal.

Consider the speculative stories that are now being told by anthropologists about the early hominids. It seems that our ancestors learned how to control fire maybe as much as a million years before they developed language. A stunning fact. It makes you wonder, What's so special about our ancestors that they could control fire, and how did they differ from other hominids, such as the ancestors of chimpanzees, which were then extant? You wonder, Could a chimpanzee be trained to tend a fire, to gather wood, to keep it dry, to put only the right amount of wood on the fire, not let it go out, not make it too big, keep it going? I've asked various primatologists and chimpanzee experts what they think, and they're divided in their opinion of whether a chimpanzee could even be trained to do this reliably. But whatever the talent for this sort of long-range project, it's something our ancestors mastered hundreds or thousands of years before they had language, or so it seems.

Now, it might be that there were really two ways of tending a fire—the way a weaverbird builds its nest and our way. If that were the case, and if our hominid ancestors had tamed fire in the dumb, mindless way, then I think we would not be here. The woods might be full of chimpanzees, sitting around campfires; but they would be like beavers building their dams. It wouldn't be like human culture. There may well have been moments in our evolutionary past—in fact, there almost certainly were—when several ways were available. There was a way that required us to become more devious and more intelligent and more reflective in the way we dealt with the problems that faced us, and ways that perhaps didn't require that sort of intelligence, say cheap tricks or combinations of cheap tricks. We are lucky to be here, I suppose, because our ancestors found the intelligent tricks instead.

*What really bothers me—and I think perhaps you also—is this: First, we have our genetic makeup, and second, we have our cultural makeup. With respect to this genetic makeup, you have quoted Richard Dawkins, who writes, "Cliché or not, 'stranger than fiction' expresses exactly how I feel about the truth. We are survival machines, robot vehicles, blindly programmed to preserve the selfish molecules known as genes. This is a truth which still fills me with astonishment. I have known it for years, but I never seem to get fully used to it." He sees genes as successful Chicago gangsters, ruthless and selfish. This is the truth that still fills him with astonishment. Do you feel the same sensation?*

Yes, I do agree. I think it's simply the truth about why we exist. We exist because we are the latest line of survival machines, designed over the period of natural selection, with ultimately no deeper raison d'être than just the preservation of the gene complexes that reside in each of us. Now, that doesn't mean that we haven't developed our own autonomy. Nothing about what we hold dear, or what matters to us, follows immediately from that claim. I have tried, in fact, to drive home that implication very clearly with a little thought experiment of my own.

Suppose you wanted to live five hundred years from now and there was no way of keeping you alive in the normal course of events for five hundred years. But let's suppose there was a way that your body could be put into suspended animation, perhaps in a cryogenic chamber. How are you going to keep that chamber properly protected and supplied with electricity for the next five hundred years? One way would be to build a giant robot that would lumber around the world, staying out of harm's way, providing itself with enough energy to preserve itself and its precious cargo—namely, the capsule in which you reside. You couldn't be in control of it, you'd have to cede control to it. It would be autonomous. You could design it as much as you wanted to, but once you got inside and closed the door, your fate was its fate and it had better have the capacity to make clever decisions, decisions that you would approve of, if only you could, via the controls.

Suppose you actually faced this design problem, you would recognize: I want to make this protective vehicle clever enough to recognize not just immediate dangers but very far-flung dangers. I want it to look very far into the future. I want it to be able to anticipate harm and to recognize its best chances. To form an alliance with another great robot, perhaps, against a third, and to be able to judge whether it makes sense to cooperate in this case.

The only real hope of success under these demanding circumstances is to make a robot that is essentially capable of learning, of taking on new projects, of devising for itself new goals and new means of communicating with other such beings. It must be able to anticipate dangers and to plan ahead.

Now the cost of giving it all those powers is also giving it the power to change its mind about what it ought to do. Maybe the robot you so cleverly constructed is going to fall in love with another robot and throw his life away, and yours with it, to get the benefits it wants. And there you go. And it was your best chance and it didn't work.

And in a similar way, there is no reason why human beings, given our extraordinary malleability and susceptibility to new ideas and new influences, should not be able to defy the genetic factors without which we wouldn't exist. We can rebel against any feature of our biological heritage, and we do it every day. Wearing eyeglasses, having your teeth straightened, having plastic surgery, getting an artificial heart, or simply deciding not to make any more babies in spite of one's urges. These are all ways we rebel, and there are many others as well.

*You have written, "Conscious human minds are more or less serial virtual machines, implemented inefficiently on the parallel hardware that evolution has provided." So what about the killer ape underneath? Who makes decisions in critical situations?*

Well, that's always the problem. And every one of us knows of occasions when the animal wins. The more reflective we are, the more we learn to plan for that. After all, one of the features of the environment that we learn to take into consideration is our own selves. I am part of my own environment and I know what my urges are and what my susceptibilities are. I know which colors I prefer, which smells I can't stand, which things distract me. I may not be able simply to banish those features of myself by fiat. I can build other features of my environment that can be counted on to overrule those features. I can harness those features in new ways. We can overcome the killer ape in certain situations.

*But at which times does the killer ape raise his head?*

What your brain is and what my brain is, is a loose coalition, an unsteady alliance of different parts, some of them very ancient, some of them of our construction in our own lifetime, some of them of our own construction within the last few days or weeks. And it is precisely because we are so reflective—because we pay attention to our own reactions to things, and then we pay attention to our reactions to our reactions, and then we plan about changing our reactions to our reactions to our reactions, and this self-reflective spiral becomes more and more complicated—that we build up new structures in our brains. How powerful are they? Well, it varies from individual to individual. Some people are impulsive and very animal and lose their temper very quickly, and we say, "He's behaving like an animal." And some people do. There are those who don't behave in the peculiar ways that human beings—and only human beings—are capable of. And of course if it's really true that some individuals are so lacking in powers of self-control and self-regulation, then this is not a moral agent, this is somebody who has got to be institutionalized and protected from himself, and society must be protected from him. Aside from people like that, a normal adult human being is quite wonderfully reliable and safe and wise. Otherwise we wouldn't go out on the highway. Think of it. Unhesitatingly we get in a car, we drive 60 miles an hour on a highway with cars coming at us. The drivers could instantly kill us. We're not afraid of that. Why? Because we trust the self-control systems in those brains. You put chimpanzees behind the wheel and nobody is going to go out on the highway.

*What about Vietnam or Auschwitz or whatever other catastrophes we have had this century?*

Yes, things break down and there is no one master. Certainly ancient animal urges rise up. But also other urges which I am afraid are actually much more human than animal.

*You simply blame your ancestors, you remove your moral responsibility.*

Oh, no, those of us who are capable of normal, minimal levels of self-control are responsible for our actions, because we build ourselves. We, and our own reflective activities, are more responsible for the product that now faces the world than either genetics or our schoolteachers. Indeed, we tend to excuse somebody who has never been to school, who has never had the opportunity to learn the culture that we consider to be the prerequisite for a moral agent. This person should know better, but doesn't know any better. But once the basic minimal conditions are met, both genetically—this is somebody who is not retarded, who has a normal nervous system—and in terms of schooling, then we automatically get an agent who simply by adopting the habits of a cultured human being has the reflective habits and the habits of self-correction and guidance that make him or her responsible for his or her own actions.

We create ourselves and then we are responsible for the selves that we create, on an ongoing basis. At any moment I can't have control of the very next syllable I say, so I have to have turned myself into the sort of person who can wing it at times like this, relying on the fact that I'm a good enough self-controller, so that what comes out will be appropriate—though maybe I'll live to regret some of it. The myth of perfect conscious, deliberate control is hopeless. But we do a very good job of it, actually.

Our main dangers grow out of our animal past, but very indirectly. Fanaticisms are the single most dangerous feature of human existence right now. If you ask why fanaticisms govern people's lives the way they do, I think the answer is in part that we crave simple answers to complicated problems. This is very unfortunate. As you can see, I'm speaking with a sort of eighteenth-century Enlightenment voice at this point. To me the goal is to impose more reason and higher standards of rationality. Human beings are up to it. It's their fears that lead them to adopt and then cling with a deathly embrace to doctrines that are just indefensible. I think actually part of our Enlightenment heritage of tolerance for this—which has been a very good thing—has been the conditions of the flowering of modern civilization. We're seeing that one of the prices we pay is an unwillingness to confront some of the ancient myths and just declare them to be the nonsense they are, because we're afraid of hurting people's feelings or offending their religious sensibilities. The rise of fundamentalisms of every stripe is tremendously dangerous. I don't think, however, that they're a function of our animal natures, except in the sense that part of the taming of the human animal has been to create susceptibilities to certain sorts of fear and to certain sorts of relief from that fear.

*Why do we have a Swiss cheese consciousness? Why do we think that consciousness is something continuous when in fact it's not at all? How do you prove that it's not continuous? According to you, consciousness is full of holes and sparse and doesn't contain half of what people think is there.*

First of all, it surprises people to learn that there are these big gaps in their consciousness, both in space and in time. People are stunned to learn that they have a blind spot in each eye, big enough to hide six full moons piled up one on top of the other. You don't notice that in everyday life. You're not aware of what you're missing.

America has Fort Knox; the fort that's filled with gold. The gold in Fort Knox is supposed to preserve the value of the American dollar. Notice it doesn't matter that the gold is really there. All that matters is that everybody thinks it's there. It's the fact that it's believed to be there that plays the role in the economy of nations.

Similarly, in your conscious life what matters is what you think is there. We think of our consciousness as being continuous. We ignore the gaps, and because we ignore them, their presence makes no difference. It's because we're so used to ignoring them that it takes a special effort to draw our attention to them. The reason you don't normally see your blind spot has several elements. One is that in order to see the spot, you have to see the edges, and in order to see the edges, you have to have receptors on both sides of the boundary. As there are no receptors on the inside of the boundary, you can't really see the boundary, so the only way you can see your blind spot is by making something disappear into it at the time you're attending to it. Well, you can do that very simply. You put two crosses on a screen or on the wall. You close one eye and focus on one of the crosses. As you move your head closer and closer and reach about the right distance, depending on the distance between the two spots, one of them will suddenly disappear. It has disappeared into your blind spot. That is one kind of gap.

*But the gaps in my memory . . . Part of my uniqueness is the fact that I have a real past. My past has formed me and it's always there, whenever I want it.*

If you go to sleep, of course, it's not there. What is it like to be asleep? Everybody knows about those sleep gaps, and they don't bother our sense of continuity. As philosophers we can reflect about this. How do I know when I wake up that I'm the same person I was when I went to sleep? How do I know it was I that went to sleep? Maybe it wasn't. It's precisely because we don't find sudden metamorphoses happening that we are comfortable in our sense of continuity.

There are gaps in time. In the course of your everyday conscious visual experience, your eyes are jumping about very fast. In a little jump called a secade, your eyes move to about three or four fixations a second; so there are fifteen to twenty milliseconds of jump three or four times in every second. That's not a big gap, but we aren't aware of those gaps at all. We are entirely oblivious of any changes that are made during those gaps. So these are really temporal gaps in our visual experience.

*As you wrote, "We will never be able to tell in fact that our brains are provisioning us with less than everything that is available in the world." That seems to me a wonderful kind of dilemma.*

There's a very simple way of thinking of this. Mother Nature is stingy, she doesn't go to needless expense. Why bother bringing the whole world or a representation of the whole world into the head when for most purposes the world is right there? All you have to do is look at it whenever you need it. Leave it out there and don't go to all the trouble of representing it and storing a representation of it. For the same reason, I buy only a few books and borrow any others I need from the library.

Similarly, as you walk around, you get a flood of information from vision and your other senses. You get more information than you can use. That's why you think you have it all, because you never have any hunger. Any information you want, you've got it. And since you are seldom put in a position where you crave more information than you get, you have the sense that your information store is complete. But it isn't, and we can demonstrate that by artificially creating a hunger for some information that you don't have. And then it can be stunning. Think of these lovely experiments that John Grimes has done where he shows subjects pictures. These are high-resolution, full-color photographs that he shows to the subjects on a computer screen. They're asked to study each picture for ten seconds, because they are later going to be asked to pick them out of a larger group of pictures. While they're looking at the pictures, an eye scanner looks at their eyes, and as soon as the eye makes one of these secades, these jumps, something big in the picture changes, something really quite astonishingly large, but it changes during that brief flick of the eye.

*And the brain doesn't register that?*

The brain doesn't pick up on it, and it's fascinating that even though something quite large has been changed in the picture, the subjects are unaware that anything has changed. Now, if they had in their brain a good copy of that picture, they would notice a mismatch. But they don't.

*What are the implications of these split second experiences for the discontinuity of consciousness?*

Well, there are many implications, but one of them is that the brain actually stores and processes and represents less than we think it does. It has a much more modest diet of information than our phenomenology at first suggests. But then we can go beyond that and say: Not only that, but the order in which things happen in the brain is not the order in which they seem to happen. There is quite a difference. The order in which things seem to happen is a function much more of interpretation than of the actual temporal order of the events happening in the brain.

We have no trouble with this idea in novels and films—we understand what a flashback is—nor do we have any trouble understanding the sentence "Tom arrived at the party after Bill did." We learn of Tom's arrival before we learn of Bill's arrival, but in actual fact Bill arrived first. There's no problem about that. We recognize how in these forms of representation the order in which things happened in the representing may be different from the order that representing represents. The brain does the same thing. It's quite possible for you to have a brain event that represents $A$ and a later brain event that represents $B$, but in which the brain represents $B$ as happening before $A$. That's the way it seems subjectively to you, even though it's the reverse of the order of the events in the brain. That's a very striking idea. I think this is one of the hardest ideas in my book to understand. It's very hard to believe and it takes a lot of strenuous exercise to show people that they should abandon this idea that the stream of consciousness really is running through a sort of projector onto a screen.

*And what, then, is the implication?*

In my book I present a theory called the "multiple drafts" model of consciousness, which suggests that all of these demons are writing things down in some sort of brain language, in drafts of narratives. That was to counteract an overreliance on pictures, which is a mistake. But the idea of writing is also a mistake. So let me give you a different version of the same theory, which is in an important respect equivalent, although it has some different images associated with it. We could call this the "multiple cuts" theory of consciousness.

Imagine a movie studio where they make films, and they've got all these pieces of film that have been shot in any order at all. It doesn't matter what order they've been shot in. And now the film is being put together by various editing processes. First this bit goes before that bit, and then that bit goes before this bit. Maybe you even have different teams working on different versions of the same story at the same time. Maybe eventually one of these versions gets released as a film to the public, or maybe not. It may just get stored. Now you may think: What is the right version? Is it the version where $A$ happened before $B$, or the version where $B$ happened before $A$? It's not important in what order the film was made, which is the correct canonical version. You might think: Perhaps the studio has a boss with his own private inner office, the "central boss meaner" of the whole show, who at some point watches a particular rough cut of the film at a private screen and says, "That's it." Now if somebody tampers with that film later and changes the order or cuts a scene out, that's tampering with the official version.

What I am saying is, there's no official version in consciousness. All the time our brains are tampering with the contents. They're revising them, editing them, some things are being dropped out all together. The question is: What was the original version you were conscious of? That's a mistake. It's a tremendously attractive mistake, but simply a mistake. The simplest phenomenon I have come across that exhibits this is called "metacontrast." Suppose I flashed a disk on a screen—flash, flash, flash. You would see each flash very clearly. Then suppose I took a ring and flashed it on the screen right after I had flashed the disk, so that the inner boundary of the ring coincided with the outer boundary of the disk when it had been there. Now if I flash the ring within a few milliseconds of the disk, you will see them together: a ring surrounding a disk. If I delay the ring until, say, a second has gone by, then you will see both in sequence. You will see disk followed by ring, disk followed by ring. But if I get the interstimulus interval just right, say about 120 milliseconds, all you will report seeing is just the second stimulus, just the ring. The disk disappears. It's a stunning effect. Now, how do we explain that?

Well, here is one standard theory. All you are ever conscious of is the ring, and the reason is that somehow the first stimulus, the disk, doesn't reach consciousness. It's ambushed on the way up. Somehow the ring overtakes the disk and prevents it from ever entering the theater of consciousness. And so you correctly remember that what you saw was a ring. And that's all you saw. Well, here's another theory. You were conscious of the disk, but the ring followed the disk in consciousness so swiftly that it simply erased your memory of that consciousness of the ring.

Now we have two theories. One says that the disk never made it into the charmed circle, and that's why you don't remember it. The second theory says: Oh, the disk made it, but then the memory was wiped clean. There is no difference between those two theories, because there is no way of drawing the line that distinguishes the inner sanctum where what happens there matters. That's the mistake, the fundamental mistake of the Cartesian theater. And it's a tremendously attractive idea and it's just wrong.

A philosopher in discussion with me recently, Michael Lockwood of Oxford, said, "Perception is the leading edge of perceptual memory." To which I replied, "Edge? What makes you think there's an edge? That's the mistake." Eventually material is deposited in perceptual memory. That memory itself may begin to decay very quickly. Moreover, it may get tampered with. But you can't draw that edge in, so that you can say: Now it hasn't entered memory yet; now it has entered memory and any further adjustments count as a memory disorder. The line between a perceptual illusion and a memory disorder simply can't be drawn. Since it can't be drawn in a principled way, we have to give up the idea of this privileged place where consciousness happens. Of course it happens in the brain. But there isn't any headquarters, smaller than the brain, which is the conscious headquarters.

*All these ants running around, these dumb soldiers carrying messages without knowing their content or their product . . . Our consciousness is the product of all these messages.*

That's right. And under normal circumstances a more or less coherent story emerges. It's the story I tell when you ask me, "What did you see?" It's the story I can tell myself. But if my demands for precision, or for unity get high, then I run into trouble. The story has only so much unity to it. There just isn't any fact to the matter of how it *really* was in my consciousness, even though I can't tell. That's why metacontrast makes such a good case, because when people see the metacontrast stimuli, they see the disk and they see the ring. And when they just see the ring, I say; "Now you tell me, or you tell yourself in your inner heart of hearts: Did you see the disk and forget it, or did you just see the ring?" They have no way of deciding that. There's nothing they can appeal to from the inside, from the first-person point of view, that will distinguish those two. I say, if you can't distinguish it from the inside and there is no principled way of distinguishing it from the outside, there is no fact to the matter.

*We have a conception of our soul as coherent, of our person as a unity. And now you say there just is no "central meaner." Consciousness is just dumb soldiers running around. What aspect of your theory creates the most controversy?*

Let's see. Getting rid of the central meaner has been less provocative than I had expected. I had expected it to be more unsettling because so much attention has gone into the fallacy of the central homunculus that's looking at a screen. Everybody knows that that's a fallacy. And here I am pointing out, yes, that's a fallacy, but there is the same fallacy on the output side—the idea of a central meaner who gives directions to the speech carpenters to make the language. Then we have to replace the central meaner with an account of how coherent language can be emitted, as it is, out of a collaboration and competition of somewhat noncentral, somewhat not-in-charge subsystems. One of the features of this which I really like is that I learn what I'm about to say at the same time you do, except for the rare instances when I may deliberately rehearse a sentence to myself before I reveal it to the world.

*Consider the wonderful example of Bertrand Russell and Lady Ottoline.*

Lady Ottoline Morell, to whom he blurted out, "I love you," and then thinks: What have I said? Then, he says, "I reflected on it and I realized that it was the truth." I think there is much more opportunism, you might say, in normal conversation, at all levels, from the most mundane to the most poetic and philosophical. We find out what we think by hearing what we say. We shape what we say next on the basis of what we just heard ourselves say, and because we have ongoing projects which require that certain sorts of conditions be met by the speech we are uttering, it comes out in a more or less coherent way. It would be bizarre to suppose that it was the product of a whole meaner, sitting somewhere in the middle of my head composing speech acts, which were then turned into English by my speech-output machinery. That's the old homunculus problem right back in full force.

*I would like to read something to you so that we won't completely misunderstand each other. It's a quotation from a Hungarian friend of mine, a writer. He once wrote, "We not only live in stories, in half-make-up daydreams or seemingly real stories. We are them. We differ in nothing from animals and stones except in that one typical human characteristic: that we tell each other stories without knowing whether they are true, whether they ever happened, but in the illusion that maybe they once happened and therefore may happen again sometime. Our position is not midway between God and the universe, not between evolution and dinner at half past seven. Our position is as if between a thousand stories that are all true or could have been true or may become true, without knowing, therefore, where we find ourselves."*

It's tantalizingly close to what I think the truth is. But I have recently learned, somewhat to my dismay, that there is a variety of views that are very close to mine and are very popular which I don't want to endorse, because they are slightly too radical. Even to the point, I think, of incoherence. First of all, I do think that in a very important sense our self-narration, our creation of ourselves, is a matter of spinning narratives. This is as much a part of our way of dealing with the world as a spider's web is the spider's way of dealing with the world. Words, words, words—we use them in the same way animals use their nests and their other ploys. The web of words is our way of making our way in the world. And out of this we construct ourselves and our lives. The important thing to remember is that for the most part we don't do this deliberately. The stories we tell ourselves and each other are for the most part not professional storytellers' stories. A professional storyteller is to what we all are roughly what a civil engineer is to a beaver that's building a dam. The beaver is not a professional dam builder, but he's a very good dam builder. He doesn't have to think about all the principles. And similarly the stories that we are, as opposed to the stories that we merely tell, are stories that are not professionally crafted, but are sort of emitted by us. This is what our brains do. Our brains govern a process that over time creates an autobiography. Our tales are spun, but for the most part we don't spin them. They spin us.

That doesn't mean that anything goes. This is not really a relativistic doctrine at all. It doesn't mean that a murderer can tell a new story where he isn't a murderer or that an evil man can tell a new story in which he's a good man. It doesn't mean that everybody's fantasies about their past are as good as the truth. Those are the outrageous versions of the doctrine that I will not associate with. I know they're popular in some quarters. I think in the end there are scientific principles that govern the interpretation of these emitted stories.

*In the beginning was the word. . . .*

In the beginning of this task was the word. The word is very recent. If you look at the actual history, words have been around for just a twinkling of time. But since those words have been around, they have played an ever more potent role in constructing what we are. It is a recent innovation which has very much taken over.

*What would we be without words? Let's consider a congenital deaf-mute who has no access to either sign language or normal language.*

Well, that is exactly the case you want to look at—a deaf-mute child who doesn't have signing. Happily, there are very few such cases, because deaf children, thank goodness, generally are taught sign of some sort immediately as their natural language.

*What happens to this little Kaspar Hauser?*

Well, this is a very important theoretical issue. And here is where we could disprove a theory of mine. It follows from my theory that the consciousness of such a human child, such as it is, would be tremendously diminished in comparison with our consciousness. It would be as different from our consciousness as the consciousness of another species would be. It's simply not a normal human mind, even though it's in an almost normal human brain. Some people just recoil from this view as if it were somehow an offensive claim. I don't understand why. It seems to me to be quite obvious that consciousness grows by degrees in a normal child, that the sentience of the fetus in the womb is something that grows by slow increments. There isn't a moment when the lights are turned on—now you're conscious. The same thing is true after you're born. The consciousness of the newborn infant is very, very different. Now one will ask: How do you know? Well, that follows from a theory I have which is based on lots of different sorts of experimental evidence.

*For instance, about those deaf-mute children?*

Remember that even a deaf child without sign language who grows up in a culture in which there is language is growing up in a very different environment than a deaf child who grows up without language users in the area. And of course there are certainly differences in the brains of deaf children, which are due to the presence of language in most of their ancestors. So the question what deaf people without language can be conscious of can be studied empirically, but the bearing of those discoveries, which still have to be made, is only indirect and problematic. It's not an easy matter. But if such people are capable of the sorts of thought processes that I claim you can get only by virtue of growing up with language, then my theory is wrong.

*We talked about computers, both as a metaphor to understand our own brains or our own mind and about the possibility of making a conscious computer. What would it take to make a linearly programmed computer into a conscious being? If you could explain that, we would in a sense know what we are. With this we leave the path of the metaphor.*

To make a conscious computer you would first need to make a computer that had the capacity to have the richness of content in real time that we do. That's already a very tall order. I think only by using a parallel machine would one have any hope of getting enough computational power to subserve a life in our world at our time scale. It's no good making a simulation of a computer that runs a thousand times too slowly. The world will leave it behind. Next, it would have to be programmed in such a way as to permit the evolution within it of indefinitely many levels of self-reflection. And it would have to be capable of devising new habits in a very simple sense, just new regularities, new proclivities to put contents together in certain ways. It would need to have a natural language.

*This could be any language, or is this just computer language?*

No, it has been one of the real gaps in artificial intelligence research that even the most ambitiously psychologically realistic models have simply evaded the question of how the system of representation that underlies everything relates to a natural language, and what the system would obtain by learning a natural language. How would that acquisition interact with what's already there? This is one of the unasked questions of artificial intelligence. I think this is a question that must be asked. I think that would really change the requirements for the architecture of the virtual machine.

*Is this all that's necessary to build a conscious computer?*

That's it. Except don't underestimate how much is involved in what I'm saying. We're talking about enormous amounts of linkage between various parts of this system. We're talking about very wide information channels and about a system that is very richly interconnected with the world. A home computer, for instance, has ridiculously impoverished input devices. There is just a keyboard and a mouse and a disk drive. That's the only way of getting impingements from the outside world in. It's deaf, dumb, and blind, it has no sense of touch, no sense of smell. Once you start adding all of these channels of input, and perhaps some new ones too, like X-ray vision or echolocation, like bats, and you add locomotion and behavioral channels of output that have to be interleaved, then you create a sort of system that we have only the palest copies of in existing computer systems. We're talking about a mammoth, unrealizable system at this time. But if you give me the $100 billion or whatever it would take to create that, I believe in the end it would be conscious. It would be much more expensive than going to the moon, but yes, we could do it in principle.

*Because we know how our brains work.*

Exactly. The only difference in the two projects is the direction in which they go. There is engineering and there is reverse engineering. Biology and psychology are reverse engineering: we have the artifact and we're trying to figure out how it works and why it's designed the way it is. The reverse is trying to make one. That's forward engineering.

*One of the things a computer with consciousness should have is free will. What about free will if one views people as large, very complicated computers?*

What about free will, indeed? I devoted a book, *Elbow Room*, to that before I worked on consciousness, because I thought just this question comes up: How can we reconcile a notion of free will, the kind of free will that matters to us? In that book I tried to show that the kind of free will we want is perfectly consistent with the idea that we are mechanisms.

Let's take the issue about determinism for a moment. Suppose we were to build a robot to protect your children for ten years while you go away. Needless to say, you would want it to be the most reliable and responsible robot you can imagine. Consider two different robots, each of which has to be capable of what you might call random or pseudorandom exploration. It's got to be capable of exploring the space of possible things that might happen and thinking of considerations that might be relevant in a way that shouldn't be rigid and patterned, that should have a large element of random exploration in it. There are two ways of achieving that. One is genuine randomness—quantum randomness. If you really want this, you put a bit of radium in there and a Geiger counter and then you have a real physical randomizer, according to quantum physics. Or you can use a pseudorandom number generator of the sort that every computer already has. The pseudorandom number generator guarantees that it isn't really random. It's a perfectly deterministic system, but it's just as good a way of getting this very desirable feature of a sort of spontaneity. I think that people at some level understand that this idea, the determinism, is not the danger.

Let me compare two different lotteries. Here is the first lottery. You buy a ticket, all the ticket stubs are put in a drum, and then a quantum randomizer mixes them up and a quantum grabber reaches in and chooses the winning ticket. That's the fairest lottery of all possible lotteries. Here is another lottery. After the tickets are printed, the quantum randomizer chooses the winning ticket, and only then are the tickets sold. The winner has already been determined. Now, is that a fair lottery? Does it make sense to go out and but a ticket in that lottery? Certainly, there is no difference. Well, if that is right, and I'm sure that is right, then it doesn't matter whether you get your lottery tickets through life, whenever you need a coin flip, or whether all your coin flips were determined by something arbitrary and random at the moment of the Big Bang. They still have the property of giving you an untrackable trajectory through a certain bit of space.

Consider the game children play in America called "rock-paper-scissors." Paper covers rock, rock breaks scissors, scissors cut paper. You go one, two, three, shoot and two children must make one of these signs at the same time. Now, if you're playing this game, you think "What is my strategy going to be?" Well, if you adopt a simple strategy like going rock, paper, scissors constantly in that order, the other side will track that quickly and then you'll lose all the time, because your opponent will see a pattern in what you're doing. It's important not to exhibit a pattern, to be random. But if you want to be random in this way, a pseudorandom process is just as good as a random process. Now, that simple game reveals in very simple terms why there are many contexts in which it's important for your brain to be able to randomize its exploration of a set of possibilities. That's the only way you can have much protection against systematic blindness to important events in your life.

I think a large part of free will, of spontaneity, and one of the reasons why we intuitively appreciate freedom, is that we don't want to be trackable. And that's right, because if you're trackable, you're not in charge. It's a very important threat to your autonomy. But you can build that freedom into a machine. Now, of course, if somebody else has the blueprint of the machine and knows in every detail exactly which number is going to come up next in the pseudorandom number table, then you need a real radium randomizer, because that's proof against any inquiring demon. But in the real world we don't have to worry about that. . . .

There is something in evolution known as the "Red Queen effect," a term derived from *Through the Looking-Glass*. The Red Queen has to run as fast as she can just to stay where she is. And there are occasions when you have to work very hard to keep yourself from getting into worse predicaments. And when that happens, one's free will is diminished, absolutely. When we think about free will and about freedom and why it's valuable, what we're really interested in is not being in prison, not being in a concentration camp, not having our hands tied behind our backs, not being under the direct control of somebody else's will. These are perfectly real threats to freedom, and they have nothing to do with mechanism or causation. They have to do with political circumstances and the way the world actually is.

People tend to mistake the hypothesis of determinism or mechanism with a particular version of how the world might be set up. For instance, people are very susceptible to the following simple fallacy. They say; "If determinism is true, then I can't change the way I am." No. If determinism is true, and if you can change the way you are, then you were determined to be able to change the way you are. And if you weren't able to change the way you are, then you were determined not to be able to change the way you are. But it has no implications at all for whether you can change. If determinism is true, then the weather is determined, in all of its changeability. It doesn't mean we're more like a clock than a cloud.

*But let's suppose I want to learn from previous generations. For instance, I want to learn something from a friend who survived Auschwitz, and I don't succeed. Or I want to prevent some problems for my children or myself, anticipation machine that I am, and I don't succeed. There is free will and there is reality. How should we look at that in the context of determinism?*

That's the human predicament. No theory of free will could ever change that. You can wish for a sort of free will where your will is omnipotent and you can make all your faults go away and go backward in time and undo all your errors and be two places at once. Of course that's a fantasy. Nobody could have that kind of free will. But the free will that you need for moral responsibility is still limited by the way the world is and the way you are. And we all have our flaws. That doesn't mean that we are not responsible.

*A simple, childish question: If nature is non-moral, where do we find morality? How do we define good and evil and decide whether something is good or bad?*

I like the way you put that very much, because your question implies that there is no morality or immorality in nature. Nature is amoral. Hobbes addressed just that question: Where do you find morality? And he answered it by telling a Darwinian story, several centuries before Darwin. He told a just-so story. He didn't have any fossil record to rely on, but he just imagined that something of the following sort had to be the case. There had to have been a time before morality, when, as he said, men lived in a state of nature and life was nasty, brutish, and short. And then, he supposed, a sort of social mutation happened, the coming together—more or less by accident, not with foresight—of some people who got the bright idea (lucky them, lucky us) that there should be a social contract. And they shook hands and thus created something that had never before existed on the planet: "society." They created a community with laws and rules and promises. According to Hobbes, they created good and evil. And not just the ideas of good and evil. In creating the ideas of good and evil, they gave birth to morality at that moment. Now, of course that should not be taken to be a historical account of something that happened at a specific date, say before or after 5000 B.C. This is a rational reconstruction of a process that was no doubt scattered in space and time. But what he suggested, and I think correctly, was that morality had to evolve with the establishment of a modern form of community. It depended on language for communication, so that the social contract could actually mean something. It depended, as Nietzsche says in his *Genealogy of Morals*, on creating a human being who could keep a promise. And this, he said, was no small task. It required lots of blood, lots of pain.

Maybe Hobbes was merely talking like a sociobiologist, saying that it was a useful innovation to create these larger social units. It's a bit like the social insects, like ants or bees. I think Nietzsche actually had deeper insight here. He said no, that doesn't get you morality. He put it slightly differently: Humankind is not yet interesting at this point. If you want to make humankind interesting and dangerous, then you have to go a step farther. And he tells a remarkable and slightly outrageous just-so story to the effect that genuine moral values had to be built on this Hobbesian foundation. Well, some such story as Nietzsche's has to be the truth, where out of a premoral period of the existence of *Homo sapiens* a new set of cultural products emerges.

Nietzsche saw that out of preexisting quasi- or protomoral social circumstances a further development had to happen, creating new cultural products, new ideas, new concepts, new attitudes. In his terms, it had to create a conscience, the idea of guild and the idea of evil—not just the idea of bad, but the idea of evil. His own account is melodramatic and culturally distorted, and yet it's the right sort of story to tell. Any such story has to show how, by relatively gradual increments, society could transform itself from a premoral society into a moral society by changing its members fundamental habits of thought. I think we see this in moral education, in the development of moral sentiment, moral intuitions in children. There are cultural differences; after all, morality is a social product. It's a *meme*. There are the memes in Dawkins's terms, they are the memes for morality. How they evolve and why they evolve is a story on which only a little progress has been made, but I think it's important to tell it. Here again we have to get rid of earlier myths. God didn't give us morality. That's cheap easy solution, like saying God created the bird's wing. It begs the question. We have got to answer the straightforward question of how we developed morality, and we did. Here it is.

*We can talk about hatred, about fear and altruism, but what about fun? You wrote, "Fun is not a trivial concept, but it has not yet to my knowledge received careful attention from a philosopher. We certainly won't have a complete explanation of consciousness until we have accounted for its role in permitting us, and only us, to have fun. What are the right questions to ask? Why should it take funny things to relieve stress, why not green things or simple flat things?"? Well, why?*

That's one of the unkept promises of my theory. I haven't yet got a good theory of fun, or a good theory of laughter. And they are, I think, very telling phenomena that will repay our attention, if we can only be clever enough to study them well. No other creature does anything like laugh. What is laughter for? And since that's a risky question, one wants to know what it's a by-product of that's so important to us. Why should we be designed so that laughter is, in Steve Gould's terms, "a spandrel that is so evident in the structure of our cognitive lives"? I suspect that the key to understanding this is to look at the role of what you might call time pressure and emotional storms. The way our control systems have evolved to overcome the design shortcomings of their ancestors is to pit one part of the brain against another in a sort of tense struggle, which creates the risks of certain sorts of impasses that need to be resolved by getting a push from some other quarter. And the laughter, the response, is simply a by-product of that. But also, you see, we become addicted to it. No reason why we should have become addicted to it, except that it's simply the price we pay for having built our cognitive machinery from bits and pieces lying around and put them to new purposes. I think that fun and laughter just cry out for a Darwinian explanation of this sort. It's as if somebody built a homemade airplane that rattled just terribly and shook whenever it turned left, almost shook to pieces. And if you asked, "Well, why does it shake so hard, what good it that?" it's not good for anything, it's just a by-product of the raw materials the designer used. And I think that that's got to be the general space in which a good theory of laughter will fall. I have some more half-baked ideas about the details, but that's enough for now.

Fun is a protoconcept, of course, and it seems to me to have to do very much with a sense of how you use time, with what time means to an organism. And of course it means different things to different organisms. Some animals sleep most of the time. You might say that plants sleep all the time. They don't have to wake up, they deal with time more or less on a seasonal basis or they track the sun maybe during the day, like a sunflower. The temporal demands are very different from one organism to the next. And by looking at this in the right way, you begin to get some clue about the conditions necessary for organisms to be able to have fun, to have the time for fun.

I'm fascinated by the recent perplexity of some biologists about what the function of sleep is. They've shot down all the plausible theories, and now some of them say, and this is very paradoxical, they can't find a function for sleep, which is such a ubiquitous phenomenon. They're not even exploring what seems to me to be the obvious first step to any theory on sleep, and that is: What is the function of being awake? They've got the question backward. Why should an animal be awake? It's got to be awake in order to get enough food, so that it can live and find a mate, if it's a sexual creature. Maybe it depends on its particular ways of making a living. It may have to care for its young, it may not. But if an animal can preform all its biological requirements in one hour out of twenty-four, then there's no reason not to sleep the rest of the time. It's cheaper. We're used to thinking that the point of our existence is to be awake. But Mother Nature doesn't care. From Mother Nature's point of view, being awake is a luxury. You don't need that. We don't exist in order to smell the flowers and enjoy the scenery. Those are values that we humans have adopted and made our own. That's who we are. To us a life without being awake is no life at all. But those aren't nature's values, so we shouldn't expect that there should be an answer to the question of the function of sleep.

*Talking about sleep immediately reminds me of dreams. What do we do with Freud nowadays? A psychiatrist wrote to me: 'His subconscious is the dung of all our ignorance. We post all that we cannot explain to that region, and in the dung every chicken may find something nutritious.'*

I'm not even sure Freud's name appears in the index of my book. It may, but he gets almost no attention. That's a good question. What about Freud? His early aspiration to have a material theory, a mechanistic psychological theory, was wonderful. He had a few dim ideas about how to do it, and they were in their time actually quite wonderful. Then he saw that he couldn't do that job, he didn't have the tools because science was not ready for that job, so he essentially abandoned it, and by my light he abandoned too much. He lowered his standards for scientific investigation and became more interested in telling a good story. Literature took over a bit too much. And yet wonderful insights abound in his work.

The one I admire most is probably one that is often dismissed, particularly by people in cognitive science and in artificial intelligence. There is a standard line of criticism of Freud which runs like this: Poor old Freud, he lived a bit too early, he lived before the computer, so he didn't have the right technological metaphor to use for his theories. If only he had had the computer, he would have been in artificial intelligence. His big mistake was to try to marry two incompatible ideas, the ideas of information and meaning on the one hand and the ideas of tension and pressure on the other—mechanical as opposed to informational ideas. So he has this impossible wedding of meaning talk, intentional talk, intentionality talk, with push and pull, pressure and tension.

I think that criticism is a mistake. Part of Freud's genius was to realize that you have to put these things together, because they are together. Some thoughts are harder to think than others, not because they have more information but because it hurts. Some thoughts are pleasant to think, not because they have fewer bits in them or because they're of a different sort of data structure or because they're more readily accessible. They're easier to think or harder to think because there are pressures. There are forces that push things around in the mind, preventing them from moving the way you would like them to move. One has to have in the end a theory that incorporates those forces at every deep level of theory.

A big mistake in cognitive science has been to treat the mind as this sort of rational, cognitive, deductive system, and to say, "Well, the emotions are simply a sort of noise, the creaking of the machinery and the smoke and exhaust fumes and the vibration in the system. That's all it is." I think that's wrong. The emotional inputs are fundamental. You couldn't get the mind to work without them and they contribute a great deal to the actual ongoing control and self-control of the agent. Now, Freud didn't have the right theoretical constructs of put together a proper theory by our standards today, but he had many valuable insights.

*Also in the sense of asking how many persons a person is made up of. You laugh.*

Well, as the philosopher Tom Nagel once asked, why should there be a whole number between one and infinity, which is the right answer to the question "How many selves are there?"

*I am myself, I am unique, I am precious. Don't tell me I am nine or eleven selves.*

That's you talking, but there may be somebody else in there whose voice we're not hearing right now—some other self of yours. Who, if it could talk, would say exactly the same thing: I am one. Every self strives for unity. That's why we get multiplication on occasion. Because what makes a self, or in my terms a center of narrative gravity, is that it is a rationalization; it's a coherent rendering of a set of events, a set of actions, a set of perceptions.

Here's an analogy I like. Think about a novel that has a character. And suppose we have a very forgetful novelist who writes about a character named Tom Smith. Later on in the novel we hear more about

Tom Smith, but what we learn about him doesn't jibe with what we learned about Tom Smith before. And now we have a problem. Is this the same person, or are there two people named Tom Smith here? There seem to be some commonalitites and then there seem to be some differences. We can't make these two pictures coalesce into one picture. Well, now, the principles of coalescing are principles of rationality. If one of them hates the opera and wouldn't go near the opera and the other one is an opera lover, we have a problem, because that just doesn't jibe.

*A frustration of the functions?*

That is right. What we're inclined to do is to say there are really two Tom Smiths in this story. There's the one that coheres around this center of gravity, and there's the one that coheres around that center of gravity. Their personalities and interests differ, what they know and believe are quite different. You can count on them to behave in different ways. Well, to some degree that's true of all of us.

*But, but, but. You wrote about multiple personality disorder—children fleeing from themselves into another self to avoid abuse. Is there perhaps a reverse similarity with the butchers of Auschwitz? Afterward people often say, "Oh, they were lovely people. They loved Rilke and Nietzsche and they played Beethoven so beautifully." And then suddenly they started killing people as if they were stamping forms.*

Indeed, Robert J. Lifton wrote about the strange ability of the Nazi doctors to bifurcate their lives in this way. Those were not normal people, but that feature of what they did was a deeply normal human response to the sort of grotesque predicament they were in. We all have a striving for coherence. That's something that's built into us. As long as our lives are composed of incidents that are relatively easy to keep together into a single coherent stream, then we're fine, then we are one, then we are unified.

The problems of self-interpretation are not great. For instance, as I have been sitting here talking to you, my arms have been moving. I haven't been making these gestures deliberately, but they're easy enough to incorporate into what I'm doing. They make sense in a way they wouldn't if I suddenly found myself punching myself in the nose or if my arm kept going up like Dr. Strangelove's arm and he has to keep pulling it down to his side. When things like that happen, then immediately the idea arises: It's somebody else who is doing that. And maybe it is. Maybe I'm a puppet and there's somebody backstage who is controlling me. Or maybe there is somebody in here who is controlling me. In cases of multiple personality, but also in normal cases, we see, I think, a whole gradation of cases from the sort that you and I are familiar with in our own lives. There is Dan Dennett the philosopher and the theorist, and then there is Dan Dennett the father of teenagers, and then there is Dan Dennett who has got a farm in Maine and sits on his tractor and mows his hay.

*And Dan Dennett the little child, always there inside you.*

Oh, sure, absolutely. And no doubt several other Dan Dennetts that I would be very reluctant to tell you about.

*The Dan Dennett who perhaps prefers perverse fantasies. . . .*

Sure, these are quite robust shapers of our ongoing cognition. Just a few weeks ago I gave a talk at Harvard Medical School, and at the reception afterward—I was completely in Dan Dennett the Cognitive Science Philosopher Professor mode—a woman who was catering the reception, putting out the trays of sandwiches and so forth, said, "Hi, Dan, what are you doing here?" I was completely dumbfounded. This was a neighbor I know very well in another context. And I was completely unable to respond to her because I just didn't have that self immediately available at the time. I stood there gaping like a fish. We all have experiences like that.

*You wrote, "For all our foolishness, human beings are vastly better equipped for the task of solving problems in advance of encountering them than any other self-controllers and it is our enormous brains that make this possible." Wonderful. But if we look around, what kind of future is this wonderful creation producing at this time?*

We are almost certainly not the species most likely to survive. Long after *Homo sapiens* has gone, the planet will probably be inhabited by the cockroaches and simpler creatures. We don't have any privileged position in that way. We do have a tremendous advantage over the cockroaches in that we have a much greater capacity to see ahead and plan for eventualities, because we have human culture, and because of the way human culture speeds everything up so much. Think about the AIDS virus, for instance. The AIDS epidemic is one of the great challenges to the species. But think of how much worse it would be if we didn't know about it. There are monkeys in Africa that are afflicted with something like the AIDS virus, but they haven't a clue about what is afflicting them.

*That's one side of the coin. But take pollution. We know what we're doing, but we don't change our behavior.*

First of all, you have to think about the time scale involved. We have known about pollution and its risks in detail for thirty years. I mean, we've had much consciousness-raising in the last thirty years. Even two thousand years is just a tiny amount of time by Darwinian standards, so in that regard, we shouldn't expect that a Darwinian account, a genetic account, of the response to pollution should be forthcoming. But now let's look at how swiftly we can respond to this problem that we've identified, thanks to human culture. And we just don't know yet whether it will be swiftly enough. We can make dire predictions, and there is very good reason to make dire predictions, because they then get reflected on by our fellow human beings and that may spur us to speed up our efforts, but they may lead to serious problems of reverberation. That is, if too many dire predictions fail to materialize, then we become the boy who cried wolf and our warnings no longer have much effect. That's one of the features of human culture.

*What is your prediction concerning this whole mess we have organized?*

Predicting the future isn't a game that I think I have any particular talent for. But I think it's a very grave mistake to say in a sort of defeatist way; "Oh, well, we're just animals and we're going to screw things up because we're just confused beasts and it's the animal coming out." No, what makes us different is that we do have culture and learning and science and communication. And that makes us many orders of magnitude more capable of responding appropriately to perceived hazards than any other species ever. We are thousands and thousands of times better at anticipating the future and at planning than any other organism has ever been. It's very important also to recognize that the properties that matter, the properties that are capturable only at the intentional level in terms of meaning, like the gold in Fort Knox, don't have momentum, they don't have mass. We tend to be somewhat defeatist about trends, and yet trends can vanish overnight.

People are defeatist because they see that we keep beating our heads against the wall trying to get progress on environmental issues or something. But there is no reason to rule progress out on the grounds of some sort of physical principle, as if there were a principle of momentum conserved. Things could turn around dramatically tomorrow. Look at the events in Eastern Europe and in the former Soviet Union. Who predicted them? The inertia of the Soviet Union turned out to be evanescent. There are inertias in human nature, of course, but the amazing thing is the extent to which human culture and communication, science, literature, and so forth can overpower those more fundamental effects. Genes work very, very slowly. Culture works very fast, with what genes give it. The genes set some constraints, but within those constraints there is almost nothing that cannot be achieved.

*Let's turn to something else. There are often phrases or images that somebody carries with him all his life that appear to unveil the mystery and yet leave the mystery intact. Have you some sort of anchorage of values that accompanies you in your life? A picture, an image, a sentence?*

There is music that I can always rely on to knit up whatever needs knitting up. I think of Bach, I love the *St. Matthew Passion*. Oddly enough, I delight in Wagner's *Siegfried*. I had a recording of it when I was a freshman in college and I found that it was a great piece of music to play when the going got tough. But also there is jazz that I love. Music accompanies my life in many ways, and I would be terrified to have to do without it.

*In* Consciousness Explained *you write that you will show why science falls short at the end of the twentieth century.*

I think that science is actually an important component of anything that can be called wisdom. Wisdom in the absence of scientific knowledge seems to me to be a commodity that is vanishing fast. I think it becomes harder and harder to be wise if you are scientifically ignorant.

# CHAPTER 3

# UNANSWERABLE

# QUESTIONS

## Stephen Jay Gould

Through no fault of our own, and by dint of no cosmic plan
or conscious purpose, we have become, by the grace of a
glorious evolutionary accident called intelligence, the
stewards of life's continuity on earth. We have not asked for
that role, but we cannot abjure it. We may not be suited to
it, but here we are.

"When I was five, my father took me to the American Museum of Natural History in New York to show me the tyrannosaurus. When we were close to the animal, a man next to me started to sneeze. I swallowed and wanted to pray: 'Shema, shema, Yisrael.' But the gigantic beast remained motionless in all its fossilized beauty. When we left the museum I announced to my father that I would become a paleontologist."

This memory surfaces at least three times in the books of Stephen Jay Gould, paleontologist, zoologist, and biologist. In one of them, *Ever since Darwin*, it even appears in the dedication: "For my father, who took me to see the tyrannosaurus when I was five."

It must have been a remarkable and decisive moment in Gould's life. If you know his work, it's impossible not to ask him about it.

Also, I have explicitly written to Gould that I want to ask him which of his childhood questions and fascinations were crucial for his later career as a paleontologist who has achieved great popularity, especially in the United States, through his sublime talent for popularizing his branch of science.

So far, so good, as the man who fell from the Empire State Building said as he passed the forty-third floor. Our interview at Harvard University, however, was to become one of the most uncomfortable encounters of my life.

The surroundings cannot be faulted. We are enclosed, you might even say entrapped, by thousands and thousands of fossils and skeletons. All of evolution appears to be a witness to the proceedings in Gould's study, in the corridor, and in the adjoining Museum of Comparative Zoology. The disorder that is Gould's study strikes a chord with me: it is a large-scale model of my lodgings as a student. The encounter itself, though, starts off both cordially and precariously.

Gould hates interviews, he informs me. He is participating in the program because the other scientists fascinate him. He views the next two hours as a necessary ordeal.

In the first thirty minutes, that promise is fulfilled relentlessly. Gould refuses to discuss that first, seemingly decisive memory from his youth. He aborts all personal questions immediately. He denies vehemently that he experienced even the slightest romantic sensation when he visited the Burgess Shale, that gigantic Precambrian fossil site, though his book about it, *Wonderful Life,* leaves the reader with the impression that Gould stood on holy ground, enthralled by "the most glorious landscape on earth" and "the boundlessly fascinating psychology of discovery."

After the interview, we leave on very friendly terms. Gould is relieved because the ordeal is over. I share his relief.

While we chat, a student waits in the corridor cradling a gigantic pink shell in his arms, as if holding a baby. In a few moments Stephen Jay Gould will discuss the shell with him, its structure, the site where it was found, its form, and its last inhabitant.

*God dwells in the details.*

The student carries his gigantic shell into Gould's study. Gould follows him in and closes the door. Inside, they will discuss details, rather than unanswerable questions about the purpose of those details or the meaning behind them.

■

*I just want to know a few things about your childhood in connection with your later career. Somewhere you write that at the age of four you wanted to be a garbageman. That was the first big goal in your life. Why a garbageman in New York?*

When I was a kid in New York they picked up the garbage every day. Every morning you'd see them come by with these trucks and the men would jump off the truck and throw the garbage into the back of the machine and it would whirl around. It just seemed like such a wonderful symbol of power. I thought it would be terrific. I didn't realize all the limitations of it.

*At eight you collected shells on Rockaway Beach and you divided your beauties in regular, extraordinary, and—*

Ordinary. Ordinary, extraordinary, and regular. That's a good classification. My grandmother owned a house in the Rockaways, so we went there in the summers when I was young. But that's not where my main interest in natural history came from. It came more from the Museum of Natural History in New York City. I went there almost every month for most of my childhood.

*Can you remember the time you have written about so often, that at the age of five you went with your father . . .*

I've never understood why everyone who's ever interviewed me asks me about that. I maybe wrote about it once or twice. I've never understood why people consider that interesting. If you surveyed paleontologists throughout the world, you would find that a very high percentage of them got intrigued with dinosaurs as children. Dinosaurs are big, and they're fascinating, and you tend to see them if you live in cities and you're taken to natural history museums. I used to talk to Al Romer, my great colleague in invertebrate paleontology who died twenty years ago at age eighty. He was fifty, sixty years older than me, and it was the same specimen that inspired him back in the 1920s.

*But it's a great story. You're standing there . . .*

No, it's a boring story.

*Well, it's interesting that at the age of five somebody knew that he wanted to become a paleontologist.*

It's common for paleontologists. You translate a childhood fascination into a career. If you surveyed paleontologists, you would find that a very strong percentage of them were childhood fossil enthusiasts, either because they lived in a rural situation on a farm or near a stream where they could collect fossils, or because they were urban people and went to museums.

*But this awestruck encounter that you wrote about . . .*

. . . is boring. I'm not going to talk about it.

*No? Very well, then. Your grandfather took you to the Friday-night baseball games, and to the Ringling Brothers sideshow, the collection of dwarfs, giants, and malformed people. Is that an important memory?*

You know, I don't like autobiography. I wish you'd get on to intellectual things. That's private family stuff that I don't want to talk about.

*And you don't want to talk about collecting shells on Rockaway Beach either?*

Let's talk about other things. I don't consider myself a celebrity whose life is interesting, but I'm willing to talk about issues.

*OK, let's move on to the theme of the unanswerable questions. I wrote you a letter and you wrote back, "I do think that you're asking too many, too deep, too unanswerable questions." I recall a point you once made, that someone with half a brain could formulate the big questions in his armchair. We now know that it's useless to ask questions about your private life, but what other questions would be useless to ask?*

Many of the most important, fascinating questions that you can think of are questions that we don't know how to answer; in principle we wouldn't know. If you asked me, "What's the ultimate origin of the universe?" I don't think that question can be addressed in any useful sense. If you inquire too deeply into the nature of infinity and eternity, I don't think our brains are equipped to think about it, certainly not in any way that science can address directly. Since I started writing these popular essays in the 1970s, I get a lot of correspondence from nonscientists, and it's fascinating to get some sense of the errors that people make. I'm talking about methodological errors that people make who are fascinated with science but don't really have training in it. They're almost always errors of thinking too big rather than too small. Science is a powerful methodology through which we've learned a great deal about the natural world. It has changed out perceptions of our own status and the nature of the universe. I guess people think that big science therefore asks the biggest possible questions.

*But God dwells in the details.*

One of the first things you learn in training in the sciences is to ask a question that's usually a little smaller, but potentially subject to evidence.

*Like is a zebra a white horse with black stripes or a black horse with white stripes? Or why does a bamboo flower every 120 years, and how does it count the years?*

Exactly, but we don't want to restrict ourselves only to questions of particular natural history. We can ask some general questions about how evolution works and how planetary dynamics operate. But truly ultimate questions like what is the nature of life . . . You know, people have been talking about that since Plato, probably since the first Neanderthal looked up at a star, and nobody has come any closer to an answer, because there aren't any answers.

*What has your own experience brought you at this moment—more questions, more answers? Or are we hunting for the most beautifully formulated question, rather than answers?*

I just always found the study of evolution and life's history fascinating. I always loved history, I liked old things, I liked old houses and old books. I guess I always felt that by starting with the past, you could get a better understanding of the present. Paleontology is the ultimate historical field because it's the whole history of life, and not just a little epiphenomenon of the history of human cultures and nations. I want to learn as much as possible about it in the short time we're given to be here.

*But is it the questions that are growing or the answers? Is there a kind of competition between them?*

I'm not as introspective as you would like me to be, or as you're pushing me to be. Introspection is a waste of time, for the most part.

*Why?*

Because good scholars have an almost intrinsic sense of what's answerable and what's beyond answerability, though it remains fascinating. Maybe philosophers do sit in their armchairs every day and think about the nature of reality for an hour. But I don't think most practicing scientists do, I think they just get on with their work.

*What was the most beautiful aha experience you've ever had? Or have you ever experienced a moment when you thought, "My God, this is really frightening"?*

You're a hopeless romantic. You really are.

*Nothing of that sort?*

It doesn't work that way. It's irrelevant. It probably happened because I had an endorphin rush for some reason that I didn't know about. There are exhilarating moments when your team wins the World Series, or when I was singing Berlioz's Requiem, and heard the four brass choirs and the ten tympani booming into my ears all at once, but I don't think that gave me any insight into the nature of life. There aren't peak moments like that. Or if there are, they're phony. They come about when people smoke too much marijuana, when they get endorphin rushes in their head. No, that's not what it's about.

*Not even when you stood in the Burgess Shale, in this wonderful landscape?*

If you're going to write a book about the Burgess Shale, the reason you go is conceptual. It's a kind of pilgrimage. It doesn't mean you're going to have a message of exultation. I was happy to be there, I thought it was the right thing to do, I was glad I saw it, and it would have been almost immoral to write a book about it without ever standing there to get a sense of it. But it doesn't mean that when I stood there I got some enormous hormonal rush that made me feel the nature of the universe. In fact, quite the opposite. I'm not in great physical shape and it's a four-hour hike uphill. I was damn tired when I got there.

*Then you must be a wonderful writer, because when I read your book about the Burgess Shale, I got the sense that it was a tremendously romantic experience for you.*

Oh, no, I'm a profound antiromantic. Romanticism is dangerous. Romanticism that is untrammeled by intellect gives rise to fascism, after all. You have got to fight against it.

*Yet I wonder even if it may be another romantic question . . .*

You seem to have a predilection for those.

*Let's imagine that you're looking for fossils, say in the Burgess Shale, and you find something peculiar. How does it feel when you hold it in your hand? Do you simply say to yourself, "Well, just another fossil," even if it's an extraordinary specimen, or . . .*

You're still looking for the aha experience. If you find an important fossil, most likely you won't realize its importance until you're back home studying it in detail. Most likely it's half past four and boiling hot and the only thing on your mind is going home again.

*That's not really the aha experience I was thinking of.*

You're not gonna get it out of me. I don't work that way, I don't think most people work that way. I think that's a romantic myth that comes out of literature and journalism. It's all a question of temperament. Some people get enormously excited when they see something new or exciting. For the most part great discoveries aren't made at the moment you find something. They're made over the months you ruminate and think about it. The item itself that is the basis of that discovery may ultimately turn out to have been the trigger, but it's unlikely that you saw it all in one single moment. Again, it's a question of temperament. I suspect that many people when they have that great insight feel nothing more than calm satisfaction that something's resolved.

*And that's your attitude, too?*

I'm not sure I've ever had great insights of that sort, but when I found out something that resolves some issue, at least for me, I usually do feel calm satisfaction.

*You wrote that you found Darwin's book on worms fascinating. Here's a quote from it: "It is doubtful whether any other species has played such an important role in the history of the world as these lowly forms of life." What was so fascinating about this book and about the worms themselves?*

It was his last book. He wrote it in 1881, a year before he died. Usually we expect that in old age, just before death, a great scientist will write a pontificating philosophical treatise on the nature of reality. Darwin didn't do that, he wrote a book on worms. You might think that he'd just become a doddering old naturalist. No, Darwin was very clever. He was interested in worms because they were, so to speak, a metaphor for his larger worldview. The worms that slowly turn the topsoil of England and make the topography, that work literally beneath our feet, that we don't notice, that we think are insignificant because they're so small and lowly, are in fact producing the very soil that is the basis of agriculture. Darwin uses them as a metaphor for the importance of apparently tiny things when you extend them over long periods of time, and that's what evolution is: the extension of small change over vast periods of time.

So the worms become a metaphor for evolution and the whole process of temporal change.

*What book will you write at the end of your days? Also a book about a tiny little animal?*

I don't know. I'm only fifty years old. Don't rush me.

*Would you devote yourself to the bigger questions, or to the details? The pretty pebbles?*

You try to do a little of both. The joy of writing monthly essays is that they're explorations of little things, although they often address very big issues. I'm not at all inclined to write large-scale philosophical books about unanswerable questions. I think that's a pompous waste of time.

*What are the most fascinating animals?*

Human beings, just because they're so enormously diverse and full of capacity. But I also happen to like land snails, because that's what I study. Some of them are beautiful.

*Do you still collect them?*

Certainly. It's a whole other phase of my work. All these boring, highly technical scientific papers on the evolution of the genus Cerion, a West Indian land snail that lives mostly in the Bahamas and Cuba. It's particularly interesting because it has six hundred named species, most of which are invalid, but the point represented by those namings is that it is morphologically the most diverse land snail in the world. It has an enormous range of shapes. Some are as thin as pencils and others are as round as golf balls. It has the greatest diversity of form within a common design among all snails, and that's an interesting evolutionary puzzle.

*Returning for a moment to the big, all-encompassing questions: You've written somewhere that if one is looking for clear, definitive, and all-encompassing answers to the problems of life, one should look for them not in nature, but elsewhere.*

Well, you can look elsewhere, but I don't think you'll find them there either. Those questions are traditionally the fields of philosophy and religion, and I don't think they have any answers either. We can debate them and categorize them, you can apply logic, but I don't think you'll find any answers to questions about the ultimate moral sense of things. Nature is nonmoral.

*One of the most beautiful questions perhaps is "Why are there so many kinds of living things?" The variety may be wonderful, but why isn't reality simpler, more uniform? Is this also an unanswerable question?*

No, because that comes out of general evolutionary theory, and it could have been otherwise. I don't say that we know all the answers, but it's certainly an addressable question. If the world is Darwinian, as we think it is, it really just works out that way. Once you get the evolution of sexuality in complex multicellular creatures, they form populations that are species. The nature of geological history is such that these populations occasionally get broken up, rivers change their course, continents split apart, mountains rise, organisms wander off. And once you get separate populations, they can then change in different ways, and so you end up with a diversity of creatures. I think variety does fall right out of the mechanics of evolution. It's not because God wants the ornaments to be diverse and beautiful. It just works out that way, and we like it.

*When I ask people in the street what Darwinism means, they immediately say, "Survival of the fittest." And behind this is the paradigm of evolution striving upwards to arrive at us.*

Well, those are two entirely different things. The first is Darwinism and the second is a perversion, which has nothing to do with the essence of the theory, but is only the imposition of our Western biases on an understanding that evolution occurs.

*You once said that the stumbling block to the acceptance of Darwin's theories is not in scientific problems but its radical philosophical message—it invalidates certain established Western norms. Which norms are they?*

I think a whole framework of norms, but particularly four, which are interlinked. Most fundamental is the idea of progress, the idea that we can see ourselves as predictably and properly on top of this biological heap. Therefore we like to depict evolution as moving upward from single-cell creatures predictably toward the eventual appearance of some self-conscious form, like human beings. Now, along with progress, there's a bias of determinism—the idea that what happens, happens for a definite cause, and that it's predictable. There's certainly a bias of gradualism, the notion that this upward march occurs step by slow and steady step. And then there's what I like to call adaptationism, the idea that everything that happens is fundamentally right and occurs for a reason. When you put those four together, you get a peculiar view of evolution as a predictable, basically directional process leading toward complexification and eventually toward self-conscious intelligence. But that's really not what Darwin meant.

In Victorian Britain, progress was a cultural certainty. Darwin wasn't totally immune to that, but basically the theory of natural selection is a theory about adaptation to changing local environments. The parasite that becomes morphologically simple so that it's no more than a bag of reproductive tissues living inside the host is just as well adapted as the peacock with its glorious tail feathers. Darwin's theory is really about local adjustment. It doesn't include any theme of necessary progress.

This very office that we're sitting in now was occupied in 1880 by Alpheus Hyatt, an American non-Darwinian paleontologist who believed in necessary progress. He had a long correspondence with Darwin, and Darwin wrote to him, "After long reflection I cannot avoid the conclusion that no inherent tendency to progressive development exists." Darwin was quite clear on that.

*I remember that quote from Mark Twain that you used in several of your books.*

Mark Twain was America's greatest humorist in the late nineteenth century, but he was also philosophically very astute, and very good at pricking with his pen of wit all the certainties we thought we had. Twain says that to think that nature, which has a history of life that extends for billions of years, should exist just to give rise eventually to human beings, and to think that human beings rule over all the rest of it, is almost like saying that the Eiffel Tower was built in order to support the skin of paint right at the pinnacle knob on top. The earth is four and a half billion years old. And *Homo sapiens*, our species, is less than a million, probably only a couple of hundred thousand years old, so we've been around for the tiniest fraction of 1 percent of the entire length of life's history. It seems absurd to think that somehow it was all meant to eventually to give rise to us.

In America there are stumbling blocks, based in certain forms of religion, to the acceptance of evolution at all. But among the majority of us who accept evolution, many people are still reluctant to give up the comforts of progress, gradualism, determinism, and adaptationism. So Darwin is not well understood. If you go out and survey popular attitudes in America among people who are quite happy to accept evolution and who might even say that they were Darwinians, very few of them understand the actual content of Darwin's theory. All these surveys show that the most popular concept of evolution is that it's a theory that explains why complexity increases through time.

*I have often told my children stories about going back in time and changing the future, without knowing the concept of contingency. It's an interesting theme. You have written about the species* Opabinia, *"Why isn't* Opabinia, *the spindle of the new vision of life on earth, known to everyone who is interested in the riddles of existence?"*

*Opabinia* is one of those strange creatures from the early history of the life of multicellular organisms. It had five eyes, it had a vacuum-cleaner-like nozzle that extended off the front and bent around underneath to bring food to the central mouth, and it had several segments behind with gill plates above body segments, which is the exact opposite of the arrangement in arthropods and other phyla. It's one of these early experiments in the history of life that was ultimately unsuccessful.

Now you can take a very conventional view and say the ones that lost were destined to fail. It was just a competition and survival of the most perfect anatomical designs, and life was off on its upward march. In the last thirty years, however, there's been a very profound reinterpretation of these earliest multicellular animals. We're talking about the Cambrian, which is 550 million years ago. Whereas these earlier animals had once been interpreted as simple and primitive precursors of creatures that came later, just contributing to that upward march, it now appears as though there was more anatomical diversity at the very beginning than there is now and has ever been since. There were fewer species, but those species were allocated to many more basic kinds of anatomy. Most of the initial experiments died out, and there's no reason to think that they died out because they were in any sense inferior. There may just have been something like a gigantic worldwide lottery going on. Gigantic fossils of animals from the Cambrian have been found. The biggest thing is called *Anomalocaris*. It's another one of those lines that became extinct. It's a very strange creature that you can't classify in any modern group. It had a mouth that operated like a camera shutter, unlike any mouth today, and it had an odd pair of feeding appendages that bent over. It was the largest predator of its time, and it left no descendants, again probably more because of bad luck that any predictable necessity.

*In Disney's film* Fantasia *we see dinosaurs hobbling to their deaths through a desiccated landscape, to the music of Stravinsky's* Rites of Spring. *Why did they die? And how is our destiny, our appearance in evolution, connected with theirs?*

Dinosaurs arose at the end of the Triassic period. They lived for a hundred million years, in fact closer to 150, and they were doing very well. Mammals arose at the same time. For a hundred million years — two-thirds of the history of mammalian life — mammals were tiny little creatures, never making any progress in competition against dinosaurs. Dinosaurs dominated the ecologies of large-bodied creatures for more than a hundred million years. Now, we've known for a long time they died out 65 million years ago, and theories have gone back and forth, but in the last ten years the theory of catastrophic worldwide mass extinction triggered by the impact of an extraterrestrial body has gained enormously in strength. We don't know why this catastrophe wiped out dinosaurs and why mammals prevailed, but there's no reason on earth to think that the eventual success of mammals had anything to do with intrinsic superiority or predictable eventual domination. After all, mammals had had a hundred million years to accomplish that against dinosaurs, and dinosaurs had continually held dominance over them. No, I think one has to assume that had it not been for this impact, which is the ultimate contingent event, the ultimate unpredictable bolt from the blue, dinosaurs would still be around dominating mammals. Why not? They had done it for a hundred million years and there's only been 65 million years since then.

Since there's no reason to think dinosaurs would have attained levels of intelligence like ours—they hadn't for a hundred million years—I think one has to assume that the impact was a lucky event that allowed the eventual domination of mammals. You can make various hypotheses about the reason why. Dinosaurs were all quite large, for example. It's true that there were small dinosaurs, but the smallest dinosaur was much bigger than the largest mammal. Large creatures have relatively small population sizes. In the face of catastrophes, small population sizes are a very good predictor of possible extinction. Large animals tend to be very specialized also, so it could be that dinosaurs died out largely as a result of their large size and attendant small populations, in which case mammals, with their smaller body size and much larger populations, prevailed. However, you can't say that small body size was an adaptation of mammals for survival through this future catastrophe. In fact, mammals were small for negative reasons: they'd never had any success against dinosaurs. So in that sense it's an ultimate bit of luck.

*What would have happened if the dinosaurs hadn't died out?*

I expect they'd still be around.

*Had there been any development toward larger brains? Or to a sort of consciousness?*

No. Why should there have been? Anyhow, I don't think it's a possibility in reptile design. You've had more than a hundred million years of birds, which are dinosaur derivatives, none of which are anywhere near those levels of intelligence. No, I think had there not been that extinction event, dinosaurs would still be around, mammals would still be little creatures, and there wouldn't be anyone to organize roundtables.

*If we played the tape of history a million times from the beginning of the Burgess Shale, the Precambrian explosion, you doubt whether anything like* Homo sapiens *would develop again. Suppose you played it a hundred million times?*

It still seems unlikely. You could calculate the combinations. If you take groups of ten out of a pool of a hundred, there's seventeen trillion different groups of ten. So you never get the same result twice. All intelligences of the conscious sort on earth are vertebrate, and have a vertebrate precursor among those early creatures. Most of the reruns of life's tape wouldn't include its existence, so you get wiped out right there. Even if that lineage does survive, what are the chances it would follow the pathways that it did on earth?

Probably most of the replays would never include the invasion of land. You get vertebrates out on land only because luckily there was a fairly obscure group of fishes that had a fin arrangement with a strong central axis that could be converted into a weight-bearing limb on land. Most fishes have a very different fin arrangement, with a bar parallel to the body and a lot of thin fin rays. Those were the dominant fishes, and none of them were converted to terrestrial creatures. If you had been living 350 million years ago, you would have seen this one odd group of fishes with the strong central bar, and you would have thought, "What a strange group! There aren't very many of them, I guess they're not destined for much of a future." And indeed, in the ocean they weren't. They still exist as a small group of selachians and lungfishes, but one lineage of them got out on land, and started this story that would never recur again.

*If you look at a film like* Back to the Future *from an evolutionary perspective . . .*

Well, that's an explicit film about contingency, in fact. I think people do grasp that theme. That's what's so endlessly fascinating, people understand that the tiniest little difference that seems utterly insignificant at the time will cause history to cascade down a totally different channel. In fact, that theme is so important in *Back to the Future* that in *Part Two* Doc Brown, the mad scientist, actually goes to the blackboard and gives an explicit lecture on contingency. This has to do with whether or not Biff Tannen has a book of the results of sporting events in the next fifty years so he can bet on them and make a lot of money, and he actually draws the different pathways of history.

*What is the relationship between chimpanzees and humans? In what respect are we identical?*

There are fascinating similarities and differences. The moment that humans split away from chimpanzees lies only some five to eight million years behind us. That may seem like a long time ago, but in evolutionary terms it's yesterday. The genetic similarity is great, and the more people like Jane Goodall study the behavior of chimpanzees, the more common traits emerge. Yet for all those similarities, man has acquired a unique status in the history of the earth because of the changes in the size of his brain and the development of consciousness. The chimpanzees are a small group who've been left behind, and who aren't doing too well, unfortunately.

*You've written that if they could talk, they might prove to be much smarter than we give them credit for.*

They are much smarter than we used to think, but they will never develop complicated techniques or write philosophical treatises. They will never achieve the same degree of consciousness as ours, which can impact this planet on a global scale, for better or for worse, mostly for worse.

*Interbreeding between chimpanzees and humans will be possible in the very near future. . . .*

I don't know. It's conceivable. I once described that as the most unethical experiment we could think about.

*Fascinating.*

No doubt about it. That's precisely why it shouldn't be done. But I don't know whether it's possible. Obviously we're very close genetically, but we have different chromosome numbers and I'm not sure that the sperm of a human would unite with the egg of a chimpanzee. I'm not sure if it would develop and would proceed. The chromosomes might not be able to pair, the developmental programs of the two species might be too different to match them, but it's possible.

*What kind of questions could be answered by this interbreeding?*

Well, the obvious speculation is that you would have a creature with enough consciousness to be able to respond to inquiries and tell you what it feels like from the chimpanzee half of its nature, but it's a grossly unethical experiment. One does not consciously make a creature who would be handicapped, because by human standards that would amount to a severe disability.

*But if somehow this hybrid were to exist, what questions would you ask the chimpanzee?*

I'd just like to learn what I could about what it's like to be a highly intelligent species without language. There's an assumption, which is probably right, that the key to the uniqueness of human cognition lies in language and its capacities, and here you have chimps, highly intelligent creatures, without linguistic ability, or with only the most rudimentary kind. In that sense, chimps are the one species below that fundamental threshold that still is obviously in any vernacular sense highly intelligent, so it would just be lovely to probe that.

We're storytellers. Perhaps chimps are too, to some extent. But they're not abstractors, that's the difference. Chimps probably can't abstract to any great extent, but maybe they can tell stories about where they've been and what's just happened.

*A fascinating subject in your books is the matter of neoteny. We humans appear to be flexible embryos. You mention in this context the 'Mickey Mouse-syndrome': like Mickey Mouse we never grow up, although unfortunately we do grow old. Reading that, I got the idea that man is simply a chimpanzee born prematurely at a time when the brain is not yet fully grown, so that the newly born gets totally confused when after birth the brain is flooded with information from the outside world for which it is as yet unprepared. Do you follow my meaning?*

Yeah, but it's wrong. There are two separate things going on, you see, in the differences between chimps and humans. On the one hand there is neoteny, which is the slowing down of developmental rates. This is a very important process in evolution, particularly of the human brain. We're a neotenic species in some respects, though not in all. But in general, the developmental rates of human beings versus other primates, and of primates versus other mammals, are very slow. We become sexually mature late in our second decade, although it's now mostly earlier for nutritional reasons in Western countries. Now, in a Darwinian world it's very strange to become sexually mature when you're seventeen or eighteen, because life and evolution are about making more of yourself. We have a very long and extended period of childhood development. As adults we have a skull form that looks very much like the juvenile form of the skull of most primates, including ourselves. It isn't that we're embryo chimps, it's that we haven't departed very far from the form of our own embryos, and the embryonic forms of all primates are a lot closer than the adult forms.

Now on top of that, there's a second trend. Because of the very rapid expansion of the brain, human babies are actually, in a sense, born earlier than we ought to be, given the general slowing down of rates of development. The human gestation period should be about a year and a half to two years—that would make it concordant with the rates of slowing down in the rest of our life span—but that's not possible, because by that time the head is so large that birth through the birth canal could not occur. So there has been a secondary speeding up of birth. We missed it for a long time, because development is so slow. Nine months looks like a long time, and it's still a little bit longer than chimpanzee birth. In relation to the extreme length of our youth and our late maturation, nine months is in fact a fairly short birth. So humans are born in a fairly embryonic state and the human baby is much more helpless than that of other primates. I think the main reason is just that, given the large size of the head, it's the only way to allow birth to proceed. After we're born, our brains continue to grow.

*And soon or later consciousness emerges?*

How do you define consciousness? Some people don't want to define it in the absence of language, in which case you would say it's later, but it's well known that even neonate babies can identify faces and can identify their own parents, so there's some level of consciousness right away.

*We are now entering the citadel itself.*

Yes, that's how Darwin described the human mind.

*A Dutch psychologist has argued that the new brains are badly adapted to the old brains of the killer ape. He uses an image something like this: our instincts derive from the crocodile, the horse provides us with feeling, and the neocortex allows us to contemplate our grief. He says that we make our decisions with those unique new brains and that we think we can control our behavior with them, even while we are getting very different phylogenetic instructions.*

I think that's a stupid way of putting it. It's quite wrong to say there's a primitive brain that's the source of everything nasty we don't like and then just pile consciousness on top of that. It's not that simple. The basic theme is right: the brain has a long history, and we've built our large one by modifying and adding quite a bit to a retained core. But it seems so foolish to identify everything we don't like about ourselves and all the emotions we don't care for with something deep in our past, and then everything we like, everything that has to do with intelligence or altruism or moral behavior, as part of the neocortex. We also inherit from our past a propensity for cooperative behavior, because that has been part of evolution from the start. We don't simply add things on top of what was there, you reconstruct everything.

*Freud claims that a child has a phylogenetic consciousness at birth.*

Yes, but Freud's theory is not so broad in scope. For Freud what you're recapitulating is the history of a human past, so if you go through anal, oral, and genital stages, they're really very late stages of a primate lineage. Anyway, Freud's ideas are all based on Lamarck, and inheritance is a justification that doesn't work. This is one of Freud's theories that are the least defensible.

*And if Oliver Sacks talks about prehuman memories that go back to the darkest corners of existence . . .*

I have no doubt there are phylogenetic heritages, maybe even very specific ones that may well be prehuman, but that still doesn't imply that there's a reptile brain on which you have added layers. There is a reptile brain that has been reconstructed, some of whose contents are retained. There is in fact a complex coordination between the old parts and the new parts.

*Richard Dawkins raised your heckles with his 'selfish gene' theory. He writes that genes have created us, body and mind, and that: "Cliché or not, 'stranger than fiction' expresses exactly how I feel about the truth. We are survival machines, robot vehicles blindly programmed to preserve the selfish gene molecules in our genes." And he adds that "this is a truth that still fills me with astonishment."*

It ought to astonish him. The reason it is astonishing is that it's wrong. As a metaphor I don't mind it, it is a way of talking about Darwinism, but as you correctly read, for Dawkins it is not a metaphor. He actually thinks it's a reality. And I think he's wrong. I think the vast majority of evolutionary biologists know he's wrong and understand it perfectly well. Darwin's argument is that natural selection works on bodies. There is a reductionist tradition that gets you down to organisms. There were older notions that selection might work on species, on ecosystems and even larger units, so within the confines of philosophical reductionism it is already quite a step to take it down to bodies. Dawkins is an advocate or an even stronger kind of reductionism, which is odd in a non-reductionist age. He wants to break it down even further, and he says, "Now we've discovered genes, we're going to break it down to selection on genes." But that's wrong, because natural selection works on many units simultaneously.

Let me put it this way: if genes built organisms in a one-to-one fashion, then you could talk about gene level selection. If each gene translated to a little blob hanging on the arm of an organism, and if natural selection then came along and determined whether that organism would live or die on the basis of the number and size and form of the blobs, then yes, you could break it down to gene level selection. But the minute you get what you have, namely massively non-additive interaction between genes, then you have emergent characteristics at the level of organisms which cannot be explained in terms of individual genes. We know that natural selection works on organisms. Organisms live, die and reproduce at a certain rate, so the only way to make an argument for gene level selection is if the death of an organism, or its giving birth to many, is formally reduceable to the differential survival of genes. That isn't so, because the organism is a collection of emergent characteristics based on non-linear interaction among the genes and it therefore cannot be reconstructed simply from the list of genes and their actions. This is really a philosophical point, which Elliot Soburn and Lisa Lloyd, two very good philosophers of biology, have written about conclusively.

Dawkins is right that gene level selection does occur, but you don't need any selfish genes for it. Gene level selection occurs since natural selection works simultaneously on a hierarchy of levels. There is species level selection, there is organism level selection—which is Darwin's notion—there is gene level selection, there is probably some lineage selection and there is local population selection, which is important in Civil Rights' famous evolution theory. But interestingly enough, most cases of genuine gene selection occur because those genetic effects do not express themselves in organisms, which are the chief locus of selection.

For example, if the gene duplicates itself without that having effect upon the external form of the organism, then Darwin's form of natural selection, which works on organisms, cannot notice it. And if the gene keeps increasing in numbers within the genetic system, that is gene level selection; that is a gene operating as a Darwinian agent to make more copies of itself in its world. That kind of gene selection occurs, but it does not translate into the adaptive phenotypes of organisms. That is where Dawkins goes wrong.

*Let us return for a moment to the citadel itself, consciousness. You wrote: "Through no fault of our own, and by dint of no cosmic plan or conscious purpose, we have become, by the power of a glorious evolutionary accident called intelligence, the stewards of life's continuity on earth. We did not ask for this role, but we cannot abjure it. We may not be suited for such responsibility, but here we are." What was that glorious accident?*

The accident is the 60 trillion contigent events that eventually led to the emergence of *Homo sapiens*. It's everything we've been talking about. It's that no species now alive is predictable, and any species that exists does so by the merest good fortune of tens of thousands of antecedent events that went one way and not the other. If the dinosaurs hadn't died out, we wouldn't be here. If some fish didn't have that strong central axis, there never would have been terrestrial vertebrates. If a different set of creatures had survived this decimation pattern of the Burgess Shale, we wouldn't be here. If the eukaryotic cell had never evolved through this odd mechanism of symbiosis, there probably would never have been more than algomaths. Even when you get to the evolution of mammals, that's no guarantee you're going to get conscious creatures. There are six thousand species of mammals, none of which—outside the order of primates—is threatening to become a powerfully conscious species with this kind of strength and influence over the rest of the earth. I think there are some two hundred species of primates, and there's only one line of primates, namely us, that has veered in this direction.

It's really a curious phenomenon. If intelligence was meant to be, you'd think it would have evolved convergently in lots of other lineages. It's just a weird invention that developed in one odd species living on the African savannas a couple of million years ago.

*Sublime and whimsical at the same time.*

It is whimsical. There's a common tendency to equate importance with necessity. Just because something is important—which consciousness clearly is to the history of the planet—doesn't mean it was meant to be. There's never anything in the history of life that's had such an impact on the earth as the evolution of human consciousness, but that doesn't mean it was meant to be. It could still be accidental, as I think it was.

*But why have only humans developed consciousness and intelligence?*

I assume become it's very difficult in terms of neuronal architecture. You have to have this head, you need to wire it in a certain way, you need to invent odd phenomena like language, I don't know what else. Also it's probably not a very adaptive trait, one that natural selection would favor in many circumstances. It's a by-product, I presume, of natural selection working in this lineage for large brains, but I don't know why the brain got large in the first place. It certainly wasn't so that we could paint pictures or write symbols.

*Why did this small group of tree-dwelling apes get such large brains?*

It's just one of those things that happen. There are a lot of trees out there, so there's a lot of potential environment of any creature that can get into it.

*So this is a question without an answer.*

Right. Well, the answer is that it just happens, so we might as well make the best of it.

*Do we?*

No, but there's always hope.

*Yes, there is always hope. That is a cliché. But how are we doing with this wonderful consciousness.*

Fairly badly in moral terms, but that merely illustrates that it didn't arise for reasons of our higher moral development. Our brain gives us the capacity to do all kinds of wonderful things and all sorts of terrible things, and we do them all.

*You have observed that morality cannot be taught by nature. If you look for morality or free will or rationality in nature, you won't find it.*

But those are all different things. You certainly won't find morality, which is a question of how we ought to behave. Rationality may be subject to definition, but moral questions are questions about oughts. Nature, as science understands it, is a factual set of properties. There's no way you can go from the facts of nature to the oughts of action. They're just different things. Nature is nonmoral. Lots of things happen in nature that are horrible by our standards. Darwin wrote a famous letter to Hooker in 1856 in which he says, "What a wonderful time the devil's chaplain would have with the immensely blundering, wasteful, and inefficient ways of nature." Of course that's right. I wrote an essay once about the famous wasps of the family Ichneunomidae, which paralize caterpillars and lay their eggs in the living flesh of the caterpillars. When the little wasp larvae are born, they proceed to eat the caterpillar from the inside, while the caterpillar's still alive. That would have to sound horrible by our standards, but you can't lay moral blame on the wasp. It's just playing Darwin's game, and has found a way to win it for awhile.

*If we can't find morality in nature, we have to find it in ourselves, you wrote. Well, what kind of job is that?*

It's not a job for scientists. It's a job for all human beings, but the answers aren't going to come from factual nature or science.

*If nature is nonmoral, why should we be moral?*

I think there are two or three separate reasons. One is to make sure that we don't end up killing each other, a very practical reason. Take a simple moral principle like the Golden Rule [Do unto others as you would have them do unto you]. Basically it's a negative feedback principle that allows societies to be stable enough so we can continue on. Otherwise everyone who seizes power just seizes more of it, and you end up in positive feedback loops that kill everybody off in the end. Another reason is that once you have consciousness, you can start thinking about those things, and there's really no way to avoid doing that. John Stuart Mill said that it was better to be Socrates dissatisfied than a pig satisfied, and that's right. Maybe the pig's happier, but we can't avoid being what we are.

*We are doomed to freedom, as Jean-Paul Sartre said.*

Yes, I think that's right. We might as well make the best of it, and find it exhilarating. Mortality is the product of the formulation of certain principles, such as the Golden Rule, that you can debate. It's a by-product of consciousness.

*How should we look upon intelligence within the framework of evolution? Is that the evolutionary accident?*

Think of it, life has been around for three and a half billion years, an immense amount of time. There has never in all that time been a species so capable of changing the earth's surface, of intervening globally in its climate, of wiping others out. Now all of this was the product of just a few thousand years, because even ten thousand years ago, there was no human culture that was altering the earth very much on a global scale. You can't even measure that geologically, that's just an instant. Basically intelligence has imposed a very different system of change.

The Darwinian system of change is a very inefficient system, because you've got this two-step process of variation, and then natural selection imposes itself on the variation. Human cultural evolution is enormously more powerful, though confined to one species, because it's Lamarckian: what you learn in one generation you teach directly to your children, and that doesn't happen in nature.

The reason why natural evolution is so slow is that whatever happens in your lifetime doesn't change your genetic structure. You have to wait for the lucky small-scale variation. But as soon as you have a Lamarckian system operating—which occurs in cultural evolution, where anything you invent or learn or discover immediately accumulates and gets passed on—you have this powerful accumulative mechanism that doesn't exist in nature. On top of that you have the possibility of joining lineages. When one culture invents something, other cultures can get it. In nature, when one species develops something, it can't transfer it to anyone else; each species is its own unique entity. There's interaction, but there's never amalgamation, whereas in human culture you have this complex reticulation. So I think it's for those two reasons, the Lamarckian character—the accumulative inheritance of knowledge and technology—and this reticulative property of discovery and invention, that cultural evolution is so fast. It takes place, so to speak, in microseconds.

*Is that the reason you once said that biology probably will not play a major role in explaining cultural diversity? That the natural sciences meet their limit?*

Well, it's related to it in the sense that there's been no change in human body form or biological construction during the last few tens of thousands of years, and therefore everything that we call civilization has been built by this unaltered body and brain. Of course, the biology of the basic body and brain make it possible, but the growth and expansion of civilization have nothing to do with biological change. We are the same people our Cro-Magnon ancestors were when they painted the caves of Lascaux.

*Daniel Dennett says that many people find it an uncomfortable idea that the self, or the soul, is in fact a kind of abstraction, a denial rather than anything positive, while in fact it has a great deal going for it. Do you feel any kinship with that?*

Yes, I agree with that. "Soul" is a vernacular word. It means something to some religions, and that's fine. If you take "soul" as a vernacular word that we use as an abbreviation for consciousness and ethical thoughts, then I suppose it will have some sort of material basis in the brain. It might even be technically reproducable. It is certainly conceivable.

What we call emotions are mostly evolved reactions. I wouldn't know how to install those in a computer. Our emotional repertoire is linked to behaviors that are part of a specific history. The greatest obstacle for replicating human behavior in a machine is that we are the highly complex products of billions of years of evolution. I don't think the complexity is the main problem.

*But in principle there would be a chance?*

I don't know.

*We'll ask Dennett.*

He won't know either. Nobody knows.

*In 1992 you wrote a wonderful book,* The Mismeasure of Man, *in which you conclude that biological determinism is on the rise again. Why has biological determinism regained so much popularity after the atrocities of the past?*

I think for the usual reasons. People of power and influence like to be able to say that they owe their position to the fact that they're built that way, whether true or not. And that the people below them are in their lowly place because they belong there. Now, the United States is, of course, a heterogeneous country. We have the greatest mixture of races and national origins of any country on earth. And particularly early in this century, when millions of immigrants were coming from mostly poor areas of southern and eastern Europe, not to mention a large population of blacks—20 percent of Americans—there were powerful calls on the part of whites in control, who were mostly of northern European backgrounds, to try to maintain their position of power by arguing for the superiority of their kind of people. In World War I the entire army was subjected to mental testing, which showed that immigrants from southern and eastern Europe did more poorly than "old Americans." That was only because their knowledge of English was so poor. In the '20s and '30s some twenty or thirty states had laws to compel the sterilization of mentally unfit people. They weren't widely applied, except in Virginia and California, where some 40,000 people were involuntarily sterilized. The texts of those laws became the basis for the Nazi eugenic sterilization laws, the Nuremberg laws of the mid-1930s, which were applied very tragically and very rigorously in Germany to some half a million people. After World War II, when people realized the horror of what Hitler had done with eugenic doctrines, the popularity of that old style of argument pretty much disappeared, but it never goes away.

Racism remains a deep issue in America. Many people really feel that those they don't like and whom they see as economically inferior to them are that way because of their biological construction, even though it doesn't make a lot of sense, given how genetically similar all human beings are.

*I once made a series of four programs about genetic manipulation, titled* Better than God. *I found that we can do in one year what nature takes a million years to achieve. I was particularly surprised by the witch hunt for social and other deviations — alcoholism, criminality, low intelligence, and so on. The old eugenic song is being sung again.*

Yes, it's such a wide issue because you can't deny that there are illnesses that have genetic bases. Some of the classic and serious mental illnesses, such as schizophrenia and manic depression, are probably such illnesses. After all, there must be illnesses of the brain as an organ just as there are illnesses of other organs. But to say that something as complex and multifarious as intelligence — which is only a word we give to this enormously varied series of capacities that the brain has — is a biological thing is nonsense. And then to rank people according to the amount of it that they possess doesn't make any sense because there are so many separate dimensions of it. So you have to sort out where you have good arguments for specific potential pathologies and where you just express social prejudice through biological guesswork.

*How would you define intelligence?*

It's a vernacular English word for this enormously complex multifarious set of abilities and capacities that emerge from the structure of our brains and the way we learn, but there's no meaningful sense in which you could ever capture it as a single entity. Some people are good at some things, others are good at other things. I'm not saying we're all the same, obviously we're not.

*If you can blame the victim — the poor, the black, the less intelligent, the malformed, the mentally deficient — simply because of their genetic material . . .*

That's the traditional biological determinism. It's a false and vicious social theory that validates or gives rise to the desire to capture intelligence as a single number. It doesn't make any sense, but if you could express intelligence as a single number, then you could say aha, my group has a lot of it and these other groups I don't like have less of it. Once you realize that it's simply not a meaningful enterprise — that's what my book on the mismeasure of man is about — then you realize that it's just an argument of social prejudice and not even potentially a biological fact.

*What about the kind of science that produces these kinds of prejudices, while labeling itself as objective?*

Science is a socially conditioned enterprise, and there's no reason why scientists any less or more than other people shouldn't have biases, which they often don't recognize. When I wrote that book, the most interesting thing for me was to learn how many scientists, who probably sincerely believed that they were only objectively depicting the natural world, made the most absurd errors based on their unconscious a priori convictions about the obvious superiority of certain groups. On the other hand, it must also be said that science did a lot to undo that mythology.

*What will be the fate, in your expectation, of this reemergence of biological determinism? What is the cause of its increasing popularity?*

The America of Reagan and Bush, with their reactionary conservatism, got a Supreme Court that is now much more conservative than it used to be. And when conservative social theories prevail, ideas about the biological basis of social stratification tend to gain popularity. I don't think there's much more to it.

*You simply say: This man's genetic makeup is inferior, so let's get rid of him. His miserable fate is his own fault, rather than that of the political or economic system.*

That's the crudest form of the argument, but there are more subtle forms, too. In Singapore a few years ago, Lee Kuan Yew, the very powerful former prime minister, discovered that highly educated women were having few children. He then made the classical eugenic mistake of assuming that high education meant intrinsic and biologically superior intelligence, and decided that his nation was going to hell as a result of the progressive decline in intelligence because women with less education were having more children. He instituted a whole set of social policies, including monetary benefits for educated women who had more children and social clubs where smart—I say "smart" but I mean "highly educated"—men could meet highly educated women. It was almost comical, because it was a repetition of some of the worst eugenic errors of the 1920s.

*What influence had what happened in Auschwitz, as a metaphor for World War II, on your own views about human behavior? We are capable of wonderful, mysterious things—but on the other hand . . .*

That's the fundamental thing that's incomprehensible. It's captured in all those old films where you get some particularly rigid and vicious Nazi—usually it's Erich von Stroheim—murdering people by the millions and then he walks over to the piano and plays a beautiful Chopin etude . . . They said that Mengele whistled tunes from opera as he decided who would die and who would live. All you can do is struggle to keep people like that out of power.

*Have the events in Europe in the early 1940s had much influence on your own views?*

Who knows? I was born in 1941, my father fought in the war, it was always part of the context of my own life. It's certainly true that World

War II was responsible for the death of the older form of virulent eugenics. A postwar period of enormous hope and optimism surrounded the foundation of the United Nations, but then the Iron Curtain descended and we had forty years of Cold War, and everything's as confusing as ever. We have this powerful attribute of consciousness, and we don't know what to do with it. Basically we're just evolved apes that are trying to deal with this powerful mechanism that no species has ever had before.

*If the dinosaurs hadn't died out and the mammals had stayed little creatures, we would not have appeared in evolution. What would the world then look like, compared to that magnificent evolutionary tree that finally brought about the human species?*

It wouldn't look much different. The continents would be in the same places as they are now, innumerable organisms would live on earth, the dinosaurs would reign supreme as they had done for a hundred million years. But there wouldn't be any conscious creatures that could talk about it. The earth would be teeming with life, but there would be no one around to map it all.

*How unique is our latent self-destruction?*

It's a function of consciousness. No other species has ever had the capacity to destroy itself and drag large parts of the earth down with it.

*You've participated in a conference on the possibility of a nuclear winter. What was it like to discuss with other scientists what happens after a nuclear war? What would be the consequences of the nuclear winter?*

The nuclear winter was only a supplement to what we already knew about the horrors of nuclear war. After all, in a full-scale nuclear catastrophe every major city on earth would be targeted, so destruction would be enormous, but to think that there was the possibility of this whole secondary level of impact through worldwide changes in climate of the sort that a dark cloud of lofted material might impose was very intriguing. For all the arguments that had been advanced about nuclear war, here was yet another aspect of global destruction that hadn't been properly considered.

*So what kind of animals are we, simply in Darwinistic terms? What kind of animal threatens the whole diversity of evolution?*

I wouldn't even look at it in Darwinian terms. The only insight you can get from Darwinian systems is that the brain evolves to a large size for some set of reasons, which we probably can't reconstruct because there isn't sufficient evidence. These capacities for destruction are not explicitly built by natural selection, they're side consequences of the complexity. You can't even say the potential is built by natural selection, except in the most indirect way. Selection builds the brain for a reason, and then by virtue of its structural complexity it can do many other things that fall outside the realm of the evolutionary reasons for its construction in the first place.

*What do you see as the most important reason that gave rise to the development of the brain?*

It has to do with the ecology and particular history of those forest- or savanna-living primates in Africa three to five million years ago, but there just isn't enough evidence. There's a load of speculation. There are male-based theories of fighting, there are female-based theories of gathering, there are social-based theories of cooperation and family structure—I wouldn't even call them theories, they're speculations. I don't really think there's a great deal we can know about it.

*You've written somewhere, "We live in an age of unsoluble tension between our connection with nature and our dangerous unicity." Would you elaborate on what you mean?*

Our connection with nature is our place in the tree of life. We are the new twig on the branch of the chimpanzees that emerged some six or seven million years ago. In geological terms that's yesterday. Our dangerous unicity is our consciousness and the power it has given us.

*What do you expect will happen, now we've come to the end of the twentieth century?*

I don't know. Really, I take contingency very seriously. Contingency tells me that there is no way to predict the future. What's more, the future is in the hands of nonbiologists. It's a matter of politics and of economic policy. I don't think that the theory of evolution will tell us anything about the course of the future. We live at a very different level of cultural rules, regularities, and random changes, and not of natural selection.

*Daniel Dennett says that we are the best anticipation machines.*

But how do you know what to anticipate?

*I'll ask him. He says that man is much better equipped than any other species for solving problems even before encountering them.*

We're better than anything else, but that's not saying very much. We can't even predict the stock market. No one can predict who'll win the world series. If you can't even predict that, what are your chances of correctly predicting what will happen to human civilization, which is much more complex?

*Think back to Rockaway Beach when you were ten years old. Are the questions that interested you then very different from the ones you're concerned with now, or would it be fair to say that there are many answers, but the questions essentially remain the same?*

I don't remember what questions I was asking when I was ten. Like any kid, I used to lie in bed and wonder about eternity and infinity and all those unanswerable questions. Maybe I realized they were unanswerable even then. I remember I used to think: How can there be infinity, because there must be a brick wall out there somewhere? But then there has to be something beyond the brick wall, doesn't there? Or how could everything have a beginning, because there must be something before the beginning? I don't think we're equipped to deal with those questions. I don't remember myself at eight or ten very well. It's almost impossible to capture what was in my head then.

*Leaving answers aside for a moment, what are the questions that interest you the most at this time?*

I want to understand the workings of evolution better, especially which other principles are necessary in addition to conventional Darwinian natural selection that work on organisms. I would like to understand better how evolution works over longer periods of geological time. I want to know how important contingent events, like the catastrophic massive extinction, are to the selection of species.

*You said once that not religion but irrationalism is the enemy of knowledge and science. I'm sorry to come up with God again, but after all, I'm a hopeless romantic.*

I know you are. I knew it from the first letter you ever wrote me. I've been trying to rein you in right from the start.

*What was the indication in that first letter that I was a romantic?*

Oh, it's full of flowery statements about the ultimate nature of unanswerable questions.

*And yet you decided to participate.*

Mainly because you had such interesting people involved in it.

*Thank you. Anyway, God. In one of your old textbooks you read that nothing in science is incompatible with God or with religion. "Whoever thinks that is mistaken about science, about religion, or about both." Has this never been problematic for you personally? God, or if you prefer religion, on the one hand, and on the other the Darwinian theory of evolution?*

It's not a problem to the great majority of educated people in the world. The problem in America is that there are many so-called fundamentalist religious groups that take the Bible literally. That's odd, because there are many conflicting things in the Bible. But the majority of believers have

101

no trouble with it. They understand that religion is about moral values and science is concerned with the factual state of the world and the universe, which are two different things. Religion is a system for finding answers to moral questions, or at least a satisfying answer to moral questions, and the factual state of the world has no influence on that at all.

Science does not deal with moral questions, but is good at answering factual questions. So essentially there is little connection between the two. Historically, religion has always intervened in the domain that we now call science, and there has been a struggle when the boundaries had to be redrawn. That's one of the reasons why people keep speaking of a conflict, when in fact there is none. Most religious people have no trouble accepting the facts that science offers, because whatever the factual state of the world, it cannot possibly threaten true religious inquiry.

*Would you define yourself as a religious man?*

Not particularly, but that's just a personal preference. I have complete respect for those who don't agree with me because these are unanswerable questions, and people reach their own personally satisfactory solutions.

*When the word "God" is mentioned, many people feel some sort of reverberation from their childhood. Does this word have any meaning to you?*

It means so many different things to different people. It spans the whole range from the anthropomorphic controlling deity, usually depicted as white and male and sitting on top of the clouds, to a very mild pantheism that identifies God with the abstract laws of nature, like that of Spinoza and Einstein. And they're such different concepts.

*But if I say God, what bells ring in your head?*

Since I wasn't personally brought up to accept such a creature of formulation, it doesn't particularly resonate with me. I just recognize it as one of the great issues of human history.

*What questions will you ask when you meet the other participants at the roundtable?*

I'd like to know if we could make some progress on the integration of the contingent and individual, and on a scientific view of nature and of the history of humankind. We're all interested in that.

*You've written, "We delight in paradox because it appeals to both the sublime and whimsical aspects of our psyche." What are the most important paradoxes in evolution or in our appearance in evolution?*

That quote refers to the important question "What is an individual?" There are many animals that are borderline cases—in one respect they're colonies and in another they're individuals. That's the essence of paradox, two contradictory things that both appear to be true. Are there fundamental paradoxes like that in evolution? Sure there are. Take the one I work on in functional equilibrium: it looks as though to define evolution at all we ought to have slowly transforming sequences, and yet the geological record is one of fits and starts. But I think the resolution is that you can climb up staircases. There is a larger-scale continuity, with each step as a discrete event.

There is a paradox in the very definition of species. If you believe in evolution and there's a single transformation, you oughtn't to be able to define species as anything other than an accidental moment in time in a transforming lineage. Yet we say that species are the real units in nature that evolve. I think the solution to that paradox is also the staircase model: that species are stable for a long time, and then transform pretty quickly.

There are many puzzles in evolution. One is the appropriate level at which selection is working. Darwin had selection always choosing among individual organisms, as selection for him works on bodies, but much of evolution goes on either at the level of genes or at the level of species. Really it looks as though you have several interacting levels. We need a theory of multiple levels or hierarchical selection, which has not yet been well formulated. There are problems involving the traditional assumption that the history of life is continuous and adaptive, because these catastrophic episodes of mass extinction intrude. There are also problems with the evolution of genomes. If adaptation rules, why does more than 90 percent of the genetic material of our organisms not code for anything? What is going on within genetic systems? There's so much we don't know.

*You've written, "I may not be the master of my own destiny, but my sense of integration probably reflects a biological truth." What is this idea of integration?*

I meant that we are so complex as to be unpredictable; that what we call free will covers a great range, and that's why we do have free will, in the traditional sense of freedom. If we were made up very simply, if each separate part went its own way and was determined by the laws of nature, then all human actions would be totally predictable. But we are so complex and integrated that there is none of that predictability. So even if we do not control our destiny entirely and though we are influenced by the amount of money that we have, the language we speak, and our socioeconomic status, we do have a considerable amount of free will in terms of the way we live our lives.

Someone who's terribly poor and who lives in a ghetto without any means of existence has little free will. But people who are economically well off and who aren't tied to their country, religion, and family to any great extent possess a relatively high degree of free will.

*What dangers lurk in a reductionist approach to reality, in seeing humankind as a machine?*

The main danger is that we don't recognize and sufficiently acknowledge the impact of unpredictable history upon us. We start to think of humans as a collection of behaviors determined through natural selection. And that's just the wrong approach. History is rich and unpredictability is great, and flexibility is enormous.

*But what are the dangers now that biological determinism is rising in popularity?*

Well, I do think that's true. The danger usually associated with it is the political effect, when repressive regimes use it to rationalize the status of the people they torture and abuse. Yet there is a definite chance of avoiding the dangers by a combination of good scientific information and decent humanistic politics. But I can't predict the future. I base myself on the theory of contingency and I believe in it passionately. And it teaches you that you cannot make sweeping predictions.

*Is there comfort in this theory of contingency?*

I think there is. Some people find it frightening. For me it's exhilarating.

*About unanswerable questions: What questions did you ask your father? What did your kids ask you, and how different were the answers?*

Oh, sure, they were very different, they were different generations. My father was an idealistic Marxist out of the 1930s, which was a common political attitude in this country and elsewhere, and I got pretty straight line Marxist answers to most of my questions. He also was a great optimist, he fought in World War II, he believed that the world could be reconstructed in a better way afterwards. He was disappointed by a lot of what happened, but I was growing up by then. My children grew up in a much more cynical age. I don't think they even entertain hopes of peace and brotherhood among all human beings.

*But what questions did they ask you when they were young, and what were your answers?*

It's as with all things. Kids ask the damnedest questions, both profound and naive.

# CHAPTER 4

# IN PRAISE

# OF DIVERSITY

## Freeman Dyson

The gospel that I preach, boiled down into one sentence, is
that of the abundance of life and the limitlessness of human
destiny. I suggest the following hypothesis about the
enigma of our existence: our universe is the most interesting
of all possible universes, and our destiny as humans is
to make it so.

Freeman Dyson is far more fragile than I thought: a small man in a slightly oversized raincoat, with glasses that seem to date from before World War I. When I meet him in a hotel in Cambridge, England, he carries two unbuttered rolls in one hand and a somewhat feminine umbrella in the other. He immediately reminds you of an absentminded professor. His wife, who has accompanied him, explains that Freeman would forget to eat if someone weren't around to remind him periodically of the concept of taking in food.

Almost all reviews and articles about him mention one character trait of Dyson's: he is obsessed with the future. He is one of the prime advisers of the space agency NASA, and stresses the importance of smaller spaceships rather than the unwieldy space shuttles of the present. "The future belongs to the birds."

At the same time he is a prominent adviser to various congressional committees on defense and disarmament. "For decades I've been rewarded handsomely for giving advice which is then ignored."

He knows the world of the warriors inside out. And he has found time, next to his impressive career as a physicist working alongside such people as J. Robert Oppenheimer, Edward Teller, Richard Feynman, and Hans Bethe, to raise five daughters and one son. He's a kind father, that's plain to see. And he has the most curious smile I've come across in years.

When he calls an autistic woman he's known since her childhood the closest thing to an alien intelligence he's ever come across, I'm struck by the same observation, looking at the man opposite me. Slightly alien, very kind and easygoing, but also rather strange. Spellbindingly strange, and at the same time spellbindingly normal.

The number of citations he's had is impressive, yet Dyson is a very down-to-earth character and a plain speaker, as we find out when he discusses his wartime experiences, when he was a scientific adviser to the RAF Bomber Command.

The afternoon is to be like a newsreel: we'll travel a multicolored path from astrochickens via Eichmann and Hiroshima to Wittgenstein and Dyson's grandchildren.

Two images will stay with me. When we walk down the stairs after a six-hour interview, I tell him that I'm looking forward to seeing him again at the roundtable. Dyson seems to take that remark as my parting words to him. He rushes down the stairs and disappears through the door.

The next day I amble past Jesus College, where Dyson is staying, just as his car drops him off. He picks up his bags, looks in my direction—I'm about twenty feet away—but doesn't recognize me.

Of all the scientists I interview, he is closest to the archetype of the scholar who studies the world without appearing to be part of it. He seems to have been parachuted into Cambridge by beings with a different kind of intelligence from somewhere around Saturn or the Andromeda nebula, where Dyson is dying to go.

*What are your earliest childhood memories?*

I had a very happy childhood. We lived in Winchester, which is a very ancient town in the south of England. As children we were running loose in the fields. There were marvelous trees to climb in. My happiest memory is of sitting up in the tops of trees with my friends, talking about this and that. That sort of stayed with me. All my life that's been a kind of metaphor for the right way to live. There's a beauty about trees, and they are useful and necessary and helpful, besides being beautiful. Our relationship with the trees has always been somehow central to my view of things, and especially now since we've started to worry about carbon dioxide. Of course, trees are God's way of getting rid of the carbon dioxide.

*I thought you would say: In my early childhood I read Jules Verne, or Edith Nesbit's* Magic City. *But you were sitting in the trees looking down upon the world. . . .*

I used to take books up in the trees and read up there. As I was the son of a professional musician, I had too much music. That was something I wanted to escape from. I admired my father very much, but still, those endless concerts . . . I remember when I was quite small I was taken to a concert and one of my father's friends asked me if I liked music. And I said, "Well, music is very nice, but too long." I didn't hate it, but I knew that wasn't what I wanted to do with my life. I was interested in mathematics and in trees and other things.

*Were you creating a world of dreams, high up there in the trees, or did you at the same time have both feet on the ground, so to speak?*

I would say we were very ordinary kids in a way, but we had great freedom, that was the beauty of it. It was a very safe world we lived in.

And we were allowed to run around more than the other kids. We used to divide the children of our acquaintance into two tribes: the Smart Tribe, which was us, four or five kids who had this freedom, and the rest of them were called the Fussy Tribe, who were always being chased after by their mothers and told what they couldn't do. We were very aware of our freedom and enjoyed it. Apart from that, I don't think we philosophized very much.

*But you also read Jules Verne and* The Magic City.

I wrote about *The Magic City* particularly, and that was important, though I don't know whether I understood how important it was until later. You always see much later what she was driving at. I remember I loved, actually, the books about girls. I always enjoyed *Little Women* and *Good Wives,* by Louisa May Alcott. Alcott wrote a set of four books, *Little Women, Good Wives, Little Men,* and *Jo's Boys.* Jo was the leading character in this whole family saga. As a child Jo was a tomboy, and then she grew up and became the adoptive mother of twelve boys. This was in fact a true story, Jo was taken from life. She adopted these twelve boys and brought them all up, and that's what the third and fourth books are about.

One of those boys was called Nat, and in the book he played the violin. This was around 1880 or so. Anyway, Nat actually showed up at our house. He came from America, he had a violin with him, and it was the real Nat. He'd become a professional violinist. He happened to be passing through and he stayed at our house. He sat by the fire and told us wonderful stories. He remembered all the things that were in the books, and they were his childhood. It was all real.

*So to you it was all mixed up, the books, the characters, and reality?*

Yes, finding out that this all was real and that these twelve boys existed. Of course, we asked him what happened to Dan, to John, to Demi, and every one of them. We wanted to know what really happened to them in later life. So he told us. It was something that came as a gift from heaven.

*Do you remember any other gifts from heaven in your childhood?*

Well, there was the sky. I remember a wonderful night we were taken up on the roof to look at Saturn through a telescope. I was probably six or seven. I loved stargazing, and of course in those days skies were darker than they are now. So astronomy was always important.

*Can you imagine the sensations you had at those moments? Were they the same as the sensations you have nowadays?*

That's of course impossible to remember. Sixty-year-old memories are completely unreliable. I know I often not only forget things, but I remember quite vividly things that never happened.

But you ask about astronomy. That wasn't just a matter of stargazing. Another character who had an important role in my life was Frank Dyson. He wasn't related to us, but he came from the same village in the North of England that my father came from, and they knew each other. They were the two local kids who had become famous, Sir Frank as an astronomer and my father as a musician. So they had a lot in common, and I heard at the breakfast table all about what he was doing. When I was five or six years old, he was at the height of his career. He was not only astronomer royal of England, but he was actually president of the International Astronomical Union, so he was the number-one astronomer at that time.

In 1930 or '31 the asteroid Eros came by the earth. It was important for the professional astronomers because it gave them a much more accurate measurement of the distance between the earth and the sun than we'd had before. To set the scale of the solar system and so set the scale of the whole universe, you needed some object that was between the earth and the sun in order to measure the distance accurately. Eros was exactly right for this. So as it came by the earth, there was serious international collaboration to measure its position very accurately and track it and compute its orbit, and finally then deduce what we call the size of the astronomical unit, which is the distance from the earth to the sun.

Frank was in charge of this whole operation. And it was talked about every day at the breakfast table. Of course, it filled me with all kinds of dreams. That was, I suppose, when I decided that I would like to be astronomer royal myself. And the fact that he had the same name made it even better. I dreamt that I would be a big astronomer myself, and become an explorer of the universe. When I was eight years old, I sat down and wrote what was supposed to be a novel, which ended up as a truncated fragment, like most eight-year-old's novels. But it was a story about Eros and the hero was an astronomer, a mixture of Sir Frank Dyson and Jules Verne. So what happened in the story was that Eros actually collided with the moon. And there was this tremendous discovery, which my hero made—he was called Sir Philip instead of Sir Frank—Sir Philip discovered ten years in advance, by computing the orbits, that Eros and the moon were going to collide. He immediately then started a great project to launch an expedition to the moon, Jules Verne style, of which he was to be the leader, and the parts of the novel that actually got written were concerned with organizing this expedition. Anyhow, I was into space travel already by the time I was eight.

*I can imagine that those fantasies about exploring the universe are still with you, as fresh as they were in your childhood.*

Yes, that's certainly true. I'm still deeply interested in astronomy, and I'm still deeply interested in getting out there and bringing the whole universe to life. It's not so much just people going out there, but the trees

109

and the potatoes and the corn and everything that's going with us. Bringing the whole thing to life.

*Are there any questions that you would say are unanswerable?*

The simple answer is no. But it all depends on how long a time scale you're thinking of. I mean, I consider that we are still monkeys; we just came down from the trees rather recently, and it's astonishing how well we can do. The fact that we can even write down partial differential equations, let alone solve them, to me is a miracle. The fact that we ourselves at the moment have very limited understanding of things doesn't surprise me at all.

If you go far enough in the future, we'll be asking totally different questions. We'll be thinking thoughts which at the moment we can't even imagine. So I think to say that a question is unanswerable is ludicrous. All you can say is that it's not going to be answered in the next hundred years, or the next two hundred years. But if you go far enough, there's no reason to think that human beings shouldn't have the mental powers of other creatures that may already be around. Let alone the ones that may arise in the future. To say there are unanswerable questions makes no sense. But if history comes to a stop, if we descend into barbarism or if we become extinct, then the questions won't be answered. But to me that's just a historical accident.

*Do you mean that such a disaster caused by humans would be a historical accident?*

Yes. Many other species have become extinct, so why not us? There's a wonderful poem by Robinson Jeffers about this. "One day the earth will scratch herself and smile and rub off humanity."

*Would it be a great loss?*

Well, for us it would be, of course. In the big scheme of things, maybe not. Whether there is other life in the universe is one of the great questions which I'd love to know the answer to.

*What do you expect?*

I think very probably yes. But it's a question you can decide only by observation, not by theorizing.

*You wrote: "My sister and I owe our lives to a sniper's bullet. If our Uncle Freeman kept his head down, we would never have existed."*

Our Uncle Freeman was captain I believe in the British infantry in World War I. He was fighting in France. He happened to be very tall, he was two meters tall. So one day he put his head up out of the trench, and a German sniper put a bullet through his head. And that was the end of him. That was I think in April of 1916. My father was his closest friend, they were colleagues as schoolteachers. Freeman was a classical scholar, my father was a music teacher. They were very close. Freeman was a sort of confirmed bachelor  and had a very close relationship with his sister. They used to wander around Europe together. By the time he died she was already 37, and she probably never would have married if Freeman had not been killed. The fact that he was killed was a tremendous grief to both her and to my father; it brought them together. And so it happened that in 1917, one year after his death, they got married. And my sister and I were the result.

*You have written much about the heritage of World War I during your childhood. "The image of Paradise lost, of unspeakable mud and blood, of unspeakable massacre, and of impoverished survival were deeply ingrained in our minds almost as soon as we could talk." You talked about sitting in the trees, dreaming about the universe, but at the same time there was this heritage, these myths of World War I.*

Well, it was certainly very much a part of the background. We had this war memorial which we walked through every day. It was a lovely cloister, with the names of five hundred boys who were killed in the War, just from that one school. When we were children, it was only ten years in the past. We lived this free-and-easy existence, but in the knowledge that the grownup world was very tragic. And we felt in some way—I think my sister more so than I did, because she was three years older— that it was carpe diem, make the best of things, because this is all you'll ever get. Every day of peace and freedom is something to be treasured, because we are probably doomed in the end. We had this feeling of doom very strongly, because another war was already threatening at that point. We didn't expect to survive it.

*You really didn't expect to survive much longer?*

Of course, we thought of World War II as a bacteriological war. If German warfare turned out to be as we expected, then Europe would be overrun with plagues. That vision of World War II was quite widespread at that time.

*The myths of World War I were still fresh. What kind of myths were they?*

Well, it was of course a gruesome war. It was a little bit like the memory of Vietnam to come in later times—regarded by everybody as a gruesome mistake. Quite different, from the way we look back on World War II.

*But we're at the end of the 1930s. Freeman Dyson is expecting chaos in Europe, plagues, bacteriological warfare. At the same time he is stargazing and trying to get hold of some mathematical books.*

I give my father a lot of credit for pushing me in the right direction. One of the most important books in my life I got from him. And that was called *Men of Mathematics*, written by E. T. Bell, a Scottish mathematician who settled in California. It was a collection of very romanticized biographies of mathematicians, full of historical errors but still a wonderful book. He made mathematics sound like a grand adventure. He had a very fine gift for describing the essence of pure mathematics in popular language. It filled me with dreams of becoming a pure mathematician. Of course, in Bell's universe, pure mathematics was the only thing that counted. To be an applied mathematician was for him very definitely second class. So I decided to go for pure mathematics.

*What was the beauty of this world you discovered?*

Abstract beauty, the beauty of numbers, the beauty of abstract structures and of multidimensional geometry. All this was like a grand vision which I had been totally unaware of.

*Was there also a connection between the vulgar, brutal, horrifying world surrounding you and this wonderful clean world of abstract mathematics?*

Indeed, and that was very strong in the book. For example, the life of the French mathematician Poncelet, who was a soldier in the Grande Armée that invaded Russia, is described very graphically. Bell describes this brutal character Napoleon who drove his men into the wastes of Russia, where they all froze to death. Poncelet was captured by the Russians and incarcerated in a Russian prison for a couple of years. Without either paper or pencil, just with pebbles scratching on the walls of his cell, he worked out all the axioms of projective geometry. That was how he survived. So all his great mathematical ideas were produced in these harsh surroundings of the Russian prison. That was a very powerful image. That made a strong impression that this could be my escape, too.

*Did you realize at the time that it was an escape, or is this backward projection?*

I think it was. I think by that time I was quite self-aware.

*Don't you find that amazing, the power that many people have to survive in the most horrific circumstances?*

Well, I never came into any of those horrific circumstances, of course. We were amazingly lucky. We came through the war without any serious damage or danger.

*But what happened during World War II? The student, the mathematician, goes into the war and ends up working high up in the operational research section of the RAF, giving advice about bombing German cities. What happened to you?*

That's a long story. I suppose as soon as Hitler took power in 1933, we saw the war coming. I was then only eleven years old. I hardly remember a time when we didn't see it coming. We thought of civilization as being doomed in some sense.

So I decided to become a pacifist. The only hope seemed to be Gandhi. He was simply against war, against violence of any kind. And he seemed to be very effective. He was both a saint and a politician. And so I quickly decided that I would be a follower of Gandhi. My politics were simply that I would have no part in the war: I would refuse to fight or to help other people who were fighting. I would become an uncompromising pacifist.

I joined this Peace Pledge Union, which meant that you signed a pledge that you would never bear arms and you wouldn't do various other things. I'd subscribed to the *Peace News,* and I tried to convince all my friends to become pacifists, without much success. If we could convert England to pacifism, then there would be a chance. Maybe the Germans would invade England, but we would then convert the Germans. We thought of ourselves under German occupation as being in the same position as the Indians under British occupation. If Gandhi could deal with the British, then we could deal with the Germans. It all looked sort of reasonable. We thought that this nonviolent resistance would work in the end, even against Hitler. I don't think it was an absurd idea, considering what we thought were the alternatives—that or a fight to the death, and we didn't see much hope in fighting to the death. But of course it became very clear that we weren't going to convert many of our friends, let alone Neville Chamberlain.

What happened was sort of funny. We wanted to rebel against these monstrous militarists who were running the country, but whenever we tried to rebel, we found that they were always far too reasonable. It was very difficult to rebel effectively. For example, we were supposed to join the military training units which were preparing the pupils of our school to become soldiers. So we decided to resist joining this training corps. But the school merely said oh, if that's the way you think, then why don't you grow some cabbages instead? And it was the time when people were, you know, "digging for victory," growing vegetables to help feed the population in case of a war. So we weren't really in a very effective position to rebel, you couldn't really morally object to growing potatoes. They handled this very cleverly.

*And your political stance was weakening?*

No, it went on much longer. If ever I'd been told, "Now you have to go into the army and become a soldier," then I could have resisted and said, "No, I'll be a conscientious objector." I never had the chance. We had had these horrible stories from World War I of the best and the brightest of our young men going into the trenches and getting killed for nothing.

So in World War II, all the young people who were going to college were told, "It's better you get some scientific training, and then you can do something useful for the war, rather than just going into the trenches." They sent me to Cambridge to study mathematics. So this pacifism became very theoretical and by that time apocalyptic visions had faded.

When the war really started, of course, it was totally different from what we'd expected. It was an incredible relief. My uncle was running the ambulance services in London, so he knew what was expected. The week war was declared in 1939, the London hospitals were emptied of all patients, in the expectation that London would be catastrophically bombed in the first week. They had calculated, based on figures from the war in Spain, that you would have 250,000 civilian casualties in the first week. And there would be another 250,000 psychological casualties, people running crazy around the streets. When the first week arrived, nothing happened. Essentially life went on as usual. Finally in 1940 the bombing did start. And even that turned out to be not at all the way we'd expected. The total number of people killed in London in the whole war was about 50,000. So it was one-fifth of the number we'd expected in the first week. It was a substantial number of people, but it never came close to anything like a total catastrophe.

Of course, it was an enormous relief. By the time I was a student in Cambridge, the war had already gone on for two years. It was obvious then that England was not going to be destroyed, and that we would somehow or other get through the war and come out of it more or less alive. And then it became just a practical question—what part in the war should I take?

I gradually abandoned this belief in pacifism. It was obvious that we weren't going to convert the British public to pacifism. The British public was at least 99 percent behind the war and was doing very well. It was a time of enormous solidarity. When I was living here in Cambridge, in the middle of the war, you never thought of locking a bicycle, everything was so civilized and friendly. People were suffering a reasonable degree of hardship, but it was shared. It didn't matter whether you were rich or poor, everything was rationed; you got your ration, and that was enough. And it was a time when the country was, in a way, more at peace with itself than it's ever been since. So in the end I felt, well, I'm one of them after all, this pacifism really doesn't make any sense.

*Such a period of crisis brings out the best in people.*

Of course. I've extremely happy memories, though it was not a happy time. So by the time I came finally to the moral choice, in 1943, when I'd had my two years as a student here, I was nineteen. I'd done my two years as a student, and then the question was: What will you do? I wasn't actually asked to serve in the armed forces. They simply said, "You will serve as a civilian." The man who put me in my slot was none other than C. P. Snow himself, the novelist. He was then responsible for technical manpower assignments. So he said, "You shall serve in Bomber Command as a civilian adviser," and I said yessir, and that was it. By that time I felt I might as well do what they said. It made no sense to rebel against this very benevolent organization which was taking care of me. By that time it was obvious that the war was going to be fought through to the end, and one might as well help as best one could. I didn't realize then how bad the bombing campaign actually was. When I went into it, I found out very quickly.

The first week I arrived at Bomber Command was the week of the Hamburg attacks, the fire storms of July 1943. These were the first really effective bombing raids against a German city. There were four attacks in one week on Hamburg, in which we succeeded for the first time in raising a firestorm, which was the whole idea, of course. I think 80 percent of the bombs we dropped were incendiaries, not high explosives. The idea was to burn down the city, and in Hamburg we succeeded.

*Do you remember the reactions afterward? Was there a kind of euphoria?*

Yes, oh, yes. At the Command people were absolutely delighted. Finally what we'd been trying to do had worked. Hamburg was a great shipbuilding center; a large fraction of all the U-boats were built in Hamburg. Of course the U-boats were the primary threat to Britain, so from a military point of view, you might say this attack actually did make some sense. It turned out that the U-boats continued to be produced after the attack, but at least there was some chance that we could have damaged the U-boat production substantially with this kind of attack. We didn't learn until later how unsuccessful it really was as a military operation. The fact that U-boat production was not really put out of business didn't become clear until probably a few months later. What happened was that the Germans had a very good fire prevention system, though they couldn't save a whole city. They could choose what they wanted to save, and so of course they saved the U-boat factories.

*Was there generally euphoria when the Lancasters came back after a successful mission?*

Yes, this was a very special mission, because we introduced a new weapon called Window, which the Americans call chaff, which is these little strips of metalized paper that you throw out of the bomber, and which produce radar echoes. It was used for the first time for these Hamburg missions. And the first job I had when I came to the Command was making pictures of the actual distribution of the Window during the attack, showing how fast it fell, and to what extent the bomber stream would be hidden. I was calculating how effective Window should be. The marvelous thing was that that first night we lost only twelve Lancasters, which was way down. Normally, we'd lose something like fifty on a major attack. So it meant that Window had actually worked, it had saved three-quarters of the normal casualties.

*Did you think at all about the carnage on the ground in Germany?*

Oh, yes, we thought of that a lot. We knew we were going to kill a lot of people. But primarily we still thought in terms of military objectives.

*And those people were invisible.*

Let's not forget that a lot of them were building U-boats, and we wanted to discourage them from building more U-boats. And this was a strong way of discouraging them. We knew very well that it was a dirty war. There were many things about the war that were brutal on both sides. But attacking a city like Hamburg, which was a primary military production center for the navy, seemed to make a great deal of sense.

*And finally you bombed Dresden.*

Yes, two years later we bombed Dresden.

*You've written, "I had been retreating step by step from one moral position to another in Bomber Command until at the end I had no moral position at all."*

That's correct.

*I am reminded of the bombings of Dresden, if you see what I mean.*

And rightly so. It's a complicated story, because the attack we made on Dresden was no different from about twenty others. By this time, February 1945, the German defenses had more or less disintegrated, so we were able to destroy any city we wished. And so we went around Germany destroying more or less whatever was left. I remember we attacked Leipzig one night, and then another night Berlin, and amongst others we attacked Dresden. It wasn't a particularly heavy attack. It was just one of many. We knew that Dresden was an ancient city with historical monuments, and that it had not much military involvement. But that was true of many other places we attacked. So for us it wasn't anything unusual. The unusual thing was that in Dresden there was another firestorm. We never understood why. There were only two of these major firestorms, one in Hamburg and one in Dresden. It wasn't because the attacks were any different. It was probably something to do with the local weather conditions. The difference was that Dresden clearly was militarily unimportant. Dresden really was wanton destruction. It was a human tragedy

116

because it happened so late in the war and it didn't affect the outcome of the war one way or the other.

*Was it necessary, in hindsight?*

Of course not. But none of those attacks in 1945 were necessary. By that time, just three months before the end of the war, there was really no point in destroying any more cities. It was being done mainly just from bureaucratic inertia. We had this enormous Bomber Command, the defenses were more or less overcome, and what could you do? We just destroyed whatever was left, that was all.

*You write that "burning down cities was all we could do; in this crazy game of murder we killed some 400,000 Germans."*

Right.

*What kind of man were you at that time, toward the end of the war? What was the metamorphosis you went through?*

I became convinced fairly early that the bombing campaign was totally mistaken. That happened largely during the Berlin raids. Hamburg was July '43. We started seriously on Berlin in November '43. All through the winter of '43 till about March '44 we were attacking Berlin. Over and over again. That was when, from my point of view, the battle was lost. The idea was that we would burn Berlin down. The fundamental purpose of our bombing offensive was to destroy the military production apparatus in Germany. A lot of that was concentrated in Berlin. And so November 1943 was really the big test of the whole campaign. Could we in fact put Berlin out of action? And the answer was no. We'd attacked Berlin with the heaviest attacks we could manage all through that winter, from November until March, and a lot of damage was done, but by and large the whole industry continued intact. By January '44 it was obvious to us at the Command that we had failed, that we were not destroying Berlin to any decisive degree. We were losing huge numbers of bombers. The Germans had already won the battle. We realized that nothing we could do from that time on would really help the war in any decisive fashion. And for me that was the turning point. After that I was merely concerned with saving the lives of the bomber crews.

*You wrote, "I sat in my office until the end, carefully calculating how to murder most economically another 100,000 people."*

What I meant by "most economically" was by reducing the losses of the Lancaster boys. The idea was to get through with this bloody business with minimum losses, that was all. We knew it was a bloody business, we knew it was militarily unimportant. But at least we didn't need to lose more crews than was necessary. That's what I meant by "most economically."

*Killing another 100,000 Germans. . . . Were you at all aware what was happening on the ground when your bombs fell?*

Indeed we were. We'd seen the same sort of things happen in London, so we knew what it was, we knew what it meant, and we knew that it was militarily pointless. It was simply a salvage operation as far as I was concerned at that point. The best we could hope for was just to save a few thousand lives.

*How did you feel about the Germans?*

We were killing them, but ours was a small part in a very brutal and horrible war, in which brutalities occurred on an even larger scale than ours.

*But at the time, you were aware that it was useless to bomb any more German cities?*

It wasn't so clear. I would say it was not cost-effective. You couldn't say it was definitely useless, because we did some effective operations. We were quite effectively putting oil refineries out of operation in the last year of the war. That may have been of some importance. But what was certainly true was that the continuation of the war for an additional couple of months would have killed far more people than our bombing did.

The war as a whole was killing people at a rate of half a million a month. So if we could have shortened the war by two months, it would have saved a million lives, roughly. That was the kind of calculation we had to do. If those 100,000 people we killed by bombing shortened the war substantially, then it would be worth it. That same calculation was done in Hiroshima in a much more dramatic fashion. In Hiroshima, of course, the case was still not clear, but at least it was a lot clearer than it was in Germany.

*When you say that you no longer had any moral position at the end of the war . . .*

I mean that I was then just taking the easy way out. If I had been morally consistent, I should have resigned my position at Bomber Command and gone out into the streets to shout, "What you are doing is not only ineffective, but also criminal." I didn't do that. I wasn't sure enough of myself and I wasn't a hero.

*Do you still remember the daily atmosphere at Bomber Command?*

Very well. In fact, my closest friend at Bomber Command was Michael O'Laughlin. I shared an office with him. He's the man I'm going to spend the night with tonight, he lives here in Cambridge. He's now the Reverend Michael O'Laughlin. He and I kept each other sane during all those months. He was the only friend I could really share all my thoughts with in those days. That's how you get through. We were both aware that this was an insane operation which had got us somehow trapped in it, but neither of us was prepared to come out publicly and denounce it. Not only out of cowardice, as we'd say, but there was also a feeling of respect for all the people who were dying in the Command, and we were, after all, being paid to save the lives of the bomber crews. We owed it to them to do our best.

*And shouting "This is insane" wouldn't help the boys in the Lancasters, but would in fact betray them.*

It wouldn't have helped them at all, no. It wouldn't have helped anybody, really, except it could have just maybe made ourselves feel a little better.

*It seems like a tragedy, to calculate how to burn down cities most cost-effectively. But at the same time there's Freeman Dyson's other self.*

Yes, that's absolutely right. This is what Hannah Arendt calls "the banality of evil." These little *Spiesbürger* in the DDR, who ruined people's lives for forty years, it's the same story. The people at the headquarters of Bomber Command were also like that. The officers who were running the show were very ordinary people. It was their job, that was all. It's just like that, I suppose, in every war and in every dictatorial regime. There are very few real criminals, but a lot of plain ordinary people who do disgusting things just because the organization says they should.

*The real evil is bureaucracy.*

Right. That was very true in Bomber Command. There was very little chance of turning the thing around once the decision had been made to have a bomber command. In 1936 the decision was made that Britain's strategy in World War II should be based on heavy bombing. The bomber would be the primary workman for World War II as far as England was concerned. So they built these huge factories to build huge bombers in huge numbers. It took about five years for the thing actually to get going. By the time you got to 1943, the bombers were streaming out of the factories. There was a huge bureaucratic organization to train the crews in Canada and bring them over by the thousands. And that was the only war we could fight, really, because that was the way the thing had been planned.

*When it became clear that the bombing raids were insane, criminal, and pointless, bureaucracy took over.*

Yes, there was no way this whole big organization could get turned around. It would have meant essentially not doing anything. As we see now, when you want to get rid of nuclear weapons, even when the will is there and the decision has been made, it's very, very difficult.

119

*What you're saying is more or less that hundreds of thousands of Germans died because of the British bureaucracy?*

Right. And even more because of their own bureaucracy.

*You have also said that you felt a certain sympathy for Adolf Eichmann. Why?*

I don't remember whether I said I felt sympathy for Eichmann personally. I felt sympathy for the people who worked for Eichmann. People who were at my level in his organization. The people who were in the concentration camp bureaucracy, who were doing that kind of job. Who were simply taking orders from above, signing papers, writing contracts, getting all the apparatus to work, to exterminate the Jews. It was the people at the lower levels I was thinking of, who were analogous to myself. Many of those people were convicted of war crimes . . .

*"They went to jail, I stayed free . . ."*

Yes, what I was doing was in a way similar. And I thought that many of them probably had the same kind of repugnance to what they did as I did. I can't know for sure, but . . .

*You wrote about your visit to Dachau not long after the war. Do you remember what kind of weather it was that day?*

It was a beautiful day. The thing I remember most vividly was the correspondence of one of the doctors of the camp administration. They have all the contemporary correspondence and the newspaper reports which actually described what went on while the camp was in operation. The doctors were performing horrible experiments on the prisoners in Dachau, and at the same time carrying on a private practice in the Prinzregentenstrasse. I remember at the time we were taking our seven-year-old daughter to a doctor in the Prinzregentenstrasse, and it made us wonder whether he was one of those. It was remarkable how there was this contact between the hell that was going on in the camp and the normal bourgeois existence in the Prinzregentenstrasse, where the doctors were carrying on their practice. That is the most vivid memory I have of that place. Again, it was the ability of people to live on two completely different levels at the same time. I'm sure those doctors were not very different from the rest of us. They were just people who had been offered a job, which had some scientific interest, or at least appeared to have some scientific interest when they started, and they gradually got sucked into it. Much like me. To have come out in public and said "This is a criminal operation we're running in Dachau" would of course have been a heroic act. It would have meant they would have joined the prisoners.

*Many people would hesitate to say that they can understand what people do in circumstances like the Third Reich, and how common evil is. Is that one of your fascinations also?*

Oh, yes. And of course there have been endless discussions about Heisenberg and his colleagues, who worked on the German nuclear program. What they did, and what they should have done. They were in the same sort of ambiguous situation. And there was never any real answer.

*But you say, and I will quote you literally, "men like Eichmann, just like me, calculating." You understand the man. You understand all the men behind him.*

I don't claim that I know enough about Eichmann to understand him, I mean personally. He may have been a very special case, I don't know. But our analogous figure whom I knew slightly was Sir Arthur Harris, who was the commander in chief of our Bomber Command. He pushed the campaign as hard as he could. He bore personal responsibility for the attack on Dresden. Yet he was a man with very strong human feelings. I know on good authority that he was seen to weep on several occasions, when talking with air crew that was going on these bombing operations. He knew what it meant.

*You also had a discussion with a general whose name I don't remember. You were there to give him strategic advice, and he kept talking about silkworms. Wasn't his name Harrison?*

Correct. This was again at the late stage of the war. He was one of the people that looking back I really admire. He was at a high level, just below Harris, a commander a bomber group. He could have driven his bomber group as hard as he could, which is what Harris wanted him to do. Obviously his heart was not in it. And what he was in fact doing was holding back, sending his boys out as little as possible. But he couldn't come out in public and admit that. So he talked about silkworms. It was a way of signaling to me that he wasn't really interested in pushing the campaign. I was adviser on keeping crew losses down, but he knew how to save the lives of bombers. Simply don't send them out.

*And in talking about silkworms he transmitted that message to you.*

Yes, he loved them, I mean he had mulberry trees and a silkworm farm that he was taking care of himself. That was his passion in life. No doubt it kept him sane.

*Did you ever talk with the boys who flew the Lancasters?*

Once or twice, yes. But it was not made easy. They thought we might contaminate them with subversive thoughts, so we met them only on rather rare occasions. And when we did, it was difficult to talk with them, frankly. Because we were in such a privileged position. From their point of view, we were just young kids who had been pampered and sent to college instead of having to fly. They had no respect for us. And quite rightly.

At the end of the war wc had killed 400,000 Germans, but we could have killed vastly more. We were sort of lucky. First of all, we were lucky we didn't have nuclear weapons. And we were lucky that the bombing was so ineffective that we killed fewer people than we had intended. So when it was all over, I could look back and say it really wasn't so bad, so let's get on with life. I felt a feeling of enormous liberation once it was over. I remember that during the war we used to joke that really, we were doing these Germans a great favor, because fifty years later they would live in beautiful new modern cities and we would still be living in the same old slums. Actually it took only twenty years. So very quickly the mood changed totally. I didn't feel particularly guilty after it was over because, in a way, the war was a great success. We achieved almost everything we'd set out to achieve, and we kept England free, we kept Western Europe free. And we got rid of Adolf Hitler.

*Eliot says: "Where does one go from a world of insanity, somewhere on the other side of despair." Does this refer to your feelings after the war?*

Yes, I think that's absolutely right. We had been feeling a great deal of despair in the last years of the war. Certainly. I felt very desperate that last winter, and then you come out and life goes on. And you go beyond despair.

*Do you still dream about what happened in the war?*

On the whole, I'm a good sleeper. There was one nightmare which I remember vividly, because it happened several times, of an airplane crashing, burning on the ground. The people inside are screaming, and I'm standing there and I can't move. I should run into the flames and drag those people out, but I'm stuck there and I cannot move.

*Stephen Toulmin said that when he saw pictures of the "pinpoint bombings" of the Gulf War, he was overwhelmed by two things at once: a fascination that the bombings could really be executed with the kind of precision he had dreamed about in World War II, and at the same time the horror of the war itself. Did you have similar feelings?*

My feelings were rather different, because I saw the truth about the Gulf War which the public didn't see. In fact, the bombing was much less precise than the propaganda pretended. Even though the bombing was aimed at undefended targets. Even in World War II, we were pretty good on undefended targets. It's always easy to hit things if they're not defended. It's much harder if they're shooting at you. So as far as I was concerned, the Gulf War wasn't so different. It was misrepresented to the public. Actually a huge fraction of the bombs missed their targets, and a lot of the bombing was just about as bad as it was in World War II. And if there had been any serious defense, it would probably have been hopelessly bad. So the people drew the wrong lessons from the Gulf War, namely, that precision bombing is a good way to go. Against any serious defense I don't think it would have worked.

*You've written, "The world of the warriors is overwhelmingly male-dominated. The world of the victims is women-and-children-dominated." How would you, on the basis of your experience in the "world of the warriors" during and after World War II, describe the female view on the world, and how the male view on the world?*

Of course, it's not all men on one side and women on the other. There are warrior women, like Margaret Thatcher, but I think it's by and large true.

The warrior view is the view that's presented of the Gulf War, of the victory of machines and of brilliant maneuvers cleanly carried out in the desert with lovely brigades of tanks driving along and wiping out the enemy formations without significant losses. I've heard that described by many of my friends, people who fought in the Gulf War and also in World War II. War is fun, especially when it's short. Everybody enjoys a short war. It's an illusion, because no war really is short. As a rule they don't come to a clean end. Very often the suffering begins only when the war is over. And I think we all know the point of view of the victims: waste and devastation and loss of a decent chance to live.

I don't know what more there is to say. I'm pleased with the way the warriors have behaved in the last year or two, as far as the United States is concerned. I've seen a lot of generals recently who have really turned around, and it's sort of fun to talk with them. They just spend their time traveling to and fro between Washington and Moscow, and talking with their colleagues in Moscow about how to handle the world. That's great, and they enjoy it too. The military people actually understand each other rather well, certainly much better than the politicians do. An American general and a Russian general have a great deal in common. The question now is how to live together, how to get things organized. And how to prevent the world from falling into chaos. For them it's rather easy to establish collaborations. For the politicians it's much more difficult. I find all this very hopeful. The military is much more adaptable than I had given them credit for.

*I remember Stephen Toulmin saying that things are happening again and again. People don't learn from history. He said, "That's the gloomiest thing I feel at the present stage of my life." You're talking about hope.*

Oh, yes. I'm always very hopeful. I think we are at a new phase of history. It's true, things tend to happen over and over again, but this didn't happen before. I don't think it ever happened before, such a big empire disintegrating so quickly. And the fact that it's happened without breakdown of the military chain of command. All those things we were terribly afraid of as far as nuclear weapons are concerned actually didn't happen. Yet. They still may happen.

*Let's slowly change the subject. We're in Cambridge right now, a few decades after World War II. Here you once met Ludwig Wittgenstein, the stubborn philosopher. Would you mind telling how you met him and what happened?*

Well, it so happened that I lived in a room in Cambridge, the top of a tower, next door to Wittgenstein. There were just these two rooms at the top of the tower, and one was mine and one was his. He was then the very famous philosopher, and I was a humble student. So I never would have ventured to speak to him. But we used to pass each other on the staircases fairly frequently, and one day quite to my surprise he asked me would I like to come into his room for a drink of coffee? I said yes, and I came in. It was a difficult situation because he had only a single chair, which was almost a horizontal canvas chair in which you were lying rather than sitting. He motioned me to sit in this chair, so there I was, lying staring at the ceiling and Wittgenstein standing still and very silent, not saying a word. And we stayed there then for I don't know how long, but it seemed like ten minutes.

Finally, I decided I would start a conversation. So very bravely I said to him, "Professor Wittgenstein, I was reading the *Tractatus Logico-Philosophicus* and I found it extremely interesting. I would really like to know whether you still agree with what you wrote in the *Tractatus.*" And Wittgenstein stood very sternly over me, and he said, "Tell me, which newspaper do you represent?" And that was the end of our encounter. I slunk away with my tail between my legs.

*Wittgenstein is one of the miracles evolution has brought us. Let's go to evolution before humans appeared. Stephen Gould has four propositions about evolutionary theory in the footsteps of Darwin: Evolution is not a gradual process. Matter is the ground of all existence. Evolution has no direction. Evolution has no purpose. What do you say in reply?*

I agree with one and two. Even though number two doesn't mean very much to me. It all depends what you mean by the ground and existence.

But the third one, evolution has no direction, I don't agree with. It seems to me it has a fairly clear direction, from the simple to the more complex. And from less diverse to more diverse. The tree of life becomes more diverse as it evolves. And the fourth one, whether it has a purpose or not . . . I wouldn't be dogmatic. We certainly don't understand whatever purpose it may have, but to deny the existence of a purpose seems to me as foolish as to believe that it has to have a purpose. I would say, we'll wait and see. Maybe it does have a purpose. Maybe we'll create a purpose. I think it's foolish to preach about questions like that.

*Why are there so many kinds of living things? Why not a bit more uniformity? You once asked your mother the same kind of question. Do you remember?*

Yes, though it was about churches. I asked, "Why do we have so many churches in Winchester?" and she said, "If God had wanted us all to worship in one church, he wouldn't have made so many different kinds of people." I liked that, and I feel the same way about life as a whole. I mean, that's the glory of life, that it always seems to tend to diversity. It seems to be one of its most basic characteristics. So in that sense I would say that evolution does have a trend.

*But why is life so complex? Or is that question unanswerable?*

No, why should it be unanswerable? It's a question that we don't know the answer to yet. Maybe one day we will. It seems to me a perfectly sensible question. There's nothing in it that makes it inherently unanswerable. Of course I don't know the answer. I'm not an expert, but the experts don't know either. Why should they? After all, we've been studying life scientifically only since Aristotle, two thousand years, and that's a generous estimate. How could you expect us really to understand it in such a short time? It's amazing how much we have discovered in a short time. The idea that you should solve these major riddles just at the first try seems to me to be asking much more than is reasonable.

*Gould's preferred evolutionary mechanism is contingency. You talk about comet shower theory. You've written, "If this theory of comet showers is right, it changes the way of thinking about life and its evolution." What exactly do you mean by that?*

It means that there's a very much larger random element than we had realized before. It confirms Gould's statement that evolution goes by jumps. And of course the effect of a comet shower is to make it easier to make big jumps. If you wipe out half of the species, then the other half rearrange themselves, so the survivors will evolve more rapidly. I agree completely with Gould about the jumpy nature of evolution. But I think the difference between us is partly just a matter of time scale. If you look at evolution as a professional paleontologist does, on a time scale of maybe ten million years or so, which for geologists is very short, then it doesn't have any clear trend. It fluctuates tremendously. If you look at it from the point of view of life as a whole, say from three billion years back until today, then I think the trend is much clearer. I tend to think in terms of billions of years, while Gould thinks in terms of millions. I think when he denies the purposiveness of evolution, and denies that it has a trend, he's rather thinking of the detail. And of course the detail is amazingly diverse and random.

*Gould says that in the Precambrian, life was not more diverse but more complicated than it is now.*

Well, I would have very great doubts about that. It's quite likely that it was more diverse in the very narrow sense that there were more finalized body plans than there are now, and therefore more distinct ones. But on the other hand, there's been this enormous flowering of diversity on a taxonomically lower level, where you have enormous diversity of trees and birds which didn't exist in the Cambrian. So just because all of those are in only a couple of phyla doesn't mean it's not diverse. I think the taxonomist's view of diversity is a very artificial one.

*You've said, "I propose that our universe is the most interesting of all possible universes, and our fate as human beings is to make it so."*

I like that as a statement, though I wouldn't say that it's a statement of fact in any sense. It's just a hope. It's a statement of what I think would be a delightful universe to live in. Every time there's a new discovery in science, whether it's in astronomy or biology or any other field, it confirms my belief that this is the most interesting of all possible universes. I can't claim that this is in any sense a sure thing. I would say it's a good working hypothesis, that's all. And it may quite well be our destiny to take charge of the universe in some sense, to direct the future of life. It depends on whether or not we meet other creatures who have greater capabilities than ours. If not, then we may find ourselves in charge.

*You've written, "If there's a God, it's a Socinian God."*

Right. Now this is a big subject. What I mean by a Socinian God is a God who's neither omnipotent nor omniscient. He doesn't know what's going to happen, and he doesn't compel the world to go according to his wishes. He is learning and evolving as the universe learns and evolves. I don't necessarily believe in such a God, but if there is a God, then he should be of that kind. I like to describe him as the "world soul"—which was my mother's phrase—so that we are little bits of the world soul. And so it may well be that we are part of the world's growth, and we are ultimately in some sense responsible for its growth. That's the kind of world I would like to live in, and as a working hypothesis it seems to me quite reasonable. In detail the world shows no evidence of any sort of conscious design. If there is to be a conscious design, it probably has to be ours.

*You once had a dream about God. Would you tell us about that dream? It says much about your vision of how the world should be or could be.*

It was a delightful dream. It happened when I was in Israel. In the dream I was at home with my four little girls. We were sitting around in the kitchen, and I suddenly said to them, "Look, we have an appointment, at five o'clock we have to be there." And they said, "Where do we have to go?" and I said, "We've got some questions to raise," and I asked if they'd like to come along. And two of them said yes, and two said no. So I went along with two little girls, one in each hand. We came to the door of a building and walked in. It was like a kind of church, except it didn't have a roof. It just went straight up. The two little girls and I floated up in this building, very very fast, up into the sky. Finally we came to the top and it was just five o'clock, when we had our appointment. And there was the throne room with a big throne at one end, a kind of wooden throne with a wicker seat. This place seemed to be completely empty. So we climbed up the stairs to the throne. When we got to the top, we saw a six-month-old baby lying there looking quite happy on the throne of God. I picked him up and held him in my arms, and I handed him to the girls. And they walked around with him a bit. And then at the end I held him in my hands, and suddenly I felt an enormous feeling of peace. Of some kind of fulfillment. I knew all the questions I wanted to raise somehow had been answered. And that's the end of the story.

*What is real science to you?*

The details. The most exciting thing that's happened in the last couple of months was that a friend of mine called Joe Kerschwink in California discovered that we have magnets in our heads. I like that. That's something very real, very concrete.

*What is the meaning of this discovery?*

We don't know. We know that many creatures have magnets in their heads—pigeons and fish, for example, as well as various kinds of bacteria. They all use them for some particular purpose, either navigation or orientation. It's a very useful device, a little magnet that the earth field orients, so the animal can tell which direction is north, or which direction is up, as the case may be. Joe Kerschwink is actually a geologist who studies rocks. He got interested in these little magnets you find in rocks, and he decided he would have a look in people's brains to see if they're there. And they are. His wife is a Japanese biochemist, and she took the most lovely electromicrographs of these little magnets. You can see how beautifully made they are, they're perfect crystals, and you can actually see the layers of atoms. The human ones are identical to the ones you find in pigeons. So the next question is: Where are they and what are they good for? That's the kind of science I really enjoy. Finding real things and asking new questions.

*You once criticized a study on nuclear catastrophes. You wrote, "Carl Sagan believes strongly in the reality of nuclear winter, whereas I am still skeptical. We both use the same mathematics and both work with the same laws of physics. Why then do we reach different conclusions?" Why?*

It's because that is a purely theoretical problem. There is no real nuclear winter. It's a hypothetical situation, so there's no way you can say definitely yes or no. It's a problem of estimating probabilities and estimating the relative importance of different factors. And so it's a dubious sort of science, but it's the best you can do. It's an important question, but it's not clear that it really has a scientific answer. Whereas if you're talking about little bits of iron in our heads, that's something real to which we can apply science in the true sense we can investigate and study it. That's the distinction I make. There are different levels of science. Making calculations about nuclear winter is a style of science I don't feel comfortable with, because you never really know whether you've got the answer right. It's not testable unless you have a real nuclear war, and we don't want to test it that way. The essence of science is to be testable. Anyway, I enjoy the details when it comes down to it. Science is at its best when studying the details of things as they are. Superstrings, for instance, are pure mathematics and they're very beautiful, but it has very little to do with the details of the real world. It's a work of art, if you like. It's the opposite end of the scale from finding little magnets in people's heads.

*Let's discuss the future possibilities in science. Daniel Dennett informs us that at last consciousness will be awakened in a computer. You write, "The building of truly intelligent machines will at last be possible. Between 2000 and 2050 there will be an artificial intelligence revolution."*

It's likely that there will be a sort of merger between neurophysiology and electronics. That's what I was talking about there. What physics can do well is to make tools. You shouldn't expect ideas from physics, but tools. And the development of artificial intelligence is almost entirely a question of tools rather than of ideas.

One of the things that's happening is that the tools of physics are being applied more and more to biology. Perhaps in the end it may turn out that electronic computers are superfluous in some ways, that biology after all can do the job better. We don't know. But in any case it's likely that there will be a merger. So that we will have neural circuitry doing the jobs that neural circuitry does well, and electronic circuitry doing the jobs that electronic circuitry does well. Very likely the two will be linked together, so that you won't be able to tell in the end whether a robot is alive or not. It would be partly neural and partly electronic. Whether you consider it to be alive is a matter of definition. That's roughly what I was meaning, so that the question whether we'll have conscious machines is in a way meaningless, because it's the question of what you call a machine. A person with a hearing aid you'd say is still a person. If you have a human brain that's so mixed up with electronic circuitry that it has a hundred times our capacity for solving mathematical problems, it still is a human being. But of course there are all sorts of steps beyond that, where you might say it's no longer human. And then you really get into problems. Do you give such a being civil rights? But anyway, I wasn't looking that far.

*Well, aren't you? You wrote once that the distinction between living and dead, and between present and past, is becoming blurred. What exactly did you mean?*

Well, that of course is much farther into the future. The blurring between living and dead will clearly take much longer. That's the stage at which you may be able to transplant memory and personality from one brain to another, so that in some sense you can record a human being's personality.

Suppose that the dreams of the artificial intelligence crowd came true, which I don't necessarily agree is very plausible, but just suppose. . . . There's a man called Hans Morovec who talks about downloading—that's his metaphor—a person, which means you transfer all his memories and his personality to a computer. And then you find an appropriate brain in which you can upload him again. You are resurrected in somebody else's head. So you get over this little awkward transition of death. I don't like that idea particularly, but I was just playing with it. If this becomes possible, then of course the distinction between past and future is blurred. And then you wouldn't know who you are anymore. Are you really the person who lived a thousand years ago, or are you the person who is living now? The whole relationship between past and future becomes vague. I think it's an interesting speculation, but I'm not taking that seriously as a program. Most likely it'll turn out to be a total illusion. I mean, we're just beginning to learn something about neurophysiology, and one of the things we're learning is, as I was hearing this morning from Gerald Edelman, who is a great expert in this field, that neural circuitry is totally different from electronic circuitry. In fact, the more we learn about neural circuitry, the less similar to electronics it seems. And so in a way it makes these dreams look very much less plausible.

*So then Edelman would disagree with Dennett, who compares the brain to a computer.*

Well, it's a totally different kind of computer. It seems extremely unlikely that you can make any sort of one-for-one transfer from the neurons to electronics. The neurons have a totally different kind of architecture. And we're only beginning to learn what that is. On the other hand, Edelman is making computer models of neurons. And on a deeper level you may in fact be able to make such a transfer. But it's not such a simple matter as some people had thought.

*You've written about the "astrochicken": "The next 100 years will be a period of transition between the metal and silicon technology of today and the enzyme and nerve technology of tomorrow." What is an astrochicken?*

The astrochicken was just a concrete example of what life might be like once it gets loose in the universe. I believe that life ought to be loose in the universe. The universe is a very dull place. We have life on only one planet, and there's all this enormous real estate out there, which would be much more beautiful and more exciting if it came alive. So my idea is that life will in the end spread, and that we are perhaps the midwives who make this possible.

The question is, what sort of life could grow out there in a vacuum? I can see no particular reason why the present types of living creatures shouldn't be able to live in a vacuum. They only need some rather radical changes on the surface. It's the surface which is difficult. Our skins are not well adapted to living in a vacuum. But as far as the insides are concerned, it wouldn't make much difference. So you have to sort of redesign the skin of a creature—whether it's a vegetable or an animal—to live in a vacuum. Well, there are three things you have to adapt to. Zero temperature if you're going out very far from the sun. Zero gravity, which may be difficult because we have adapted ourselves to living under earth gravity. But there again, some tricks could enable one to live in zero gravity. And then, finally, zero pressure, which is living in a vacuum. That's the hardest. Somehow you have to surround yourself with an impermeable skin, so you don't lose air and water all the time. And you have to be able to live on some kind of chemicals that you can eat and drink without exposing yourself too much to a vacuum. So there are all sorts of practical problems, but in the end it looks as though the thing ought to work. It would be a wonderful expansion of the diversity of the universe if the life would move out.

The astrochicken was just an example of a kind of creature which could live. It would have essentially the body of a chicken, but appendages which are quite different. It would have enormous wings, to act as solar sails with huge extended membranes, with which it could fly in space using sunlight instead of air. And it would have radio antennae, long little thin wires sticking out, so it could communicate by radio instead of by sound. It would do all the things a chicken can do, including laying eggs, but it would do them in different ways. This was the idea. This would be something that could come into existence within maybe a couple of hundred years, and would then be a viable species for colonizing different parts of the solar system. It could fly from one asteroid to another, it could settle down and raise a family. And it could live on whatever it happened to find there in the way of chemicals.

However, one species wouldn't do the job. You need a complete ecology. Of course plants are essential, so there's another creature which I call the Martian potato, which is a potato that's adapted to having its leaves in a vacuum. The potato is underground, of course, buried in the Martian soil, deep enough so that it doesn't freeze. You'd have all sorts of microorganisms to keep the ecology going. So the idea is that you could have a complete ecology of these rather weird-looking creatures, which could then spread out. And once you have the freedom to move in space, then there are really no limits to how far it could go. And then evolution would take over from there.

*We would need artificial intelligence and genetic engineering, and what else?*

Well, a good system of space propulsion to get you off the ground. At the moment, of course, launching into space is very expensive. We have to invent cheap ways of getting from here into space. So that's the third technology. I regard that as the easiest, actually. Of course artificial intelligence is helpful, because it means that you can have this marriage of electronic with neural circuitry, which is probably what you would like to use. So that these creatures can communicate by electronics, by radio over large distances, and still function with ordinary brains for their daily sex life and all the rest of it.

*Because there must be some fun in the universe if we're spreading life through space.*

Indeed, yes. I mean, the whole thing is no fun if it isn't fun.

*"Genetic engineering will fulfill the promise of a cleaner and more liveable world for mankind," you wrote. First the good news about genetics. What can we achieve with the genetic engineering revolution?*

I was thinking of industrial processes mainly. Biological processes are generally very much more economical, less wasteful than industrial chemistry. For example, if you take the question of burning coal, which is a very messy process as it's now done, you could imagine a bug which is programmed to use coal as its food—which biochemically could be quite feasible—and which would convert coal cleanly into, say, methane and other clean fuels, and could deal with the sulfur and other contaminants in a clean fashion too. In the end, instead of a large smokestack through which all these noxious gases are going up into the atmosphere, you'd just have a fermentation plant in which these bugs would be eating coal at one end, and out the other end would come cylinders of natural gas, or a pipeline of clean hydrogen. And you'd get waste products, in the form, say, of bars of solid sulfur, which could then be used for other processes, which in themselves are not damaging to the environment.

The crystals of iron oxide in our heads is a wonderful example of this process. We make absolutely perfect crystals in our heads called magnetite, that's the magnetic oxide of iron. And that's something we don't know how to do by ordinary chemistry, but our cells know how to do it. We have this enormously fine-tuned technology which we still are not really able to exploit. I think when we learn to exploit it, a whole lot of industrial processes will become clean, as well as mining and garbage disposal. My favorite example is the turtle with diamond teeth which is programmed to eat up old automobiles. That's a joke, of course, but there's no reason why such creatures shouldn't take over the job of chewing up the garbage and converting it into clean by-products. It's the sort of thing that organisms are doing naturally. In a natural forest dead animals are disposed of that way, and we could learn to do it equally well.

*And we could bring flowers to the Sahara.*

In principle, yes. You can argue that it's good to have some deserts, but in principle we could let the Sahara become a garden. The raw materials are there. I would think it's likely it'll be between fifty and a hundred years before this really becomes a major factor.

*What about "monkeying around with the humans," as you dubbed it?*

This is far more dubious, of course, but we're already doing it. For medical reasons there's an enormous push toward what they call gene therapy, and I must say, if you look at the horrors of hereditary diseases, there's every reason for using gene therapy if you possibly can do it. I think this kind of gene therapy will come very quickly, but then the question will arise: Do you consider subnormal intelligence a hereditary disease? Then it becomes really tricky.

*Yes, should people with deviant genetic makeup be allowed to reproduce?*

It's a question of what you call deviant and what you don't. There we really get into deep problems, and I'm not advocating that one rush into that.

*How long will it take before social pressures rise? For instance, on people who are at risk, but don't want to be genetically analyzed before they have children.*

In the United States the laws about experimenting with human subjects are very strict. You just are not allowed to experiment on human subjects without informed consent. The lawyers are very, very tough if you try to do that kind of thing. Also they're very strict on the privacy of medical information. You're not allowed to force people to be tested for AIDS, for example. The legal obstacles are very strong. In the United States, of course, everything is in the hands of lawyers. So for us it's a legal problem. For other people it's a social problem.

*Yes, but about this monkeying around . . . What experiments should be forbidden, however tempting they are to scientists?*

There are two things one could think of happening. First of all, there is restricting childbearing to people who are certified as genetically healthy. That's eugenics, of course, and that I think is likely to stay illegal in the United States. There's a very strong tradition now to keep the laws on that kind of subject strict. On the other hand, there's the question of positive interventions. If a couple of parents decide, "We'd like to have a child who is an artistic genius, let's have a try," are you going to forbid that? I don't know. I think that's a much more acceptable kind of intervention. If a couple of parents decide to try for a child with superior endowments, using some kind of genetic manipulations, the question becomes: Are they prepared to take the risk of it not working? If it doesn't work, then the child is burdened. Do you allow parents to take a risk which may involve the suffering of the child?

*And what happens if the child does come out a prodigy?*

Then you can't really raise any moral objection. If it's guaranteed to work. But even then it'll cause social problems, because you may not want so many artistic geniuses.

*No. Monocultures are highly dangerous.*

Yes. But one could say there will be enough diversity in people's wishes for their kids.

*This monkeying around, this world of DNA, of cloning, of producing hybrids. We're not permitted to do such experiments, but how fascinating is it? When I talk to scientists, they say it must be forbidden, it's perverse, but it's fascinating all the same.*

My feeling is that in the long run it will be done, because one will learn what makes sense and what doesn't. In a way it's like contraception. It's messy and it's repugnant to many people, but after awhile you get used to it. Things that to one generation seem perverse become accepted in a hundred years or so. My hope is that when human beings spread out to other parts of the solar system, when we have space colonies and are living in remote places, then these activities will become much less dangerous.

The problem on this planet is that we're all so close together. If some of us are much different from others, it causes enormous social problems and conflicts, as we see every day. Even slight racial differences cause enormous problems. If you had genetic engineering producing radically different kinds of people, it's hard to see how our political systems could handle it, but if you had a colony of pioneers somewhere out beyond Jupiter monkeying around with their children and producing superior brains, that wouldn't bother us to anything like the same extent. So one could make it a condition of genetic engineering that you go off and do it somewhere else. That it's prohibited within some well-defined zone, but beyond that, anything goes.

*Cloning yourself into potential immortality—isn't that tremendously seductive?*

That doesn't appeal to me personally. I have six children and they're all different, and I find that much more interesting than if I had six more of myself.

*"My own feeling is that physics is passing today through a phase of exuberant freedom," you wrote. What are the developments you never dreamed of in your childhood?*

Well, we've just discovered some real planets beyond the solar system, and that was marvelous. I've been waiting for that for fifty years. This discovery means the world does have all this diversity that we've been talking about. The stars are not just dull little balls of fire, but they have interesting places revolving around them. There's an enormous variety of things we have discovered that we never dreamed of, like black holes, pulsars, quasars, all these unbelievably active goings-on in the universe.

In Aristotle's time the sky was supposed to be quiescent, perfect and peaceful. Nothing ever happened in the celestial sphere. That remained the general view of astronomers right through Copernicus and Galileo and Newton until just the last thirty years, and now we know it's not like that at all. In fact, the universe is full of violent events and fantastically strong gravitational fields and collapsed objects and huge outpourings of energy.

*What are the queerest things in the universe at present?*

The things we understand least are the quasars. These are the most violent and the most energetic objects in the universe, and they're still totally mysterious. All we know is they're there, and they're rather frequent. Nobody ever dreamed they existed until they were found, and even after they were found, it took a long time before people took them seriously. Nature's imagination is always richer than ours.

*Scientifically speaking, you once lived in a city and now you are in the rain forest.*

Yes. The image of the rain forest was more concerned with particle physics, where things have got steadily more complicated. Instead of having just a few fundamental particles, we seem to be getting more and more, and the scheme of things has gotten more and more complicated in the last twenty years.

*If I asked you, "Are the laws of nature immutable, or are they evolving, as the universe is evolving?" what would you say? From Descartes's day until the beginning of the twentieth century everybody knew the laws of nature were eternal.*

This has now become an experimental question, since we can look at quasars, very close to the beginning of the universe. You can tell from the shapes of the spectral lines that the atoms were exactly the same as they are now, so that the laws of physics have not changed since very close to the beginning.

*Rupert Sheldrake says quite confidently, "The cosmos now seems more like a growing and developing organism than like an eternal machine." It's a matter of taste, I suppose, but what would you like? If you're talking about a Socinian God, that would seem to imply that the laws of nature are not immutable, but that they evolve.*

It depends what you mean by the laws. I was speaking of the laws of physics in the narrow sense of the rules of the game governing atoms as individuals, and the most elementary laws of physics. We have no evidence to suggest that those laws change. But of course the universe is so much more than that. I agree with Mr. Sheldrake that it's actually more like an organism and that the laws on a higher level—that's the laws governing life and society and the laws governing the enormous variety of structures—evolve as the structures evolve. You can't have laws of economics and sociology until you have human beings and societies for the laws to govern. So the laws grow as the objects grow.

*You've said that minds are getting control of matter. What do you mean exactly? Is mind different from matter? The mind organizes matter, but it's not matter itself.*

We don't know that. You see, I dislike philosophical statements altogether. I'm not interested in the question of defining words. I'm merely saying that "mind" is a way of talking about things, and "matter" is another way of talking about things. I don't care whether they're the same or different. The mental world is something I believe in very much, and as intelligence develops, the mental world gets more and more powerful.

*How do you feel about the illusions of the Cartesian theater? For three centuries, starting with Descartes, Newton, the Enlightenment, we've been hunting after an all-encompassing theory, after the ultimate answers—the certainties Montaigne would have got rid of, but Descartes, Leibniz, and Newton wanted to hang on to. Are we leaving the Cartesian theater at the end of the twentieth century?*

No. I've never read Descartes, so I don't really know what he said, but I would agree with Montaigne. The idea that we're anywhere close to any ultimate understanding of things is a kind of delusion of grandeur which I don't like.

*Someone once asked Oliver Sacks, "If you were frozen now and revived after fifty or sixty or seventy years, what's the first thing you'd want to do?" He said he would immediately ask for a copy of* Scientific American. *What's the first thing you would be interested in?*

I'd like to meet my grandchildren. That would be the most exciting thing for me. I have three grandchildren, who are now between the ages of zero and three, and I'd love to know what they're like fifty years later and hear about all their life histories.

*And what's the next thing you'd want to know about?*

I must have disappointed you in not dealing with the big problems, but I think it's true, I'm always more interested in the details than in the big picture. So my grandchildren are more important to me than any of these big philosophical questions. If you ask what I'd be most interested in knowing about scientifically, I would probably say, "Did we get to Mars yet?"

*You haven't changed much since you read Jules Verne.*

No, that to me is still very central.

*You once said, "I came upon a scene and found myself playing roles which were half serious and half preposterous, and that is the way it has continued ever since." Is this the definition of your life?*

Yes, and even more so now. I mean, I've become a television star! That's something I never dreamed of, and I find it delightful. For me it's a new career. I've reached the age where I get invited to talk on television. I was just in Tokyo talking on Japanese television with Stephen Hawking, who's of course a real superstar. I was just a minor figure in comparison. We were talking about the future of humankind.

They were asking us very specific questions, so I was compelled to sound pompous.

*You said: "I'm living half serious, half preposterous." Steve Gould writes: "We delight in paradox because it appeals to the sublime and whimsical aspects of our psyche." You have told me that you once came to Hiroshima with guilt in your heart. We are talking now about the sublime and the whimsical, the serious and the preposterous . . .*

My wife and I arrived in Hiroshima of course intending to pay our respects to the dead and to visit ground zero and see the evidence of destruction, and to feel suitably solemn and guilty. When we arrived, we found that everybody was dancing for joy in the streets. It turned out it was the day of the final game of the world baseball series, the last game of a series of seven between the Hiroshima Caps and the Osaka Braves. This final game had been played that afternoon and Hiroshima won. All the department stores declared everything was half-price in honor of the occasion. It was just terrific. The time we spent in Hiroshima was the most cheerful of all the time we had in Japan. I found it wonderful how adaptable these people are. They've left the past behind totally. The monuments in Hiroshima are there, but they're really for tourists, and not for the people of today. Anyhow, it's a lovely place to raise kids. It has nice wide-open streets and there's absolutely marvelous countryside around—little islands and the sea where you can go out in a boat and visit the little shrines. It's a place of great beauty and, in a way, more relaxed than other Japanese towns. That's the paradox. If there is a God, he obviously has a sense of humor. . . .

*Cruelty and a sense of humor.*

Yes.

*Sublime and whimsical.*

Yes.

*Ridiculous and majestic.*

Yes.

*Would you agree if we chose for your part of the narrative the motto "In praise of diversity"?*

Yes. That is my guiding principle, if I have one at all.

*Speaking of diversity and different cultures, you were bombing Dresden. Why did the Japanese bomb Pearl Harbor?*

I'm not a historian but I do know that it was a work of art. Everything I saw in Japan had this character of doing things unnecessarily beautifully. You buy a little bag full of oranges at the train station: five little oranges beautifully wrapped up in a little paper carton, and then an additional little bag where you put the peels so can discreetly throw it away into the appropriate receptacle. They just worship beauty. I find that very attractive. Of course it's the same with their gardens, with the little flowers they grow in front of their houses. Wherever you go, it's hard to find anything ugly.

*And the same applies to the way they bombed the Americans?*

Right. When they came to bomb Pearl Harbor, it was a work of art. With a minimum amount of force they created a masterpiece. The way they destroyed the maximum number of American ships with a rather small number of airplanes was amazingly efficient. The whole thing was carried through to perfection. It was lunacy in the sense that it was pretty obvious that in the end it would be a disaster. But the mere fact that it was so elegant was probably a strong reason why they went ahead.

*Do I detect a hint of jealousy, when you think how you bombed Dresden?*

Oh, yes. There have been very few bombing operations as good as that.

*OK. On October 19 you will come to Holland. What is the first question you would like to raise in this company of wise men?*

I'm no less interested in what those people will be discussing than in who they are. I would raise personal questions primarily, to find out what's going on in science in all the various areas those people represent.

*I gather that you've talked to Oliver Sacks these past few days.*

Yes, I've been spending quite a lot of time with him. The thing I find most fascinating to discuss with him is an autistic lady that I know. I have a long-standing interest in extraterrestrials, in intelligent creatures who might be living out there in the universe somewhere and what they might be like. I've always felt that this woman, who is now thirty-five years old, whom I've known since she was a little child, is the closest I'll ever come to an alien intelligence. It's a marvelous thing to know an autistic child. Her universe is radically different from mine. Concrete social relations are for her very difficult to comprehend. On the other hand, with anything abstract she has no trouble, so we can talk very easily about mathematics. She's also a very gifted painter. It's a marvelous mixture—strangeness and familiarity. It has enormous importance for the kind of thing Oliver Sacks is doing. He's trying to explore the neurological basis of personality, and I think this autistic syndrome comes as close as you can to that central problem. These people's intelligence is essentially intact, but something at the center is missing, which is why they lack the capability for human relationships of the normal kind. I find it absolutely fascinating.

*When I said, "Thank you for this interview," you said, "A whole part of mine is missing." What part is missing?*

It's simply my work as a scientist. I believe that science has much more in common with art than it has with philosophy. When I'm really doing science, I think of myself as practicing a craft, much more than following a method. That somehow didn't come through in the interview. To give an example, we've run out of ideas in physics just for the time being. But we're producing marvelous tools. That's really the main excitement to me as a physicist—that we are producing tools for other scientists to use to explore the universe, both in biology and in astronomy.

I'll take quickly two examples. The digital sky survey which I'm involved with at Princeton is a new survey of the universe which will be about a thousand times as extensive and a thousand times as complete as anything we've had before. It's being done very cheaply—it costs about a hundredth as much as the Hubble space telescope. It's clever, it's cheap, it's quick, it has all the virtues, and it will be finished in five or seven years or so. That's made possible by the development of new physics tools, particularly good data processing and good electronics. As a result, astronomers will have an enormous enlargement of their view of things. And to me that's terrific.

A similar thing, which I think is even more important to the general public, is called oscillator-coupled magnetic resonance imaging. Magnetic resonance imaging is, of course, a very useful tool in medicine. You take magnetic images of people's brains in order to see what's going on inside the brain or in other parts of the body. My daughter, who is a medical doctor, uses it all the time. It's now being used extensively all over the world. But it has one great weakness: it has low resolution. That is, from outside the body, you can see things only on the scale of millimeters or centimeters. You can see a lot, but not enough for many purposes.

A new idea being developed by a friend of mine, John Sidles, at the University of Washington in Seattle, is the oscillator-coupled magnetic resonance imaging I mentioned. It's essentially coupling together the idea of magnetic resonance and the idea of the atomic force microscope, which is a very sensitive microscope which was also developed in the last few years. It looks as though we actually can have magnetic resonance imaging with a million times better resolution, which means being able to look at the insides of molecules and individual atoms magnetically, without destroying the molecules. An intermediate resolution, on the scale of cells or neurons—which would be exactly what the neurophysiologist would most happily use—would open new windows into biology and medicine.

*What's the most fascinating thing you could think of in terms of tools in the next twenty, thirty years?*

The development of the nondestructive sequencing of molecules, sequencing DNA in particular. This magnetic resonance idea makes that possible. There's a chance that that actually might give you a very fast and efficient way to sequence DNA. That would make it feasible to sequence the whole genome in a few months. And maybe in a few years it wouldn't be the human genome, it would be the whole biosphere genome. We would map the genetic sequences of all the interesting species. That to me holds great promise. I think that the physical sequencing of DNA will turn out to be enormously cheaper and more powerful than chemical sequencing, which they're doing now.

*What are the implications or applications, both positive and negative?*

If we have abundant DNA sequences, it's very much like this digital sky survey—it's the same kind of thing for medical people. Whenever you want to investigate a hereditary disease, you first of all find where it is in the genome. You have the genome in your computer, and so you find out where the gene is and find out how it's controlled. And so then you can go on from there to devise a therapy. So it will be an enormously useful tool in medicine and also in the evolutionary discussions. If you know the sequence of a chimpanzee and an ape and of a gorilla and a human and various kinds of other creatures, you'll settle a lot of these evolutionary questions.

*You have said that science could provide us with a philosophy of hope for the next century. What did you mean by that?*

The fact that science provides tools for so many different purposes means that as long as we have active science, we can always hope that new solutions to problems will arise. I mean, you never can be sure, but it gives you new hope. Science will keep things from stagnating and from ever being too peaceful.

# CHAPTER 5

# REVOLUTION

# OR

# SIDETRACK?

## Rupert Sheldrake

Do the laws of nature evolve? Or does only physical reality evolve and are the laws of nature eternally fixed? What do we really mean when we talk about "the laws of nature"? I will show how my hypothesis of formative causation leads to a new and radically different evolutionary understanding of ourselves.

"There's a niche in our culture for Rupert Sheldrake," said Daniel Dennett. "He's extremely clever but totally wrong." Stephen Jay Gould concurs.

Stephen Toulmin doesn't know Sheldrake's books, but he has heard that they're not up to scratch. Neither Oliver Sacks nor Freeman Dyson knows who Sheldrake is, but Dyson sits up when I tell him Sheldrake advocates holism. "Well, I hate isms of any kind. I detest things like reductionism and holism."

One thing may be clear: during the roundtable Sheldrake will be met with enmity from all and sundry with respect to his hypothesis of formative causation.

I have to admit that I expected to meet a New Age disciple full of vague statements. Sheldrake is a leading thinker of that movement. But his words and actions prove that prejudice wrong: he talks sense, he talks to the point, and even for an Englishman he has an understated sense of humor. He doesn't speak, he teaches. My questions are largely interruptions of his lecture, but he accepts them graciously.

I remember those hours in Hampstead in London, I remember Sheldrake's voice, the trees behind him that I've looked at for hours, the green of the trees that shone through his hair, the green design of his jacket, the green chair in which he sat. Everything was green that afternoon.

But even more I remember Rupert Sheldrake after the roundtable. The same man who told me, "I do not as yet regard my hypothesis as an absolute truth" suddenly turned into a raconteur, telling story after story about the weirdest experiments and constantly exploding with laughter, though not so often or so long as the rest of the company. In shirtsleeves and with a glass of wine in his hand he sheds the understated humor and emerges as a man who can sublimely put himself and the world into perspective without ever showing signs of nihilism.

"I love him as a human being," said Gould. Dennett, too, spoke with genuine fondness of Sheldrake. I suddenly understood why.

Is he a twentieth-century union of Darwin and Einstein, as many people believe? Or is he the highly intelligent inventor of an ingenious theory that is totally wrong?

"The truth is a matter of taste," my late grandmother would have said. The other five participants in the discussion thought otherwise.

■

*"We are such stuff as dreams are made of, and our little lives are rounded with a sleep."*

Actually I think it's the other way around. Before we're born and after we die it's probably like a dream. It's as if our lives are rounded with a dream. In between waking life with more dreams and fantasies as well. A dream enters into a realm of possibility, of imagination. There's a sense in which all our lives are an interface between that and the life of embodied existence in the physical world. I suppose part of the business of science is to explore that interface, because you could say scientific theories come from the dream realm. Some of them in fact come to people in dreams. But any scientific theory must be tested against reality, you have to do experiments, and experiments are not quite so much like dreams, they're more like oracles.

The experimental method is best seen as a modern form of divination. In Roman times people cut open animals and examined their entrails. Nowadays scientists cut open animals and examine their physiology. You do an experiment, you look at some feature of the world, and you ask for an answer; that's just what diviners did and what the purpose of oracles was.

Somehow these experiments modulate our scientific *dreams*, at any rate. The ordinary idea of a dream is that it's free, independent, and has nothing much to do except with one's memories and possibly one's future, one's desires. But it's somehow unlimited by reality. Well, science is limited by reality through the experimental method.

*Have you ever been struck by the question: Why are there so many kinds of living things? That's a fascination from my childhood.*

I feel that too, and I actually get it in a double dose, because I often go walking on Hampstead Heath with my sons, who are four and two years old, and the two-year-old says for everything "Why?" He's in the phase where he just says *why* all the time. The four-year-old is very observant and knows a lot of flowers and plants. He focuses his attention on many things as we go around. So it's not just remembering the state of my own childhood. The presence of children with quite far-ranging curiosities gives it another dimension. It's a great experience.

*Why is the grass green, why does the moon have phases, why is the sky blue? Do your children ask you the same questions you asked your father?*

I can't remember what I asked my father, but I imagine that they must be the same kind of questions. These are very fundamental questions. My children are fascinated by death; for example, they ask about what happens when you die. And they're very interested in stories of witches and giants that eat up children, they're very concerned with the whole question of being eaten and eating, killing and dying. I think that's partly because we don't eat meat, so they think about why people kill animals. Why do animals kill other animals? To eat them. I explain that in nature things have to eat something and animals either eat other animals or they eat plants. Even if you eat plants, you kill them, but all this eating and killing is part of the structure of nature. If you look at the fairy tales that young children read, it's amazing how many of them involve stories of killing, eating, or life-threatening situations of various kinds.

*When your son asks, "What comes after death?" what do you say?*

Well, he asks that quite often. Part of the answer is, of course, that your body decays. When we go to the church on Sundays, he likes playing in the graveyard of Hampstead parish church. There are yew trees and old tombs that are overgrown with ivy. He loves hiding behind those tombs and he's very interested in whether they've all got skeletons in them, which they have. So he know that bodies decay, that you bury them in graveyards and the body decays.

So the real question is: Does he have any sense of *life*? My best explanation to him is that it's like dreaming, since I believe there is some kind of conscious survival of death. The best way I can conceive of it is that our life is rounded with a dream, as I said at the beginning, in the sense that death may be rather like dreaming. If you have a nightmare, then that may be rather like hell. Only in death you can't wake up, so you're trapped in dreams permanently. When we sleep our physical body is lying in our bed, but when we dream we have the sensation of going to other places, talking to other people, seeing things, walking around, even flying. Most of us don't pay much attention to dreams, yet we all have a dream life, parallel to our ordinary life. We have an implicit body in our dreams, even if we're not aware of it, and this dream body then comes back into our physical body, and when we wake up we forget about the dream.

One way of thinking about the way we survive bodily death would be in a kind of dream body. I leave aside the obvious question of what's the physical basis of the dream body. I'm just now talking about what we experience.

Most people in most cultures for most of human history have believed that in our dreams we do in some sense travel outside our body.

Sorcerers and shamans and witches have perfected the techniques of traveling consciously in dreams, so-called lucid dreams. If you know you're dreaming, it's possible to take control of the dream and use it to go visit people in distant places and see what they're doing. There are reports in all shamanic traditions and in all psychic traditions that people can really find out things they didn't otherwise know through this kind of dream travel.

So, just sticking to the evidence as we experience it, leaving theories about the brain aside, we see that when we die there's this sense of continuation of the dream state.

We all have our own kinds of dreams, depending on who we are, what our interests and desires are. The postmortal dream state would depend very much on the kinds of people we are and the kinds of memories and experiences we've had. I think that the traditional doctrines of life after death fit quite well with the dream state. You continue after death to have some kind of psychic life that may resemble more the psychic life of the dream state. And then sometimes you have totally blissful dreams, when there's a kind of liberation from the ordinary limitations of dreaming. That may be the final liberation, a kind of mystical experience within the dream, which is possible, and which some people have. I've had some myself.

This analogy is my starting point. You asked me how I talk about it to my four-year-old son, and that's the answer. Now, if I were talking about it to someone like Daniel Dennett, I'd obviously have to be talking about it in a completely different way, because he'd immediately bring in the brain and his theories about the brain.

*Dennett calls the dream an illusion without an illusionist, and consciousness an abstraction caused by neurosynapses, this army of dumb idiots that form our brain experiences.*

Exactly. I would say that is just as much a theory as the other one. But one can start with experience, and we all have experience of dreams. I think it's better to stick with the experience for awhile before we rush into theories or conclusions. The whole point of science is that you start from experience—at least, that's supposed to be the point of it.

*Immanuel Kant once said that this universe is as majestic as it is ridiculous. Does this sound familiar to you?*

I don't really think in those terms very much. Kant was influenced by Newtonian astronomy, and this sense of a vast mechanical universe going on automatically over vast distances, quite independently of us, gives you this kind of astronomical sense of physical immensity. That was probably what he was thinking of. It's much harder to get a sense of it from actually looking at the stars or the planets. In fact, it's rare today to find anyone who's got any sense of the universe from actually looking at it.

Most people I know are completely ignorant of the phases of the moon, the positions of the planets, the names of the constellations. I was having dinner with a friend who's a professor of astronomy once and afterward we went out. There were some particularly bright stars and I said, "What's the name of those stars?" and he said, "Don't ask me, I've no idea what they are. I can tell you how the sun works, I know all the equations for galaxies and so on, but I don't know what those are." The actual observation wasn't part of it. And much the same can be said of astrologers. They have an ephemeris, they look it all up in a book. But they don't really look at the heavens either. I think if we want to have a sense of the heavens, we have to form a direct experience of looking at the stars.

Whenever I do that, I do get a sense of majesty. For me there is the sense of the sheer realms of possibility, when one looks at the stars in the sky and realizes that all the stars we can see in the sky are in our own galaxy, and there's only one other galaxy that we can see with the naked eye. That's the Andromeda galaxy, a faint cloud like a little patch of misty light in the sky. With telescopes we can see millions of other galaxies. When we realize that each of these stars may have a planetary system, and on these planetary systems there may be limitless forms of life, all sorts of imaginations, all sorts of mental life of every kind throughout the universe, then it becomes much more interesting. If we see it as a mere panorama of inanimate matter, then I can't get terribly excited about that.

*But if you see life as an instrument of matter, just molecules and atoms dancing cheek to cheek, and that dance forms life and forms our consciousness . . .*

I don't find molecules and atoms terribly interesting. What is interesting is the dance they do. It's like going to a great city like Jaipur in India. The fact that it's made out of stone or brick isn't the point. What's interesting is the actual forms, and those are not determined by the material.

*You talked about your children's questions. When I was very young, one of my fascinations was that our universe was just one atom in the eye or the ear of somebody else in another universe, and that an atom or a molecule was a universe in itself. Did you have similar fascinations?*

Yes, I did. I vividly remember that when I was maybe six years old, I was lying in bed in the summer and I saw the dust in the sunlight as it came through the window. I was watching these dust particles and then the idea came to me quite spontaneously that each of those particles might be a whole world like our world, and in those worlds there might be people lying in bedrooms looking at dust particles, and each of those would be a world. This was probably the biggest idea I'd had in my life

146

by that time. I was suddenly struck by this idea of infinite worlds within worlds, like Chinese boxes, stretching infinitely in all directions.

*If you think back to that picture of universes within universes, like Chinese boxes, is there any development, or have your amazement and conclusions remained the same now that you're grown up?*

I wouldn't put it in quite the same way, but I do believe that the right approach to nature for science is the holistic approach: to see that everything is nested within something else. The earth is a unit, but the earth is within the solar system. The solar system is a unit, but that's within the galaxy, and the galaxy is a unit, but it's within a cluster of galaxies, and then all these are together within the whole universe, which is the ultimate physical unit.

Then if we look at the earth, we have ecosystems that are units, and then societies, and then within those there are organisms that are units, within them organs, within those are tissues and within tissues cells, and within cells molecules and within molecules atoms, and then subatomic particles and then complexes of subatomic particles disappearing into the realm of the very small, until they disappear from our ability to detect them. The smaller they get, the bigger the apparatus you need to find them. The ultimate limit is set not by nature herself but rather by the willingness of the U.S. Congress to go on funding ever-larger particle accelerators. So from the small to the large, at every level in the universe there's a wholeness which contains parts which are themselves wholes which contain parts. This view of nature is the background to all my scientific thinking.

*I want to start talking about consciousness, as a prelude to discussing your theory of formative causation. If you think back, do you remember the odors of your childhood, the colors, the songs?*

With a particular smell you have a rapid evocation of memory, but I don't know if I remember the colors of my childhood. I certainly remember vivid episodes and scenes. There's one particular fascination I remembered quite recently. I was about five or six; and I was staying on the family willow farm. My grandmother grew willow trees for making baskets. And I was outside with an uncle and I saw a row of willow trees with rusty wires hanging between them. So I said to my uncle, "Why is that rusty wire hanging between those trees?" and he said, "Well, we made a fence out of willow stakes, and the fence came to life." I looked, and of course then I could see that each of them had been a fencepost; and those wooden posts had formed shoots and roots and it wasn't a fence anymore. It was a row of living trees. And this really made a tremendous impression on me, this sense of the dead things coming to life in such a vivid way.

But when I remembered this particularly vivid incident, I then saw, both to my surprise and delight and also to some extent horror, that in this childhood memory was summarized much of my subsequent scientific career. I spent years working on plant development, on the behavior of isolated stem cutting. Much of what I did subsequently was foreshadowed in this particular memory. This kind of childhood revelation affects many people for the rest of their lives, usually without their knowing it, because we don't usually pay much attention to positive memories from childhood. Certainly in retrospect, one could say that these moments of epiphany or revelation or insight condition much of what one does afterward.

*You have written, "Memory is both everywhere and nowhere in particular. Memories must be stored somehow inside the brain, but in the continuing absence of any direct evidence, it remains more a matter of faith than of fact." Where does memory reside?*

I think that *where* is the wrong question. Memory is a phenomenon of relation in time. When we realize that memory has principally to do with the interrelation of events in time, it's not immediately obvious that the question *where* plays much part in this. The question "Where is memory stored?" immediately traps us in a whole set of spatial metaphors. The problem is that we think of time in terms of spatial metaphors: the near future, the distant past. So people think there must be a memory store. So where is the memory store?

I don't think it's in a place, I think it's a relation in time. I don't think it's stored in the brain. I think we tune into our memories in a kind of transmission in time. This is a key part in my particular theory of morphic resonance. I think that the past is potentially present everywhere and that through similarity or whatever we then tune into, we access aspects of past experience. But it's not in the meantime stored anywhere in particular.

*Freud said, "Prehistoric times have found their psychic repercussions in a heritage that in each generation needs only to be revived, not acquired. Children in many ways react not according to their own experiences, but according to instinct comparable to that of animals, in a way that we can explain only by assuming that they have phylogenetic knowledge at their disposal." Oliver Sacks writes about prehuman memories that go back to the darkest corners of existence, that provide his patients with images from the prehistoric and prehuman landscape. How familiar does that sound to you?*

It sounds entirely familiar to me. I think that we inherit a great deal of collective memory from our ancestors and I think it goes back a long, long way. For example, the experience of a child at its mother's breast, a very fundamental experience very early in life, I would say is in resonance with the experience of young mammals sucking from breasts for sixty, maybe a hundred million years of mammalian history. There's not much difference between a human baby sucking at a breast and a piglet sucking at a breast. This has been the defining characteristic of mammals ever since the mammals first evolved. This experience is so utterly fundamental and is so similar to that of phylogenetic memory going back many millions of years that I think it would almost inevitably invoke or be related to this long series of memories.

*But Sacks is talking about prehuman landscapes; even premammal landscapes, even predinosaur landscapes.*

I'm not quite sure what kind of experience he might be referring to. People who have taken psychedelics and see astonishing visionary states often describe things that could be regarded as prehuman. Most of us would spend a lot of time suppressing these archaic memories, but they might come out in dreams, and in certain unusual and altered states of consciousness they may become clearer.

*There are people who believe that they have memories of a previous life. Usually they are explained in terms of reincarnation or rebirth. We are slowly approaching your theory of morphic resonance. How would you explain these pictures from previous lives?*

Well, let me say first that I regard it purely as a question of empirical evidence. Do people remember previous lives in a way that can't be explained in normal terms? I think at least as regards young children, the evidence is positive. The American psychologist Ian Stephenson has shown in very careful case studies that in many cases these memories couldn't have been acquired by the children normally. There seems to be something paranormal and unusual going on here. I would interpret the evidence myself in terms of picking up the memories of previous people.

Just as Jung thought of the collective unconscious as a kind of collective memory, in my own work I think of a kind of collective memory as well, through morphic resonance. In a similar way you could see how it's possible for somebody to tune into the memories of a particular person in the past. But I wouldn't necessarily interpret it as reincarnation. I would prefer to think of it as accessing somebody's memories.

*To make sure that I don't misunderstand you, do you claim that we possess memories not only of our direct evolutionary godfathers, but also of the organisms that preceded us, trilobites, single-cell organisms, perhaps even the crystals that existed before life emerged? How far does our memory reach back? What have we inherited?*

I think that we are the products of an evolutionary development, and that there's a kind of memory inherent in the whole process. The vast majority of that memory is unconscious, just as the great majority of our own memory is unconscious. Most of us can't remember how we developed inside our mother's womb, most of us remember almost nothing from the first few years of our lives, and if we can't remember even our own ordinary personal history, we're not likely to have vivid memories of life as a trilobite or as a cell in the primeval slime.

The kind of memory that's implicit through this evolutionary history is essentially a memory of unconscious habits. You could say that the cells in our bodies participate in the unconscious habits of cells right back to the first cell, including the way cells divide and many features of cellular organization and behavior. But these memories are not expressed as conscious reminiscences in any sense. They're more like the kinds of memories expressed through our own habits, like riding a bicycle: you can't say how you do it, you can just do it. That's a kind of memory, but it's not a conscious reflection. I would say the kind of memory we inherit from our forebears and way back from prehuman ancestors is much more of that general kind, to do with habits. These are expressed in animals as instincts—unconscious patterns of behavior.

*We'll put memory aside for a moment, but we shall return to it later. Let me quote you briefly: "I show how the hypothesis of formative causation points towards a new and radically different understanding of ourselves and the world we live in." That is quite a promise. Could you try to convince us?*

I have to start with a historical description. We've recognized since Darwin that there's a general evolution in the biological realm. Before Darwin, it was generally accepted that there was an evolution in the human realm, an evolution of human consciousness. In the eighteenth century the progressive philosophers were obsessed with the idea of human progress: from barbarism to civilization and then to science. But they didn't think then that evolution occurred in the biological realm. Darwin showed you could have a scientific theory of biological evolution, so now human evolution was embedded in a much bigger evolutionary story, the evolution of life. But the physicists resisted the idea that physics or chemistry evolved, they were locked into a view of the universe as eternal, a great machine that went on forever, but gradually running out of steam, running down thermodynamically. So they had a great machine that was gradually devolving, governed by eternal laws of nature that never changed, and by particles of matter and a quantity of motion that never changed.

*Life evolves but the laws of physics do not.*

That's right. The basic principles of physics are totally nonevolutionary. That was the idea until the 1960s. Then the Big Bang revolution occurred in cosmology, and we now have a view that the whole cosmos evolves. At one time even the fields of nature, the electromagnetic and gravitational fields, were not separate and distinct in the way they are now. According to superstring theory, they were part of a primal field. In the chemical realm, once there were no atoms, and certainly at one time there were no zinc atoms or iron atoms or aluminium atoms. These all evolved historically in time as the cosmos developed. And then molecules and crystals. Once there were none of them, now there are many kinds. So the whole of physics and chemistry has also undergone an evolutionary development.

We now have a radically evolutionary cosmology, but a relic of the old thinking is still there in that most people think that the universe is governed by eternal laws of nature. What I'm suggesting is that the so-called laws of nature are not fixed. If we live in a radically evolutionary cosmos, then why shouldn't the laws of nature evolve as well? And my view is that they're really more like habits; that what happens in nature depends on what's happened before. There's a kind of memory in nature, rather than eternal mathematical laws.

I would say that the universe is not a machine, it's more like an organism, and the Big Bang theory is like the traditional myths of the cracking of the cosmic egg. It tells us the universe began small and that ever since that beginning it's been growing, and as it's grown, new structures and patterns have developed within it. This is like an embryo. No machine starts small and grows and forms new structures, but a tree does as it grows from a seed, and an embryo does as it grows from a fertilized egg. Effectively our modern cosmology has given us a view of the whole universe as a developing organism.

The old idea of eternal laws fitted very well with an eternal universe. Physicists have resisted the evolutionary idea tooth and nail because it's so alien to the traditions of physics, which are radically nonevolutionary. But now they've finally gone over to an evolutionary idea of the world. Still there's this residue of the old idea of eternal laws. That's what I'm challenging. I'm arguing that the idea of formative causation give us a sense of memory in all aspects of nature, so we can think of the evolution of nature as being accompanied by the evolution of the habits of nature. So when I say this hypothesis gives us a radically evolutionary understanding of ourselves and the universe, I'm trying to extend the evolutionary model to its limit, because what we've seen is a series of extensions: first it was confined to the human realm, then to the biological realm, now the realm of physical phenomena.

*What does formative causation really mean? What are the consequences of your view that not only the world but science too is subject to evolution? Take, for instance, the question: What was there before the Big Bang?*

I have no better answer for that than anybody else. I think the problem of the creation of anything, including the Big Bang, is a profound mystery. The creation of new forms and patterns, new species, new ideas is one of the ultimate problems. I don't think that science can address it, because science confines itself to the study of regularities and repetitions. Creativity always happens outside the normal order of things, it has no precedent. The Big Bang is the primary creative event, but in an evolutionary universe there are many creative moments, because every new pattern, every new idea, every new form, new species, new molecule, and new crystal implies a creative jump.

Many people deny that there is any intelligent or formative principle in the evolution of nature, but they're prepared to accept that the whole universe with all the laws that govern it sprang from nothing in an instant. Well, if you'll believe that, you'll believe anything.

I think that the Big Bang theory requires us to put all the mystery in one single event so far away and so remote from our normal existence that you don't really need to think about it very much. It's to create one gigantic creative event where the whole cosmos springs from nothing, owing to some chance fluctuation, and all the laws of nature appear as if from nowhere. This is a thought so big that you can't really grasp it, and yet I find people who otherwise are utterly skeptical in their way of thinking perfectly happy to accept this gigantic mysterious event, as long as you don't let mystery get beyond the first ten to the minus thirtieth of a second of the cosmos. Then it's so far away, you can keep it at bay.

*What are morphogenetic fields? What is morphic resonance?*

It's a question of form, order, pattern, structure. Science has been quite good at telling us what things are made out of. It's rather like trying to understand a city like Amsterdam by analyzing the bricks, and believing that the fact that they're made of a particular kind of mud or clay will tell you something about the nature of the city, the potentialities of building in that material. But it won't tell you anything about the pattern the streets make.

This is the aspect of nature which has been largely ignored by science. Science spends a lot of time breaking things down and analyzing what they're made out of, and of course everything's made out of something, so you can always find answers that way. But when you break things down to look at the bits, you lose the form, the structure. If you knock a house down to analyze the materials it's made of, then you've lost the structure of the house in this very act of analysis. And in studying nature, especially in biology but also in chemistry — chemistry is a science of forms, because molecules have particular forms, as do atoms and crystals — you require an understanding of the formative principles that give rise to them. That's what I'm talking about in formative causation.

Formative causation is the kind of causation responsible for form, structure, or pattern, and the causal influence on this process is what I call the morphogenetic field, or more shortly the morphic field, from the

Greek word *morphē*, meaning form. Each kind of thing has a field that gives it its form, pattern, structure, or order. This field carries the shaping influence of a kind of memory. So an animal like a giraffe is shaped as it grows as an embryo, and as it grows up after birth, by morphogenetic fields of its species. But then how do those fields get the form they do? I would say they get them from previous giraffes, by a process I call morphic resonance: an influence of similar things on subsequent similar things. So the fields that organize things have a kind of inherent memory within them. These fields are nonmaterial, but they're physical.

*Like gravity is physical but nonmaterial?*

Yes, the gravitational field is physical, it has physical effects, it's part of nature. But it's not material in the sense that it's made of matter. When Newton first thought of gravitational force, the question arose: What is it made of? How does the moon affect the tides on the earth, what's in between? And some people said: "It must be made of matter, so there must be a special subtle matter, the ether." Einstein showed that we don't need the ether as the basis of electromagnetic or gravitational fields. They're themselves made of space, or space-time. Fields are patterns in space or space-time. Matter is made of fields and energy, rather than fields being made of matter. So I would say the morphogenetic fields and morphic fields in general are part of nature, but they're not made of matter any more than gravitational fields are made of matter.

*Can you give some examples of experiments that have been done to prove the hypothesis of formative causation?*

The example of rats learning new tricks is the easiest to understand. The animals within a given species draw on a collective memory and in turn contribute to it though morphic resonance. So if you train rats to learn a new trick in London, then rats in Holland and Germany and America, in Australia, in Russia, all around the world, should learn this same trick more quickly. And this happens just because they're rats learning the same thing. It doesn't depend on rats teaching other rats or letting them squeak over the telephones to rats somewhere else. It should happen anyway, and the more rats that learn it here, the easier it should get everywhere else. That's the basic prediction in the realm of animal behavior.

There's a lot of circumstantial evidence, from studies of rats and other animals over the years, of a dramatic improvement in learning rates in standard laboratory tasks. These improvements have been found all over the world, but as there was no theory in science that could explain it until morphic resonance came along, these results have simply been ignored. I've dusted off a whole lot of existing experimental data that provide quite good circumstantial evidence for morphic resonance.

The case of the blue tits is one of the few we have of a new pattern of animal behavior spreading and the rate of its spread being carefully monitored, thanks to the efforts of hundreds of amateur bird-watchers all over Europe. Round about 1920 these little blue-headed birds had discovered that they could tear the tops off the milk bottles delivered to doorsteps in England and drink the cream. They only discovered this about twenty years after milk deliveries began in England. Then a blue tit in Southampton, in southern England, discovered this and it spread locally until lots of them were doing it. Then the habit turned up somewhere else, far away, much farther than blue tits could have flown. The rate of independent discovery, which was carefully documented, accelerated until by the late 1930s this was happening practically everywhere in Britain. The rate of discovery accelerated in such a striking way that Sir Alistair Hardy, a professor of zoology at Oxford, came to the conclusion that something like telepathy might be involved.

But the most interesting results are the Dutch ones. Once British blue tits had started doing this, then Continental ones started in Holland, in Sweden, in Denmark, and other countries. The habit spread in Holland in a pattern similar to the one in Britain. The difference is that when the Germans invaded Holland in 1940, the delivery of milk bottles stopped, so there was no more milk for the blue tits to steal. The habit didn't begin until 1948. Blue tits don't live more than about three years, so after eight or nine years there were no more blue tits left that could remember the golden age of free cream before the war. Yet when milk deliveries began again, within two or three years blue tits were stealing milk all over Holland. The habit spread much more quickly the second time around than it did the first time.

*What kind of experiments on humans prove your hypothesis of formative causation?*

First I should say that this hypothesis applies to human learning as well as bird learning, so it should be getting easier for children to learn to program computers or to play video games, because many have learned how already. These predictions in the human realm are supported by a lot of circumstantial evidence, but to control for all the other variables, you have to do specific experiments. Two or three have given inconclusive results, but something like 90 percent have shown quite clear effects in the direction of morphic resonance.

The experiment that is easiest to understand is one that was done with crossword puzzles at Nottingham University two years ago. The person who did it, Monica England, reasoned that if morphic resonance exists, it should be easier to solve today's crossword puzzle tomorrow than it would have been yesterday, because so many people have done it today. Now, hundreds of thousands of people do newspaper crosswords, so to do this experiment, all you need is to persuade a newspaper to supply their crossword in advance, so you can test people before it's published and after. We persuaded the London *Evening Standard* to supply their crossword in advance for this experiment. The day before it was published in London, students in Nottingham were tested with this crossword and with a control crossword that was not published during this period. They got ten minutes on each crossword to solve as many of the clues as they could. Then you mark it to see how many they got right, and that gives you a score. And then other students were tested after it had been published in London. This newspaper is not circulated in Nottingham, so none of them would have done the crossword.

It turned out that the score on the test crossword increased quite substantially, by about 20 percent, whereas the control crossword didn't change at all. This shows that the test crossword became easier to do after people had done it in London. The control crossword served to control for individual variations in crossword-solving skills, and that didn't change.

This result is something I've subsequently found from people who do crosswords habitually. A lot of people have written to me saying that they regularly do the *Times* crossword puzzle, which is very difficult, and they've often found that they do better if they do it in the evening of the day it's published, or even the next day, rather than straightaway in the morning. When the results of those crossword experiments were published, these people suddenly found an explanation for something they had discovered by themselves.

I've also done some experiments with Japanese nursery rhymes. The reasoning there was that if you take a nursery rhyme that's been known to millions of children over the centuries, and they've all learned to sing it, it should be easier for English or American people, or Dutch or German people, to learn that nursery rhyme than some other similar rhyme. Now a problem with this experiment is to find another rhyme that's equally easy or difficult. To do this, I had the help of Shintaro Tanikawa, one of the leading poets in Japan, who wrote some other rhymes with a rhythm and word pattern similar to those of a common Japanese nursery rhyme. He gave us two false rhymes and one real rhyme—I didn't know which was the real rhyme myself—and then we got groups of people to memorize these rhymes by chanting them in the way children do. Later they were tested to see how much they could remember of each of the rhymes. And sure enough, they were able to remember more of the genuine nursery rhyme than of the other two—about twice as well as the others. So this is the kind of effect one would expect.

*You wrote, "When people learn something new, such as windsurfing, then as more people learn to do it, it should tend to become progressively easier to learn just because so many other people have learned to do it already." But let's take the Industrial Revolution, which has been continuing in the Western Hemisphere for two centuries. Why did it not show up at the same time in Africa, India, Indonesia, or Latin America?*

The general question is one of parallel inventions and discoveries. There are many examples of cultural patterns that have evolved independently in different parts of the world, and archaeologists are often very puzzled by them. That's why you get theories of people floating around the world on little rafts carrying cultures with them. In a world with morphic resonance there's no need to have all those hypothetical rafts floating around the world, because people could pick it up anyway. The key feature of morphic resonance is similarity. If people are confronting a problem that other people have already solved somewhere else, they'll be more likely to find the same solution. But if they're not confronting that problem, they won't come up with the solution. So if you have two groups of people trying to solve the same kind of scientific or mathematical or technical or economic problem, you have ideal conditions for morphic resonance. But if you have a tribe of hunters and gatherers in Africa, and you have entrepreneurs in Victorian Manchester in England trying to find ways of spinning cloth more cheaply using industrial looms, there's such a difference between the problems that they're confronting that you wouldn't expect any resonance.

*But when a culture is directly confronted with aspects of the Industrial Revolution, for instance, what happens then?*

The remarkable thing is that the Industrial Revolution has spread to all parts of the world so phenomenally fast. Part of this is of course through ordinary communication. I would never claim this as an example of morphic resonance because a lot of it depends on perfectly normal means of human communication, but the remarkable thing is that as soon as these things are introduced to other cultures and people are introduced to these ways of doing things, they get it so fast. In New Guinea, for example, there are people driving lorries and operating machines whose fathers were living in a Stone Age culture. In a single generation, people have jumped about 20,000 years of human history. I personally think that in many ways it's a disaster.

*How big are morphogenetic fields? Miles, light-years, do they stretch to the ends of the universe?*

Every organism—a crystal, a cell, a giraffe, a cow, a person—is organized by a field within and around it, just as a magnetic field is within and around a magnet. It's quite local. What involves moving over great distances is morphic resonance, the influence of one organism on another. This resonance is, I think, independent of distance in that it doesn't fall off with distance in space or time. Now, if that's the case, then people learning something in one part of the world should influence people all around the world as long as they're in similar conditions, without showing any diminution due to distance. And more generally, if this is the case, it means that events on one planet or on one star could influence those on other stars or planets even in other galaxies. Morphic resonance could work over huge distances in the universe.

*You wrote, "There is the possibility that most, if not all, known patterns of activity that appear on earth have already appeared frequently elsewhere in the universe or in previous universes. Morphic resonance from these systems may swamp the predicted effects." "Elsewhere in the universe or previous universes"—for you it's simply a possibility?*

I think it's a possibility that everything that's happened here has happened somewhere else, and my reason for thinking that is the empirical fact that apparent morphic resonance effects do seem to be detectable. If morphic resonance effects are not detectable, if there's no improvement with time, there are three other possibilities. One is that morphic resonance is wrong as a theory, which I'm sure most people think. Probably I would, too, if the experiments didn't work. The second is that everything that's happened here has happened somewhere else so often that there's nothing truly new happening on earth, so you wouldn't see these effects, because everything would already be governed by established habits. The third possibility is that morphic resonance works from the future as well as the past, in which case everything that's going to happen will also influence what's happening now. And since we don't know what's going to happen, this makes the theory untestable. Still, it's a theoretical possibility.

What I'm concerned with here is the fact that if morphic resonance experiments yield positive results—in other words, if things get easier and easier, if we can see habits building up in nature—then either this shows that morphic resonance doesn't work over astronomical distances, or it shows that what's happening on earth is truly original in the cosmos. That opens up the theoretical possibility of an institute of cosmic novelty that could be set up on quite a low budget, where you could find out what's happened over the whole of the rest of the cosmos by testing for morphic resonance with the crystallization of thousands of different chemicals, for example. Now if some of these chemicals turn out not to show a morphic resonance effect, if the crystals form the same way at the beginning and go on forming the same way, showing no habit, no tendency to crystallize better or faster, then we can infer these compounds have existed in a crystalline form elsewhere in the universe.

If we find ones that do show this learning experience, that show this buildup of habit, we can infer that they have occurred for the first time here on earth. So we can actually map what's happened elsewhere in the universe in a low-budget terrestrial laboratory, without any need for billion-dollar space probes.

*I don't want to seem too sceptical, but you write: "The assumption of the hypothesis of formative causation that morphic resonance takes place only from the past may be wrong. It may emanate from the future as well, or even instead." Would you mind explaining how we might be influenced by events that will take place in the future but that seemingly have already happened?*

It might be possible that we're influenced by morphic resonance from the future, but I'm advocating the theory that morphic resonance happens only from the past. The reasons why I think that is so are, first, that the future and the past are asymmetric in their relation to the present. All our experience shows that we can remember the past, and we can have plans or desires about the future, but our knowledge of and relation to the future is radically different from that of the past. The second reason is that there's an in-built arrow of time in all developing organisms. We grow up from embryos into children, into adults, and then we grow old and we die. If you look at the history of the whole cosmos and its evolution, exactly the same developmental arrow of time applies to all of nature.

Classical Newtonian physics is to a large extent reversible. You assume that matter and energy are always there in the same amounts, that the laws of nature don't change. In theory most things could go backward as well as forward. But in evolutionary physics, in an evolutionary universe, time has a real meaning and a real direction. Now, in such a universe, the past bears quite a different relation to the present than to the future. The future is one of openness and possibility, but the past is one of causal influence from what has happened before. I think through morphic resonance, this kind of habit or memory effect comes from the past. And so I'm postulating a theory of memory in nature through morphic resonance from the past, and the experiments I'm proposing are designed to test this theory.

I'm not saying that it's not possible to have a theory of morphic resonance from the future as well, it's just not the theory I'm advocating. I leave the possibility open, but I think that it's very unlikely, first, because any kind of future causation creates logical paradoxes of the kind that science fiction writers enjoy: if you travel back in time and murder your grandmother, how can you be here today, you know, that kind of paradox. Second, the idea of future causation leads to different predictions. It means that new things that happen now won't get easier to happen as time goes on, because they'll be influenced by so many things in the future that you won't see the kind of change I'm predicting. On the other hand, there's some evidence for future influences through precognitive dreams and premonitions, so I don't totally rule out the possibility of influences from the future.

Now to complete this, I should say one more thing. Very often what we do in the future is a repetition of the past, and you could say that when an acorn grows into an oak tree, the morphic field of the acorn contains, as it were, the future form of the oak tree. In a sense the tree form toward which the acorn develops lies in the future for that acorn. But in a sense it's a memory of all the past oak trees that have contributed to the morphic field. So in the normal course of nature, most of what happens is a repetition of something that's happened before. There's a loop whereby what lies in the future for any given organism is in a sense a memory of what similar organisms have already done in the past. In any repetitive kind of activity, and most of nature is repetitive, the past and the future are not so clearly separate. In most cases, desire is based on memory, so the desires that one has of things one wants in the future are very often attempts to recreate or reenact memories from the past.

*The Darwinian theory of evolution holds that evolution has no purpose. Every individual struggles to increase the representation of its genes in future generations, and that's all there is. Your comment?*

The urge to reproduce and survive is an obvious basic truth of life. The real question is: Is there more to life than that? The problem is that most people who think there's a purpose in evolution think that the purpose is to produce modern scientists or modern Westerners or something like that. I personally find it hard to believe that the purpose of the entire cosmos culminates in a President Bush. Theories that are too human-centered seem to me inadequate to explain any purpose of evolution. But if there is a purpose, well, what is it? Perhaps it's greater complexity, consciousness, self-consciousness—one could give answers like that.

The strength of the Darwinian view seems to me that it emphasizes the importance of diversity. If you have a purposive view of evolution, it's difficult to see why it should require so much diversity, unless diversity is itself a purpose. If we think the purpose of evolution is the evolution of human consciousness or the evolution of self-reflective intelligence or something like that, then why do we need five million species of beetles and butterflies in the Amazon alone?

*Darwin wrote once in a letter, "What a book a devil's chaplain might write on the clumsy, wasteful, blundering, low and horribly cruel works of nature." We're still talking about purpose.*

Darwin was very keen to expel purpose from nature, because he wanted to keep God out of it. He started by reacting against the idea of the watchmaker God. He was reacting against a theological view that treated animals and plants as machines made by an engineering God. And in rejecting this image of God, he wanted to reject purpose from nature and any sense of sudden jumps or any surprising creativity in nature. We can see in the world what we want to see. If we think everything in the universe is organized in polarities, we see polarity wherever we look. If we think it's all organized in threes, we see patterns of threes and trinities wherever we look. If we want to see destruction, waste, and cruelty, we can see it wherever we look in the human and the biological worlds. If we want to see cooperation, symbiosis, and mutual help, then again we can see it wherever we look. I think Darwin particularly emphasized the destructive aspects of nature because of personal psychological motivations, and partly because he made destruction the primary creative power.

*When I ask people what Darwinism is all about, they say survival of the fittest, ergo human beings are the best-adapted species and are rightfully at the top of the ladder. How deep-rooted is this straitjacket myth of linear progress?*

It's terribly deep-rooted, because the evolutionary idea in biology started from the evolutionary idea in human affairs. The idea of human progress came first and was generalized to biology and then to the cosmos. But now the idea of human progress, which was part of the ideology of the Enlightenment, was the idea that through reason, particularly through scientific reason, moral man has risen above the superstitions of the Middle Ages, and that those notions in turn had risen above the superstitions of savages. So the idea of human progress culminates in the eighteenth-century gentleman as the ultimate peak of human development.

This is still the standard ideology of the whole mainstream of Western thought, and given the fact that that kind of ideology came first and the evolutionary picture of life was added on, you then get the progression from the primeval slime, as animals then crawled out onto land, and then monkeys swung in trees, and finally it ends up with civilized men and women. This evolutionary progression is so deep-rooted in our ideology that it's extraordinarily difficult to get away from it.

As soon as anyone discovers there's a backward tribe living anywhere, if there are any left, they move in, build roads, have development agencies, UNESCO will set up schools and so on, so they can be turned into people just like everyone else, and within ten years they'll have television. It shows an extraordinary intellectual and cultural imperialism on the part of the technologically advanced societies. If our supposedly advanced development is taken to give us the right to exploit the rest of nature, use it as we like, we then have the roots of the ecological crisis. It's one of the things that has caused the great problems of the modern world.

*We're indirectly talking about consciousness. Stephen Gould wrote, "Through no fault of our own, and by dint of no cosmic plan or conscious purpose, we have become, by the grace of a glorious evolutionary accident called intelligence, the stewards of life's continuity on earth. We have not asked for that role, but we cannot abjure it. We may not be suited to it, but here we are." What would your approach be?*

A lot of it depends on your ideology. None of us knows how consciousness came into being, so we can read into the mystery of the past whatever we want to, and people of course do just that. There are two basic theories of creativity that we find again and again. One is creativity from the bottom up, the idea that new things emerge from a lower level. It's essentially a feminine metaphor of creativity: the new emerges from the dark womb of matter, or the darkness of nature, like a child coming out of the womb. This theory of the spontaneous emergence of higher levels through accident is essentially a materialist theory of creation: "matter" comes from the same root as *mater*, mother. I think materialism is essentially a kind of unconscious cult of the Great Mother, and it says that everything comes from matter, or Mother Nature. Gould would have no alternative but to say that, because of his whole ideological background. In Marxism it was made quite explicit through dialectical materialism that through tension and conflict, you have the appearance of a new synthesis from a lower level.

The other traditional view of creativity, found all around the world, is the top-down model: creativity coming from a higher level moving downward. That's the view in traditional creating myths—for instance, in the Judeo-Christian tradition, where you have the consciousness of God as the prime creative power. Creation is made by division of a primary whole. You start with the undifferentiated unity, and then there's a series of splittings or bifurcations, as in the book of Genesis, where light and dark are separated, then earth and dry land.

We see exactly that same pattern in physical evolution theories. Superstring theory postulates the idea of a primal creative "unified field" that has ten dimensions, nine of space, one of time. And then this is split through what they call symmetry breakings to give the gravitational field, the electromagnetic field, the fields of quantum field theory, the nuclear forces. Unified field theory invites us to contemplate a top-down type of creation. Then the question is: How does the unified field come about? Physicists would say it's because of these "overarching equations," these cosmic rational principles that somehow govern the whole thing. These are supposed to exist even before the whole universe does—a kind of Platonic overmind, from which the rationality of the universe starts—and then there's a kind of descent into matter from these abstract unitive principles.

*So matter is not the ground of all existence, as Darwin wrote.
Something existed before it.*

Yes, something existed before it. According to the traditional view, that is
the laws of nature, which are not material. Then in the Big Bang you
have the rising of energy and fields. Matter, in the limited sense of stuff,
comes much later. There's no matter in a fire of billions of degrees
centigrade, at least not matter in any normal sense of the word. There
are fields and energy and vibratory structures of activity, but there's no
brute stuff.

I would say that the traditional view is that human consciousness is
a lower aspect of some higher form of consciousness, that the cosmos
itself is pervaded by a kind of mind or consciousness. The earth certainly
has one. Ultimately there's the consciousness or mind of God. There are
hierarchies of intelligences, traditionally conceived of as the angels,
associated with the stars and the planets. So there are many higher forms
of organized mentality in the cosmos, and human mentality is one of the
lowest of these. Insofar as there are jumps in human consciousness, they
come about through inspiration from higher levels of consciousness,
which are usually unknown to us precisely because they are beyond our
normal means of conceiving. But this is what mystics and visionaries in
all cultures throughout all the ages have talked about. So this is a kind of
descent from above. When Gould says, "This came about through no
spark of divine consciousness, only through accident," this is pure
materialist dogmatism. He doesn't know any more than anyone else
knows, he's just stating his ideology.

My own view is that there's a lot to be said for both theories of
creativity. There's a sense in which you can see a bottom-up aspect to
creativity, the way it's rooted in physical and bodily realities. It doesn't
come out of nowhere or come into nowhere, it's concerned with the
ongoing reality of physical existence. But I think there's also an element
of descent from a higher level. There's always a higher context, a larger
context within which creativity happens.

*Higher or larger? There's quite a difference.*

What would be the higher context of human creativity? What's the more
inclusive context of an individual human having a bright idea? That
human is part of society and you could say that there's a collective
consciousness that maybe works through individuals within a society,
rather than simply coming out of individuals. If there's a human
collective mind or consciousness, it's embedded in the larger nonhuman
environment and ultimately within the planet, Gaia. So the collective
human experience is shaped by the conditions of the environment, by
history, and by the characteristics of our planet. It's not a disembodied
kind of biological intelligence, it's entirely terrestrial. It's evolved on
earth, it's conditioned by the conditions on earth. The fact that we sleep

and wake in twenty-four-hour cycles, for example, is a very obvious way in which our whole psychic life is conditioned by our terrestrial environment. And the earth is part of a larger system, the solar system. Who knows that there isn't some kind of intelligence guiding the evolution of the solar system. So you could say that it's both larger and in some sense higher, in the sense that it's more inclusive. And then the solar system is part of the galaxy and so on. But if there are these different levels of organization in nature, each more inclusive than the last, how are we to say that at each level—the solar system, the galaxy—there's absolutely no intelligence, that these are simply blind aggregates of matter? That we alone are the only conscious intelligent beings in the cosmos? This seems to me to be an incredible species arrogance. Humanism in its scientific, secular form essentially amounts to saying, "We're the only conscious beings around, at least on this earth and probably in the whole cosmos." How on earth does one know that? In my opinion, it's pure self-serving arrogance to assume that. It may be so, but to assume that without evidence, because we like the idea, seems to me a very narrow and limited view.

*You have written, "No one knows how embryos progressively take up their forms, how instincts are inherited, how habits develop, or how memory works. And of course, the nature of mind is obscure." I think Daniel Dennett will totally disagree that "the nature of mind is obscure," since he wrote, "It's obvious that no teddy bear is conscious, but it's really not obvious that no robot could be." He informs us that it will take a long time before computers cry, but finally perception and human consciousness can be awakened in a computer. Is there anything here that you might agree with?*

Well, I don't like it. Dennett's approach shares this obsession with the machine as the central paradigm. The problem with the last three hundred years of mechanistic science is the assumption that the only valid way of thinking about nature is to use machine metaphors. Previously, people had always used organic metaphors—metaphors of animals, of plants, of trees, of people, of families. Since the seventeenth century there's been an attempt in rational scientific thinking to impose a single source of metaphor, manmade machinery, as the only valid source of thinking about nature. It's intensely anthropocentric. It takes one very recent aspect of human activity and projects this human obsession with machinery onto the whole of nature. So then the ultimate question is: Are we ourselves machines?

*Yes, says Dennett. Which implies that we can rebuild ourselves into robots.*

Yes, but in a sense he's carrying out the Cartesian research program. He's a latter-day Descartes, with all the problems that Descartes had.

163

Descartes thought that animals were simply machines and that people were machines but with this God-given rational mind somewhere inside the head that controlled the machinery.

The Cartesian dualism has been the dominant model in the West ever since the seventeenth century, and the main way people try to deal with it is by denying that there is anything autonomous about the rational mind. The materialist says, "We're machines just like everything else in nature." Then you have to explain the thinking conscious mind, so then you have to say, "We're intelligent, thinking, conscious machines," but there aren't any intelligent, thinking conscious machines, so then you have to invent them, just to prove that we're intelligent, thinking, conscious machines. Developing artificial intelligence to make intelligent, thinking, conscious machines is ultimately aimed at proving we're nothing but machines.

It seems to me a futile exercise, like a dog chasing its tail. I can't get very engaged with this quest to try to prove, through enormous intellectual convolutions and frightfully clever arguments, that we're nothing but machines by imagining that our brains are some kind of self-programming computer of a type that doesn't actually exist, but of which we're promised there will be examples at some time in the future. The point is that we're not thinking machines and there are no thinking machines. But materialists have to keep pretending that they will exist.

Then, of course, the question will become: How do we decide whether it's fully conscious or not? That is a philosopher's dream. You can write tons of books on this subject, because it's hard to prove that even another person is conscious, let alone a machine, so there's enough mileage in this for philosophers to argue about it for centuries more. I just don't think it's a very fruitful debate. If you say that we're like self-programming computers, you've still got the bit that does the programming. The compute metaphor is inherently dualistic: the software is like the mind, the hardware is like the brain or the body. You keep landing back in the same old Cartesian dualism. Thinking of the brain as a computer is just a way of trying to update the machine metaphor using the latest technology.

A lot of this computer thinking was started by Alan Turing, the British mathematician, during the war. He laid the foundations of modern computing theory. Interestingly, Turing was motivated by a desire to prove the immortality of the soul. Turing was homosexual, and when he was at school, his dearest friend died at the age of about eighteen. He was obsessed with in what sense his friend could be said to survive the death of the body. He came to the idea that if the self was nothing but a kind of logical structure of abstractions that you can program into a computer, then you can take this program from one computer to another, and thus have a kind of immortality of this system of abstractions, independent of the physical base in which it's realized.

So there's a sense in which this dualism of body and soul, or machine and program, which is present in the computer metaphor was built in right at the beginning by Alan Turing. In fact, it was part of his motivation for doing it. He searched for a kind of abstract, mathematical basis for an abstract immortality.

Dennett does the same thing, but there's something a bit more interesting as well in what he's saying, which is to see the self as a construct. That's not only Dennett's idea, it's the basis of a great deal of traditional philosophy as well. The Hindus, for instance, and the Buddhists certainly would say that the ego, the sense of the self as a unified ego, is a construction. Many Western psychologists would say this as well, that our sense of self is an intellectual construction based on reflections from other people, on language and our modes of thinking. Some traditions of Buddhism say that to dissolve this illusion of the ego is the purpose of the path; that it's a liberation to realize that this is not an ultimate truth. So there's a sense in which some of what Dennett's saying resembles some religious philosophical traditions. Maybe it's a paradox that he arrives at such a similar position.

*Gould says, "Since we cannot find any morality in nature, we have to find it in ourselves. If nature is nonmoral, then evolution cannot teach us any ethical theory at all." In other words, how lonely are we despite our unicity?*

A lot of secular humanists have to prove that human beings are radically different from everything else in nature, and the usual concepts they use are consciousness and morality. But most of the things we think of as moral features we can find foreshadowed in the natural world. For example, parental care and affection, which are a basic aspect of moral responsibility toward children, are a key part of all human societies. The behavior of birds and animals in looking after their young may be unconscious or instinctive, but we certainly see the principles of parental care and responsibility at work.

*But if you look at caterpillars eating their own parents, then you can say, "Here we are back again with Darwin's horribly cruel world." It depends what you look at.*

I don't know whether more caterpillars eat their parents than people kill other people. If you look at human wars, humans do not have a distinctly better record than other animals in terms of not killing each other. We're probably worse than most, in terms of our record in killing members of our own species. The problem, if you take morality as distinctively human, is that you fall into a kind of narcissism, because we look at an idealized reflection of ourselves. The reality of human behavior is that for a long time people have killed and brutally massacred members of our own species, and the so-called modern civilized world has done more of it than most. The Iraq war showed that it was considered perfectly alright to massacre tens of thousands of retreating soldiers with weapons of mass destruction. Things that in the past would have been considered inconceivably brutal are now considered perfectly normal. So there's no growth of morality with the advance of technological civilization.

If you ask, "Do human beings on average kill each other more or less than the members of the other species?" the answer is, I think, they kill each other more than the members of most other species do. Very rarely do animals kill other members of their own species, but it's quite common for human beings. So I find the morality argument as a kind of species badge of honor not a very strong one.

Morality as conceived by Enlightenment philosophers seems to me a kind of abstraction. If you look at morality as practiced in traditional societies, it's not usually elevated into some enormous moral code, it's more a matter of custom or habit. The natural state of human morality is closer to the kind of implicit behavioral norms that we find in animal societies. Bees, wasps, ants, flocks of birds—all of them have ways of cooperating. The individual members of the society work together, usually fairly harmoniously. And this we find in human societies, too. We're social animals, and as such we find that our societies are influenced by social bonds and social norms, like any other social animal. We make it conscious, and we elevate it to the name of morality, but the word "morality" is quite a recent invention. In traditional human societies the word "morality" isn't exactly used in our modern sense. There are certain norms of behavior, and if you do things that are prohibited, you're ultimately expelled from the society. I think the abstract notion of morality is not very helpful.

*Dennett says, "For all our foolishness, we human beings are vastly better equipped for the task of solving problems in advance of encountering them than any other self-controllers, and it is our enormous brain that makes this possible."*

It's a curious paradox that many materialists like Dennett are extremely keen to emphasize the unique features of human consciousness and morality, and at the same time try to deny them as mere aspects of mechanism. It's extraordinarily ironic.

*Because at the same time we are nothing but selfish and ruthless gene machines who try to survive?*

That's right. And to say that we're better because we've got bigger brains ignores the fact that brain size hasn't increased that much for twenty or thirty or more thousand years, so the same brain capacity as Einstein's was present way back in the Stone Age. The evolution of modern culture has no particular correlation with brain size. What we're talking about is the extraordinary phenomenon of cultural evolution over the last five, seven, ten thousand years. Now, this cultural evolution is certainly amazing, but to try to root it in something to do with the size of the human brain seems to me to beg the question, really.

*What is this cultural evolution really? We've got slow Darwinian evolution, and suddenly some ten thousand years ago consciousness was awakened, and cultural evolution ensued. How important is that evolution, apart from the obvious fact that we can destroy everything on earth?*

I think it's an example of our cosmic arrogance. It shows that because we're so obsessed with innovation and creativity, we should learn from the human process something about a speeded-up version of creativity. We've somehow enormously speeded up the creative process, and we've done that partly by diminishing the power of custom and tradition, which in traditional societies restrain creativity. The purpose of an individual in a traditional society is to live in accordance with the myths and the way the ancestors have lived. Innovation is a deviation from an established path. That's dangerous, because if a society puts great emphasis on innovation, each new generation feels somehow better, wiser, cleverer than the last.

Our societies are evolving with the dissolution of the old social structures, hurtling into the future in directions that nobody can foresee. The dissolution of traditional morality and traditional social and family patterns is happening far faster than I think anyone imagined in the past, and in the future will lead to a kind of society that no one can really envisage. Clearly the traditional family system is breaking down, and nobody has any idea, since it's never happened before, what happens to a society if the principal socializing influence on children is no longer present. Yet this is a logical outcome of the dissolution of traditional forms of social order.

*Stephen Toulmin has written, "Looking back at the received view of modernity after fifty years, my inclination is to retort: don't believe a word of it. The defects become more evident with each year that goes by." Do you understand why we continue on the stage of the Cartesian theater, although we can see the theater burn?*

It has to be understood in terms of a reaction. Modernity has put us in the privileged position of being in charge. There's no God, we're basically the conscious beings who run the world. We find this humanistic self-glorification, this cult of modernity everywhere. It's based on a rejection of what went before. The seventeenth-century mechanistic revolution involved the rejection of traditional religion and especially the medieval synthesis, the reigning philosophy of the medieval schools and universities. I'm sure that for many of the people who broke out of it, this seemed like an incredible liberation. And because there's still some continuing presence of the Jewish and Christian traditions in our culture, many individuals find themselves breaking out of a religious background that they find restrictive morally, because it says you can't sleep with whomever you like, there's a value in the family, there's a value in traditional social institutions. They would rather believe they're free to do exactly what they please, as long as it doesn't harm anyone else too much.

On the one hand, there's this personal moral liberation. On the other, there's a sense of a larger conscious presence, that one's human life is part of a much larger system of consciousness, involving ultimately a kind of divine consciousness; that human consciousness is a limited part of a much larger purpose and a much larger whole. For many people, rejecting that is a kind of liberation. You can see the whole history of religion and traditional culture as one of appalling superstition and oppression. And then you can justify the modern position as being one of liberation from all that.

This dynamic still continues, but there's now a new movement going on, which is surely not overdue, of seeing that this attitude of modernism is itself a kind of cultural phase that can imprison people in alienation and despair. If you're sick of a modernist world, then you'll want to go beyond it into some kind of postmodern view, which can somehow restore a sense of wholeness and meaning in life.

*How does all this relate to formative causation? Should your hypothesis prove to be right, what would be the social and individual implications for the lives of people and for rebuilding the future?*

Formative causation has many implications, the first of which is that our minds are much more permeable to the thoughts of other people than we usually assume. We all know we're influenced by other people's actions and by their words, but we usually assume that our thoughts are entirely private, that they go on in the privacy of our brain, and that the mind is encased in the brain. From the point of view of formative causation, even our thoughts and attitudes influence other people, and we're in turn influenced by countless other people's thoughts and attitudes. So our minds are not insulated and separate in the way many modern people like to imagine, they're far more permeable to each other. Now this is what many traditional societies have believed.

*We read each other's minds without knowing it?*

Yes, we're constantly influenced by the Zeitgeist, the spirit of the times, the fashion, the cultural norms, the thoughts in other people's minds around us at the time. Jung's theory of the collective unconscious said very much the same thing, but from the point of view of formative causation, this connection of the individual mind with the collective becomes much more explicit. Now, in some sense that gives us a new basis for at least a kind of individual morality. Kant talked about the categorical imperative as the basis of morality—that if you will to do something, the categorical imperative puts it to you whether you want others to do the same thing. According to morphic resonance, even your thoughts have the capacity to influence other people, they make it more likely for others to think in the same way. So that would force us to take a certain responsibility for our thoughts, as well as for our actions and our words.

*So thoughts become dangerous, since they are no longer private.*

That's right, but all traditional moralities have recognized that. Modern morality doesn't. It makes our thoughts entirely our private business; they are of no concern to anyone else and no influence on anyone else.

Formative causation makes us see societies and social groups as having a wholeness, a unity, and enables us to think more about the reality of the social forms in which we live. We all know that we're influenced by our social group and culture. Formative causation enables us to understand and to appreciate more how their influence may work. It also enables us to accept that this is a necessary feature of our human condition, that we're social animals, that the social forms—which can evolve and change, usually more slowly than an individual does—are an extraordinarily important part of our being, and that many of the dangers our species faces depend on collective myths and collective norms. These need to be changed on the basis of old habits. It's no use from this point of view to simply change the way individuals behave, because the collective has a dynamic of its own, and that needs to be addressed as well. There's a New Age idea that all you need to do to change the world is for individuals to change. It's a kind of atomistic view of society. It gives us a different sense of the role of society, and it also gives us a different sense of the relation of human society to the larger living system in which we're embedded.

*Do you manage to live by these standards you're formulating, or is your belief in the hypothesis of formative causation not yet strong enough?*

The hypothesis of formative causation is not a belief system or a religion, it's a scientific hypothesis, and I don't know if it's right or wrong. Obviously I think it's more likely to be right than wrong, otherwise I wouldn't have spent years of my life developing it and doing research on it. We need to improve our understanding of the role of memory in nature.

As for me personally, I don't think it's possible to build a personal faith firmly on a scientific hypothesis, because scientific hypotheses are provisional. My own particular hypothesis is still very controversial and needs to be tested more, and although I think it's a probable indication of the way nature works, I don't take it as an absolute truth. I do think, though, that it enables us to understand better and to appreciate better many traditional teachings of various religious traditions. I would say that my own personal morality and belief are largely influenced by the religious traditions that I've been exposed to.

I was brought up in a Christian manner. My parents were very devout, and I went to quite an orthodox school of an Anglo-Catholic kind—a Church of England school, but of the more Catholic kind of Church of England. My parents were more Protestant. Like many young scientists, I rejected all this when I was about fourteen or fifteen. Science is the future, religion is the past; science liberates, religion binds and enslaves—superstition, the Inquisition, you know, all the standard stuff. I believed all that for quite a while.

But later, first through a sense of the inadequacy of mechanistic science and then through the need for a more holistic approach, I started thinking about holistic philosophy. I became interested in Oriental religions, I started doing meditation. They said, "You don't have to believe anything, just try it, see if it works for you." It did, and it changed the way my mind worked. I became much more aware of the way my mind was working through the practice of the Hindu form of meditation. Then I lived in India for seven years, and was fascinated especially by the Hindu culture, and also by the Sufi culture, the mystical branch of Islam. I tried to find out as much as I could about those traditions. I was fascinated by the rich religious culture of India. But unexpectedly and quite paradoxically I found that I was drawn back to a Christian path while I was in India. Much to my surprise, I found that this was the path that seemed more natural to me. I suppose largely because it's my ancestral path, it comes more naturally to me than Hinduism. I realized I could never be a Hindu because I'm not an Indian. Hinduism is grounded in India, its sacred places are all in India, its traditions are all in Indian languages. I could visit it, appreciate it, learn from it, but I could never actually be a Hindu. So I found myself drawn back to a Christian path.

For a while I lived in an ashram in South India with a British Benedictine monk who'd lived in India for many years, Father Beade Griffiths, and this for me was a way of finding how to make a bridge between the Eastern and the Western ways of thinking. For me it was a very important discovery that it's possible to learn from other religions; that it's no longer for me necessary to say this is right and all the others are wrong, that you can say there are different paths, and that each path merely emphasizes certain aspects of the religious life, which other paths may have done implicitly.

There's a sense in which all religious traditions admit a plurality of nonhuman or superhuman intelligences, whether you think of them as the gods or the angels or the shining ones or the devas, but all traditions would also recognize some underlying unity behind all these different gods. All the Hindus that I met would say that there are many gods and goddesses, but the Brahma, or however they conceive or name the ultimate principle, is shining through all these different forms. In traditional Christianity the fundamental sense of God is not seen as an undifferentiated unity, but rather as an organic set of relationships, as is illustrated by the doctrine of the Holy Trinity.

*But it's still a moral concept of God.*

Any concept of God is a complex one, because it combines many aspects of human experience, and one aspect of the Judeo-Christian God is morality and justice—not just human morality but a sense that there's some ultimate justice in the cosmos, even if you regard it as an ideal.

*Since the ideal exists, it's real in a certain sense, is that what you mean?*

Well, I think you could say that. But myself, I don't take the moral aspect of God as the principal defining characteristic of the divine. It's one of the aspects that are important in human affairs. But the point is that any system that takes divine justice seriously doesn't just take this life seriously. If you have some sense of an afterlife, then the workings of divine justice become easier to understand. If you say, as the materialist does, Our brain is all there is, the mind is just an aspect of the brain, therefore when we die, that's the end," then the whole of justice and the whole of the drama of human life and consciousness have to be played out just in this life on this earth. There's no other frame of reference or context. If we had no sense of the possibility of society becoming fairer, then the whole dynamics of the better aspects of Western society would lose their meaning. Although the state is supposed to be neutral, most modern states are informed by some Christian notions of equality and fairness, some ideal of justice. The basis of the whole Western doctrine of progress, the whole purpose of social reform—both in secular and in religious contexts in our civilization—is the idea of moving toward some kind of millennial state, where things are better.

This Judeo-Christian millennial dynamic, the idea that history is moving toward some kind of culmination, is so fundamental in our whole civilization that it's impossible to escape it, unless you become extraordinarily conscious of it. Most people are unconscious of it, and therefore entirely passive toward it. The dynamic that ultimately underlies all of the motivation for progress, social reform, justice, New Agery, ecoactivism, all the rest of it, is based on the sense that it's possible to move toward a better kind of society, and even those who don't believe in an actual literal messiah are still within the field of apocalyptical, millenarian thinking. Even the idea that through science and technology we can progress, we can understand more, we can solve problems, we can feed everyone, clothe everyone—these traditional ideas of science are very strongly influenced by this model of history, which in a sense is a kind of evolutionary model of history, leading toward some end. Take that away, and you're left with nothing but the most abject despair and futility.

*So it's a kind of illusion without which we would die or be utterly alone?*

I think it's more like a self-fulfilling prophecy. Not all cultures have it. It's a feature of Judeo-Christian culture. The view in almost all other cultures is that history starts with a golden age, and then you have the myths of the ancestors and the heroes who lived in this golden age. The purpose of life thereafter is to repeat the basic pattern that was given at the beginning. In Hinduism and Buddhism you have the idea of an endless cycle of things, which are gradually getting worse. The Hindus talk of Kali Yuga, the dissolution, the dregs of time, as a whole age that is exhausted and decadent. The hope for individuals is that you can undergo some kind of spiritual vertical takeoff through meditation, through liberation, and you can leave this futile world behind, which is just continuing in endless cycles, gradually running down.

That's a totally different model of history from the Western one. Where Christian missionaries failed, the missionaries of technological progress have succeeded in converting people to a totally different model of time—that what your parents did is out of date and you can do much better with modern technology, gadgets, television, industries, urbanization, and what have you.

*In one of your books you quote Jacques Monod: "Man must at last wake out of his millenary dream and discover his total solitude, his fundamental isolation. He must realize that like a gypsy, he lives on the boundaries of an alien world, a world that is deaf to his music, and as indifferent to his hopes as it is to his sufferings and to his crimes." Why this quote?*

Because Monod puts very explicitly the natural outcome of a mechanistic, materialistic view of nature and of humanity. This is the development of the movement started by Galileo and Descartes, which has now worked itself out in our society and indeed has been exported to the rest of the world.

*We can't predict the future, but how afraid are you of a total collapse of Western ideology, including the Cartesian theater, which we've enjoyed for three centuries?*

I believe that it's possible to envisage an alternative and better view of things. I wouldn't say the mechanistic view is totally wrong, but I'd say it's much too limited. We need a much larger view of nature, of evolution, and of human nature. This is one of the things I'm trying to do in science, in my own limited way—to look for a larger kind of science in which the virtues of mechanistic theory are still there, but where we have a much broader view of nature and of ourselves.

*What is the paradox or the most fascinating problem you're dealing with at the moment?*

The central question that my scientific work is based on is this question of evolution and memory. Do the laws of nature evolve? Is there a kind of memory in nature? Are we influenced by an unseen presence of the past? Do we, through religious rituals, reconnect with those who've done it before, which is the belief in all religious systems? Is there a kind of memory and habit principle in nature? These questions are part of a larger question, of finding a scientific way of expanding science, because I think science is much too limited. I think there are many things that science has hardly begun to study, simply because of this narrow focus, this obsession with the mechanistic side of things. But it's no use just saying that. My central goal is to find scientific ways of expanding the realm of science, and so to renew present-day science, which has had many negative effects. We need a science that is much more friendly to our life in the world, that helps to dissolve the gulf we've set up between science and religion, or between machinery and consciousness.

*How much faith do you have that finally you will manage to believe in the hypothesis of formative causation?*

Well, my mood changes from time to time. Sometimes I'm oppressed by the sheer weight of scientific conformity. Billions of pounds are spent every year, there are hundreds of thousands of people whose jobs depend on this enormous institution. It's a bit like Soviet Russia, there's this huge bureaucratic system in place, and there are a lot of people within science who don't really believe in it as it is now, but if you value your job and your career, it's better not to say so in public. If often seems difficult to change. On the other hand, the Soviet system collapsed too.

I think all that could change quite fast, a scientific revolution could sweep us very rapidly. If it then becomes a matter of everyday activity, then the theory behind it doesn't matter. It's no use arguing that computers don't exist when lots of people have got them. There's no use arguing that you can't send messages through empty space when people have got television sets. Technological development faces you with a fait accompli. If there are unseen, unknown aspects of nature, as I think there are, there will be ways of applying them once we learn more about them. My primary aim is not to find applications of morphic resonance, but when it reaches the point where it can be applied, it will take on a kind of reality in our present cultural context that it wouldn't otherwise have.

*What kind of applications of formative causation do you think would suddenly convince people: Sheldrake is right?*

There are two possibilities. The first would be an educational application. If morphic resonance is involved in learning, then we may be able to find ways of enhancing morphic resonance so that we can increase the efficiency of learning or training procedures. Already some experiments have shown that people learning tasks on computers can learn them quicker after other people have learned the same thing, and if we can improve the conditions for learning or training, this could be applied within a few years, at least within commerce, where people are interested not in theories but in what works. For schools and universities it will take longer.

Another area would be a technical application, on the borderline of what's possible. It's possible that morphic resonance is at work in the pathways lasers make when they go through certain kinds of crystals. If this is the case, then it might be possible to develop a new kind of memory chip based on morphic resonance technology, which would fit into modern optical computers, the new generation of computers. A computer that worked on morphic resonance would paradoxically come far closer to what Dennett and other people dream of, an organic machine that would be capable of thought, memory, and indeed communication with other, similar machines, because they'd resonate with each other around the world without any need for telephone lines, satellites, or other normal means of transmission. But this would mean that we had to accept a basically organic way of thinking about the whole of nature, and leave the old machine metaphor behind. I'm discussing that kind of application with one of the leading Japanese electronics companies that is actually doing research on this. It's an outside chance, you know, one in ten, one in a hundred, but if this happened, the world would be changed quite fast.

*Yours would be one of the greatest scientific revolutions of the twentieth century.*

Well, perhaps, but that's not my principal concern. My principal concern is to bring about this revolution in thinking. My theory may only be a stepping-stone to a bigger and broader view. You don't change science simply by arguing, and you don't change science simply by evidence, because if people want to ignore evidence, they will. Science is changed first through technological application and then because the social context changes. That's the other important thing, because there are very important and powerful socioeconomic and political reasons why the present form of science can go on indefinitely. It's closely associated with disregard for the environment, with environmental destruction and all sorts of things that are arousing a popular revulsion.

Genetic engineering, for example, is no longer the leading edge of technological progress, it's an abomination that Frankensteinian scientists have got into. The social support for that kind of science is waning, and with it the financial support, since much of it is supported by taxpayers' money. In Britain the amount of money for research is declining and the number of scientists is declining. People are fired from jobs and institutes are being closed. The social context of science is changing completely. All these things together mean that a change may not be very far off. A growing general demand for some new kind of science will favor the emergence of a new kind of science.

*As far as morphic resonance is concerned, what ideas would you want to break, after all these years of thinking in the Cartesian theater?*

First, the idea that there's no memory in nature. That's the first assumption of the Cartesian type of science. That nature is governed by eternal laws, and that the past is merely a kind of causal platform for the present state of affairs. That it's machinelike rather than organic. All organic phenomena have a kind of memory as part of their nature— crystals as well as molecules as well as feathers as well as computers as well as human beings. We are built on memory. Of course, we also have an activity in the present, and we have an openness to the future, but memory is the basis of regularity in nature, it's the basis of the predictable, if you like. Now the unpredictable, the creative—that's another story.

# CHAPTER 6

# DESCARTES,

# DESCARTES . . .

## Stephen Toulmin

The third millennium is only a few years away; spectators may expect us to draw up the balance, to reassess our place in history, to come up with new ideas about the direction we should go in. Not purposes that we can pursue separately, but reasonable and realistic plans that we can embrace together. Instead, with eyes lowered, we are backing into a new millennium without giving serious attention to the questions: "Where shall we find ourselves in the year 2001, and where will we go from there?"

Where do you start with someone who is the superlative of everything you yourself always wanted to be: a man who wanted to comprehend reality fully in all its fascination as well as horror, in all its antinomies and contrasts, in all its paradoxes and frustrations, in order finally to come to terms with it and, who knows, even understand it.

It was a long afternoon in Lisbon, where we were to discuss a range of subjects. But afterward, exhausted from an interview that lasted more than six hours, neither of us could remember exactly what subjects had come up. We had dinner at a seafood restaurant, where my credit card wasn't accepted, that much I do remember. Of our conversation I remember little. My brain couldn't take it in anymore, apparently.

A physicist by origin, Stephen Toulmin quickly became a philosopher of science. But to call him that does him great injustice. He is much more: historian, philosopher, neo-Aristotelian. He yearns back to the time, or at least the ideas, of Erasmus and Montaigne. A kind of nostalgia, you might say. If you ask him about Montaigne, his face changes. We are entering a world that is familiar to him, a humanist perspective that is also his, a world in which philosophy didn't just exist for itself but had to have practical applications to achieve meaning.

"We should recapture the wisdom of the sixteenth-century humanists; we should develop a view in which the abstract strictness and accuracy of the seventeenth-century 'new philosophy' is combined with a practical interest in human life in all its concrete detail. Descartes's fundamental agenda has lost its credibility. Therefore philosophy finds itself back with Montaigne's skepticism."

However many subjects came up in Lisbon, that city was never so much as mentioned that long afternoon. The conversation was pervaded by Toulmin's deep conviction that the "modern world," which started with the materialism and rationalism of such people as Descartes, Newton, and Leibniz, has run aground.

"We seem to have run aground without knowing where we are. And yet many people still find the dream convincing. Their trust in industry and science is founded on the concept of rationality, which was advanced by the English 'natural philosophers' and which promised intellectual certainty and harmony." We'll be discussing that all afternoon, even when we don't actually talk about it.

A few weeks after our meeting, I read somewhere, I think in the *New York Times Book Review*, that Stephen Toulmin is *the* philosopher of postmodernism. We never even mentioned it that afternoon.

To me he has remained the man who yearns back to Erasmus and Montaigne, to a world in which "the inescapable complexity of concrete human experience" played a part; a world so different from that of Descartes, Newton, and Leibniz, the thinkers who founded our modern society and who were under the illusion that rationality and materialism would one day lead to a comprehensive view of ourselves and of the world.

That afternoon in Lisbon, Stephen Toulmin was especially that a man who despises a univocal materialist and rationalist view of modernity and considers it to be dead, and who yearns for a science and a philosophy that will rediscover what Erasmus, Montaigne, and Aristotle described long ago.

"We have Descartes and Newton to thank for good examples of well-formulated theories, but humanity also needs people who realize how theory impinges on practice in ways that make our hearts beat faster."

■

*Immanuel Kant once stated that our appearance in time and space is as majestic as it is ridiculous.*

I think I understand what he was trying to say, but poor Kant was caught in a philosophical situation from which he was only half able to escape. Whenever I read anything of Kant's—leaving aside the *Ethics* for a moment—I have a sense that I'm reading two quite different texts that have got printed in the same words. On the one hand, he still has one foot in the Cartesian rat trap, and on the other hand, he's trying as hard as he can to move in the direction of pragmatism. I would have preferred it if he'd said that it was as ridiculous as it was majestic. I think he's trying too hard to be edifying, in his good Protestant way.

*Dennett writes, "We are all faced with the baffling phenomenon: how could anything be more familiar and at the same time more weird than our mind?" The same approach as Kant.*

Yes, Dennett's caught in the same trap.

*He's leaving the Cartesian theater but coming in again through the back door?*

The question about which I have a much more skeptical attitude than Dennett is the question about the interiority of the mind. I think the interiority of our mental life is very largely an artifact. A very interesting Russian writer called Lev Semenovich Vygotsky, who died at the age of thirty-six in 1934 of tuberculosis—of all the grotesque things to die of then—wrote a series of wonderful essays. Vygotsky was this kind of Mozartian genius who had the central idea—which one also finds in some of the early pragmatists—that we live in the public domain, and find it convenient to internalize for some purposes activities that would normally and naturally be part of us as visible participants in the world.

Much of what's gone wrong with philosophy since Descartes is a result of not understanding how our mental life originates in practical life which has become internalized. This was a point to which Wittgenstein drew attention in his classes, because of his sense that it was really not possible to see how anything could be said to have a meaning unless this meaning was conferred on it within a group of language users or practice users. Many philosophers had long taken for granted that all meaning came from the inside out, instead of existing in a world in which we learned how to participate and which we then made our own.

*Before we start talking about the Dennetts, the Kants, the mind, the brain, the Cartesian theater . . . Steve Gould writes that when he was five years old, he went with his father to the American Museum of Natural History in New York to see the* Tyrannosaurus rex. *At that moment he decided to become a paleontologist. Did you have a similar experience in your childhood that was decisive for your later career?*

Well, I have one slightly touching memory which had a lot to do with the course my career actually took. My father was an interesting and a very just man. In a different generation he would have been a professor of economic history, but he ended up working as a lawyer in an industrial firm in England run by Quakers. He had four children, and he decided that it was very important that we should have intelligent conversations at family mealtimes. So he would sort of open up topics and expect us to talk about them. The only trouble was that the moment any of us said anything that he disagreed with, he would leap in and correct us. He would say, "Excuse me," and then tell us the truth. My poor elder sister used to burst into tears and run out of the room and go and lie under her bed. I learned simply to shut up and think about those things to myself.

So there's a sense in which my entire career has been motivated by what the French call the *esprit d'escalier*, figuring out all the things I should have had on the tip of my tongue to put my father right when he started telling us things dogmatically. In a sense, this inevitably made me an epistomologist. I hate to be told something by anybody unless I have a feeling for how it could be that way. People think I'm very versatile because I've written books about the history of physics and about argumentation and about seventeenth-century history, but I feel that they're all about the same thing. They're all about *how* we come to be able to understand the things we come to be able to understand, and just what the limits of theory are, and just how we have to be prepared to back up the things we say. I also feel very acutely the injustices that human beings do to each other in the name of doctrine. It's terrible watching the wreckage in Yugoslavia, all caused by the things that tore Central Europe apart in the first half of the seventeenth century. People refuse to learn from others' mistakes. This is the gloomiest thing that I feel at the present stage of my life. And yet in areas where there is a tradition of learning, that tradition does carry many of the fruits of history forward, if the tradition is transmitted in a self-critical way. This is where the natural sciences succeed at their best, in passing on from generation to generation a set of ways of thinking about the world—thinking not only of the world, but also of handling it. People don't just accept it on the say-so of their teachers. What they pick up from their teachers is a feel for how all of these words fit in, mesh with things, so that they can recognize in nature how nature lends itself to our understanding. But the words are never magic words. I have developed a terrible intellectual irritability. When I see journalists, when they hear the name Einstein, automatically reaching for their pens and writing down $E = MC^2$, I turn away and say a little prayer and worry why they do this. Why can't they understand that the man was trying to answer real intellectual questions? He wasn't just discovering formulas.

*I'm briefly coming back to your father. What kind of truths did he preach?*

It would have been easier if he had been a dogmatic man, with a message that we could reject. No, it was the manner in which the views were presented, not the content of the views. If he'd insisted on some outrageous religious opinion, I could have reacted against it, I could have worked the thing through. As it was, I never really had the chance to be anything except an agnostic, because he wasn't telling us a lot of cobblers. He was being very reasonable, but in a very dogmatic kind of way. I've had to piece things together, but I remain interested in a lot of the things he interested me in.

*For instance?*

His favorite book, I am happy to say, was Mottley's book on the rise of the Dutch Republic. Especially during the last twenty-five years living in America, I've thought a lot about the differences between the Netherlands as the country it is today and the United States. It seems to me that both countries started off along the same road, but they ended up very differently, and I think the reasons why are extremely interesting. They have to do with what at the moment is my main preoccupation, which is what happened early in the seventeenth century with the invention of a particular kind of intellectualism by the likes of Descartes and Hobbes—the worship of universal theories and this search after a certainty that's not there.

There are two very interesting things which I see as connected. On the one hand, the United States was founded by people who had read deeply Hobbes and Locke and Rousseau and the Encyclopedists, whereas William the Silent lived before Hobbes's work was published. When the United Provinces insisted on separating themselves from Philip of Spain, the arguments they used were thoroughly medieval ones—none the worse for that—about what made a sovereign illegitimate and how he could forfeit his right to the loyalty of his subjects. They'd never heard of Hobbes, because Hobbes hadn't written yet. The intellectual context for the foundation of the United States only came into existence about fifty years later. The founding fathers of the United States knew the theories of Hobbes and Locke and Rousseau. As a result, the way in which people think and talk about politics in the United States is dominated by this theoretical tension between the individual and the state, which happens to be the federal government usually, the Leviathan. This is a model Hobbes imposed on political thinking, a model which one certainly doesn't find in Machiavelli.

Holland was founded as an alliance between provinces and cities and all kinds of intermediate institutions. To this day politics in Holland runs in a way that is inconceivable in the United States, with religion and trade unions represented in the political process. This is something that's ruled out in America. All of these intermediate institutions are prevented from playing the role in the political life of the country that people in many European countries take for granted. I feel that the individualism of Hobbes and Locke in the realm of politics is part of this extraordinary transition that took place in Europe—this search after a theoretical system which would make everything clear and which was to achieve a kind of certainty that Montaigne certainly had imagined was impossible. Erasmus would have regarded it as folly to seek after this.

So I find myself turning more and more into a sort of late-Renaissance skeptic. This happens also to be an intellectual position that I think is really quite close to the one Wittgenstein was putting forward in his later years, when I went to his classes at Cambridge.

*I just want to return for a few moments more to the years of your childhood. Do you remember dreams you had? Sheldrake got the idea that our universe was just one atom in the eye of a giant in another universe, and that an atom in our universe was a universe in itself.*

I remember sitting up in bed year after year reading books with titles like *The Mysterious Universe* and *The Restless Universe*. My imagination was very much seized by the whole cosmological project. But even then I had one foot in both camps. On the one hand, I was fascinated by what people said; on the other hand, I was afraid some wrote a bit like my father talked. I wasn't quite sure I could believe the things they were telling as a very nice kind of fable, but the fables certainly fascinated me. I used to go down weekend after weekend to the science museum and play with all the machines there and put coins in slots and make the steam engines run. I was always a bit of a spectator.

When Wittgenstein was the same age, he actually built a little model sewing machine with his own hands. He really had what the computer people call a hands-on sense of things. His family marveled at their little brother's facility with his fingers. In fact, one of the reasons I gave up being a physicist after World War II was that if I had to handle apparatus, I always broke it. When I went to do physics at Cambridge, the first thing one had to learn to do was to join two pieces of glass by heating them red hot. I could never do that. They always fell apart. If you gave me an expensive measuring apparatus or something, I would destroy it. I was in good company, though. When Dirac, the theoretical physicist, whose classes I went to at Cambridge, was a student, they sent him out to Metropolitan Vickers in Manchester, this big engineering firm, and they found out early on that he was a danger to himself, so they employed a small boy to go around with him to make sure he didn't put his hand in any of the machinery. This is something I have a great sympathy for.

*Did you decide to read physics for want of a better subject, or was there a real fascination behind it?*

There always had been this fascination, but the other reason I gave it up eventually was that I discovered that my interest in physics arose rather out of its philosophical connections. I was interested in the larger issues on which I had hoped physics would throw more light than it turned out to do. Physicists do useful research, but I was more interested in understanding how there could be these limitations on what we could do, that we couldn't leap straight to a kind of full-fledged view of things.

I have a feeling that in the years since I left Cambridge in 1942, I've branched out in all kinds of different directions from the scientific starting point that I was taught at Cambridge, and that really only now I understand what it was they were teaching me.

*What was the essence of it?*

I couldn't fully get to the heart of what they were teaching me at Cambridge unless I placed the physics that I was required to study for exams first in a philosophical context, then in a historical context, then in a context of social history, then in the context of general intellectual history. . . . Only when I started to understand why Montaigne and

Descartes and Leibniz and Newton were locked in these intellectual struggles in the seventeenth century, and what it was that led to the temporary victory of the Newtonian point of view, and what all this has got to do with the background to chaos theory, for instance, could I feel at home in physics. That is to say, I feel that I can naturalize the ideas of physics, so that they're not just technical notions. I feel I understand how they fit into everyday human life and grow back out of them.

*What happened before the war? How did your father talk about it?*

As a family, we understood much better than many people what was going on, because my father worked for a business that had connections in Stuttgart. He used to go over to Germany all through the early years of the Nazi regime. He knew what was happening, he knew about *Kristallnacht*, so we knew Hitler was up to no good when members of the Conservative party were still inviting Mr. Ribbentrop to their country house parties and thinking that Mr. Hitler was really a perfectly reasonable fellow, and if you just made a few little concessions, all would be well. That was a luxury our family never had the chance to indulge in. It was clear to us that bad things were coming.

*What kind of bad things? Mass extinction?*

Well, you know, I'm not jewish, though I went to school with a lot of jewish children. I've always felt very much at ease with jewish people. Many of my jewish friends have an attitude towards intellectual commitments that I find very congenial, but the holocaust is not part of my inheritance. I mean, my father understood the general nature of German antisemitism, but of course nobody could conceive of the lengths to which it was going to be carried. I will only say that when we heard about it, we were not incredulous. It didn't come as much of a surprise to us, because it was just a more horrific part of the picture that we had grown up with. But alas—I don't know why I say alas—alas it wasn't my people.

Unfortunately, the more I read of history, the less I'm convinced that the events of the Holocaust were unparalleled. I think to say that is to underestimate the capacity of people to be beastly to each other. I think there are other things that have happened in history that are as awful, and likely to happen again. It's a very optimistic view to imagine that the Holocaust is unique. I'm afraid it's the kind of thing that could happen again in the name of a different gospel and with different victims.

*Do you remember the moment you heard about what really happened in Auschwitz? Your father predicted something, but weren't you shocked to find that it really did happen?*

Surely, no, none of us who lived through that time will ever forget the first newspaper photographs of Belsen, of the pits full of bodies. In some ways, to have known beforehand that this kind of thing was likely to happen made it worse. I couldn't be incredulous about it. In this respect, Father had been more than right. He gave me a good point of view. My only trouble was that I needed to understand for my own sake why this was the right point of view.

*What was your father's reaction when he saw the first pictures?*

By that time I was twenty-three and going back to Cambridge. After my work on radar I went to Europe and did a bit of technical intelligence work, going round talking to people who'd been doing physics in Germany and Austria during World War II. Some of that was quite amusing, I'm sorry to say. It turned out that some of the scientists in Germany were quite smart at getting money for their own research, even when it was quite useless. There was a small team of people who had a very nice little castle not far from Weimar. This was at the stage when the Americans had occupied Türingen and the Russians hadn't yet moved in. They had succeeded in convincing Goering's Reichsluftministerium that atmospheric electricity might pose a danger to German aircraft, so they spent a very happy war in the countryside of Türingen doing totally useless research on atmospheric electricity with funding from the Air Ministry. Anyway, I spent a bit of time doing this kind of thing and then went back to Cambridge. That was when I switched to philosophy and attended the last year and a half of Wittgenstein's classes at Cambridge.

*But did you talk with your father about . . .*

No, you see, the thing with him was that he never listened, he preached.

*Did you love him?*

He was not a lovable man. His own mother had been a terrible woman, I hate to say it, a terrible mother. He had really not known what it was to be loved, but he was not by temperament inclined to use her sort of psychological weapons against his own children. The result was that in order to avoid using her kind of psychological pressure tactics, he kind of removed himself from the emotional lives of his children. I respect him enormously, and the more I go on, the more I can see his virtues and strong points, but he found being part of the world of love really very difficult. I didn't understand the situation well enough to court him. He was just this rather wise, if unintelligible, figure who from time to time would produce dicta that were always plausible enough to set me thinking, even though he wasn't able to explain why he believed the things he believed.

I realize, looking back over my own rather complex emotional transactions later in life, that with two sisters and a mother and a nanny, I grew up in a world in which the world of love was always the world of women. There were all kinds of different mirrors to reflect oneself from,

185

and all kinds of different ways of learning to deal with the people who were there to deal with. But they were mainly women, because Father was in the back room at his desk doing his accounts. So this was really how life started off, and if there's one perception that Plato and Freud and the Jesuits share, it's that if things start off in one way, they tend to go on that way.

*And now?*

And now I'm rather Epicurean about things. One gets eventually to the stage at which your own emotional reactions are something that happens to you. It's not that you disown them, but you get a sense of why they're happening at the same time that they happen. Then life becomes a bit like skating, you know—you stay on your feet, you don't always end up going in the direction you thought you might go, but you're less liable to take a tumble, you're less liable to find your reactions destroying the situations in which you find yourself. To that extent, one learns to figure skate. That's still compatible with being enthusiastically involved, only in ways that offer less danger of becoming catastrophic. You go through a terrible series of gauche phases when you find yourself feeling obliged to say things to people that turn out in retrospect to have been wholly destructive, even when you meant well. These are the kinds of episodes in life that can haunt you long after everybody else has forgotten about them, sort of exemplars of disgrace that one creates for oneself.

I did this once to myself professionally by letting myself accept an invitation to talk about the philosophical significance of Arthur Eddington's book on fundamental theory, only to find myself with an audience of about six people, all of whom knew much more about the book than I did. Fortunately, it was not a public meeting of any conceivable society. I remember on another occasion when I was trying to play the flute and I was invited to join an amateur orchestra that was going to play the Bach Fifth Brandenburg Concerto, again to discover that I was really not good enough to play my very prominent part to the standard of the rest of the people. A bad habit of being too ready to enter into other people's games on the basis of insufficient skill.

*Just after the end of World War II you started studying philosophy and you learned about the Cartesian theater, about modernity. What did you expect from modernity?*

I think we assumed that technical progress would continue, as indeed it has done. However much our general view of the world has become more complex, more varied, more colored and shadowed and dark and light, it still is the case that the technological changes which have taken place—even that's putting it too narrowly—even the intellectual achievements which have taken place since 1950 have really been in many ways extraordinarily positive.

The whole computer business has really been extraordinary, and also in many ways has given the lie to the people who hate technology. We've gone through this stage when people were sure that technology was giving power to the powerful and robbing the rest of us of power. This seems to me to be quite wrong. In a curious way, the history of the development of computers is a nice illustration of how in the long run the emancipatory effect of this technological development has far outreached its contrary effects. Everybody was afraid of the KGB and the FBI getting hold of IBM 360s. In the long run, few things did more to bring about the disintegration of the Soviet Union than the personal computer and electronic mail. I have friends who've worked for a long time with International Physicians for the Prevention of Nuclear War and other such organizations, and for years they've been having electronic mail contact with their colleagues in Moscow and Tajikistan, and they organized peace demonstrations in the Soviet Union, collaboratively across the world.

But to return to modernity, in the 1930s and '40s we believed in technology, but we didn't understand much about the rest of life. People in England have always had a very pragmatic view of politics, and as a result, until recently there hasn't been any kind of significant sociology in England. One of the curious things about England is that they were very good at anthropology and hopeless at sociology. Why? Because for the English, anthropology was the sociology of other people, and the question was "Why don't other people behave like us?" You know, we just behave, we just run things in a reasonable way, and we really need to study why those funny people in the Kalahari Desert and Brazil do what they do.

*Did that also infect you?*

Well, you know, people in England in my generation weren't brought up to think in terms of social structure, to think critically. There was this sense that if technical progress went along all right, then finding institutions within which it could work was not a problem. I still feel very good about the fact that in the last thirty years or so, basically since the publication of Rachel Carson's book *Silent Spring*, we really have been able to develop the argument about ecology. If Rachel Carson were to come back to life, she would have to feel a certain quiet pride in the fact that scarcely a government in the world now dares to be without some ministry taking care of environmental questions. Historically speaking, thirty years is an extraordinarily short time.

*You wrote, "Looking back at the received view of modernity after fifty years, my inclination is to retort: Don't believe a word of it. The defects become more evident with each year that goes by."*

What I mean by the received view of modernity is what we were taught at school, not what was actually happening. I don't believe that in the time of Galileo religious oppression was less extreme than it was in the time of Copernicus, quite the contrary. Or that seventeenth-century Europe was economically more prosperous than sixteenth-century Europe. In that particular passage I was discussing the fact that people were much more tolerant in the sixteenth century than they were in the seventeenth century. They were much more able to laugh at their own religious differences and didn't regard them as a killing matter.

I had this lovely optimistic picture of how, when Galileo and Descartes and Newton came on the scene, this was a sign that people were really making progress and that all that medieval stuff which had gone on beforehand could be conveniently forgotten. That was the doctrine that was handed down. It was kind of the collective version of my father's unsubstantiated assertions.

*What exactly went wrong when Descartes and Newton appeared on the stage and Montaigne and Rabelais disappeared into the darkness of the Middle Ages?*

That's very difficult to make plausible without going over the story at length and in some detail. I don't think this revolution happened slowly. On the contrary, it happened rather rapidly. In my book, I use two assassinations as emblematic episodes in the history of modernity.

At the end of the sixteenth century, everybody in Europe continued to have this comfortable sense that things were going along OK, although there were a lot of difficulties. Montaigne had Protestant and Catholic relatives, and when Henri IV asked him to run diplomatic missions between the Catholics and the Protestants, he had no difficulty in doing so. Regrettably, the Protestants and the Catholics couldn't be persuaded to sit down at a table together and reach a final agreement, but there was no sense that this was going to be impossible. And then Henri IV was assassinated. And I think at that moment people realized that cooperation was not just going to be hard to maintain, but it might even be bad policy. A situation that had appeared difficult came to appear unmanageable, and that's why the Thirty Years' War lasted thirty years. People just despaired of being able to handle the situation. In particular, they had no intellectual framework within which they could frame issues that could go across the boundaries between people's ways of thinking. It was the kind of final fracture—the vase broke, the glass shattered.

In some ways, the assassination of John Kennedy had a similar effect. After 1963 people were never really able to convince themselves that there was a plain road ahead.

*But Descartes's and Newton's appearance as symbols of the new age gave people a new impulse.*

Well, Descartes and Newton are really not the same generation. People like my colleague Alisdair MacIntyre talk about the Enlightenment project as though everything that happened from 1630 to 1789 was the product of a single generation of people with a single set of ideas. For me, it's much more interesting to look at the ways in which people were reacting to the situation.

All but the last two years of Descartes's professional career was spent during the Thirty Years' War. After leaving the Jesuit college at La Flèche, he studied law for a year, and then gave it up to become a young gentleman with Maurice of Nassau's military schools, where he learned the latest tactics. Then he became an officer in the Duke of Bavaria's army. He was part of the general staff side in the Thirty Years' War, and really only gave it up when people convinced him that he was wasting his time and he should go and live in Holland and talk to Beekman and other interesting mathematicians. So he settled down in Holland and wrote the great works of the 1630s, which were to leave such a stamp on people's minds. But they left a stamp on people's minds because he convinced them that if only we pursued some kind of abstract rational method, we'd be able to find general recipes for getting out of these difficulties.

Descartes was of course quite a subtle man. If you look at what he says, it's clear that his personal ambitions were much more qualified and much easier to understand than those of his followers. Still, the general impression people carried away was that there was this art of being rational which was going to provide us with general procedures for solving not only intellectual problems, but tactical and practical problems as well. There was some kind of general intellectual recipe for dealing with problems, which when I was a young man was called the scientific method.

*And which was very seductive.*

Certainly, especially for people who see the world falling apart around them. Leibniz was born in Leipzig two years before the end of the Thirty Years' War, in 1646, and he grew up in a devastated country. I can well imagine that for him as a young intellectual, the most important thing was to figure out how you could prevent people's inability to talk to one another and to share ideas, and how you could reconcile different theological systems. He must have been afraid that as long as this went on, the Thirty Years' War was liable to break out again. None of the causes for which the war had been fought had been victorious. The Catholics hadn't persuaded the Protestants, the Protestants hadn't persuaded the Catholics. They stopped fighting out of sheer exhaustion.

So for Leibniz it was a major project to figure out a universal language, a *characteristica universalis*, a language which would be an expression of how experience comes to all human beings of whatever persuasion. If only we could construct this language, people could talk to each other without misunderstanding.

He spent thirty years trying to organize what we could call the first ecumenical congress of people from all the different religious persuasions. In short, Leibniz had two projects. On the one hand, there was an intellectual one, to create a universal language and solve the problem of communication. On the  other hand, there was a practical one, to find a way of bringing all these different theologians together in order to defuse the ideological aspect of the wars that had devastated Europe at the beginning of the century.

Then Newton came along, and Newton did what Descartes had wanted to do for physics, but much better. It's a mistake to think that Newton was doing physics in a strictly empirical way, whereas Descartes had been doing it in a narrowly mathematical way. What Newton actually does in his *Principia mathematica philosophiae naturalis* — a very grandiose title, as Leibniz no doubt thought — is very much the same as what Descartes had done in the *Principia*, only on a much more powerful intellectual level, from the standpoint of both the mathematics that he did and the level of critical analysis. The whole of Book II of the *Principia* is Newton's account of what Descartes's theory of the world should have been if Descartes had really worked it out in detail. Nobody ever wrote a better mathematical treatise on Descartes's view of the physics of astronomy than Newton did, with the destructive aim of showing that it would never work. What he really ends up showing is that his theory of motion and gravitation is the story we have to have if Descartes's program for physics is right.

So everybody at this point breathed a sigh of relief, because the epoch that had opened when Copernicus made people doubt that they really understood the nature of the physical world at last came to an end. Newton had finally resolved the intellectual quandaries that people had been left with ever since 1543, when *De revolutionibus* was published. At that point also, people were ready to breathe a sigh of relief because between 1650 and 1678 the temperature of European politics had lowered considerably. Nobody was prepared anymore to quarrel about the new power of the nation-state. Everybody was settling down into a new regime of diplomatic maneuvering. Nobody believed any longer in the spiritual authority of a universal church. Every country went its own way in this respect. A new pattern of life emerged that most people were comfortable with.

*A new pattern that was to last for three centuries.*

Indeed, and this is why I find myself being invited to talk to all kinds of people, even managers, about the historical significance of uniting Europe. We are now creating institutions in Europe and in the world which operate much more effectively than the ones that were founded in the seventeenth century. We know that states can't go their own way now, that no national government can afford to carry on without understanding that all of its policies are affected by what's going on in other countries. One rightly hears words like "supranational" and "multinational" and "international" and "transnational," because the job now is to find functional ways of building up networks of action and networks of loyalty that are different from those of the last three hundred years.

*How would you describe the illusions of the Cartesian theater, the big mistakes and failures? What kind of metaphor comes to your mind?*

There's a very nice metaphor that comes to my mind. I had a student who wrote a very interesting paper for me about the transition from the apron stage to the proscenium stage, which took place at precisely that time, between 1600 and 1640. Shakespeare worked with an apron stage. In a Shakespearian play you saw a slice of life that was going on in your midst. The audience was all there, and this slice of life was going on just there.

On the proscenium stage there's a curtain, and at a certain point the curtain is drawn apart and a mysterious set of events in a world apart from yours is revealed to you. I think that our images of the mind are closely associated with this proscenium idea. Everybody presents a stage face to us, but what's going on in the mind remains hidden behind the curtains of a proscenium stage. We no longer feel that things that go on within us all are part of a public activity. This seems to me to be a key intellectual transition. You find this idea in one of John Donne's poems:

> 'Tis all in pieces, all coherence gone,
> All just supply and all relation,
> Prince, subject, father, son,
> 'Tis all forgot, and every man alone
> Thinks he hath got to be a Phoenix,
> And that there can be none
> Of that kind of which he is, but he.

It's a curious kind of narcissism to think that every individual creates his own mind and personality from scratch in his own lifetime. There's none of this sense that we are the inheritors and transmitters of traditions, that our world is shaped for us by the things we grow up into, and which we internalize and make our own. I think we're recapturing that now, and that we're creating a pragmatist rather than a Cartesian world.

*When did you begin to feel uneasy about what is shown in the Cartesian theater? What changed your view?*

I'm very conscious of having been a skeptic from the beginning. It's been very annoying for people I work with, but my general attitude is: If there's something everybody believes, it's almost certainly wrong. When I read Bertrand Russell's book *Our Knowledge of the External World* and Marx's book on the analysis of sensation, I could see the charm of this

191

way of thinking about the world, but I've always felt uncomfortable about the unanimity.

Wittgenstein's classes at Cambridge at the end of World War II confirmed me in my skepticism in that respect. The success of those classes is easy to explain. The content is much harder. The mannerisms are what most people talk about, but he was very influential, and for a very good reason.

It was a strange spectacle. He'd come into class with scarcely more than the desire to state a question for people. Even to state the question took him about three minutes. He'd begin to state it, then break off in the middle of a sentence and struggle with the question of how he was going to end the sentence. This always caused him great difficulty, but the most important thing was to understand that here was somebody who was applying standards higher than we understood to his own thought and his own ways of expressing himself. Eventually those of us who stayed with the class came to understand why he found it so hard even to frame a philosophical question.

I sometimes use the image of a slow bicycle race. When I was a child we had bicycle races where we tried not only to go faster than one another, but also to go slower than one another, and the point about the slow bicycle race was to go farther than the other fellow without falling off. I think of Wittgenstein's philosophy lectures as being like a slow bicycle race, at which he was an absolute master. "You may think you can go straight from A to B, but I'll show you that you can't even go from A to A prime." He showed that things people took as self-evident were based on all kinds of unjustified assumptions. You can see that with my father behind me, this was meat and drink for me. It was about understanding how language and thought and mental habits all fit together, how they so easily lead us into deceiving ourselves into thinking that the mind is essentially in the head, or whatever it may be.

Coming to understand these things was something I found very liberating, and it convinced me that in fact a decent intellectual account could be given for the skepticism that until then had come naturally to me. And I found that same account later in Montaigne in the *Apologie de Raymond Sebond*, where he explains the position of Sextus Empiricus and Pyrrho in antiquity. This again was to the effect that if you find yourself compelled to ask a philosophical question, the thing to do is not to try to answer it, because whether you assert something or deny it, you're making the same mistake. What you have to do is to ask yourself: Now, why should I want to put it that way? Why should I think that this is the question? And then when you stand back, you learn to understand better the intellectual confusions that bred the kinds of philosophical questions that Descartes landed us with.

*We have plenty of beautiful answers, but formulating the most beautiful question is what it's all about.*

Well, certainly this man's struggle even to get a question stated was a mark of an extraordinary talent. You must always be self-critical about what you're asking. Always dig below what you first think you can ask and try to understand how much you're already taking for granted. Then you go back behind that, and strip yourself clear of the unjustified assumptions.

This was what you saw him doing for himself. There are other aspects of Wittgenstein's thinking that I personally have moved away from, but his classes were an irreversible experience. In contrast to professional philosophers who would tell you what Wittgenstein says, what I learned from Wittgenstein is that he isn't teaching us anything—he hasn't got any doctrines—but he's helping us to see our way out of a whole lot of traps.

One of the main traps was indeed this Cartesian trap, the idea that the world begins in the mind of René Descartes, and in the minds of other individuals whom God has kindly given clear and distinct ideas. To that extent, Wittgenstein brings us back out of the proscenium stage onto the apron stage, where we live surrounded by the rest of the world and act out the episodes of our lives in this public domain. Of course, from time to time we stop to say something to ourselves under our breath, to wonder what to say without yet saying it. But we're basically doing all the things we've learned to internalize as part of a public world, not as part of a kind of narcissistic rehearsal behind this curtain. The most impressive single topic he was discussing during those months I was in his class was the question about what personal experience would have to be like for the Cartesian story to make sense, and he fired off many examples of things which really just didn't fit into that. He showed us how much we could liberate ourselves by understanding that language is a social medium which we make our own as individuals, but whose meaning entirely comes from its being in the public world.

Eventually one came to see that sensations were similar to the thought that what gives money value is the sentimental value we attach to it. What we have in our head is all promissory notes that have no currency value. This was how my own interest in Wittgenstein led me to Vygotsky and more recently to people like Bakhtin, who at the same time were making a similar kind of transition in the field of literary criticism.

*What are the myths that we have constructed concerning our unique and precious consciousness in this Cartesian theater? What have they cost us?*

I think this is the point at which I part company with Dennett. The point is, I think, the word "consciousness" as a general noun covers just too many different kinds of things. I know what it is to be conscious rather than unconscious. If somebody hits me on the head, I lose consciousness. I also know what it is to do something consciously as opposed to without thinking. But I'm equally conscious whether I'm doing something consciously or without thinking. I know what it is to engage in a conscious conspiracy with other people, to share intentions, to engage in common actions.

Consciousness is not a single function. It's less miraculous when you understand  that it's at least four functions, which different organisms could develop separately. We happen to have all four, and that creates an intellectual creature of remarkable capacity. I would love to hear Stephen Gould talk about the different aspects of being conscious or acting consciously or engaging in conscious collaboration and so on, and especially about how all these different aspects entered into paleontological history and human history.

*Do you also mean the killer ape and the crocodile that still bring their influence to bear on the decisions the neocortex makes?*

Well, crocodiles are interesting. I'm told by people who ought to know that crocodiles don't dream but birds do; that the bird brain is capable of rapid eye movement sleep, but the crocodile brain is not. It's clear that not everything that makes humans uniquely human is already fully fledged in the transition from crocodile to bird. If we were able to give an adequate neurological interpretation of the paleontological evidence, I think we could see that the transition to being fully conscious creatures has involved multiple steps.

Some of those steps have been quite recent. St. Augustine tells us that St. Ambrose of Milan used to sit on the steps of the cathedral in Milan and read through the missal to himself so fast that the people who looked at him decided he must be a magician. Why? Because he was reading to himself, without actually forming the words with his lips, as people then did.

There are good reasons—which have to do with the development of manuscript writing and the ways breaks were introduced between sentences and paragraphs for thinking that before St. Ambrose and even for quite a while afterward, reading to yourself was not part of the generally shared cultural heritage. And I think that thought is a result of internalization, including the internalization of the ability to read.

Many aspects of what we call consciousness are in fact cultural and historical products, which no doubt were possible only for creatures with certain kinds of brains, but nevertheless things whose appearance we find only at a certain point in the history of human cultural development. For me there isn't a single miraculous consciousness that distinguishes human beings. The idea of a consciousness as a unitary function seems to me to be to repeat the Cartesian mistake with the word "consciousness" substituted for the word "brain." You can find this in Bertrand Russell's biography, when he talks about himself as a young man of seventeen or eighteen being driven, as he says, to the conclusion that consciousness is an undeniable datum. I think that consciousness is an undeniable part of our experience, but that this undeniable fact of our experience is itself a very complex one. We need to know much more, partly from the paleontologists, partly from the neuroanatomists, partly from the cultural historians, and partly from the cultural anthropologists, because it may well be that this is something that varies from individual to individual. In fact, at some point the same brain injury produces different psychological effects in people who grow up with Chinese, an ideographic language, from people who grow up with an alphabetical language. Thinking to yourself is a different process for people whose primary language is ideographic.

*Dennett writes, "The idea that the self or the soul is really just an abstraction strikes many people as simply a negative idea, a denial rather than anything positive. But in fact it has a lot going for it, including a somewhat more robustly conceived version of potential immortality than anything to be found in traditional ideas of the soul."*

Well, clearly what I've been saying rather goes in the other direction. It does seem to me that there's a lot of evidence that we acquire all kinds of mental functions independently of one another, and we can lose them independently of one another. In aphasiology and other branches of clinical neurology you see how people lose what seem to us to be indissolubly connected skills. With some kinds of injuries, for instance, people can be in a state in which you can dictate to them a passage, which they can then write down, but immediately after that they can't read back to you what they've just written. For us that's almost as hard to imagine as what it's like to be a swallow.

I would never be able to say whether I agreed or disagreed with anything Dennett said about consciousness unless we could first of all sort out which of the many different senses and aspects of consciousness he's talking about. This is where Wittgenstein's influence on me is irreversible, when people start using these big words. I remember Wittgenstein once saying in class, "What philosophers *mean* is always right." The trouble is they use language that makes it impossible for other people to understand straightaway what they're saying.

*Dennett also says it will be a long time before computers start crying, but eventually we'll be able to awaken consciousness in a computer.*

For me the question is not: Can you give computers consciousness? The question is: Do you allow computers to have these more complex kinds of mental activity? If they were all combined, needless to say, in some sense or other this computer would be conscious, but again, one has to look at the different components separately.

When people talk about the "experience" of computers, they fail to understand that so far we've denied computers the opportunity to be the kinds of things that these arguments are about. Computers are expected to stay sitting on the desk or anchored to the floor. How can we ask, "Wouldn't the computer prefer to go swimming?" If you came in one morning and turned your computer on and it said on the screen, "I'm really feeling quite bored with all this calculating, I don't think I'll work today," you'd know that one of your colleagues had programmed it to do this. But a computer could be like that. It would be very unfortunate to make a computer like that, because it wouldn't be marketable. There's nothing inconceivable about it, it's just that we like computers to be perfect servants, always at our beck and call. To that extent, they're a great substitute for an underclass. And in fact, they're doing the underclass out of a job.

*Dennett points out that if you make a conscious computer, you also have to give it human rights.*

That's way down the road. By the time we understand all the different things that make up what we call consciousness in ourselves, we'll have had to make all sorts of choices. One of the things about children that parents find very hard to accept is that children talk about their parents behind their backs, and eventually conspire to do things that either the parents don't know about or even frustrate the parents' plans. And this is part of human life, learning that your children are not totally under your control, and that they can even enter into a conscious conspiracy to frustrate us. We have to be grown-up enough to live with the consequences.

Now, it would be different if we found that the computers were banding together after hours and deciding that from now on they weren't going to run certain software or that they were going to generate certain gremlins from time to time. I suspect that some of these young computer people would already be able to write the software that would enable computers to do this. If this really started happening, we'd have to secure ourselves against it, because it would destroy the social utility of computers as perfect servants. However, there may come a point at which we would say, "Isn't it a bit unfair to neutralize this virus? Aren't computers happier if they have this virus?"

*How persistent is the myth of the "central meaner" in our brains?*

That's the great error. If you look at the whole historical development of language about mental function, it was only at the point at which this mechanistic physiology that Descartes invented was used to develop some kind of very crude neurophysiogical model that the image of the mind as a little man inside the head achieved dominance in intellectual history. My beloved Montaigne doesn't have it, it would make no sense to him. This is a by-product of seventeenth-century mechanistic theory, and not even physics these days takes the central axioms of Descartes's mechanics and Galileo's mechanics as the last word.

It's a tragedy that neurophysiologists and psychologists and philosophers still image that we have to operate with this image. It was a by-product of a particular moment in history. It's really sad when we find people's popular arguments sidetracking these issues. There are a lot of other fascinating things—for instance, the nature of attention. We're scarcely beginning to have any conception of what, neurologically speaking, is involved when we attend closely to something. For instance, if you're listening to music, sometimes you can follow the viola player in a string quartet, or listen for the bassoon in a Mozart serenade. You pick out one voice in a polyphony of musical voices. We would have made some marvelous progress if we really knew what's involved in paying attention, and how auditory function and the neurophysiological mechanisms for it are brought into play.

My fascination is with these questions about the elements that seem to constitute our conscious lives and experience, and our ways of acting consciously. But they're not all going to be part of a single tidy model, let alone about a little man inside our head.

*What kind of picture of morality did you have in your childhood, and how has it changed through the years?*

First of all, ethics as we learned to talk about it at home was never religious. My parents were married in 1917, and they were part of a generation that was horrified by the ways the organized churches behaved during World War I, the wicked things that the Anglican church said about the Germans, and the wicked things that churchmen in Germany said about the French and the English. So my parents resolved not to bring their children up within any institutional religion, and for us, therefore, learning to understand how one lived was something entirely independent of any theology.

The religious group I increasingly feel a deep sympathy with are those people popularly known as the Quakers, the Society of Friends. This group has a very interesting history that goes back precisely to this period in the 1640s. They first became an organized and self-organizing group during Cromwell's Commonwealth, and they were very much associated with the Cromwellian rebellion against the royal and ecclesiastical establishment in England. The Quakers have never accepted the authority of the nation-state to tell them to go to war. After 1657 they became pacifist, and to this day, when there's a war, the Quakers go out there with ambulances to bind up people's wounds. They are conscientious objectors. They have a practical approach to ethics which is entirely undoctrinal.

197

As a philosopher I get more and more bored with philosophical theories about ethics. I'm much more interested in seeing the historical development of people's concrete ideas about how people live with one another. In fact, a few years ago I specifically wrote a book called *The Abuse of Casuistry* with Albert Jonsen, a colleague in America, about the practice of forming particular ideas about ethics, and how they change over time. In this respect, I found my way, but again in a manner that involved little religious or philosophical doctrine. I'm much more concerned with concrete problems and particular solutions.

Ironically, this puts me in a very curious situation, because when I reread Aristotle's *Ethics*, I feel a great sympathy with the way he talks about ethics in all the different kinds of relationships that people enter into with one another, and how the ways we act in those relationships vary from case to case, from circumstance to circumstance. For me pragmatism creates the possibility of looking at the particulars of things.

*Is perhaps one of the reasons for your rediscovery of Aristotle that you're bored with philosophy as simply a kind of sophistry?*

Oh, I think what I'm doing is philosophy. It would have been called philosophy for much of the history of philosophy. I really do regard this digression that we get with Descartes as a pathological phase. It's exciting that Descartes was doing two things: he was launching mathematical physics and sticking us with this particular epistemological agenda. The development of mathematical physics has gone ahead splendidly, but the epistemological agenda has led us into a prolonged dead end.

The point is not whether what I'm doing is philosophy. I'm just bored with seeing the same old mistakes repeated again and again, and I wish with some impatience that the emancipatory aspect of Wittgenstein's teaching would make more progress. Poor old Wittgenstein thought he'd been sent into the world to make philosophers unnecessary. He had this picture of himself as Hercules cleaning out the Augean stables, after which nobody would need to ask these questions anymore. He'd be horrified if he came back to life and saw that there are more professional philosophers now than ever before, and that most of them are making precisely the kinds of mistakes he was trying to rescue the intellectual class from.

It's very helpful from some points of view to put Wittgenstein alongside Tolstoy. If you read *Anna Karenina*, there are chapters that Tolstoy devotes to Katavasov making his professional philosopher friends look ridiculous, and Tolstoy does so for the same reason that Wittgenstein did. Wittgenstein learned a lot from Tolstoy, because for both of them, no philosophical thesis was any good unless it could be put to some use.

*And you take the same view?*

Yes. I think theory has to be justified as a form of practice, instead of practice having to answer before the high court of theory.

*Gould said that if nature is nonmoral, we have to search for morality in ourselves.*

I don't think we have to look for morality, it builds itself up for us in the course of our lives. We needn't seek for it unless we think we've got to have some kind of theory into which we can fit morality as one of the subcomponents. This is all part of this overintellectualized image that we're grown up enough to grow out of.

The view of modernity that I grew up with was the idea that nature was simply factual, and value questions were only human. Again, this seems to me a mistake. Certainly for the Stoics everything in the world was rational, and human rationality made sense only if human conduct fitted in with the rationality of everything else that was going on in nature. They certainly didn't think that nature was nonmoral. Sometimes I'm tempted to say that the development of the ecology movement represents a kind of return to a Stoic view of the world. Many people of my children's generation have a very strong sense that human practices, in particular industrial, technological practices, are open to criticism to the extent that they don't treat nature as nature should be treated. As though nature itself had rights.

I think Darwin would have welcomed the sense people have that the loss of species is a moral issue. It might have eased his loneliness somewhat. Darwin's loneliness grew from the fact that his insights pointed beyond the general sense of his time. If Darwin could come back, I'd give him Rachel Carson to read, and tell him about what's happened since 1962, and how his ideas played such an important part in changing our conception of nature, so that he need never again think of nature as totally nonmoral.

Those things Darwin said about nature—wasteful, blundering, inefficient—those things apply to human beings as well. I think calling behavior brutal is very unjust to the brutes. Human beings like to unload onto the other animals their capacity to act, as we like to say, "inhumanly." The whole notion of brutality as inhuman implies that humans have invariably acted in a way higher than loyal beasts and kindly animals. It seems to me that it's not so. Antiquity was full of stories about other species coming to the aid of human beings and feeling themselves to be part of a community. It's not part of my own experience, but people who swim alongside dolphins or who go in boats out with the dolphins end up in a social relationship with the dolphins. When we are kind in the presence of dolphins, they're prepared to let us

join in their play and their collective activities. I don't take that as
something mysterious, it's what one would hope to be the case. But it's
not part of any picture in which all animals except humans are written
off as purely mechanical brutes. Quite often when I'm teaching I take my
dogs into class and they sit quietly while I lecture, but I don't like to take
them in when I'm lecturing on Descartes, because I'm compelled to say
that Descartes thought dogs were merely machines, and this is an insult
I'm not prepared to expose them to. I'm quite sure that Descartes never
owned a dog. He couldn't have said the things he said about animals if
he'd had any kind of firsthand experience of the attempt to live on a
social basis with creatures of other species.

*What did you learn from your dogs? I don't mean this in any
sentimental way.*

Oh, no, no, no. . . . People say that dogs remain rather like children
throughout their lives. They don't ever develop the ability to turn their
backs on you that cats have. Cats are very happy to have owners, but
walk away from them and do their own thing.

    Dogs are different, they're very much like children who want to be
played with the whole time. My dogs always have one ear ready for the
moment when they can leap up and say: Isn't it time to go for a walk
now? I've learned what it is to be emotionally blackmailed by the dogs,
they know how to get to me to do things. This is not entirely frivolous.
There's an interesting book about the domestication of animals which I'd
love to have Stephen Gould's view about, because it has an evolutionary
argument. It's based on the perception that what we call the
domestication of animals was maybe equally a case of animals
discovering the advantages of tagging along with human beings. Once I
read this argument, I understood a lot about the dogs, that for them it
was very handy having these humans around who would give them
meals and take them for walks and otherwise make their lives a pleasure.

*Talking about morality or the lack of it, Hannah Arendt has described
the everyday appearance of evil—how people could play Mozart and
quote Rilke and Shakespeare but were capable of turning around and
killing people as if they were stamping forms. François Cavanna, the
French writer, says that people don't don different masks in peace or
in war or in bed or at work, they are all these different masks.*

One can't help being fascinated by it in the way one's fascinated by
snakes. I think this use of the word "masks" is exact. The point is that
one has to learn to use masks. I don't think we're all born with an evil
streak. We have to study under what kinds of circumstances people learn
to dissemble, learn to put a misleading face on their actions. Or how
their personalities become dissociated. It's a social matter, not a genetic

problem. My own perception of it is that people develop dissociated personalities or this habit of wearing masks in characteristic kinds of circumstances, which we need to learn more about. I'm not seeking to excuse them, I'm only saying that if we want to understand what kinds of evil people there are, we need to understand in what different ways the world—that is, we ourselves—can create evil people, or in what ways we ourselves are participants in the situations that actuate the potential evil in people.

*Have you ever looked yourself in the eye in the shaving mirror and said, "Stephen, you really are a bastard, and didn't even know it."*

I've never been a violent person. I hate and despise violence, though partly as a way of excusing other defects. But I've certainly been forced to recognize at times that I've treated people in ways that I felt remorse about. One doesn't go through life without that. I've been married more than once, and to some extent my matrimonial misadventures have been products of my own inability to deal with situations I wish I hadn't got into in the first place, but since I did get into them, I wish I had been able to behave less gracelessly. I've also been on the receiving end, but that's another matter.

*How many times were you surprised by your own reactions or actions, so that afterward you said to yourself, "My God, did I do that?"*

Oh, again that is something that happens to us all. I was in psychoanalysis for a few months, sorting out the fact that I wasn't able to accept as mine the feelings that that kind of situation left me with. And that helped me to recognize the things that trigger those reactions of mine that left me feeling so bewildered. None of us ever totally gets to the point at which we lack these buttons that can activate us.

On the other hand, you learn to steer your way around your own shortcomings. Montaigne has a nice passage where he says he does his best never to do things he's not prepared to speak about. This is a kind of measure I would like to be able to apply to myself. But of course this also involves having the opportunity to avoid getting into situations in which you're liable to react in ways you find hard to speak about. Epicurus told everybody they ought to practice detaching themselves from their feelings, and looking at their feelings as something that was happening to them, rather than something they were doing. You should learn to adopt enough distance from your own feelings so that you could even circumnavigate them if you recognized a situation of danger. True, you can't guarantee that you'll recognize it. On the other hand, I suspect that you get a little better at it. The world is made up of getting a little better at things. There aren't any universal solutions, there are no guarantees. . . .

*Daniel Dennett says that we humans are the best anticipation*
*machines, and that our enormous consciousness makes this possible.*
*We are the best self-controllers. Shouldn't we say at the same time that*
*we are the best denial machines?*

This is just the thing. Why doesn't he say we're the best anticipating
organisms? Why this preoccupation with the mechanical analogy? If
you study mechanics now, at the very least you use quantum mechanics,
not Newtonian mechanics. The people who talk in mechanistic terms
about physiology, neurophysiology, psychology, and cognitive science do
so despite the fact that in physics the whole situation of predictive
success and determinism has changed.

One of the very important things about this recent development has
been given the bizarre name of "chaos theory." This is the final
mathematical working out of a problem that has been there from the
beginning. The foundation for the modern discussion of this whole set of
problems was a paper that Henri Poincaré published in 1889 as a
contribution to *Acta mathematica*. What's interesting is that the
problem he was concerned with is precisely one of the problems that
was at issue between Leibniz and Newton in 1714 and in the
correspondence between Leibniz and Clark. Mathematically speaking,
Newton's account of planetary astronomy took for granted certain
assumptions that are as unfounded now as they were then—namely, that
because we can solve the equation for a single planet going around the
sun, the combination of all the planets going around the sun at the same
time and interacting even in a minor way with one another is in
principle mathematically equally powerful. From the beginning it was
known that this so-called $n$-body problem cannot be given the same
mathematical treatment as the two-body problem, of a single planet
going around the sun. And to this day, if people want to make
predictions about the future motions of the planets, they have to make
allowances for the mutual interactions of the planets on a step-by-step,
basically empirical basis.

As Poincaré saw, this $n$-body problem was a major intellectual
obstacle to the philosophical interpretation of the Newtonian system.
When Laplace gave us this image of the perfect calculator—that given
the position and velocity of every atom in the universe at the creation,
we can calculate its entire history using Newtonian methods—he was
quite mistaken. So all of the philosophical discussion of mechanics and
of physics and of physical nature based on the assumption that Newton's
mechanics led to perfect predictions in all cases was just wrong.

In this 1889 paper Poincaré states very nicely in the very last chapter
how even with very small planets that are exerting very little influence on
one another, if there are enough of them and if they get close together,
they'll behave in ways that are totally different and radically
unpredictable by the methods of mathematical physics. Now, chaos

theory is precisely about the radical unpredictability you get in these critical situations. The world is basically not like the planetary system. The whole philosophy of the people who talked about nature after Newton was based on the assumption that the planetary system was a paradigm of a natural system. It wasn't. It was a totally exceptional situation. It happened to allow Newton to do his calculations with convenient ease, but the idea that everything else operates with the kind of regularity and predictability of the planetary system was always an incorrect extrapolation.

From the time that Poincaré came back to this problem in 1889, this should have been obvious to everybody. Of course, it didn't stand in the way of Planck and Einstein or of Hisenberg and Schrödinger, who got onto quantum mechanics. But the trouble is that philosophers continued to talk as though Poincaré had never written—as though this whole nineteenth-century image of a mechanical universe grinding out physical events in ineluctable sequence were unimpeached.

*You studied physics. What is your greatest amazement when you look back on what you thought then was physical reality, compared to what reality has since turned out like?*

I wish I'd been given this work of Poincaré's to read. People went on studying the things they knew how to explain, and when they didn't know how to explain something, they said, "Oh, that's a special case." You have a millstream that flows steadily. At a certain point it breaks into turbulence. Why does this change happen? What's the difference between turbulent motion and smooth motion? We were taught to believe that turbulent motion is just a special case of smooth motion. "There are too many variables, it's easier to study smooth motion." There was a certain insistence that everything was basically universal and uniform and governed by constant laws, and intelligible in the way the planetary system was intelligible.

When I'm feeling kind, I'll say this was a methodological program. But when I'm not feeling so kind, I'm inclined to say it was a convenient out, because otherwise you'd face some very difficult philosophical questions. You see a clear blue sky in which a storm begins to form. Why does that storm begin to form at precisely that point, at precisely that time? They tell us if only we knew the exact temperature gradients and humidity changes and the rest, then we'd know. Maybe, maybe not, we don't know. There are lots and lots of things that happen out of a clear blue sky.

The world is predictable within limits. But the limits begin to appear larger and larger. Scientists once thought you could find out what somebody was thinking by having enough electrodes attached to their cortex, without seeing them in a context. When we talk about what people are doing, about their desires, their thoughts, their feelings, we talk about them on the apron stage. We talk about them as people who are engaged in tasks in a world that's full of other people, and in which their own past life history plays a crucial part. This is what psychology is about, it's about how people act in the light of their past, and given the circumstances and situations they currently find themselves in. Their neurophysiology makes them capable of acting as they do. But you don't find out where a car is going by looking in the carburetor, even though, if the carburetor wasn't there, the car wouldn't go anywhere.

*In one of your books you say that "with eyes lowered, we are backing into a new millennium without giving serious attention to the questions: Where shall we find ourselves in the year 2001, and where will we go from there?"*

One tries to draw people's attention to new questions, or to questions they ought to be asking. This is rather different from the question about individual freedom of action. It's a healthy step, because in many ways the space we have for making choices on our own is very closely related to the space that exists in the world for our institutions to work differently. The best way to free ourselves up to act in new ways is to deal with the problem on the social level first, and then create a situation within which individuals are free to act differently.

Look, if I were half my age but still had the ideas I've got now, maybe I would really ask myself whether I shouldn't go and work for Amnesty International or one of those nongovernmental agencies that seem to offer so much more positive and helpful contributions to human affairs than any of the official governments.

*You once said that the political supremacy of Europe has ended, and with it the hegemony of European ideology.*

I'm not sure I'd put that last bit again in quite the same way. It refers to the business of learning to accept the limited character of national statehood. The idea that every state should correspond to a nation and that a nation has to be an area populated by people of the same culture has reached its reductio ad absurdum in Yugoslavia. This was always true of the Balkans, but we had the Habsburgs and the Ottomans between them to thank for keeping the lid on it. And now we're paying the price for their acceptance of that myth. After 1919, people insisted that every nation was entitled to its state, and there was this thing called the principle of nationality, which was used to justify setting up these states in Eastern Europe. Macedonia was always, as the French say, a *macédoine*, a collection of chopped fragments alongside one another.

But Europe is really learning to develop the institutions and the institutional habits that make living in Europe now totally different from what it was before World War II. The United States is quite a different story. In the United States people are still very confused about the nature of nationality, and about the nature of their statehood.

*Schopenhauer says, "The true motto of history should be 'The same in a different way.' We sit and talk, and our eyes light up and our voices betray our excitement. Others have confronted each other exactly like this, a thousand years ago, and in another millennium it will be the same again. The mechanism which prevents us from realizing that is time."*

Schopenhauer was a wise man with a humorous capacity for capturing disagreeable truths. And there's a lot in what he says that I wouldn't quarrel with. I do think, though, that the situation has changed in ways that make it almost qualitatively different.

Harry Truman used to say that his favorite reading was Plutarch's lives of the noble Greeks and Romans, because he learned more about his contemporaries in politics from Plutarch than he did from any other source. At the same time, many of the problems of the twenty century have arisen as a result of industrialization, the bureaucratization of society, and the whole scale of human interaction with nature. Maybe the scale of population growth has got to a point where the old solutions can't do the job anymore. That's why we have to think about how our institutions can be adapted to deal without present problems.

*It's not history donning another misleading mask?*

I don't think we should allow that possibility to discourage us from doing our best to deal with the situation, however different it may be from earlier situations. Let me give you an example. If in 1815 you wanted to get a message from Rome to London, it would take as long as it did in the time of the Roman Empire. The best you could do was to give it to a man riding the fastest available horse. Rothschild made a killing on the news of the battle of Waterloo, because their carrier pigeons arrived from Waterloo before the official military messages, which had been taken by horse and boat. I find it rather tiresome that now we know about everything that's happening on the other side of the globe within a few minutes of its happening. In some ways, that makes it much more difficult for us to act. In the old days an ambassador wasn't called plenipotentiary extraordinary for nothing. Nowadays an ambassador would be on the telephone to the Foreign Office straightaway. The decisions are all taken back at the head office, out of the hands of people who understand the situation on the ground, and put in the hands of the people who only know general principles. For me as a neo-Aristotelian, this is very much a regression.

*We've had carnage in Vietnam, in Auschwitz, mechanical destruction of people. We've had carnage all through human history, but this century it's talking a different form.*

Let me give you, as an example, my own reaction to something sufficiently recent for us all still to be unclear about our judgment about it: the war in the Persian Gulf. For me this was a kind of replay of a part of my life. In World War II I was working with people who were developing microwave radar for the purpose of producing very accurate pictures of the ground from a bomber, so instead of obliteration bombing you could direct a bomb to a particular place. Of course, you only had to solve this problem mathematically in order to see the possibility of "smart" bombs. So that watching these grotesque television displays of bombs going down the chimneys of the buildings was a fulfillment of an intellectual dream of 1943, the dream of a group of people of whom I was one. It was fascinating to see American military technology doing what for us had been a professional fantasy.

On the other hand, I felt deep disapproval of the whole operation on larger grounds of history and policy. I found myself torn between technical fascination and admiration, and the deeper disagreement with the policies that had led up to this.

*At that moment, did your old profession raise its head again?*

No, it was impossible to see it without being conscious of the irony. I was aware that the world was different and that I was different. In World War II I had deep reservations about my own involvement with death and destruction early on. The Dresden bombing seemed to me to be almost enough to disgrace us as allies in the war against Hitler.

*What did you think when you realized after the war that the transportation lines to Auschwitz and other extermination camps had not been bombed either by the Americans or by the RAF, when it could have saved hundreds of thousands of lives?*

I thought the reason was bureaucratic. But not bureaucratic in the sense of what Eichmann did. It was the business of Air Chief Marshall Harris, as commander in chief of Bomber Command, to bomb the targets that the War Cabinet decided had highest priority in the effort to destroy the German military power. Delaying the destruction of German military power was not going to make things any better for anybody. In that sense, of course, the situation of the Jews in Europe was truly tragic. I've never heard of anybody in the U.S. State Department or the British Foreign Office who understood enough about the nature of the extermination machine for that possibility to have occurred to them.

*They knew about mass destruction.*

Who is "they"? Not the commander in chief of the Bomber Command. Maybe somebody in the Foreign Office. But at critical moments people may be unable to get the message through, or may come to understand that it would do no good to try too hard to get their message through. It's easier for a politician—politicians always look after each other—but if you're a simple official in some foreign office with a wife and five children, you're in a difficult position. You can be a saint, but on the whole it's better for a saint to not have a wife and five children. It makes their moral position easier to carry through into action. On the whole, saints don't get into that kind of civil service job—they're obviously going to be fanatical and untrustworthy.

We have much more to learn from Max Weber than we have from Karl Marx. The question is the nature of a bureaucratically organized society. When people attack technology and science, more often than not they're attacking what happens to these things once they get into the hands of a bureaucratically organized system or society. That's why, for me, the central problem is how we redistribute power so that our institutions will be better adapted to what actually has to be done. The central practical problem is how we can change the executive structures of our societies and cultures so that the needs of human beings really are met, instead of the desires of an oligarchy of politicians or preachers or mullahs or whoever it may be.

*What childish questions are still with you after all these years? I mean questions like why is the sky blue, why is the grass green, why does the moon have phases?*

Basically the question that's still with me is: Why are people so nasty to each other? When I look back, I can see why I've come to feel so critical about the late seventeenth century: much of what we now think of as human inequality was institutionalized at that point.

*Why* are *people so nasty to each other?*

I think the only answer is: That's how it worked out. I feel terribly bad on behalf of the victims of injustice, but behind that, my heart bleeds for the fact that history worked out the way it did, that people came to act so miserably. And usually that happened for the reasons I hinted at earlier, that their eyes for some reason or other were shut or distracted. I don't know what to do about that except bleed.

*But the question remains.*

There is no general answer. That's why we find it's so hard to anticipate. For a long time in the middle period of my life, I used to hate institutions from the bottom of my heart, because I think most injustice springs from the fact that institutions work in ways we can't control.

I realize now that's too easy a way out. One has to try at a certain point to prescribe for institutions. Tolstoy puts this same case in *Anna Karenina,* in an extraordinary series of chapters where Levin goes to the meeting of the county council. Tolstoy describes in detail the corrupt manner in which a new president is elected to run the council. He has Levin talk to himself in ways that make it clear that Tolstoy thinks it's an illusion to think that there could be any morality in politics, that political corruption is always going to foil our best attempts. That's too hard a message for me. . . .

*By the way, is the same music from this morning still playing in your head?*

Yes, it is.

*What kind of music is it?*

It's still Schumann's piano quintet, it's still the same movement, the happy one. E. M. Forster had this wonderful phrase to go with it: "The world will yet be saved, be saved." It's in *Two Cheers for Democracy*. I used to know Forster at Cambridge. He was a fellow at my college at Cambridge, at King's. He was really a sweet, curious man, like a dormouse. He had a little moustache that twitched like a mouse's bristles. He had one of those glass biscuit jars by his bed, and a friend of mine gave him a packet of biscuits to put in his biscuit jar. When she called him down to dinner he was a bit late, and she asked him what was up. He apologized that he was late because he found the biscuits were slightly too big for the jar, so he'd had to nibble round the edge of all the biscuits so they would fit in the jar. That's a characteristic picture of him.

*You write somewhere, I can't find it just now, that if you had to spend time with some philosophers or thinkers . . .*

If I was forced to spend eternity with any group of intellectuals, I would rather spend it with Erasmus, Rabelais, and Montaigne than with Descartes, Leibniz, and Newton. Which isn't to say I don't respect and admire the work Descartes, Leibniz, and Newton did, but in different ways they seem to me to have been very strange people. Leibniz would merely be annoying, but Descartes and Newton were rather curious people. Both of them lost parents very early. Descartes's mother died either shortly after his birth or after the birth of the next child. Newton's father died before he was born, and his mother, wanting to remarry, gave him away to be brought up by his grandmother. So he felt like a child with no parents.

This kind of contingency has all kinds of deep effects. I don't think that Descartes's mechanical theory of the passions as by-products of physiology would appear plausible to somebody who hadn't been robbed of the basis for much emotional development by losing his mother. I say this not in any kind of cheap reductionistic way, but with a sense of seeking to feel my way inside how his thought came to develop the way it did.

*Schopenhauer saw life as a lesson we haven't asked for. Let's discuss this lesson.*

If it comes down to the choice, I'd rather be kind than clever. I don't let myself be cleverer than is compatible with being as kind as I know how.

I wasn't always like that, but that's what one comes to at the age of seventy.

*You look much younger.*

Maybe I've succeeded in being kind rather than clever for longer than I think.

I think I've been very fortunate. The scholarly life is tremendously advantaged. I'm amazed that people have been prepared to support this habit of mine. I feel like Gibbon in that wonderful story in which he goes to the royal library at Windsor to present George III with his most recent volume of *The Decline and Fall of the Roman Empire*. George III, who was a notoriously bad conversationalist, feels he has to say something to Gibbon, and so, Gibbon having paid his respects, the king says to him, "Another damn fat thick square book. Always scribble, scribble, scribble, eh, Mr. Gibbon?" Sometimes I feel this about myself, always scribble, scribble, scribble. And the world has let me do it. If I hadn't been allowed to go my own way, it would have been a different story. If I'm ashamed of anything, it's that I really have taught for the sake of buying the time to write. Although other people say I'm not a bad teacher, I've never felt this myself, because in the last resort I was always trying to think my way back to answering the questions that first arose out of my relationship with my father and subsequently out of my relation to my education. Fortunately, other people have been prepared to listen to the things I had to say over the years.

*What question or paradox fascinates you the most at the moment?*

Well, I think for me the central question is still the question about what we should be doing rather that what we should be thinking.

*Is this another expression of the boredom you feel about philosophy? That is to say, philosophers can answer many questions, but they can't offer us any real solutions for something like grief or cruelty, or for how we can behave in a different way either individually or collectively.*

I do feel a certain impatience with many of my philosophical colleagues, because they see no other possibility besides their way of doing philosophy. There was a wonderful conversation I heard repeated recently. Allegedly Alisdair MacIntyre visited Magdalen College, Oxford, and had dinner with Peter Strawson there. It's said that at a certain point in the evening Peter Strawson turned to MacIntyre and said, "The trouble with you, Alisdair, is you're interested in too many different kinds of things." Now, for me, you can't be interested in too many different kinds of things. I feel that as a philosopher you can't do your job unless you're prepared to be interested in anything it takes to throw light on the central questions we're concerned with. It seems to me that

209

my philosophical colleagues remain stuck in continually discussing questions that are no longer the active questions for anyone who's read enough, whether it's physics and biochemistry and evolutionary biology, on the one hand, or clinical medicine, law, or psychotherapy, on the other hand. Unless you're prepared to take a serious interest in how philosophy feeds into and feeds from these other subjects, you're just impoverishing yourself.

# PART II

# THE

# ROUNDTABLE

## AN ATTEMPT AT SYMBIOSIS

*We wonder, ever wonder why we find us here.*
Thomas Hardy

I find it deeply mysterious: you arrange to meet six people on a day months ahead, people who live in very different parts of the globe, and on the appointed day they wander in through the door at exactly ten o'clock, as if stepping into the office. Nobody has died in the meantime. And everybody looks at me expectantly: "OK, here we are. What's up, doc?"

I gaze at them in bewilderment. Once, on a languid summer night, I had had a ridiculous daydream that they would one day sit around one table. Now here they are.

Oliver Sacks and Stephen Jay Gould look as if they're on their way to a funeral: conservative black suits. The others, too, except Dennett, wear a suit and tie. So there they sit:

The timid, strange Freeman Dyson.

The quick-witted, ever-smiling Stephen Jay Gould.

The belligerent, energetic Daniel C. Dennett.

The thoughtful, dreamy Oliver Sacks.

The formal, precisely formulating Rupert Sheldrake.

The well-mannered *homo universalis* Stephen Toulmin.

Nobody has any idea what this discussion will bring—who will fall silent, who will carry off the laurels, whether the judgments they voiced about each other when I talked to them individually will be brought into the open or covered up.

I expect that virtually no one will take Rupert Sheldrake seriously. Dennett's ideas are declared to be outdated by at least two others, while he believes himself to be a radical. Dennett believes that all five others are romantics, who recoil from the consequences of a materialist view of life. Oliver Sacks expects that a reconciliation with Dennett will be impossible. Sheldrake expects a madhouse of six overblown egos. Dyson has warned me that the six participants may have considerable differences of opinion, but will cover them up once they're together. Stephen Jay Gould expects a good discussion ("Why else would I have participated?") but doesn't understand why I have invited Rupert Sheldrake to take part. Oliver Sacks is the most phlegmatic: "Whatever happens, it will be fascinating."

Having talked to each of the men individually, I lost any idea of what to expect. I looked at the faces around the table and was astonished once more that they were there; ten hours later I realized that there had really been an attempt at symbiosis. Seated at a nineteenth-century table, the men searched for consensus rather than for differences. As I had hoped long ago.

In the next few days I was inundated with questions from people who knew about the forum.

"Was the atmosphere tense?"

"Did they go for the jugular?"

"Did anybody walk out?"

"When did they start fighting?"

I had to disappoint them all.

"So it was boring, then?"

Well, if it's boring that people are well behaved, if it's boring that they confront each other with arguments rather than rancor, if it's boring that people talk about each other's ideas rather than their characters, if it's boring that people search for consensus rather than differences, if it's boring that people respect each other despite totally divergent views on life, then the conference was almost impressively boring.

■

*Stephen Jay Gould, one of the reasons for you to participate in this project was that you were dying to meet Oliver Sacks.*

GOULD: Well, we only live two hundred miles apart, in Boston and New York, but you never meet someone when it's easy, so you have to wait for a circumstance like this. The main reason, aside from the fact that ever since someone gave me *Awakenings* I've regarded Oliver Sacks as the greatest writer and person of insight about case studies of human medical histories, I feel in a deeper sense he's trying to do exactly what I'm trying to do in science—namely, to broaden its definitional bounds, so we no longer see science only in the light of that set of techniques that comes from the quantitative disciplines of physics, chemistry, and such. Those disciplines see science as ultimately simplification, generalization, and pure experiment. They ban from the realm of science those explanations of complex individualities that are what make up history.

I'm a paleontologist, I study historical sequences through time. There are classical scientific generalities to be found, such as the recurrent causes of mass extinctions, but so much of life's history is the narrative of the highly contingent, individual, improbable events that occur, that are unpredictable before they happen but are eminently explainable afterwards, if the evidence is good enough, and that therefore fall into the domain of science. When I read Oliver's case studies of human beings, I think he is making the same point: that the case study not only is a device of literature—though when done well it's good literature—but in fact is the classical mode of the medical science that we've lost because we've gotten a model that insists more on predictability.

Medicine is not even seen as science and I think Oliver has tried quite explicitly to bring back into the domain of science this basically natural history activity of the individual case study, which is essential also in clinical treatment. People don't fit into categories entirely, they have their ontogenies that are contingent and complex and unrepeatable, though explainable, in the same way that organisms have their phylogenies that fall into the same explanatory modes.

*Oliver, I remember your saying about Stephen Jay Gould, "I think of him as a brother." What kind of brother is he?*

**SACKS:** Well, I think Stephen's already said quite a lot about the sense of parallelism which we feel and which perhaps our work is about. As a physician, I'm forced always to deal with the particular. The patient says, "Look at me. I'm not a syndrome, I'm a particular person, living my life under these conditions," but equally I am drawn to theory. There seems to me an odd, sometimes uneasy tension between the two of them. But my background, perhaps like Stephen's, is one of somewhat old-fashioned natural history, and in particular the grand narratives of the last century, which perhaps weren't too informed scientifically but were enormously rich in detail and suggestion. I think this sort of narrative has become rare in medicine in the present century.

My own background originally was partly in the hard sciences, and I've had to deal with a sense of uncertainty as to whether the descriptive, narrative mode can rank as science at all. I now think it can, but in some sense I think I cringed under the might of the physical model.

213

**DENNETT:** Don't you think it's important to have a theory in order to do the narrative well? That is, don't you think that a narrator needs to have theoretical axes to grind?

**SACKS:** Well, yes and no. I mean, Darwin always said you can't be a good observer unless you're a good theorist. But then maybe theory is always implicit in narrative. If it's explicit, I think it can be worrying. I'm thinking of a particular example in neurology. Sir William Gowers, the great descriptive neurologist in the last century, on several occasions described a very elaborate attack of epilepsy. First of all, the patient became conscious of the beating of his heart, then of two lights pulsing and drawing nearer, and then suddenly of a vision of an old woman in a brown dress, who offered him something with the smell of tonka beans. And then he lost consciousness. But what's interesting is that when Gowers described the seizure in 1881, he was in a sort of theoretical passion, under the strong influence of research science. When he redescribed it in 1904, he wasn't. The two descriptions are quite different. One wonders which is the more accurate one, the one he wrote in a state of theoretical animus or the one he wrote when he was sort of unbuttoned. I think the latter one is probably the more correct, and I think the first one is deformed by theoretical presupposition.

**DENNETT:** But to return to Darwin's point, if you don't have a theory at all, you're not going to know what you're looking at unless you're extremely lucky or an utterly inspired genius.

**SACKS:** Stephen, you'd be the person to tell us. Is Darwin's book on barnacles different in tone from his book on orchids, with the pre-imposed theoretical framework?

**GOULD:** Yes, it is, but I don't think it is in the sense of pre-imposed theoretical framework. The barnacle book—four monographs, two on fossils, two on modern barnacles—is written in the mode of the taxonomic monograph. He still felt that he had to establish credentials before publishing *The Origin of Species*. Yet when you go through its details, he's asking so many questions. He discovers, for example, minute males that are in a sense attached to the females, forming almost a sexual pair, and he wonders how they got there.

The orchid book, the first book he wrote after *The Origin of Species*, is disarming, and I think consciously so. It has this odd title, *On the Various Contrivances by Means of Which British Orchids Are Fertilized by Insects*. Yet it's a mordant satire, as Giesling showed. Orchids are very complexly adapted to pollination by insects. Yet Darwin shows that these orchids are not all gorgeously designed, as they might have been if they'd been done from scratch, but jury-rigged "contraptions," he says in one place, because they must be the altered parts of ordinary flowers that are fit for other purposes. And so that book

214

really is an explicit evolutionary treatise, though a subtle one. Yes, they're different books, but I would say that even the barnacle work is more theoretically informed than Darwin himself might have recognized.

*Oliver, you said in New York, "When I'm at the roundtable, I'd like to know the form of passion in my colleagues there." I wonder what the passion is with the philosophers.*

TOULMIN: My passion? I think one of the worst things about the intellectual world is that people are continually being snowed. I'm a kind of Pyrrhonist emancipator. I think the important thing is to give everybody as much elbow room as they're entitled to and not to make them think they have to believe things where there isn't sufficient reason. I think this is really what makes me tick ultimately. I've hated so much having things imposed on me that I had not come to feel convinced of.

*You're talking about your father.*

TOULMIN: I'm also talking about my father. But I feel deep indignation toward tyranny of all kinds, intellectual tyranny as much as political tyranny.

DENNETT: My passion is a little different. You use the word "emancipator," and essentially that's my passion too, because what I see, particularly in philosophy, is an occupational hazard. Philosophers would like to work the way mathematicians work, purely a priori. When they do this in the various realms of philosophy, they ask themselves, "Is such-and-such a thing possible?" Then they try to imagine it and they say, "Well, I can't conceive of that. If I can't conceive of it, then maybe it's inconceivable." And then they move from their own inability to conceive of something to a judgment that it's impossible. All too often in the history of philosophy these apparent insights into necessity have actually been failures of imagination.

I like to think of my role as an imagination stretcher, showing people that more things are possible than they first think, and that they shouldn't be so ready to dismiss a large area of actual possibility just because they can't conceive of it. People respond to my theory of consciousness, for instance, by saying, "That's all very interesting, but that's not the way it is with me. My mind is entirely . . ." They can't believe that I'm actually talking about the very phenomenon they know so intimately on the inside. I may be right or wrong, but that's what I intend to be offering theory of, and it's fascinating to me that some people just are unable to entertain the hypothesis that this might be true.

*Freeman Dyson, everybody is a philosopher, isn't he? What about your passion?*

DYSON: No, I don't consider myself a philosopher. I just came from three days of hard science, from a conference in which all the experts from all over the world in the field of gamma ray astronomy gathered together in one room. And it's exactly like paleontology: we're looking at the past and we're seeing marvelous things that we don't understand at all. And it's mostly case histories. I enjoy this tremendously and I think it has something to say. Even in the hardest of science, theories don't actually help a great deal. The world is much stranger than we imagined.

**TOULMIN:** Even in quite easy parts of physics. For instance, we know what makes gases gaseous and we know what makes solids solid, but we're still quite rocky on the question of what makes liquids liquid. I think it's important that people understand that the things we don't understand include some of the most elementary, everyday things.

**DYSON:** In fact, particularly those. If you look at almost anything that's plainly obvious and look at it in detail, you find we don't understand it.

*Rupert, what's your passion?*

**SHELDRAKE:** I suppose my passion is really the sense of the richness and power of life, of animals and plants and people. And indeed of the whole cosmic evolutionary process. As a child, I was fascinated by plants and animals, and I kept pets and collected plants and so on. From the earliest stage I knew I wanted to be a biologist. I loved making these relationships with animals and plants, but as I studied biology, I learned that they were just inanimate machines and that they'd all evolved by blind chance. It was unscientific to form any personal relationship with them. All qualities should be expelled in favor of quantities. I found this narrow, dogmatic, cramping style of science more and more restrictive. Then one day in the biochemistry department at Cambridge, I saw one of those metabolic wall charts, with all the biochemical reactions of the body on them, and someone had written across the top, "Know thyself." And that drove home to me quite clearly the gulf between conventional biochemistry and biology, which I knew pretty well. I was in an emotional turmoil at the time, I was in love, there were some beautiful plants I liked in the garden of my college in town at Cambridge, and it just seemed so unrelated. This gave me the sense that science as we know it, especially biology, has got itself in this tiny, narrow, cramped way of trying to cram life into this terribly narrow thing. There's so much more there. So my passion is to find ways of thinking about life scientifically still, but no longer in this theoretical straitjacket.

*OK, we'll see if you're a scientist or whether the others disagree. Stephen Jay Gould, your passion is love for all the forms of life, like Oliver Sacks?*

**GOULD:** Well, passion means suffering—I can't forget the original etymology.

*Oh, it's a romantic question, I'm sorry.*

GOULD: Well, that's important. You don't really get at things unless you invest that kind of devotion, the kind that implies some suffering, if only because you have to cast off other things that you very much like to do. If I had a better voice, I'd probably be singing Wotan today, and if I had better bodily skills, I would have played professional baseball. I ended up doing what I do because of the various passions that I had as a child. Fortunately, I had skills in one of the areas that excited my interest, and that was paleontology—unlike baseball and opera. When I saw the skeleton of a tyrannosaurus when I was five, I found it thrilling in that ultimate childlike sense of being absolutely overwhelmed. Nothing rare about being a childhood dinosaur nut. What's rare is to stick with it. I think the reason I stuck with dinosaurs is that when I was ten or eleven I learned evolutionary theory, which I found thrilling because it was that wonderful mixture of science and narrative.

*Oliver, your passions in life?*

SACKS: Well, as with all of us, I suppose, they've been a bit divided. For example, last week I was at CERN, and a few months ago I went to Fermilab. One part of me likes to look at that sort of big science. But I think my epiphany was seeing the periodic table in the science museum in London when I was ten or eleven. And after a somewhat disturbed period in the war when I was evacuated, like so many kids in England, I loved the sense of stability and security and constancy there in the family relationships of the elements.

My first passion was collecting the elements. I had a lot of elements, and those I didn't have physically I tried to appropriate mentally. I wrote down all their qualities and I thought of them as friends, although I guess the relation wasn't too mutual. The first bit of thinking I ever did was to work out the properties of some of the missing elements. I didn't know it had been done before, but I was tantalized by the blank spaces on the table, and that gave me some sense of the coherence of nature and the fact that it wouldn't play a dirty trick on one. But my background was more biological and medical, since both of my parents were doctors, trained in neurology. The house was full of clinical stories and anecdotes, and I'm afraid sometimes clinical specimens. When I was about fourteen or fifteen my passion moved to that. About that time the modern synthesis came out, and I found this synthesis of evolution and genetic mechanisms thrilling. I loved physics and then I loved chemistry and then I loved zoology. I still like wearing the banana slugs of Santa Cruz on my tie. And I still like to go scuba diving at the Great Barrier Reef. If I weren't a neurologist, I'd be a botanist.

Rather slowly and reluctantly and belatedly, I finally got to patients and people. Now I have a strong feeling of inevitability about that, but I still enjoy my excursions to Cape Canaveral or CERN or the Great Barrier Reef. I once thought in terms of some overarching theory. I struggled through Russell and Whitehead at one point, and wondered whether one might have a *principia symbolica,* which would be about being human. This paradox of the theory of the particular has always been in me somehow.

*My proposal is to be chronological in our discussion, starting from the first beginning of life and . . .*

SHELDRAKE: Why not the beginning of the universe? If we're going to think big, we might as well think really big.

*Well, why not? OK, if we raise childish questions . . . Daddy, why is the grass green, why is the sky blue, why does the moon have phases? Stephen, why not this one: What was there before the Big Bang?*

TOULMIN: Well, if there was anything before the Big Bang . . . We don't know whether the Big Bang was the beginning of time or whether it's one of a sequence of events in time. That question is already a stinker. That's going to keep us going all day.

*Gentlemen, what was there before the Big Bang? A kind of Platonic archetype? Nothing? Or God?*

GOULD: It's not a question we can take up. Anything you say is marginally expressive of a whole set of personal biases that it would take hours on the couch to unravel.

DENNETT: And it may not even be a well-formed question, which I think was Stephen Toulmin's point. Can you use the word "before" in that context? It may be simply an inappropriate use of the word.

TOULMIN: Unfortunately, we don't know whether it is or not. We can only show that the question, whether it's well formed or ill formed, is at the moment undecidable.

SHELDRAKE: But it's a very profound and important question for science. My own starting point is that if we take evolution as a theory referring only to life, we're dealing with a very, very narrow section of a cosmic evolutionary process. And when we actually take the view of the Big Bang, assuming there was one . . . Most scientists refuse to discuss metaphysical questions and certainly don't want to have God in the picture at all. In fact, there's an implicit assumption throughout the whole of science that all the laws of nature are fixed and that they were all there at the moment of the Big Bang. It's present in the implicit assumption that any experiment ought to be repeatable anywhere, anytime, and that the laws of nature are the same everywhere, at all times and in all places.

**DYSON:** That's really not so. That's something we are testing all the time.

**SHELDRAKE:** I've not met anyone testing it. Can you tell me how you're testing it?

**DYSON:** Well, by looking at these ancient objects in the sky and verifying whether their spectra follow the same laws as the ones down here. We have very direct knowledge of things that were going on at only one-quarter of the age of the universe.

**DENNETT:** Can you be sure that the speed of light is constant, for instance? In order to arrive at any judgments about these early events?

**DYSON:** You can compare the things you observe with things that happen nowadays, and so far, the evidence is very strong that they behave the same way. But that's by no means taken for granted. In fact, it's one of the interesting open questions.

**SHELDRAKE:** But so much of it is circular. I've recently been looking into the question of whether the constants of nature *are* constant. Eddington and Dirac suggested that the gravitational constant changes with time, but even then, they assume there's a constant law governing its change. But many of the arguments for the constancy of constants depend on assuming that they or at least other constants are constant in order to do calculations. So there's a great deal of circularity.

**DYSON:** No, that's not so. I've written several papers about this, so I should know. It's really not true that the arguments are circular. You're testing directly the notion that the laws are constant. There are very few really good tests, but such as they are, they've always turned out negative. For example, the fine structure of the lines in the quasar. When you look at the fine structure of carbon at one-quarter of the age of the universe, it turns out to look exactly the same as it does now.

**SHELDRAKE:** I think it's perfectly possible that the behavior of carbon hasn't changed for three-quarters of the age of the universe, but since I think the regularities of nature are more like habits, I would have said that's a habit built up much earlier on, and over time they get pretty constant.

**DYSON:** That's a perfectly sensible hypothesis. We don't get back that far, of course.

**SHELDRAKE:** But when we come to the nature of living organisms on the earth, to jump from the constancy of spectral lines in carbon in quasars to a universal fixity of all natural law is obviously a big jump. Many people make it. I'm not saying you make it, but I find that among my colleagues it's a deeply implicit assumption which is never even questioned. And it seems to me that if we have an evolutionary universe, the evolution of the regularities of nature is implied. There is a kind of overhang from a Platonic, static, or changeless universe of eternal laws, like Platonic forms or ideas. Then we've had an evolutionary universe, which physics resisted for decades, until the 1960s or so, when it finally came in. We now have a radically evolutionary universe, but the old implicit assumption of fixed laws of nature has stayed in place in the thinking of most scientists.

GOULD: But I would reject your view that change in them was implied by the evolutionary universe. It's testable, it could be so, but I happen to disagree with you that it is so. Your very idiosyncratic view on that is exciting and needs more tests, but evolutionary theory in biology is about the history of contingent change of organisms, and there is nothing unsensible about the view that that change should operate under certain regularities about modes of inheritance and other so-called natural laws. It is not implied a priori that those laws should alter as the organisms alter.

SHELDRAKE: Well, this is a different question. Your very strong case for contingency in evolutionary history leaves open the question of how inheritance works. It seems to me that the answer to the question of whether the universe is being made up as it goes along, in some sense, is much more radically evolutionary than you think.

GOULD: I don't disagree that your question is sensible, but your preferred solution is not implied by the nature of things.

TOULMIN: You raise this question of the constancy of laws of nature. It does seem to me that the attitude adopted by your friends among the scientists whom you criticize is crucial. I mean, one can be dogmatic about this or one can simply treat this as a rebuttable presumption. Functionally speaking, so to say, assumptions about the constancy of laws in nature are rebuttable presumptions, and in some cases matters have come to light which have rebutted the presumptions, so we no longer assume that the geological structure of the earth must always have been as it was at the creation, which Newton undoubtably assumed.

GOULD: That's narration, not lawlike behavior.

TOULMIN: Well, no, but at the end of the seventeenth century and very early decades of the eighteenth century, it was taken for granted that a lot of things had been so ever since the creation. And all of that has been chipped away. We still are left with a kind of general presumption that those laws of nature which haven't yet proved to be variable can be presumed to be fixed. We also have some epistemological reasons that people like Poincaré are good at analyzing—namely, that we need some kind of set of presuppositions even to be able to construct coherent theories at all. So we're probably never going to get rid of all these presumptions, if only because some of them are used to establish the vocabulary in which we're able to give a physical account of the world. I agree with you that there are plenty of scientists who still go on saying in a rather dogmatic tone of voice that of course laws of nature are constant, but I think you're exaggerating this particular epidemic of dogmatism.

**DENNETT:** Rupert, I'm sure you must have been asked this question many times, but if you're putting forward a theory where the regularities exhibited by carbon atoms, say, are really just habitual, doesn't that presuppose a sort of law of habit? Why should habits behave the same from the Big Bang to the present? Aren't you yourself actually presupposing a regularity, which you then use as the basis to explain these other regularities?

**SHELDRAKE:** I'd say that there's a principle of habit in nature, but without specific content. The law would simply be that self-organizing patterns become more probable through repetition, but it wouldn't say which self-organizing principles come into being. I've applied a radical contingency that Steve emphasizes in "Life to the Whole of Nature."

**DENNETT:** I'd love to believe your revolutionary view, because it's just so wonderfully iconoclastic, but I still have this suspicion that there's something of false allure to it. If you look at explanations of habit, such as there are, they all seem, like the standard assumptions about evolutionary theory itself, to presuppose a basic set of assumptions about physical laws of one sort or another. Then one explains the laying down of habits on that basis. Whether one talks about grooves being worn in soft plains or strengthened connections or something like that, one has a mechanical model, which itself presupposes the laws of physics. You seem to be sort of helping yourself to the idea of habit and making it fundamental, when insofar as we understand what habits are, we understand them against one background or another of immutable mechanical law.

**SHELDRAKE:** Well, it depends who understands them that way. The question of habit in biology is interpreted in the current mechanistic paradigm in terms of some kind of changes in nerve connections or whatever. These are all assumptions, so one can say here's a theory of habit—not a very well proven one—and that indeed assumes constant mechanical laws. But that's exactly what I'm challenging. I think habit is a much deeper and more important principle in nature than we usually think. Law is the preferred metaphor in science—an extremely anthropocentric metaphor based on human laws, which in fact do evolve, of course.

**GOULD:** Animal isn't anthropocentric?

**SHELDRAKE:** No, because animals have habits. Animals don't have laws. Only human beings have laws, so I would say the metaphor of law is much more anthropocentric than the metaphor of habits.

221

**TOULMIN:** But if you look at this historically, it's not anthropocentric but theocentric. You may say that when the idea of constant laws was seriously emphasized in the sciences, which wasn't until well into the seventeenth century, it was part of a particular theological vision of the universe. What's interesting is your choice of the word. I don't know if you've looked up Aquinas on the subject of *habitus*, but I suspect that you have a more respectable intellectual ancestry than you'd like to believe.

**SHELDRAKE:** I've nothing against Aquinas, I'm in favor of him.

**TOULMIN:** Fine, because what we're interested in understanding is a good part of the Aristotelian tradition, which was thrown into the shade as a result of this rather unhappy overemphasis on the particular theological model that especially the Protestant natural scientists thought was an indispensable part of their mission to get across. It's interesting how late people came to this conviction that the laws of nature were constant. There was absolute doubt about it before about the middle of the seventeenth century. One reads Sir Thomas Brown on how the entire universe is in decay, how the greater part of time has gone, what is to come, and how we may expect the present dispensation to be dissolved any day now. In some ways the conviction that the laws of nature were going to continue working was also part of the new humanistic vision. Until you were prepared to believe that the universe was capable of going on for thousands of millions of years in the future, you were open to these kinds of apocalyptic ideas that it was all going to fall apart, because there wasn't anything like laws of nature to sustain our conviction that the thing would keep going.

**GOULD:** Or if there were laws, they were only for that short period of a few thousand years between the divine creation and the coming suspension of those laws for the end of things.

**SHELDRAKE:** I agree with you entirely. The idea of eternal laws of nature is a theological-mechanistic-scientific seventeenth-century mixture, and now that the mind of God has been dissolved from the world machine, it's left free-floating in the minds of most scientists.

**TOULMIN:** Yes, but I think Steve hinted at something very interesting by implication—that, thinking jurisprudentially, the laws of nature as they were conceived in the seventeenth century were not like medieval natural law. They were the positive law that God had imposed on the universe at the creation, which he was at liberty to suspend and presumably would suspend when he decided to wind it up, or when things had got to the point at which you could have the new Jerusalem.

**DENNETT:** Rupert, I want to see just how radical your thesis is. In your view, do right triangles just gradually acquire the habit of having the square of their hypotenuses be equal to the sum of the squares on the sides? Is pi just a habitual ratio between the circumference and the diameter?

**SHELDRAKE:** Well, this is a big question, isn't it? Is mathematics constructed or is it discovered? It's a huge philosophical question and it's not one that I'm terribly concerned with myself. I don't think there are many right triangles in nature, you see. We're dealing with the history of human mathematics. It's very easy for mathematicians to be Platonists, to assume that what they discover is somehow a kind of eternal, self-subsistent realm of truth. This is where it all started— Pythagoras and the Pythagorean school getting this vision of eternal maths, and then Plato getting eternal ideas, then mathematicians rediscovering a sense of an eternal realm of natural law of a mathematical kind. This is the persuasive basis behind the whole thing, this argument about triangles, but I'm not very interested in right triangles and pi. I'm more interested in nature as we observe it rather than mathematical theories per se.

**DENNETT:** Scientists who want to go on believing in timeless regularities at least have one other foundation on which to place this belief. Now that they've abandoned an eternal God, they can say, "Well, it's just like mathematical truth, really."

**SHELDRAKE:** Absolutely, I totally agree. That's the most persuasive argument in favor of it. But even in the philosophy of mathematics, it's not an undisputed position. There are those who think mathematics is a construction rather than an eternal self-subsistent realm of ideas.

**DENNETT:** Yes, but those who think it's a construction don't think it's an evolving construction, at least not in your sense of the word.

**SHELDRAKE:** I think they do, at least some of the ones I know do. They'd say, for example, the realm of chaos and fractal mathematics is evolving right now, and it's evolved because of computers. I'm sure you like that point about it: computers have made this kind of modeling possible. You just couldn't visualize these mathematical realms before. Now, are we just discovering new realms of maths that were already there, or inventing new realms because we've got the techniques to visualize these things? I don't have a strong opinion one way or the other, but I'm more inclined to the invention than the discovery of Euler.

**SACKS:** I wonder whether some of the secret history or secret agenda of some of this is indeed theological. I wonder about some of our own religious propensities in childhood. But, in particular, listening to some of this conversation, I'm reminded of some of the tensions in Jewish theology between the rabbinical God, who is a body of law, fixed and immutable, and the caballistic God, who is an organism and who evolves. In some sense there's a change in the air between the vision of the universe as static and principled and the universe as an organism.

Certainly in adolescence I originally believed in the static, Platonic vision of the universe in the periodic table. Many Hebrew prayers end with *leolam wa'ed*, forever and ever. The wish that things should be the same forever and ever is very attractive, especially after a sort of disturbed, unstable childhood. Later the feeling of contingency—and, as you say, radical contingency—rushed in on me, but this disposed me to look for laws of change and not changing laws.

**TOULMIN:** I think what Oliver said is very interesting. There is this kind of standing tension within the Jewish tradition. It's a tension that still exists. There's a famous controversy of only about five years ago between J. David Bleich and Rabbi Gordis about whether the Torah, the system of laws, is open to reinterpretation. Gordis—who, as I understand, is Conservative if not Reformed—was pleading for reinterpretation, to which David Bleich's reply was: "In that case, your God is a different God from my God." I suspect that the possibility of putting either of these interpretations on the basic presumptions is one we're not going to argue away. We're not going to be able to say one of these can be shown to be superior to the other. Beyond a certain point it becomes a matter of temperamental difference. The J. David Bleichs of the world are going to continue to hang on with rigor to positions that other people want to be more flexible about.

**SHELDRAKE:** Steve, surely the idea of time as an arrow implies a directional movement or at least a process.

**GOULD:** There are clearly directional processes, at least in the history of the earth. Historically the discovery of them was very important. At least in British and American geology, Charles Lyell's vision had been canonical—namely, of an earth in steady state, in which there was change but no directionality. Nonetheless, the validation of vectorial properties to time doesn't presuppose anyone in favor of directionality and changing values to the constants of nature's laws. Maybe those laws are set up such that time's directionality would be implied, as has always been stated of the second law of thermodynamics.

**TOULMIN:** A signpost doesn't have to be moving itself. A signpost defines an option to move in a particular direction.

**SHELDRAKE:** As Freeman will know much better than any of the others, the cosmological arrow of time surely is given by the expansion of the universe. Wouldn't you say that was the underlying arrow of the evolutionary process?

**DYSON:** Well, we really don't know. In the hard sciences we mostly talk about models rather than laws. And if you talk to the people who are working on foundations of mathematics, they also talk about models. It's certainly true of physics and astronomy in particular that a law is just a model that we've got used to.

TOULMIN: That we're habituated to.

DYSON: Yes. There is no sharp distinction between models and laws, I would say.

SHELDRAKE: But even so, cosmically speaking there are several time's arrows, aren't there, but one of them is the cosmological expansion, which is a kind of driving arrow for the whole cosmic evolutionary process. Wouldn't you say that?

DYSON: Yes, but it's very unclear whether that's all there is. There are other kinds of asymmetries in time, which are necessarily connected with that. And it still is very much an open question. You have roughly three types of asymmetry in time—the cosmological one, the thermodynamic one, and the basic violation of time reversal in the particle interactions. And the three don't appear to be closely connected. But we still have a great deal to learn, obviously.

*Freeman, you've written about your image of a "Socinian" God, a God who evolves along with the universe. Our consciousness would be a contribution to him and his growth.*

DYSON: It's an image that I took from a recent conversation. I thought it was an important idea, but it's not my idea.

SHELDRAKE: This question of the evolutionary nature of God is a big issue in Christian as well as Jewish theology. There's a whole school of evolutionary or process theologians who are trying to get away from the idea of God as totally fixed, and have an evolutionary dimension to God within the evolutionary process.

GOULD: Or they feel forced into such a view. He's such a nasty man in the early books.

TOULMIN: I'd hate to believe he was still like that.

SHELDRAKE: Well, very few gods are just purely loving, they always have this negative or destructive quality. But you could say they are forced into the evolutionary view by an evolutionary cosmology in the same way as some seventeenth-century theologians thought they could conceive of God as the maker of eternal laws of nature, kind of Newtonist laws and that kind of thing. So theology and science interact continuously.

SACKS: There's an ironic twist, because of course the mind of God as conceived by Newton was an immutable, boundless, structureless sensorium, while the whole point of Paul Davies's *Cosmic Blueprint* is that there is no blueprint, but that the universe organizes or generates or creates itself continually, though I think not in an unlawlike manner.

**SHELDRAKE:** Well, Paul Davies is a neodeist. He holds this eighteenth-century view that God sets all the laws of nature and starts the whole thing off. So you only need God to create it. Both Paul Davies and Stephen Hawking, *A Brief History of Time,* end up with a kind of neodeism, it seems to me: if not God, then something fine-tunes all the constants of nature, so we get just this kind of universe.

**DENNETT:** Something bothers me about the direction we're going here, as a professional philosopher among people with philosophical ambitions. I sometimes get the sense that scientists, when they become amateur philosophers, think that different rules apply. One of my philosophical colleagues, Ronny D'Souza, reviewing a book on philosophical theology recently, described it as intellectual tennis without a net. Let's put some nets up, please! . . . I realize, as I say these words, "There's the uptight philosopher who doesn't have his own discipline trying to impose discipline in these areas." It's a galling stereotype, but there's a lot of truth in it.

**GOULD:** I think you're right in this case, we should discuss things we can answer.

**DENNETT:** My feelings exactly. And that's why I much prefer that we start with a set of presumptive nets that have apparently done some pretty good work, and just play as hard as we can with those nets. And when we can't play any more with those nets, we'll replace one of them.

**SHELDRAKE:** This is a very, very conservative strategy.

**DENNETT:** Absolutely right.

**SHELDRAKE:** You adopt it, Steve adopts it. But if one's ever going to find new models of reality in a radical way, one has to look at where the nets are and what they are. And your rejection of metaphysics is, I think, a way of avoiding questions you don't want to discuss.

**GOULD:** I don't avoid them, Rupert. Each of us has to have a personal metaphysics. There are questions that are formally unanswerable on which nonetheless every individual must take a position in order to integrate various pieces of his life. We're not going to answer your big metaphysical questions—they have no answers. There's a lot else we can discuss that's interesting, that's all.

**SHELDRAKE:** You do it all the time. Radical contingency is one of your great slogans. And radical contingency, in the way you portray it, seems to other people rather like Providence.

**GOULD:** Look, we can talk about it. I can make you a proposal about where I think it exists and you can tell me why you think it doesn't. But if you want to discuss the nature of God's change through time, we've got to define what he/she/it is. That'll take forever, it's not gonna go anywhere.

**SHELDRAKE:** All right, but the fact is that theological and metaphysical questions are bound up with science. The fact is that the basic questions as to whether the regularities of nature evolve are scientific questions — they can be tested.

**TOULMIN:** Hang on a moment, Rupert. There's a very important point I remember Peter Medawar making. One of the great things that you have to learn if you want to become a good squash player is to find players to play against who are just a little bit better than you. In that way you get just a little bit better. If you spend your whole time playing against people who are far better than you, you'll never improve because you'll lose all your games. Now, Peter made the same point à propos of some of his biological colleagues who had a great talent for choosing questions that were for the time being insoluble. He said they were often very talented, but they just didn't have an eye for what was within reach. When he himself was going to become a research student in Oxford, he was much suborned by people who wanted him to go into embryology, and he knew in his heart of hearts that at that stage we weren't ready to deal with the basic problems of embryology. So he went into immunology, which *was* manageable. And of course once the molecular biology story came on the scene, it was apparent why he'd been right all along to say that embryology was out of reach.

It does seem to me that the questions you want us to ask and answer first are questions that are perennially out of reach, or rather, you insist on formulating them in such an overly general way that some part of them is going to remain out of reach. Whereas what Steve Gould wants us to do is to let us specify what this question about constancy would amount to in a particular case, where there's some hope of dealing with it in a way that's going to lead to some kind of answer.

This is a way of evading it. For instance, in the Middle Ages many people interested in natural philosophy thought that we should try to find a theory of change, kinesis or *metabolē*, you know, an answer to the question "What is the nature of change as such?" And they were very indignant when others wanted to focus on locomotion rather than change in general. We know now that the only way of finding out about change is to look at the different ways in which different kinds of things change.

So I just beg you to ask yourself whether you aren't asking us . . . You know, there's the father who says to the child, "Fetch that orange from off the mantelshelf," and when the child takes it and brings it to him he says, "No, this orange is no longer the orange on the mantelshelf." There are ways in which a problem can be forcibly made insoluble.

SHELDRAKE: I'm not trying to do that, I'm trying to set up a testable theory.

TOULMIN: Yeah, but it shouldn't be overgeneral in its initial mode of formulation. Maybe the questions you quite rightly want to have answered together can be answered piecemeal, by taking them one step at a time, looking at a lot of different cases, and seeing whether, after we've been working at it for two or three hundred years, we're in a position at last to generalize. Does it seem to you an unfair move I'm making.

SHELDRAKE: Oh, yes, absolutely. It sounds just like your father, saying it and illustrating it with questions.

TOULMIN: He didn't even realize there was a question. There was only him and the truth.

SHELDRAKE: All right, you're not saying that, then. I think you can ask it in a variety of ways and test it in a variety of ways. For example, one of my predictions is that the melting points of new chemical compounds should increase for awhile when you first make them. The melting points are not physical constants. The usual assumption is that they are. You can test this theory in the realm of chemistry. Do melting points of new compounds change? They do. There's a lot of empirical evidence for it. Then chemists come along and say, "It's got nothing to do with habits in nature. People get better at making purer compounds, which have higher melting points." Then you say, "How do you know they're purer compounds?" and they say, "They must be purer because they have higher melting points." So here's one example of an empirical question one can actually get to grips with, where these issues can be focused and asked in a scientific way.

DENNETT: Except, as you point out yourself, that the problem with this as an empirical issue is that there are alternative explanations, and it's very hard to see how you're going to rule them out. One of the things that strikes me as wonderfully quixotic about your revolution is that you offer revolutionary explanations even of things that we have pretty good explanations for. Like evolution by natural selection. You want to replace that, and you want to replace accounts of learning, you want to replace sort of mundane regularities that we think we have pretty good physical explanations for. If you could point to one really baffling mystery that nobody has a clue how to deal with, and show how your revolutionary theory dealt with that, that would be very impressive.

**SHELDRAKE:** I think there are many baffling mysteries in biology. Morphogenesis is one of them. How do organisms, how do embryos develop? Something you said Medawar avoided because he thought it was not possible to solve. I think he was wrong. I think that Waddington, who was one of his opponents, was a broader and deeper thinker, and that his contribution will last longer. It is very fashionable to think that embryology is soluble in molecular terms, billions of dollars are spent on it as the basis of the human genome project, but I think it's a passing fashion.

**GOULD:** I'm not even talking of molecular answers, Rupert, though there may be a molecular basis to it. I wrote a book on ontogeny and phylogeny in 1977. It was immensely frustrating because there were no data on the construction of ontogeny. I'm not talking about sequencing nucleotides, but about what we understand about basic patterns of gradients and the development of large-scale morphology. We're getting to the point, not of understanding in full, you never do, but of being able to put together the morphogenetic basis of fairly complex organisms. It's now a tractable subject, not because we've come to molecular reductionism but because we have a proper integration of the molecular basis with good old-fashioned descriptive natural history.

**SHELDRAKE:** I just disagree. I spent years working on plant morphogenesis, and I found out as much about gradients in plants as anyone in terms of embryological chemical gradients. But I disagree that it can be solved this way. You asked for an unsolved problem. Embryology is one. But your answer to that is "Well, we're going to solve it soon." That's an act of faith. It's equivalent to saying there isn't an unsolved problem.

**DENNETT:** Let me just recast my point, just as a sociological observation. It's unfortunate for you, in terms of your chances of getting other people to get on your bandwagon, that you're claiming that your theory can deal in a revolutionary way with very difficult problems which have started to appear to be tractable by more traditional methods. That is, just as the embryological juggernaut that Steve Gould is talking about gets rolling, you come along and say, "Don't get on that train, it will never get there." Now, if you'd said that back when Medawar was a student, you might have had a more convincing case. What you really need is a case of a problem on which we're not only agreed that it's unsolved, but about which people are just throwing up their hands and saying, "I don't have a clue." Embryology just isn't like that.

**SHELDRAKE:** Well, you said an unsolved problem. We disagree, obviously, on how successful we will be in embryology. Maybe we should construct a bet. Define goals within a five-year period. And I bet you that you're wrong over a five- or ten-year period.

**GOULD:** Well, I'll take it on five and count my money now. I don't know about twenty years in the future.

**SHELDRAKE:** My way of planning the future of science would be to have bookmakers on the job. I'd have won a lot of money if I'd actually done that. I think they should have the odds published in *Nature* every month.

*I'm sure we'll continue this argument, even if it's only fleetingly, but for now let's have a look at common evolutionary theory for a moment. Steve Gould, you said that even today the theory of natural selection is widely misunderstood, misquoted, and misapplied. If I say, one, evolution has no purpose; two, matter is the ground of all existence; three, evolution is not a gradual process; four, evolution has no direction—do I misunderstand what you're meaning about natural selection?*

**GOULD:** You don't misunderstand much of what I'm meaning, but if you asked the general educated public what Darwinism is, you wouldn't hear any of those four. The major vernacular misunderstandings of Darwin, and many professional ones as well, have to do with the fact that evolution deals with questions that are at the heart of those troubling issues everyone has to figure out to construct some sense of meaning for their lives. Why are we here? Insofar as science can deal with that question at all. What are we related to? How did we get here?

The background of this is the frightening fact that people do understand—that we've only been here for a millimicrosecond of life's history. This leads to the plain conclusion, which I think is true, that maybe we weren't destined to be here, and maybe, if you could replant the tree of life from seed, our species would never develop again. Mistaken interpretations of Darwinism arise in the context of those fears, and of the traditional psychological comfort that we humans are on top of the heap and therefore rule the rest of the world by right, or that we are at least the end product of a predictable process meant to arrive at us. We're not willing to abandon any of those notions, and so we read them back into Darwinism.

After all, Darwin's theory, in its bare-bones mechanics, is a theory about adaptation to change in local circumstances. That's really all it is. To caricature it: If it was cold in Russia a long time ago and some elephants were there that had slightly longer hair, as a statistical average, these do better at leaving offspring, and a thousand generations down the line we'll get woolly mammoths. But they're not better elephants, they're just better suited to the transitory environment of that place. Since the vector of environmental change through time is effectively random, if organisms under Darwin are tracking those environmental changes, you're not going to generate a directional pattern eventually leading up to human beings.

Now, Darwin was also an eminent Victorian, not quite willing completely to divest himself of those psychological comforts and sociological presuppositions, so he in fact did manage in a different way to insinuate progress back into his system by arguing that most competitive interactions were not between organism and environment, but between organism and other organisms. And when organisms struggle with organisms, a kind of biochemical improvement in the long run might result. But that conclusion is quite separate from what I call the bare-bones mechanics of natural selection, which does not validate that notion of progress. This radical philosophical message of his theory is one of the reasons why Darwin has been so difficult to assimilate. Among educated people evolution has not been difficult to assimilate. But many alternative evolutionary mechanisms are much more consonant with traditional Western hopes.

Take Teilhard de Chardin, who had his momentary run of popularity. It was basic old-fashioned mysticism put into such an incomprehensible prose that people thought it was profound. But Teilhard puts forward the notion that the history of life was the inexorable progressive increase of spirit over matter, which will eventually culminate in the union of that growing spirit with God. It's something he called the omega point. That's a kind of evolutionary theory that's much more acceptable to people who want to see the history of life and the universe as progressive. Darwinism is indeed challenging.

**Sheldrake:** What about Alfred Russel Wallace? Like Darwin, he discovered the principle of natural selection and believed in it. And yet in his last book, *The World of Life,* he talks about the evolutionary process being guided by intelligences which he identifies with the angels. We hear a lot about Darwin's materialism, but not much about Wallace.

**Gould:** Wallace is a remarkably idiosyncratic and interesting thinker. He was more hyperselectionist than Darwin. The caricature of Darwin is "Everything's adapted, we've got to figure out why it was built by natural selection." Darwin never said that. He certainly was primarily adaptationist, but Wallace was the hyperadaptationist. Anything you presented to him, he would try to find some mechanism whereby you could find adaptive purpose in structuring by natural selection. However, he made one exception. Perhaps one of the reasons he made that exception for the human mind is that he had a long-standing interest in spiritualism. But there is a logic to what he said, which ironically comes out of the hyperselectionism that was his main difference from Darwin. You see, in the hyperselectionist's view, an organ has to be constructed by natural selection for its immediate use. Wallace, who was not a racist—which was a rare position in the nineteenth century—felt that the brains of so-called savages—his terminology—were equal to those of culturally advanced Europeans.

231

But Wallace *was* a cultural chauvinist—he thought that Gilbert and Sullivan and tea and crumpets were far more advanced than whatever those he called savages were doing in other parts of the world. So since the brain of the savage, though as good as ours, is doing so much less than ours, natural selection couldn't have built the brain, because there's so much unused capacity. And therefore there must have been some other force. You see, there's a curious logic to it.

Now, I think Darwin immediately saw what was wrong with that argument. First, what Wallace was calling savage culture was a lot more complex than Wallace was admitting. He then realized that it's absurd to say that natural selection can only build up to the point of immediate utility. Natural selection builds this complex computer called the brain for a set of highly complex things. But being the complex computer that it is, it's surely capable of doing orders of magnitude more things by virtue of its internal structure, and not immediately by the construction of natural selection. And these side consequences, these spandles as I call them, can overwhelm the original adaptive meanings. That's the fallacy of Wallace's argument.

**DYSON:** To me it still is very mysterious that we have this capacity for solving differential equations.

**GOULD:** It wasn't built by natural selection directly. I agree.

**DYSON:** I don't think anybody should pretend to understand it.

**DENNETT:** Steve, one thing about your diagnosis of the anxiety of the lay people about evolution has puzzled me in the past. You suggest that it's oppressive to some people to suppose that if we ran the tape of time again, human beings would not be created again. But it seems to me it's just as oppressive either way. What bothered Nietzsche was the idea of eternal recurrance—the horrible idea that it would all happen the same way again and again and again. He viewed that as such a nauseating prospect that he really contemplated never revealing what he'd discovered. Now you seem to think that the ordinary person is oppressed or becomes anxious at the prospect that *Homo sapiens* is a unique and unrepeatable phenomenon, whereas it might be the other way around.

**GOULD:** No, I think the fear behind the *ewige Wiederkehr* of Nietzsche and others is that there's no directionality. Borges captured that wonderfully in the *Book of Sand,* where he gets this vulgar book that has a picture every two thousand pages, but you can never reach its end. Finally he realizes it's a completely vulgar book because of its incomprehensibility, because there is no directionality, no pattern. So he loses it in the stacks of the Argentine National Library. I think that's a different kind of fear that we certainly have.

I don't mean to sound elitist, but Dennett and Nietzsche are one group, and then there's *Homo ordinarius,* which is also Dennett and me and everyone else. It seems to me that most folks—at least in Western culture—are seeking to validate Protagoras' old dictum that "man is the measure of all things." We want to find things in terms of ourselves; we want to see ourselves as paramount. Folded into that is the necessity of thinking that four and a half billion years of history of the earth and three and a half of life's explicit fossil history may not necessarily be generating us, with two cycs and two feet, but are nonetheless likely to move toward a complexification that will eventually end in a self-conscious creature very much like us. Then our existence makes sense, then we're here for a purpose. I think most people are not willing to abandon that. There was an interesting survey done of hundreds of newspaper editors in the United States. They were asked various things about evolution, and one of the questions was "Which of the following five statements best expresses your view of what evolution means?" The one that was checked by almost 50 percent, a vast majority, was in fact the worst of the five answers. It said—I'm quoting it almost exactly— that evolution means "the progressive complexification of life's history, beginning with single-celled creatures and eventually ending up with a conscious creature like human beings." That is still the standard concept in vernacular culture among opinion makers as to what evolution means. And it's profoundly wrong.

**DYSON:** Well, I wouldn't quite agree. I would say that one should make a sharp distinction between human beings on the one hand and complexity and intelligence on the other. Certainly one can see progressive aspects to evolution without believing that human beings are the culmination of it.

**GOULD:** Let me give you a different perspective even on that. Obviously it would be a curmudgeonly thing to deny that since we began with single-celled creatures that didn't even have organelles in their cells and we now have petunias and hippopotamuses, in some sense there are increments in complexity. But I think it's wrong to say that it's a driving fundamental trend in the history of life, for the following reason. Let's allow that you have a lower limit of conceivable preservable complexity. That's where life begins, coming from inorganic constituents. It has to. Take anything, any form of the primordeal-soup hypothesis. For chemical and physical reasons you can't begin with a lion or an oak tree. You've got to begin with some really simple thing. And the thing we're beginning with is sitting right next to this lower limit of conceivable complexity. And that's a bacterium. What's the modal organism on earth today? It's still a bacterium. It's never changed. I like to say there are more e-coli in the digestive track of everyone in this room than there have been human beings on earth.

All that can happen, Freeman, is that because that modal organism is sitting so close to the lower limit of conceivable preservable complexity, the only possibility of occasional increments is in the open direction. And that indeed does happen. So you have this remarkably right-skewed distribution. Every once in awhile, as you add new creatures here, a few of them flow off in the domain of complexity. Now, because we happen to be sitting up here, we have an inordinate but perfectly legitimate parochial interest in those few creatures that are sitting on the right tail, because there has been expansion in the only direction available. The real phenomenon in life's history is its success. It's the increase and expansion of diversity. There has therefore been some falling over into the only direction available. So in that descriptive sense it's true that the most complex thing at any one time tends to get more complex through time.

But that is not an evolutionary sequence. The evolutionary sequence is bacterium, eukaryotic cell, multicellular algae, ediacaran organism, sponge, trilobite, eurypterid, some kind of fish. None of them is evolutionarily linked to any other, there is no genealogical sequence leading inexorably up toward that complexity. It's just an occasional cumulation of a few very rare creatures at the right time. Now, I don't deny that the most recent and important of those creatures, *Homo sapiens,* has through mental power had enormous impact on the surface and history of the earth. But impact is not the same as inevitability.

**DYSON:** No, I see what you're saying. But I think it's really a difference in words and not in facts. What I understand by evolution doesn't mean that I have to be descended directly from you. But it's simply that I am a later branch of the tree.

**GOULD:** That's fair enough, but suppose, when you look at the entire tree of life, these branches that lie on the right tail of complexity are just extraordinarily rare, peculiar, oddly occurring. And therefore in the general story of things are exceptions.

**DYSON:** Of course they're exceptions, but often the exceptions happen to be very common.

**GOULD:** That's a fact, but it doesn't mean the process is directed toward their attainment. It means that when they occur, they have extraordinary effects.

**DYSON:** Yes, and in fact very often the big animals dominate the landscape.

**GOULD:** Before human beings, I'm not so sure that's true. Perhaps the big trees. I think bacteria have a much greater effect than brontosauruses. We just have a tendency to focus on brontosauruses.

*Consciousness is sublime and whimsical, as Steve Gould wrote; it's a weird invention. That it's powerful doesn't mean it was meant to be. It wasn't developed to paint or write symphonies. Do we all agree on that?*

**SACKS:** The ghost of final causes is haunting us all at this table. I'm afraid I may be a step behind the conversation. I'm still vaguely thinking about embryology and the notion of entelechy, this mystical notion of a total organizing principle. Perhaps now entelechy has been replaced by homeoboxes. But Rupert, it's not clear to me whether you're unhappy with the existing mechanisms postulated or whether somehow there's something teleological at the back of your morphogenetic fields.

**SHELDRAKE:** Something teleological is at the back of it, but there's a difference with the direction toward which a system develops, like an acorn developing into an oak tree. The oak tree is a final form, a telos toward which it moves. Now reformulated in modern science in the language of dynamical attractors, teleology has been reinvented and smuggled back into science by mathematicians with attractors. In morphogenetic field theory, which is a far wider theory than my own interpretation of it, the standard modeling technique now is in terms of attractors. Now mathematicians like to have it both ways. They want to have a suggestive term that suggests that things are attracted toward goals or ends. But when you say, "Hey, isn't this interesting?" they then say, "Oh, we don't mean that at all." But the fact is that the standard model now in many morphogenetic field theories is of attractors. Now, even if we conceived that the acorn is drawn toward the attractor, the form of a mature oak tree acting as a morphogenetic attractor, even if we can see that that kind of teleology is becoming increasingly predominant through this rather underhanded way it's been smuggled back, that still leaves quite open the question of whether the entire evolutionary process has a goal. That's a different question. The repetition of morphogenesis, which is what biologists study, is how time and time again a chick embryo turns into a chick and a hen. But the question of whether the evolution of the hen itself in the first place, or of the feather or of the eye, was part of a larger telos is another question.

Many people who would accept a more limited teleology about an inherent goal-directedness—or, if you like, movement of organisms toward a dynamical attractor—would not want to say that this implies an overall direction to the evolutionary process.

I think there are two separate questions. I myself don't take a teleological view of the whole evolutionary process. I think it's an open question. There could be an overall organizing principle immanent within the cosmos, maybe transcending the cosmos, maybe immanent within the earth or the solar system, that draws evolution toward the evolution of human consciousness or consciousness in general. On the other hand, maybe there isn't. Materialists will always say it's chance. It's a philosophical position that I like to have an open mind on.

**SACKS:** I read somewhere that as a child Clerk Maxwell liked to say of everything, "What's the go of it?" and sometimes "What's the particular go of it?" And we're all in one way or another talking about the go of it, from the go of individual bacteria to the go of the universe. Again, I'm sort of worried—perhaps we all are—by the ghost of final causes and perhaps by some urge to transcendence, which so often hovers round science. This was very clear in the last century, when so many physicists, Oliver Lodge and J. J. Thompson among others, were driven toward psychical research. But to come back to the point where the conversation was I probably agree that we've arrived here by a series of chances, coincidences, concatenations, although perhaps the tendency is always toward greater complexity.

**SHELDRAKE:** But we don't know, do we? Even our own individual lives have many elements of contingency in them. It's a favorite subject of fiction. But whether or not each of us has some underlying entelechy or goal is a question that most of us couldn't even answer about ourselves, let alone about the whole evolutionary process. There are many people who think that they're just responding to circumstances living in the present, and then psychoanalysts will come along and say, "Well, actually there's some childhood programming here that you haven't been aware of." Many of us are influenced by unconscious patterns.

**GOULD:** But those are personally contingent, unconscious patterns. You can't analogize that into externally universal ones.

**SHELDRAKE:** Why not?

**GOULD:** It's an illogical move. I'm not saying that it's inconceivable that such exist. But it is not evidence.

**SHELDRAKE:** I wasn't using it as evidence. I was saying that even in our own case, where there's a large play of contingency, as we'd all admit, it's an open question as to what extent there's any overall telos or goal in what we do. I would say that to show contingency in the history of life, which you do convincingly and repeatedly, still to my mind leaves open the question as to whether it's just blind chance or whether there's anything more at work.

**GOULD:** The question is at what level predictability enters. There are broad-scale predictabilities. I'll grant you bilateral symmetry in moving organisms. I'll grant you predator–prey ratios in functioning ecosystems. What I won't grant you is the inevitability of *Homo sapiens* rather than some other lineage; of trilobites rather than anomalocarids, which didn't make it.

Contingency rules in all the details of particular lineages. Now, that wouldn't be a problem if we could just say, "I don't care about the details." Science, after all, is fundamentally a search for generalities. Sure, the details are contingent, but they're not below our notice for one fundamental, historical, sociological, and psychological reason, and that is that man *is* the measure of all things. We happen to be enormously interested in ourselves, no matter how general we make our theories. They are in some fundamental sense about ourselves. And ourselves are *Homo sapiens,* one of those little contingent twigs. So we can't claim we're only interested in the generalities. We want them to relate to us.

**DENNETT:** In any case, the role of contingency—as I understand Steve's account, and I agree with this—is that it doesn't play a uniform role through all of the processes. Natural selection as a process can be compared to a noise amplifier. Once it begins amplifying a particular bit of noise, then there's a great deal of regularity in the way it happens. I have no difficulty agreeing that human consciousness is in some respects the amplification of events that were ultimately just contingent, just random. Not only that, but every thought we think probably has a contingent seed, or many contingent seeds, in its own development in our own brains. That I chose exactly these words rather than some other words probably depends on contingent states in some part of my brain. But once the process of designing this very utterance begins to get rolling, then all sorts of regularities are imposed, because what comes out is roughly a grammatical sentence in English.

**SHELDRAKE:** But one of the criticisms of your contingency view is that some people would see Providence as some guiding principle that doesn't have to have a plan made up in advance, doesn't have to be designing human beings. Maybe it works rather like we do, responding to new circumstances with choices and decisions and movements in one direction rather than another.

**GOULD:** There's an obvious response to that, Rupert, which, although conventional, I think is correct operationally in this case. In principle one can always say for any sequence, no matter how peculiar with respect to any expectations of regularity, "Maybe it's the workings of preordained plans so complex that we can't possibly discern the directionality," as in the old line: God works in many ways his wonders to perform. At that point it's not a useful hypothesis. I can only say maybe it is, but since formally we'll never know, I can't work with that and therefore I have to work without it. If it's only a plan that's being made up as it goes along, and if the mechanism whereby the planner chooses to operate is nothing different from natural selection of the other mechanisms we know, then that system is formally no different in terms of anything you could ever know about. It's nothing that science could ever adjudicate.

A fine solution was offered by Pope Pius XII, who is not one of my heroes for other reasons. He decreed in an encyclical in the 1930s that Catholics were free to believe anything science discovered about the evolution of the human corporeal form, so long as they continued to accept that at some point God infused the soul into this sequence. I'm totally comfortable with that notion. I can't deal with souls. In my own personal theology there is no such concept, but it doesn't threaten anything I can do in science if some people accept that directive. The issue that we're concerned with as scientists is what we can say about the evolution of human corporeal form. The soul then just becomes a subsidiary hypothesis, comforting and coherent for some and perfectly fine.

TOULMIN: I think that's too easy a way out. The word "soul" isn't just a theological term that has arbitrarily intruded. We must be able to study, for instance, the question "what does it mean to say that somebody develops a conscience?" I don't think you can just say, "Oh, well, if he wants to talk about soul . . . "

GOULD: I meant "soul" in the good old theological sense.

TOULMIN: Theology is much more of a pedestrian, down-to-earth subject than you're allowing it to be! You're talking about it in a sort of nineteenth-century rationalist way, as if this is something we can just push aside.

GOULD: But that's what was meant in that particular context. If by "soul" you mean the origins of feelings of morality and consciousness, that's a different subject.

TOULMIN: I think you would find that people who are of Pius XII's way of thinking would have been very uncomfortable to see scientists studying many of the things that we would regard as legitimate scientific issues.

DENNETT: Steve, why wasn't Pope Pius XII's declaration about the soul either a complete capitulation in the face of science or at least the first step in such a retreat? The notion of soul that the faithful were supposed to maintain as science progressed was already completely denatured and no longer played any, as it were, observable role in people's lives. It was just a sort of abstract passport to heaven that you somehow had. Then that was really a complete capitulation to science, wasn't it? On the other hand, maybe all he was saying was "Go ahead, believe what science tells you about certain aspects of the human body, but not about human psychology." What do you think he meant?

GOULD: First, I wouldn't call it a capitulation. It's only a capitulation in terms of the actual pathways of Western history. Of course, there was a time when the domain considered by religion included a vast amount of what is now done by science, because people with religious credentials

238

did try to explain the tides and the seasons and the history of life. Much of the history of science has been a withdrawal of theology from those disciplines. And in some formal sense that's a retreat.

But you could say—and I would say, and I'm not personally an irreligious person, either—that such a formal retreat was necessary because theology, properly defined, never should have been there in the first place. It was there only by default. To me it's just a proper resetting of the boundaries that theology will take up the subjects of ethics and morality, and science will take up the subjects of the empirical constitution of the universe.

**DENNETT:** My own attitudes toward religion are no doubt largely shaped by my own childhood experiences. I may be the only one in this group to have been brought up in the tradition that I like to think of as liberal suburban Protestantism, which had become so well educated and sophisticated and liberal that it sort of was vanishing into thin air. Peter De Vries wrote a wonderful novel, *The Mackerel Plaza,* where the Reverend Mackerel has a sermon, the last line of which is "And so, dearly beloved, we see the true proof of God's power is that He need not exist to save us." That seems to me the sort of reductio ad absurdum of enlightened sophisticated religion but that is the very reductio that Pius XII's declaration is setting in motion.

**GOULD:** It seems to me the domain of ethics and morality is a pretty darn big one, then.

**TOULMIN:** Perhaps we ought to talk about the domain of ethics and morality at a later stage, because you're making it too labile and too outside the world of the intellectually critical. I think that medieval theology, which is quite different from post-Kantian idealistic theology, was a much more solid, down-to-earth kind of thing than you make it out to be. When Aquinas talks about the animation of the embryo at quickening, he has something really quite empirical in mind, of an observational rather than an explanatory kind. To ride my own hobbyhorse, really it was only after the Council of Trent that the intellectual rot set in and one was really compelled to make everything either explanatory or failed explanation. Traditional medieval theology really didn't have these explanatory ambitions in the same way.

*Does everybody agree with Steve Gould—perhaps except Rupert Sheldrake—that "through no fault of our own, and by dint of no cosmic plan or conscious purpose, we have become, by the grace of a glorious evolutionary accident called intelligence, the stewards of life's continuity on earth?" A kind of unconscious design of consciousness, so to say.*

**DENNETT:** I agree only up to a point with that.

239

SACKS: I don't know whether the word "design" in any sense can be allowed. I'm afraid I rather think in tangents. Steve wrote of the Burgess Shale that if the tape of life were rewound, it would take a different form. I get this feeling in the few minutes of migraine aura: each time it has improvised differently. You never see the same aura twice. Somehow I think the most difficult thing is to get rid of a notion of design, somehow.

I'm afraid I have another irrelevant irrelevance and then I'll shut up. Once when I was driving down into Baja California there were many beautiful cactus gardens by the road, and one of them was particularly enchanting. I got out with a friend, a zoologist, to look at this immense garden. The range, the ingenuity, and the beauty were quite extraordinary. We were amazed at the brilliance of the gardener who could have made such a huge, various garden. And then we came over the brow of the hill and we saw that it was nature. I'd mistaken nature for a garden. I don't know what that might say about design or telos or aesthetics or anything else. Incidentally, I think the subject of aesthetics needs to be wedged somewhere in the middle between biology and stewardship and morality and all that.

DENNETT: I want to go back to your citation of Steve Gould's point. One very important thing about human beings tends to get lost in this discussion: one thing that does make us unique as a species is that for the last five or ten thousand years we have been the beneficiaries of conscious planning by our parents and their parents and the cultures in which we've resided. Today we are actively concerning ourselves with what the world is going to be like in the future. We have strong beliefs about this. They play a role in what *Homo sapiens* is going to be like a thousand years from now, if it survives. And if a thousand years from now some *Homo sapiens* were to sit around a table and say, "We are not in any sense the product of any planning," they'd be wrong. Because cultural transmission is really, with very modest exceptions, exclusively a feature of our species.

GOULD: That's a discordance from the natural process that's come up to now. That's why I've been calling it cultural evolution, because I want to emphasize the differences. There are two features that natural biology doesn't have. One is the Lamarckian inheritance. We teach our children what we learn. And the other is the anastomosis of lineages. Once a species is separate, it's separate forever. Both of those enormously accelerate the process and make it plannable.

DENNETT: Sure. But then you also agree that that process is one of the main factors that contribute to what we are. Is a human being just the genetic foundations? No. The cultural contributions are immense.

TOULMIN: I think Dan Dennett has introduced a crucial distinction at this point. Too much of the discussion about consciousness is conducted under the assumption that there's only physics on the one hand and thought on the other hand, which Descartes may have encouraged us to believe. But if you look at the history of the concept of consciousness, consciousness is always radically situated. It's *conscientia,* it's knowledge shared and planned. There's a big piece of conceptual history that has only been very partially done which has to do with the progressive refinement of ideas of consciousness. But certainly the idea that consciousness is a feature of the totally desituated individual is a very extreme one in a long spectrum of possible views. Most of the paradigmatic kinds of senses in which we talk about people knowing what they're doing, people paying conscious attention to what they're doing, and so on, have to do—as Dan rightly says—with the exercise of skills that have been learned in a very definite cultural situation. These have been developed and refined by the individual in his or her own idiosyncratic way, but the roots lie in a conceptual history that has deep cultural affiliations.

**DENNETT:** A trivial and obvious example would be that none of us have invented arithmetic for ourselves. And not just arithmetic. There are literally thousands of other cultural products that so invest our minds. If one asked what makes the stream of consciousness proceed in the way it does, the answer is that these cultural embeddings in our brains are certainly doing the lion's share of the work.

**TOULMIN:** There's a bit more to it. We know what the content of the stream of consciousness is only if we see this question within a particular *Lebensform.* When we talk about having arithmetic handed down to us, what is handed down to us is the ability not just to recite the numbers in the correct order, but to know what's involved in counting out objects of the kinds that we use these numbers to enumerate. Learning arithmetic in the course of the average child's life is a question of becoming habituated to a set of forms of life within which the mathematical procedures have a meaning. If I may pitch a googly in Steve Gould's direction, the language of baseball is fully intelligible only to people who really know what baseball is about.

**DENNETT:** I know what a googly is.

**TOULMIN:** I deliberately sent you down a cricket ball, because it's a different *Lebensform* from a baseball.

**DENNETT:** There are a lot of similarities.

**TOULMIN:** Yes, there are similarities. They are parallel evolutionary products. But one has to understand the language of consciousness in the context of the kinds of activities within which consciousness is exercised.

*Before we dive deeper into consciousness and language, I'd like to ask one question. Stephen Jay Gould, this famous letter Charles Darwin wrote: "What a wonderful time the devil's chaplain would have with the immensely blundering, wasteful, and inefficient ways of nature." Do we define nature as unconscious and nonmoral and our own species as conscious and moral? Can we really make this distinction?*

**GOULD:** You have to understand the context of that letter he wrote in 1855 to Joseph Hooker. It was a sardonic and sarcastic comment, and I think Darwin had a very definite solution in mind. He points out that one shouldn't try to extract moral messages from nature, as William Paley did in his book *Natural Theology* of 1802, which had been Darwin's great textbook as a young man. Paley goes through all the wonderful designs and harmonious ecosystems of nature, thereby telling us that we can infer not only God's existence from them, but also his benevolence, his goodness, his omniscience. Darwin says if you really look at nature, there's so much out there that's ugly. He chooses two examples, and they're very interesting. He says: I do not see how a loving God could create the ichneumonids with the express intention of their feeding within the living bodies of caterpillars. The reference was to these hundreds of species of wasp that inject their eggs into the paralyzed living bodies of caterpillars. The eggs hatch and the juvenile wasp larvae very carefully eat the caterpillar, which is still alive, because they don't want to kill it and cause it to decay, saving the heart and the nervous system for last.

The second example Darwin gives is why a cat should play with mice. When we watch cats playing with mice that are not yet dead, usually some sense of horror arises in us, even if we understand that might be an inappropriate reaction. Darwin's saying that if you actually look at nature in the raw and more fairly, you will see many natural phenomena that would be very hard to see as the results of a kind, loving, and efficient God. But Darwin's solution is that therefore nature is neither moral nor immoral. It's amoral. We shouldn't be trying to extract moral messages from nature at all.

*Does everybody agree that nature can't teach us ethics?*

**TOULMIN:** We're in bad trouble here, because you're talking as though the word "nature" were univocal and as though it always meant nature as distinguished from humanity. Again, this is a seventeenth-century move that we've spent much of the twentieth century digging ourselves out from under. Before 1600 and certainly since 1950 it's unforgivable to use the word "nature" as though humanity were not part of nature. There's a sense in which everything is natural, including even human reason, as Aquinas thought. It's clear that Aquinas thought there were certain kinds of basic moral insights which were shared by everyone, including people of all religions. The medieval moral theologians were perfectly prepared to accept Cicero as an authority on ethical issues without having to pretend that Cicero was a hidden Christian. So I think we have to be careful to avoid insisting on asking questions which arose with the kind of force they did only because of the seventeenth-century mistakes that lasted on into the early twentieth century, which we are now in a position, thank God, to get away from.

*Once more I ask Oliver or Dan: Is nature nonmoral?*

**TOULMIN:** Which nature? The nature that includes humanity or the nature that excludes humanity?

*Nature that excludes humanity.*

**DENNETT:** I think Hobbes had it just about right, that the state of nature is a world in which there is neither right nor wrong. All kinds of bloodcurdling things happen in the natural world. But morality is a human creation or discovery. In fact, I think that Hobbes can be seen as the first sociobiologist, because he created a sort of just-so story about how this arose. But he was saying in his just-so story that by a sort of rational reconstruction we could imagine *Homo sapiens* in a premoral condition when we were not distinguished from the other beasts in this regard. And then he tells his story about the social contracts.

**TOULMIN:** You think he's right, I think he's wrong. We have to do some justice to Kropotkin as well as to Hobbes. And I'm sure Steve Gould can tell us lots of stories about other social species within which there is mutual aid.

**GOULD:** But it's because they are both right—because Kropotkin is right *and* there is *bellum omnium contra omnes*—that there are no messages. Everything evolved naturally, presumably by natural selection of the reproductive success of individual organisms. And therefore it contains no messages for us.

**DENNETT:** In fact, when we look at nature, we can get some curious examples or messages. For instance, I actually think it's legitimate to look at trees as an instance of the tragedy of the commons. See, if only those trees could have gotten together and agreed not to compete with each other for the sunlight, then they wouldn't have had to waste all those resources and growing those great big tall trunks. The formal properties of the tragedy of the commons are right there in the forest. From our anthropocentric point of view, we should be grateful that those forests are there, but from the tree's point of view, it's a terrible waste.

**GOULD:** Not to mention the billions of seedlings that die! . . . which Tennyson noted and Darwin expatiated on.

*Humans have souls, the other species have not. . . . Dan, you said
there isn't such a sharp edge.*

**DENNETT:** I think one of the artifacts of our culture is the idea that
consciousness is a light which is either on or off. I think there are all
sorts of gradations. But that means that one should be very cautious
about supposing that the same questions that are properly asked about
our sort of consciousness can be meaningfully asked about the
consciousness of the bat or the dolphin or the spider.

**TOULMIN:** Leibniz was really good about this. For him, all different kinds
of monads had more or less clear and distinct apperceptions. It wasn't a
question of either having apperceptions, which were by definition clear
and distinct, or not having them. He was in favor of a kind of continuity
in respect of mentality as well as in respect of other characteristics.

*I remember Oliver saying that what he likes in nature is that nature is
nonmoral, while our human morality is such a burden. For that
reason it's wonderful to walk around in nature.*

**SACKS:** I don't know about messages. I think nature doesn't encourage
sentimentality. I think one does have the feeling of extreme divisions
between the plant and the animal worlds. A few days ago I was driving
around in upstate New York. It was very beautiful fall weather and I was
conscious of trees and meadows. I didn't realize that I hadn't seen an
animal—I mean a macroscopic animal—until after about an hour I
caught sight of a cow. And suddenly its animation seemed a thing of
extreme wonder to me. I had the feeling of it sampling the environment,
of sensory sheets lighting up. . . . What an incredible thing, a cow!
There's nothing like it in the vegetable world. I can't get the same feeling
from insects as from mammals. I think there is something deeply
different about their nervous system and mind in the way they've gone.
I'm not sure about octopuses.

**GOULD:** I think it's pure aesthetics. That's why I think that people who
try to construct moral arguments for vegetarianism, for example, will just
never succeed. Carrots are as highly evolved as a lot of things we eat. But
I respect the aesthetic arguments. You look into the eye of a mammal,
and because the genealogical relationship is close enough—and the
homologously shared emotional reactions—we see enough of ourselves
in the cow. There are many vegetarians who will eat fish but not so-
called red meat, and I think that's very much the same point. If we look
in the eye of a fish, we don't see it. I don't think there's as much
homologously shared. From an evolutionary point of view, arthropods
are wondrous in their complexity, and many of the groups of arthropods
are far later evolved than fishes. So I don't know that one can make that
distinction.

**TOULMIN:** You can suggest that there's no way we could empathize with a bat. On the other hand, it's not unreasonable to think that different species have kinds of experience that in certain crucial respects are more or less like ours, which we choose to regard as typically human. This is itself a respectable enterprise in comparative psychology.

**DENNETT:** I don't think it's intractable even to the cold, hard, objective methods of science.

**TOULMIN:** I think much of what Steve chooses to call aesthetics is also part of science.

**DENNETT:** I think we're making tremendous progress on getting information so we'll be able to say exactly what it's like to be a bat. It's still a long way off, but we can already say a lot about what isn't like, and this is already progress.

**SHELDRAKE:** I find this discussion a little provincial. We're assuming that consciousness is confined to animals on earth. What about the consciousness of the sun, for example? If people are happy to agree that the interface between mental activity and brain function is changing electromagnetic patterns, there are plenty of those on the sun. The more research that goes on on the sun, the more we find about the tremendous complexity. So what about the idea that the sun might be thinking, or have some kind of mental activity associated with those electromagnetic patterns? Well, I can immediately hear Steve's response: "Meaningless concept. You can think of it if you like, but . . . "

**GOULD:** It's close to that, Rupert. But I'll make you a challenge: The moment you can propose to me some way to have the sun talk to us so that we'll know about its consciousness, I'm willing to take it up as a subject. Before then, frankly, I'm not.

**DENNETT:** I'd put it stronger. If you can give us any reason to think there's a raison d'être to the sun's consciousness . . . The reason we're conscious is that we are the evolved products of evolution, we've had to fend for ourselves. If you go back to what Oliver said about the division between plants and animals, basically that's a division between a very conservative strategy—hunker down and put your hands over your head and hope for the best, which is the plant strategy—and then the guerrilla warfare strategy of the animals. When the animals became locomotory, they developed distal perception systems. There's no use in having eyes if you don't have feet. Trees with eyes would just be in despair because they couldn't run away when they saw danger coming. So if you can give us a reason for thinking that the sun has some use for its mind, then I think we can take it seriously that it might have one. Otherwise it seems to me to be just an idle fantasy.

**SHELDRAKE:** Well, the thing is, it rather goes back over ground we've already covered. Is there some guiding principle in the evolution of life on earth? If the sun has a mind, maybe it's the brain of the whole solar system, not just of the earth. And if one looks for a guiding intelligence, then I would look for it first in the sun and the whole solar system, rather than leaping straight to the view of a mechanical God. And then there's the galaxy. The sun is like a cell in the entire galaxy. We don't know what the mind of the galaxy might be like. Its thoughts would be "vaster than empires and more slow," considering the speed of light and how big it is. But these are possibilities that one can speculate about. It seems to me they may be very relevant to this whole question of the evolutionary process. So that may be an answer to your question of what the sun could be doing.

**DENNETT:** There's a philosophical distinction which I'm not always happy to invoke but which seems to be appropriate here, between rule-following behavior and rule-described behavior. The standard example that philosophers use is that the planets obey the laws of planetary motion. But they don't calculate what the law prescribes for them to do and then do it.

**TOULMIN:** They can't make mistakes.

**DENNETT:** That's right. So planets don't need a mind in order to figure out how to stay in their orbits. And it doesn't seem to me that the solar system needs a mind in order to maintain its regularities, whether they're habits or laws.

**SHELDRAKE:** I wasn't thinking of the regularities of the planets' orbits. I was thinking of the details of evolution on earth, on Mars, Jupiter, or any other planet. We know that sunspot cycles affect cycles of events on earth. That's a very crude example everyone could agree on. But I think it may go much further than that.

**SACKS:** I wonder whether one needs to bring in some new words, such as "spontaneity," in relation to organisms. This was specifically done by Harvey in a fascinating book on animal motion which he wrote in the same year as he wrote *The Circulation of the Blood*. As a young man he'd been to Galileo's lectures in Padua, and the first half of the book is an analysis of animal motion in terms of inertia and momentum and so forth, and the fact that the physical determinants are always obeyed. But in the second half of the book he says there's more here, and he speaks of spontaneity and grace, and he can no longer call on physical models. And then he starts to use metaphors. He talks about the silent music of the body. This strikes me as a rather nice early treatise on animation, and on the nature of the animate.

**TOULMIN:** It's the same with Barelli on animal motion. He makes it plain that all he can do is to show how anatomy is relevant to an understanding of animal motion. But he insists at the same time that the fact that an animal moves at all is not to be explained in these anatomical terms. This shows us that it's quite wrong to think that vitalism and animism and so on were medieval superstitions. These were by-products, forced on scientists as a result of having overinterpreted the mechanical philosophy of the seventeenth century. It's just because somebody might try to say that everything about animal motion had to be intelligible in Galilean terms that some kind of complementary account of the source of vitality becomes necessary.

**DENNETT:** You know, there's been a nice breakthrough on one interesting aspect of animal motion coming out of artificial intelligence. In a most improbable research program, a young artificial intelligence researcher, a roboticist named Mark Weber, decided to solve the running robot problem. And his bizarre first idea was that he was going to make a one-legged running robot. You start simple. What he made was basically a robot pogo stick. And it actually works, the thing hops away quite handsomely, and it maintains its balance. That's what the software does. Then he thought, "Well, I've solved the one-legged robot problem, how about the two-legged robot problem?" So he simply took two of these contraptions and put them together. "And now," he said, "I've got a software problem. I know how to control a one-legged robot, but how do I control a two-legged robot?" And he realized this was his real breakthrough, he had actually already solved the problem. He simply had this robot make the same calculations as it was making in its one-legged form, but now with a virtual leg, as it were, an imaginary leg in between the two. And then of course it had to keep making corrections, because its real legs weren't where its imaginary leg was. But this one hopped on two legs just fine. And he thought, "Now I've got the two-legged robot problem solved, what about the four-legged robot problem?" So he put four of them together, sort of like a horse. And now the question was: Should he put the virtual legs—it's going to have two virtual legs now—between the two front legs and the two back legs, between the left legs and the right legs, or crisscross? He didn't know, so he said, "I'll try it all three ways." And what he got was walk, trot, and canter. Now, before he did that, I would guess that most people who thought about the complexities of walk, trot, and canter would say, "That's such a complex problem, just forget about it. It's beyond robotics, it's just much too complicated to figure out the control structure in the horse's brain that could tip it into these three different gaits with a little nudge." Now, maybe Weber doesn't have the answer, but I'll bet he's got a part of it, because it fell out so naturally from this program.

**SACKS:** I think that the transition from walk to trot to canter can be modeled relatively simply. But having said that, I think that walking and animal motion are not just an alternation of limbs. The opening sentence in *Leviathan* is something like "Life is a motion of limbs," isn't it something like that? Specifically, if one has Parkinson's disease, one's walking does then become rather mechanical. One has this peculiar gait called festination. Typically, when people have this, they use the passive tense. They say, "I am walked." I had one patient, a former music teacher, who became Parkinsonian. And she said that she felt her gait had become robotic. She said she had become demusicked. Or unmusicked. And that she needed to be remusicked, which she could be by listening to music or imagining music to walk normally again. And whether these considerations of rhythm and kinetic melody can be reducible to Galilean robotic terms, or whether some quite other sort of organization is needed, I don't know. But I think that some of the problems of living organization come up even at this level of locomotion. And that you don't yet have to move to consciousness.

**TOULMIN:** But the use of the word "music" in this context is a very helpful one, and obviously Harvey didn't choose it for nothing. There's a lot to be said for simply concentrating on what's involved in teaching somebody to be a fine pianist. There are some people who get to a point at which one can say: "From the point of view of fingering and velocity, they're as good as the best, but for one reason or another it's very difficult for them to learn to play musically." We have terms like "musicianship" which have to do not with fingering and velocity, but to what use the capacity for fingering and velocity is put. One doesn't have to leap straight to a spiritual account of this, one needs to look and see what people are pointing out when they say, "Here are two pianists who have an equal level of technical proficiency. This one is a true musician, but the other one, although he's a virtuoso, will never touch the hearts of the audience." Harvey really had his eye on something.

*How would you feel about a short pause?*

**GOULD:** In baseball we believe in seventh inning stretches. Yes, it's very light in here and it's dark outside. I could do with a short walk.

∎

After a twenty-minute break, the roundtable resumed.

**DENNETT:** When we were out walking, Stephen, you said that one of the problems of the earlier sort of case history tradition was that there was a lot of implicit, unrecognized ax-grinding in the narratives that people wrote. There are many examples of that. But are you saying that there's a way of doing it which isn't ax-grinding? Is there a sort of pure observational narrative? A theory-neutral narrative?

TOULMIN: There is a pretheoretical vocabulary for medicine with words like "wound" and "awake." There is a kind of everyday phenomenological vocabulary that forms part of the vocabulary of medicine, but that has to enter into a medical history if the thing is to have any verisimilitude at all.

SACKS: A folk psychology, and a sort of folk neurology.

TOULMIN: A wound is a wound is a wound. If you don't say that somebody has a wound, you're not giving a correct report of what his condition is. But you don't have to have a theory in order to have a wound.

DENNETT: But precisely in neurology you get these conditions that leave you slack-jawed when you first see them, and it's extremely hard to figure out how to describe what you've just seen. I've been doing rounds with various neuropsychologists in the last five or six years. One of the most fascinating things about it was to realize that I would stand there puzzled, watching some patient in action, and I couldn't tell what I was seeing. And then the neurologist in charge would say notice this, notice this, notice this. And then of course I would notice those features, but not until I had a vocabulary and until I had a hypothesis to consider. Otherwise I was simply left speechless. And I'm not usually left speechless.

SACKS: There are certainly many conditions which are completely unimaginable. One of the most striking is that a patient with a lesion up here on the right side of the brain ignores left, you cannot draw their attention to the left. And you feel that they're in a bisected universe. In a half universe. They don't feel this, because they feel complete. People like this will sort of say, "Where's the coffee, you haven't given me the coffee." You say, "It's there, to your left." But somehow this can't be taken in. And one patient like this finally came to some intellectual recognition of her condition, and she would then rotate to the right, and then the coffee would come. And similarly with her food, she would literally keep bisecting the portions and would have to do a rotation.

GOULD: She would always have to rotate all the way around?

TOULMIN: She couldn't go counterclockwise to bring the thing into vision?

SACKS: No, the simple and obvious thing she could not do. But even on a sort of peripheral basis, if one has a heavy spinal, you don't just become numb from here down. You terminate. You terminate, and what lies below is not you, not flesh, not categorizable, not anything and also not anywhere. And in a way not anywhere. It sort of disappears, taking space and time with it.

SHELDRAKE: Don't you get a phantom, though? You do with losing limbs and so forth.

**SACKS:** Yes, but that's at least partly because some of the neurological apparatus is left in the stump.

**GOULD:** Do people get phantoms with a spinal?

**SACKS:** One of my colleagues, a very fine quadriplegic woman, sometimes has to have mirrors around so she can take what she calls a visual sip, otherwise she gets the illusion that she's in some sort of strange crumpled position, or just not there. But I don't think they're phantoms in the extreme vivid way. Like a wonderful phantom that one of his pupils described in *Paul Wittgenstein, the One-Armed Pianist*.

*Ludwig's brother.*

**SACKS:** Yes. When he went over a new piece of music with her, a piece which was new to both of them, he would first do it with his left hand, and then he would do it with his phantom right arm, the stump twitching furiously as he did so. And then he would complete it, and he would say, "I felt every note, here's the fingering." And so there seemed to be almost a sort of veridical sort of phantom.

**DENNETT:** Let's just look at that story a little bit more, because there's one feature about it that might be misleading us. Take a pianist who's got both his arms and don't anesthetize him at all, just tie his arms down to his sides, and then show him a new piece of music. I dare say that most good pianists would be able to play it in their head and figure out the fingering. It's not a phantom-limb experience for them, it's just an imaginative exercise. So we don't yet know whether Paul Wittgenstein's accomplishment here is more than what people who have two arms can do differently.

**SACKS:** One wonders also how much this imaginative exercise innervates the arm.

**TOULMIN:** I think it does. If you watch people who don't actually have to have their arms tied down but who know they're in a situation where they're not supposed to make a noise, very often you can see residual finger movements going on.

**DENNETT:** I'm sure the more you can do, the better it is, the more robust, the more secure the practice is.

**TOULMIN:** And also maybe the less necessary it is to move the fingers. There's this interesting fact about blindfold chess playing, that you imagine that anybody who's playing blindfold chess must be visualizing the chessboard. This is true at an early stage in learning blindfold chess. But people who get good at it say they no longer even do that. In fact, this gets in the way, it eventually becomes an obstacle to doing it. Because otherwise you ask how it's possible for somebody to play twelve games of blindfold chess at the same time, which the really skilled people can do. It's not because they can remember exactly which visual field, which visual representation to summon up.

DENNETT: Presumably even the novice blindfold chess player is not going to burden his imagination with the shape of the knight or the crown of the queen. It'll be more abstract already. Presumably this research shows us that the better you get at blindfold chess, the more of the visual details you leave aside until you get down to the crude abstraction.

SHELDRAKE: But what are you left with?

TOULMIN: Well, I don't know, I'm not good at it. Our language is not well adapted to talking about this, anyway, so I'm not quite sure how much notice I take of the story that somebody told me about exactly how he was doing it. All I know is that there's a substantial body of material which shows that, as Dan puts it, this part becomes progressively abstracted from all the visual detail of the thing. Also there's the question "What is it like?" I'm sure you've gone into all that, the question of what it is for somebody who uses sign language to think to themselves.

*Let's address consciousness and computation, consciousness and language, and all these other relations. Freeman Dyson, you wrote: "To me, the most astounding fact in the universe, even more astounding than the flight of the monarch butterfly, is the power of the mind, which drives my fingers as I write these words." I quote Daniel Dennett: "Every stage magician knows you can do a rather small trick which is almost instantly blown up in the minds and memories of the audience into something it never was. And then they have a much harder thing to explain than they actually need to. I think this is what happens again and again and again with our minds. We think the phenomena that need to be explained are much more stupendous than they are." You're saying that our minds fool us. How?*

DENNETT: Our sense of our visual world is of a whole visual field which is roughly equally detailed and filled in. Now we know that in fact color vision doesn't extend to our whole visual field. There's an area out to the peripheries where we can see motion and a little bit of shape, but we don't have any color vision at all. We know, moreover, that the detailed portion of our vision is just what falls on the fovia, the high-resolution central part of the retina.

And yet our experience of vision is not of little spots of detail surrounded by a sort of vague penumbra. Our sense is of a completely detailed visual world. And so then if we think, "Where will we find all that wonderful detail—in the brain?" we're making a mistake. All that wonderful detail doesn't have to be in the brain. We're actually fooling ourselves in thinking that we've got that much in here. We can leave a lot of that detail out in the world, it'll take care of itself. When we need it, our eyes can dart over and get it. We have this illusion that we've brought it all inside, and now we've got to find a place for it somewhere in the cortex. It doesn't have to be there.

**SHELDRAKE:** Where do you think it is, then?

**DENNETT:** It's in the world.

**SHELDRAKE:** Ah, yes, I like that idea. So then how does it work? You're saying the mind is extended in the world, are you?

**DENNETT:** I'm saying that the mind takes advantage of its deeply embedded relation to the world, to leave all other information out there. Let the world store its own information about itself. The brain doesn't have to keep detailed records inside. The metaphor I use is an interlibrary loan system. If you have a really fast and user-friendly interlibrary loan system, you don't have to keep the books in the library. If any user wants a book on such-and-such, almost instantaneously he's got that book right in his hand. It's as if all the books were in the library, but they are instantly retrieved on demand. I say that the brain retrieves on demand most of the information that it uses, and it doesn't keep it around. And at the end of my book I made a prediction that would demonstrate this in order to satisfy my scientific friends that I was willing to go out on a few limbs. I suggested that viewers who looked at pictures on a high-resolution computer screen, if an irrelevant but large part of the background were suddenly shifted in color from blue to red while their eye was in the middle of a secade, they would be oblivious of this. There were a few more conditions, but that's enough to give you an idea.

I tried this idea out on a lot of people in the sciences, and I found this wonderful bimodal distribution of responses. Everybody said the experiment wasn't worth doing, because it was too obvious how it was going to come out. But they completely disagreed on what they thought the answer was. Some people were sure that if you went and changed a huge portion of the background in a picture while somebody was looking at it, even if you changed it while their eyes were darting, of course people would notice. You can't turn a bright-red car bright green while somebody's eyes are looking at it without their noticing. Other people, who tended to be vision psychologists and visionary scientists, said that of course they would be oblivious.

John Grimes has done the experiments now, and it comes out better than I ever hoped. High-resolution full-color photographs are shown to subjects, and while the subjects are looking at them, an eye tracker, which is a little beam directed on their lens, keeps track of their eye movements. The subjects are given the following instructions: "We're going to show you a group of photographs. You shall look at each one for ten seconds. Study the pictures carefully, because later you're going to be tested for recall." And then they're told: "Oh, and if you ever see anything change, even if you don't know what it is, press this button." And then he started running subjects, and he started with little subtle changes in the background. Nobody ever pressed the button. The computer would shift something either on the first or the fifth or the tenth secade—the jump of the eye. Right in about that twenty-millisecond interval. He got to the point where he could show people a photograph—this is one of my favorites—an aerial photograph looking down at a crater lake in a volcano, a beautiful, perfectly round bright-blue lake. The lake changes to black. The lake isn't in the background, it's the focal object in the picture, and it probably occupies 10 percent of the visual space in the picture. Only about 20 percent of people notice the change. It turns out that you can make enormous changes in the visual world that people are completely oblivious of because they're not bothering to store that information. They're using the periphery of their eyes as a sort of sentry system. Any time the sentries see change, they say, "Oh, change, we'll take a look at it." So these attract your attention. But if you can sneak something by those sentries, you're home free, because there's no record inside to compare it with. You haven't bothered to keep a record of what it was before. So if you get by the first line of sentries, you're free. That's an experimental demonstration of the sort of way in which we fool ourselves about what's actually going on in our minds.

**DYSON:** I remember having a conversation with my daughter in the car. She plays the oboe, and she was suddenly told that the chief oboist had failed to appear for a concert, and she had to perform without any warning. So during this ride in the car she had to go over the music. And I asked her, "How the hell do you do that? Do you listen to it to yourself, or are you thinking of the fingering, or what is it?" She said she didn't really know, she just looked at the music, and that was enough. She was neither listening to it nor fingering, but she just somehow prepared herself mentally, and she could go on and play.

**DENNETT:** In fact, I've been trying to get development psychologists to do some experiments that ought to be done, to study trained musicians' capacities to read scores silently and appreciate the music. It stuns me that in composition contests the judges don't hear the music, they just read the scores, and then they give first, second, and third places. Now, what we don't know yet, and what I'd love to see experiments on, is how good are they really? What if you took unfamiliar scores and put in typographical errors, musical anomalies, things that would sound odd, you know? Where are they going to notice them, and where are they not going to notice them?

**GOULD:** I had some experience with that once. At a conductor's contest in Besançon in France they had snuck in little errors. And these were youngish conductors, and some picked them out very well, and some didn't. Now the fallacy of the test was whether this had anything to do with whether they were great conductors, but it was an interesting phenomenon. By the way, your computers will get over that now, because you may now introduce a full score to a computer, designate the instruments, and synthesize something very close to the score.

**SHELDRAKE:** How long does it take them to do this? I mean, can they read through a whole symphony in a minute or two? Can they do it faster?

**DENNETT:** I don't know. I talked to some composers about this, and certainly they can do it faster than real time. But just how fast they can do it I don't know. There's a sort of speed reading.

**SACKS:** There's the story of Mozart conceiving the *Jupiter* Symphony in a moment.

**GOULD:** But that's easy for us to believe, because surely the outlines of articles come all at once. It always takes me awhile to write out those outlines, and I imagine it takes most of you awhile, too. I don't think musical composition is different, especially in Mozart's age, when there were certain formulas. You'd take a theme and apply certain formalisms to work it out.

**SACKS:** The experience I've sometimes had when suddenly I've been bereaved—perhaps all of us have—is seeming to see the shape of someone's life in great detail. In a flash.

**DENNETT:** Well, I'll be the wet blanket on this score and say that such an experience seems to have a lot more detail than it really does have.

**SACKS:** I thought you'd say that.

**DENNETT:** I'm at least consistent.

**TOULMIN:** It could be that you added the detail. The important thing is that the shape is of such a kind that one is in a position to fill in the detail.

**SACKS:** Perhaps this is just a special example of revelation, you know, a sudden sense of a deeply new shape, dramatic, theoretical, historical. I don't know how much detail one needs to support this.

**DENNETT:** Well, it's important to realize that the illusion of detail is a ubiquitous human foible. Then one realizes that in these stunning declarations that one gets from people who've had visions, who've just imagined something wonderful in great detail, the conviction they have that it was all wonderfully detailed doesn't really give us much, if any, reason to suppose that there actually was anything that detailed happening. You can have the illusion that it was detailed when it wasn't.

**GOULD:** Interpret this for me, because I have been very much on your side. I'll never write an essay until I have a complete outline, and when I get the outline, I just know I have it. I then sit down and it takes me half an hour to write down the ideas. Now, I'm perfectly willing to admit that when I get that aha moment which tells me I know I have the outline, it's not all there, and yet I can then sit down and write it out. So what's happening.

**DENNETT:** I would say, first of all, that probably there are two varieties of this phenomenon, the veridical and the nonveridical. Maybe you only experienced the veridical ones. I've certainly had the experience of thinking, "Ah, I see how that argument goes," and then tried to flesh it out and realized halfway into it, "Mmm, wait a minute, I thought I saw a path through here and now I don't see it anymore," and decided that maybe I had had a sort of false illumination. Now maybe that never happens to you. You have the feeling of "Aha, yes, it's all clear to me now, just a minute, I'll set it right down." And then sometimes it does set right down, and this of course confirms your trust in your own phenomenology. When I have another aha experience, I'll trust it. But you might also have false aha experiences, which don't work when you go to set them down.

**SACKS:** Freeman, you describe an aha moment in *Disturbing the Universe* when you were on a Greyhound bus. You suddenly saw a synthesis of Feynman's approach, and you said you had no need to write it down, it was there. And then you were able to sleep, knowing you had it.

**GOULD:** On a Greyhound bus?

**DYSON:** Yes, but of course with mathematics you're doing that all the time. That's what mathematics really is: you have sudden intuitions about connections between things. You don't see the equations written down, it's just a feeling that the structure somehow connects, and then laboriously you go through the details and find out if it works or doesn't work. And sometimes it doesn't. But that's very much what a mathematician does, and I believe it's true of music. I've learned nothing about music from growing up in a musical household but a great deal about musicians. And it was quite clear to me that musicians work in the same way.

**TOULMIN:** Can we get back to something that Dan said? It seems to me that what Dan calls the illusion of detail can be turned around and looked at from quite a different angle. A complementary way of viewing this is by talking about the illusion of inwardness. Because people think that what they call consciousness has got to be an inner picture, they're tempted to attribute detail to it. And then afterward they discover it lacked the detail. The insistence on treating all mental skills as

255

concerned with the manipulation of inner pictures seems to me to be a temporary phase in the history of philosophical psychology. What you're talking about, in fact, is in many cases situations in which one becomes aware of the availability of detail, and only once you are aware of the availability of detail, you find that by acting appropriately you're able to fill the whole thing up. As you say, sometimes you find out as you go along that you kidded yourself that the detail was going to come out the way it did. But it does seem to me that what is inward is quite a separate question from what is mentally available to you. The contrast to what is permanently in the interior is these things that are internalizable. There are skills that we master, first of all in the public domain, which we can, or have occasion to, or have motives for internalizing.

I used to walk my elder daughter to school. She was fascinated by arithmetic at that stage, and she would ask me to give her sums to do. So I would say, "Polly, what is 17 plus 32?" And then she walked along with her eyes closed, so I asked her why. She answered, "That way I can see the numbers against the darkness." On the other hand, the skill she was performing by generating this inner representation was a skill she'd already mastered with pencil and paper, or with chalk and blackboard. The primary skill is the skill we have in the internal domain. It's not that we have to be able to do things in our minds which we then externalize. We acquire skills in dealing with the world which for certain purposes and on certain occasions we internalize. But this means that there is a great deal of our mental life which we need not internalize—namely, the mental life that's just concerned with exercising all the skills we have in the public domain. So it's only those aspects of our mental activity which we've had occasion to internalize that can be said to be inward. Obviously I'm grinding an ax, which I suspect we share to some extent. Too many of our colleagues in philosophical psychology were tempted for too long to assume that everything that went on in the mind was like the products of internalization. Which just ain't so.

**DENNETT:** A nice case happened to me not too long ago. My son used to have a chinning bar on a bracket on the doorway going into his bedroom at just about this height for me. I banged my head on it once or twice, and then after a long time had passed, as I was walking into my son's room I suddenly discovered that I was doing a sort of reflexive duck for a bar that was no longer there. Now, obviously there was something above my neck, between my ears, that had been laid down by those earlier experiences. All I had to do was to be put into this circumstance, and even though I was thinking about something else, it triggered the response. It's little bits of machinery of that sort that I'm saying actually compose the mind. And, as you say, they're not internalized in this traditional sense at all, they're internalized in another sense—there's something in your body that ensures their maintenance. I know this is a point that Rupert very strongly disagrees with. But it's the standard assumption.

**SHELDRAKE:** It's a mere assumption, yes.

*If you're talking about machinery, just to make things clear, let's take two steps back. You said, "I think a robot could definitely be conscious in exactly, unmetaphorically the same way we are. We are organic robots created by a research-and-development process called natural selection, and also, of course, by a learning process in our own lifetimes." One of the reasons you won't make a robot with our consciousness is that you would have to give it human rights.*

**DENNETT:** Of course. Of course.

*At the same time, Oliver is saying, "Mechanical models break down hopelessly before the sheer creativity of the brain." Before we continue on internalization, let's have a look at the mechanistic and other models of the brain.*

**TOULMIN:** But the mechanistic model again is not univocal. I mean, what we can conceive of as mechanistic models covers an enormous range. Take the point that Dan made earlier about the difference between plants and animals. For a long time our philosophical colleagues were arguing about the conceivability of a thinking machine, or a machine having feelings. All the time they took it for granted that computers had to be anchored down to the floor. Now a computer anchored down to the floor is like a plant. There are all kinds of skills that (a) are useless to it and (b) we wouldn't know whether to say if they had them or not. If you had a computer that was able to drive itself around, and we came into the lab one day and found a message on the table saying "Gone fishing," then our attitude toward the computer would change very much.

**DENNETT:** If it said, "Gone to the baseball game," even Steve might believe it.

**GOULD:** I might take two seats or something.

**TOULMIN:** I'm sure what Dan was saying was that down the road somewhere, we shall get to the point at which we shall know how to specify what a computer would have to be able to do in order for us to be able to say, "It's lost consciousness," for instance, or "It's recovered consciousness."

**SACKS:** But I think that terms like "mechanism" and "mechanical" and "computer" and "computational" maybe have to be redefined. Perhaps long before we get to consciousness one needs to talk about emotion and feelings. For example, when J. Z. Young gave the lectures that were later published as *A Model of the Brain,* which was based on his work with octopuses, on the one hand he has circuit diagrams and feedback and talks about the brain as a computer, but he then talks about the movement and motive and emotion in an octopus. He says one must think of the octopus as an exploratory computer. Now, is the word "exploratory" in a radically different domain from a computer? Is one muddling the whole thing? Does one first need to say, "What is exploration? What does it mean to be in the world, and sample the world, and construct a world, and adapt to the world?" I think there's a danger in bringing in a mechanical model of perceptions which would grind perceptions. I think there's a danger in bringing in our latest technological device too early.

**DENNETT:** That's just it. The terms "mechanical," "mechanism," and "computer" have connotations that are actually much narrower but also more powerful than the terms technically ought to have. When we think of a computer, as Stephen says, we think of a boxy thing on the floor or a boxy thing sitting on your desk. But we don't really think of a leaping, galloping robot.

**SACKS:** Perhaps one shouldn't.

**TOULMIN:** The word "mechanical" is just a concertina word, that's the trouble. If Leibniz had seen my Macintosh, he'd certainly have said, quite rightly, "That's not what I call a machine at all." The point I'm making is that everybody in the seventeenth century who studied mathematical mechanics was doing it to some very constricting presuppositions, which have gradually been eroded with the progress of physics. There's a sense in which something quite radical already happened with Maxwell. The problem of reconciling Newtonian mechanics with electromagnetic theory was the prime stumbling block that led to the transition to twentieth-century physics, the transformation equations for these systems being quite different. When you were talking earlier about imagining computers that would do this, that, and the other, I was thinking of Kelvin, who used to say that he never felt he really understood the phenomenon unless he could see how he could make a machine that would replicate it. And when he said "a machine," he really meant a Newtonian machine with at most a bit of hydraulics built in. So there's a sense in which once you put field theory right into the center of the picture, which is, as you know, what Newton was always scared of being accused of doing . . .

**DENNETT:** But that's what he did.

**TOULMIN:** Of course he did. No, Newton was in an embarassing position. He knew he couldn't get along without fields, so he took the desperate step of saying that the operation of fields is self-evidently the action of God in the universe. Fields are the device by which God maintains order in a universe which, if it were purely Epicurian, would be totally random.

**GOULD:** But in his correspondence with Bernard he was willing to permit true angelic action for certain aspects of the very earliest history. To get the sun's rotations right.

**TOULMIN:** I'm just still responding to the way the question was initially posed: Does it make sense to talk of producing a machine or a computer that's capable of manifesting consciousness?

**DENNETT:** Well, take an easier case, then: self-replication. There is a notion of mechanism in which at least orthodoxy today would say they had a pretty good handle on the machinery of reproduction. There are still lots of things to be done, but we know enough so that by and large people don't suppose they're going to have to switch to some sort of field theory to explain heritability. Of course, if we look at Neumann, we see that one of his great insights was his paper on self-replicating machines. He described in some detail what the necessary and sufficient conditions for a self-replicating machine would be, and it turns out to have been a prescient abstract description of the very process that one discovers in DNA and RNA. Now, there's an enlarged and I think up-to-the-minute version of mechanism.

**TOULMIN:** Do you really prefer the word "machine" to the word "process"? I noticed you used the word "process" just now.

**DENNETT:** Well, maybe that's a stylistic foible that I should try to stifle in myself, because my claim, for better for worse, is that in order to explain consciousness we don't need any more revolutionary science than we already have for explaining replication. The biology and the microbiology and the organic chemistry that will explain growth and self-repair and replication will also explain perception and memory and learning and intelligence.

**SHELDRAKE:** They might do that if we had them. This is spinning speculation on speculation. First of all, there's the assumption that there is an explanation of morphogenesis and reproduction. I don't agree that these problems are already solved. And I wonder, as Stephen said, why you have to keep using the word "machine." It's so anthropocentric. Only people make machines.

**DENNETT:** I guess I disagree with Rupert that the only machines are manmade. I think that the right way to think of biology is as a sort of reverse engineering. Learning about all these amazing artifacts that have been created by this long process of design and redesign and redesign. I think that biology as a science is really much more closely related to engineering than it is, say, to physics. And that it's reverse engineering, it's all this asking "why" questions. Why is this piece like this, why isn't it like that instead? How does this thing work? I would want to take the benefits and accept the costs of saying that organisms are machines.

**SHELDRAKE:** Well, it's a very conventional view to take, of course. Most biologists would agree. I personally think that these machine and engineering metaphors are not particularly helpful. But it's very curious that in many ways physics has moved on beyond narrowly mechanical views, and biology has got more into them. These mechanical metaphors are helpful up to a point, but I think it's good to remember they're only limited models. We may get more illuminating views of things without forcing everything into this model.

**SACKS:** Of course you can explain the word "machine" until it means the same as "organism." But to be more specific, I think that by and large the brain is nonalgorithmic, at least in its higher functions, and that it categorizes everything from the start in relation to the self. Or rather, some sort of self emerges through the categorizations. And this would be peculiar behavior for any sort of machine.

**DENNETT:** Well, most computers are nonalgorithmic at some level. Your standard chess-playing computer is nonalgorithmic. It doesn't have an algorithm for checkmate. It takes chances, it's a heuristic program. It'll beat me every time, but it doesn't have an algorithm for beating me—just an algorithm for playing chess.

**SACKS:** I also want to bring in the word "meaning" somehow. It may be that a number of performances that are felt to be meaningful, such as playing chess, can be simulated by use of a set of rules or some other heuristic device that is not meaningful. But the fact that a computer can beat a grand master doesn't mean it works the same way.

**TOULMIN:** It may or may not, and then the interesting question is: Can we find out in what respects? The significant thing, it seems to me, is that after the computer has beaten the grand master, it doesn't go off and drink a glass of champagne, it doesn't show signs of victory.

**DENNETT:** That's one of the unfortunate aspects of the historical fact that chess was taken as the toy problem for computers. I have a feeling that people would be less inclined to dismiss out of hand the claim that there is real meaning being considered and appreciated if instead the toy problem had been in robotics, if the computer had been an autonomous self-protective firewood gatherer, which would go out and live in the wild for indefinite periods of time. If that had been the case, the protestation "It's only a machine, of course it doesn't really understand anything about its inputs and outputs" would be a bit more hollow. In that case, the social context would sort of drop out. Chess lives in this rich social context where there are rules and going out for a drink afterward and throwing a game because you want to cheer up your opponent who's depressed and so forth. But there are other activities that are more naturally removable from such a context, in which you could see the meaning was really being appreciated.

**TOULMIN:** Yes, but the interesting thing is that to shift from computer to robot requires the use of some very novel features. A robot that did what you said would have to have been built with a command of Aristotle's practical reason, not just a computation. One of the things about the Cartesian view of rationality is that rationality becomes almost entirely computational. This is one of the reasons why people are unhappy to talk about computers having emotions, because it involves the philosophical implication that having an emotion is just having a mastery of a certain kind of computation. Which we don't want to be the case. The interesting thing about the problem "What would it take to design a robot that could ensure its own survival in a hostile environment?" is that you'd have to give it all kinds of skills.

**DENNETT:** You'd have to give it emotions. Fear and despair. And you can. In fact, I've been working with artificial intelligence experts on a project to describe the specifications of an emotional robot. And I'll go even further. I have imagined a thought experiment of creating an emotional word processor. Now you ask how in the world could you ever make an emotional word processor? First of all, you'd have to deliberately degrade its performance in ways that would make it barely suitable for human use unless it were very carefully operated. What makes word processors nice now is that they just obviously don't care. You can't overload them, you can't put them near their limits. So I imagine a word processor that, say, lives on keystrokes. If it doesn't get keystrokes, it's gonna die. You just build it that way. And it has memory limitations and so forth that mean that certain states of affairs in its world are threatening to it. And I want to make this quite real, people are going to throw the computer away if it doesn't work anymore. So in order to survive, it must find a way of living in this world. I'll cut all the details short and just say I imagine it would be possible to create such a word processor. I'm not going to let it talk, by the way, I'm not going to let it communicate verbally with its users, but it can maybe flash the screen or make a little beep. It's going to have some ways of reacting.

There are basically two ways that users can treat these things. One is considerate. They will come to appreciate the needs of this thing, and to treat it well. And they'll get rewarded for this. The other way is to sort of beat the tar out of it, the way some people treat their horses. And in effect this word processor would be always on the edge of despair, always on the edge of death, but just making a living. I predict that if you did this right, that if one of the nasty users then came and used the word processor of one of the considerate people, it would very much upset that person. He'd say, "You mustn't treat it that way, this is unconscionable. Can't you see that this is an abuse of this system?"

Now, of course this is just a thought experiment at this point. But I think the sympathies and the reactions that are so important to us when we think of emotions would be evocable, and not as an illusion. I think that it would actually be getting at something that is fundamental to emotion—that emotional reactions in us would be evoked when we saw the circumstances that those systems were put in.

**GOULD:** But this is already the case now for musical instruments and many other things. The point is, would the word processors notice and behave differently?

**DENNETT:** Well, certainly musicians would cringe to see a violin or a piano being abused. But there's really a different dimension, because there's interaction of a different sort in these cases. I'm supposing that these devices have ways of adjusting their own behavior in order to protect themselves from the things that can hurt them in their environment. That's why I chose a word processor, because it was putting it in a real, not simulated, context. But these things actually would have to earn a living in a world where people had other purposes.

**SACKS:** I confess I was thinking of dogs and wishing we would change the subject from these sort of fictitious word processors to real animals, and that we would think together about the lives and adaptations and growth and emotions and capacities and perhaps consciousness of animals.

**TOULMIN:** Does anybody at this table truly believe that dogs don't have feelings? As opposed to having theoretical reasons for feeling that they have to say dogs don't have feelings? Dan, would you think that dogs don't experience joy, shame, curiosity? You know, the basic seven-odd repertory of emotions?

**DENNETT:** They certainly manifest them, but to say that they experience them is actually to say something on top of that.

**SACKS:** You don't have to report an experience to experience it.

**GOULD:** "Manifest" is the important decision. When Darwin wrote his book, remember he called it "expression of the emotion." I don't think there's any doubt about the homology of expression.

**SACKS:** Well, let's go a bit lower. I was mentioning to Stephen earlier, a friend of mine has adopted a giant African snail as a pet. But I cannot imagine what sort of relationship he has to it.

*Steve, you can imagine, I think?*

**GOULD:** Yes, but the giant African snails are some of the world's most horrid agricultural pests. They've been responsible, mainly through misguided attempts to control them, for the extinction of hundreds of indigenous land snails throughout the world. So I don't like those particular ones.

**SACKS:** But what about its homologies in terms of emotions?

**GOULD:** I'm sorry, I was temporizing to get beyond the difficult point. You see, I don't think it's really definable, because there is truly a continuum. It is indeed the homology of that perceived similar expression that draws us to mammals. Where do we stop along the genealogical connectivity? Some people probably may see sufficient homology in a fish's eyes. I don't. By the time you get to snails, they have eyes that may or may not be homologues in the sense of being independently evolved. But there you're dealing with at least 550 million years of evolutionary separation.

I think it doesn't trigger most people's emotions. In part it's the simple homology of genealogical resemblance, but then there's another system that overrides that and can fool us. There are certain morphologies that trigger our affection, the main ones being the features of babyhood, probably because we must care for our children. Some animals have short faces and big eyes and evoke the features of babyhood that are appealing to us. I think it's fundamentally aesthetic, based on both evolutionary distance and certain features of our evolved biology.

And that also gets into the question of consciousness, which to me is a very troubling one. To me it's largely semantic. Of course, animals that are close enough to us, because of the homology of similar emotional expression, have features that in some legitimate vernacular senses of the word "consciousness" must be conscious. And yet the gap between that and what we can do with our ability to reflect self-consciously and abstractly is so great that it's quite reasonable to talk about a meaningful gap.

**TOULMIN:** Before we leave this business of emotional response, I don't think the story you tell in terms of homology covers enough ground here. What I'm saying is that we know something about animals' emotions because of their successes and failures in acting, not simply on the basis of what we see when we look in their eyes. I mean, on the basis of their successes and failures in acting, we may infer some things about what kinds of central nervous systems they presumably have. But that's a presumption. It seems to me that the emotions manifest themselves in the patterns of life and response, not just in the musculature of the face.

Though, as Darwin was right to point out, the musculature of the face itself plays a part in evoking responses from other individuals, not only within the same species but even across specific and generic boundaries. But I do think we want at a certain point to get beyond this, to step sideways and realize that alongside any story you can possibly tell about the central nervous system, there are the stories about the phenomenology of reactions and successes and failures and the rest, which constitute the life patterns in the course of which different operations of the neural system are called into play.

**GOULD:** And we see the differences in cognitive rules that in some instances almost make us cringe. In birds, for example, there are many learning rules that lead to behaviors that are horrendous in human moral terms. Many birds, for example, make judgments as to which are their young and which they protect only by the simple rule whether they're in or out of the nest. If you take the youngster and put it outside the nest, it shrieks and appeals—or so we read it—but the mother ignores it and it dies. If it's inside the nest, it'll be fed. And of course that whole system is then subverted by other birds. The cuckoo will not only throw out of the nest the true children of the parents, but then cause the parents to feed it, until sometimes the cuckoo is ten or twenty times heavier than the parents that are feeding it. And yet the parent is still operating by the cognitive rule "Feed what's inside the nest, don't feed what's outside the nest." It's like the old joke about how you treat a not particularly intelligent guy who'd never been to sea and suddenly finds himself in the navy; he only had to follow one rule: if it moves, salute it, if it doesn't move, paint it. It's a simple cognitive rule. It's a different mental system that they're following. But there's mentality there, there are rules.

*Let us try to approach those rules and that mentality from a slightly different point of view. Daniel Dennett says there's not a little man in our heads that is all-powerful. There are a bunch of little men in our heads that are partly powerful, and you can break them down and break them down until you finally get dumb, stupid ants running around that can't even count to two. And then you can replace the whole thing by a machine.*

**DENNETT:** In principle, yes. And that's the point.

**SHELDRAKE:** I can't understand why you should want to make that claim. Why do we need any little men? Why do you want to reduce it all to a machine?! Why should this metaphor be so hypnotically attractive?

**SACKS:** Yes, I want to know: Do you have a dog?

**DENNETT:** I have had dogs, in fact. One was Charlie, and one was Duffy. Right now I'm dogless. I'm also a father and grandfather. Look, the homunculus is merely a heuristic bridge, an explanatory principle.

Psychologists in particular have learned to scoff at a theory that had a homunculus, because manifestly you weren't explaining anything. If you had a theory that there was a TV screen somewhere in the head which was watched by an inner homunculus, you clearly had simply postponed the whole problem. So people got the idea that homunculus theories were bad. What they were missing was another option, which is that if you can break the problem down so that you have a team of homunculi, and each one does less than the whole job, then you actually can make progress. Then you can take those homunculi in turn and break them down. They are simply bits of machinery that can be treated as having a sort of intelligence, and as capable of performing certain tasks. You ask why I want to reduce it in the end to a machine? Because that's the only way you discharge this otherwise offensive metaphor of the inner homunculus. If you can discharge the homunculi, then you're home.

**TOULMIN:** The natural word for you to use at this point, the noun your verbs demand, is "agent."

**DENNETT:** "Agent" is fine.

**TOULMIN:** But in colloquial usage "machine" and "agent" are not interchangeable. You break the overall agency down into smaller subagencies. If that's what you're saying . . .

**DENNETT:** If finally you get down to agencies that are no bigger than a neuron, then the question is: Is a neuron a machine? It can be replaced by a machine, I think that's pretty clear. If it can be replaced by a machine, then we can replace it by a machine, and we can replace all of them by machines. And then we will have one great big huge thing, which is made up at the base of nothing but machines, but since ex hypothesi they really were replaceable, we will end up with a machine that is conscious.

**TOULMIN:** But the replacement of a single large task by a lot of subtasks, each of which is mediated by a particular subagent—from the outside this looks like a very different program from the one you were presenting us with at the beginning. I do think you must choose with care the colloquial words that you use to expound your point of view. You may end up by saying things that are deeply misleading in ways you do like, or in ways you don't like.

**DENNETT:** Well, show me what the conflict is that you see. I mean, I have all along argued for a strategy that is ubiquitous in cognitive science and artificial intelligence—breaking a task down into subtasks that are initially simply assigned to agents. Then one understands the task better and better and is gradually able to replace agents with something that's just a bit of a computer program, let's say.

**TOULMIN:** Well, I'll tell you what the problem is. Everything you're saying on that level is just fascinating and one may be perfectly happy to accept it, but the fact is we inherit from the seventeenth and eighteenth centuries a whole battery of prejudices about the words "machine" and "mechanical," and you needlessly keep rearousing this conditioned reflex when you don't have to. If you talk about major tasks being broken down into and analyzed in the subtasks, and if you attribute overall agents and subagents and so on to do these tasks . . . I mean, a computer program is a set of operations, and *operare* is an action word. What was objectionable about machines was that they were able to do things only to the extent that they were moved from outside. This is repeated again and again in the seventeenth-century literature. The point about the Archimedean machines was that they were all tools that somebody could use to transform an input of one kind into an output of a different kind. It was because the machines were simply intermediaries in the course of operations that they got this bad name.

**DENNETT:** Well, fine, but there's another side to this. You see this as a needless provocation on my part; I see it rather as a sort of antiseptic to keep people from positing what I call "wonder tissue." In these large theoretical projects in the neurosciences, at one point or another they postulate a little wonder tissue to get them over the embarrassment. I'm talking about apparently card-carrying materialists who nevertheless permit themselves to postulate wonder tissue at one place or another in their theory. In fact, they don't know what they're talking about and they don't apparently mind. What I'm really getting at when I use a term like "machine" is the prohibition of the postulation of wonder tissue.

**SACKS:** It may be in a similar sense that Gerald Edelman talks about spooks, which also mustn't be permitted. He is particularly worried about quantum theories of consciousness which somehow omit all the real tissue of the nervous system and maybe replace it with wonder tissue. I think one has to hold tight to the real tissue of the nervous system and the known anatomy and physiology and the evolutionary and ontogenetic history. Certainly decomposition one way or another occurs in all sorts of activities that are seemingly seamless. Perhaps in a naive way, introspectively we would say, "The world is given to us." You've shown very nicely that there's all sorts of detail that is not given. Now, one can show very easily that color and movement and shape and other modalities are separately constructed. Nothing is more illuminating in this way than certain clinical conditions which specifically knock out one of these. For example, I saw one man, an artist, who had lost the cerebral capacity to construct color. Not only could he no longer see color, he found himself in a gray-and-black world, and he could no longer remember color or imagine it. Color as a dimension had been pulled out of his life. It was as if he had an amnesia for color. There was a strange sort of contradiction in the way he spoke, because he did and he did not know color.

**DENNETT:** Is he still alive and communicable? I've had some puzzles about that case of yours and I'm aching to ask him some questions.

**SACKS:** Alas, he's not, but there must be other such patients. One can have a specific motion-blindness that is quite extraordinary. In such cases someone may see a car clearly until it moves off, and then it vanishes. Instead there's a series of stills. Now, there are thirty-two visual centers in the brain, at latest count, but there doesn't seem to be any master area on which they all converge. So then there's a problem of composition or coherence. How is it all brought together in the absence of any convergence? Now, Edelman would see this in terms of what he calls "reentrance signaling," a massive sort of intercourse between parallel centers, so that the final visual construction—one probably ought to avoid a word like "image"—is a process of incessant negotiation. Here, then, there's no homunculus. Somehow there may appear to be—and I say appear to be—only a what and not a who. So that one might say, "Well, yes, I have these thirty-two areas that are communicating, but there's me, you know, where do I come in?" An answer roughly would be that these thirty-two areas and their connectivity and their communication are yours from the start, and they bear the impress of your experience and your unique place in the world and your "values" from the start. So in this sense the first sensory consciousness, perceptual consciousness, is a synthesis into a scene of objects and events that are related in terms of your experience. So your consciousness is yours from the start, but in a different sense from, say, a phenomenon like bioluminescence. An organism may happen to be luminescent, but it doesn't own its luminescence in the way you own your unique perceptions.

**TOULMIN:** There is also a more inner sense still. There's a lovely story about Morris Cohen, at City College of New York. A student in his class one day put his hand up and said, "Professor Cohen, how do I know that I exist?" Morris Cohen instantly came back: "And who is asking?" There is that kind of possession; it's you who are the subject of this. So that question at least is settled. What the nature of the possession relation is, that we can go into.

*Dan, just to come back to the computer metaphor or the computer, and then we'll go into the depths of the soul and the ambiguity of consciousness—I remember that on the question "Can we become immortal?" you said, "Yes, because what we really are is the information contained in our brains, abstractions. It follows, marvelously, that you and I could be immortal. This is scientifically respectable."*

**DENNETT:** I think so because the alternative is not scientifically respectable. The alternative is that of all the media of information that there are, there is one that can't be changed, that above and beyond the competence that that medium has to store or transmit the information, there's something else that's special about it. Now, I think everybody here would agree in principle that there could be, say, an artificial ear. It would not be made out of organic materials, but as long as it reproduced the receptivity and the sensitivity, as long as the same information channels were there, and so long as the more central areas had not atrophied, a deaf person could be provided with an artificial ear. The idea that we could replace any little bit except one, that there's one area in the brain where the self resides which is not replaceable, I think is a mystical idea and simply a vestige of earlier bad ideas. In fact, Oliver just now was expressing the idea that what you are is the sum total of your attitudes, your memories, your reactions, your hates and fears and hopes. All of that could in principle be preserved, transmitted, reembodied in some other medium, and you would go right on living. Of course it's a science fiction cliché and it's really remarkable that some people, when they read about teleportation or about the idea of a mind being recorded and stored and then later reembodied, they have no trouble at all with this, they think, "Yes, that's a nice implication." While other people find this an utterly intolerable idea. I'm fascinated to see what those who find it intolerable would put in its place.

**SACKS:** I do think that we are, if you want, the sum of the processes and activities in us, but I also think these are not only uniquely marked by our experiences and values but uniquely coded. And I therefore think it would be difficult or impossible to transfer the information to another brain or download it to a machine. It is not information in that sense. It's a unique organization of incredible complexity, which sort of dies with you.

**DENNETT:** I agree entirely that we're talking about the most rarefied of possibilities in principle. The information we're talking about is of such a complexity and so intricately interwoven, the skills with the fears with the hopes with the memories with the loves with the sense of one's own body, that we are not going to do mind transplants by simply booting up some new software and some other brain. Obviously, that's impossible. But the question is whether the impossibility of that is a monumental technical, practical impossibility or whether it's an impossibility in principle. I'm saying it's a monumental technical impossibility, not an impossibility in principle.

**DYSON:** Well, I don't know how anybody can possibly know. But I'd like to come back to that question of wonder tissue. The fact is that in physics we're dealing with wonder tissue all the time, because ordinary matter behaves in very counterintuitive ways when you look at it carefully. It's not at all like electronic computers and it probably does things that are of some use to the organism. It would be strange, in a way, if our central nervous systems didn't make some use of these very strange properties of matter. I think it's not unreasonable that quantum mechanics has something to do with it. But nobody yet has a model for a quantum mechanical neuron.

TOULMIN: Freeman, you seem to be on the verge of saying something very exciting, and I'd love to elicit a bit more. I remember being at a presentation back in 1966. There was a physicist from Berkeley whom Frank Schmitt involved in one of his neurosciences meetings, and he was talking about the possibility that it would be scientifically helpful to give some kind of quantum mechanical characterization of miosis and mitosis. He thought that in these biochemical processes a quantum mechanical description of these icon function switches might well throw some light on things we wouldn't otherwise have noticed. Has any of this kind of thing happened? Do you have the sense that the quantum mechanisms have really managed to develop their physics in a way that illuminates biophysics?

DYSON: No, on the contrary. Almost everything that has been said publicly about this is rubbish. But in spite of all the rubbish that has been written, there may still be a substratum of truth there.

TOULMIN: It certainly comes under Dan's category of things possible in principle. Presumably at a certain level the most subtle processes that take place in the course of physical and biochemical operations of organisms will include some that eventually we'll come to understand.

GOULD: But what about wounding and repair? If one were talking about neurological tissue, I assume that in each human being, to get back to one of Oliver's points, the tissue becomes so conditioned by thirty or forty years of an absolutely personal and irrecoverable history that unless you happened to have mapped every last atom of it before the injury, you never could recover it. You might implant new tissue. That would allow the person to hear again, if that was the kind of tissue it was. But you can never recover the person, surely.

DYSON: I don't know, you may well be right. I don't know anything about neurological repair.

*Oliver, when you saw the sleeping disease patients, you wrote that all the certainty of predictability and having things under control was escaping from you. What happened at that moment? Because that's what we're talking about now, even if indirectly.*

SACHS: Well, I've been thinking, we may need to talk about critical moments when infinite sensitivities appear for the individual and the organism, and possibly phylogenetically as well. What happened with my *Awakenings* patients was that at first, one would see a rather predictable linear dose-related response. And then something would happen. They would get past a particular point and then fluctuations would occur, deepening oscillations that no longer had any clear relation to the time or dose. Sometimes one would see other phenomena that tended to multiply more and more. You saw a sort of incontinent complexification. Sometimes the extreme susceptibility and perhaps an infinitesimal increment or decrement of dose or some infinitesimal environmental circumstance could change the picture. In fact, I was puzzled by this enormous sensitivity. My personal association was some experiments with liquid helium I'd once seen, which partly moved me to use the term "macro-quantum." Now I was sort of ignorant, I think, and also at that time, in 1969, chaos theory hadn't been invented. I'm inclined to think that most of the situations were far-from-equilibrium situations; one was seeing chaotic processes that would sometimes get strangely, interestingly reorganized.

We talked about animals and plants and morphogenesis a bit earlier. I saw some rather pretty pictures in the *Scientific American* recently which were computer simulations of cacti and other plants growing. I think these things probably follow genetic determination fairly closely. But this isn't the case with the development of the nervous system and the neural tube, where 50 percent or whatever of the neurons die or migrate, so that even in identical twins you end up with brains which in their microcircuitry are quite different. The circuitry of the brain doesn't look like any manmade machine. It looks much more like a jungle. This sort of circuitry is incompatible with programming in the ordinary sense . . .

**DENNETT:** In the ordinary sense, absolutely.

**SACKS:** . . . unless we find a radically different sort of engineering, in which variation is of the essence and not an aberration.

**DENNETT:** And that's just what's coming along. There's a new movement, the artificial life movement, and one of the key features that distinguishes AL from AI is this different attitude toward engineering. AI traditionally starts at the top, it describes a problem and then tries to decompose it and decompose it and decompose it into its functional parts. It's a very bureaucratic idea of decomposition. And when you design systems that way, you don't have any featherbedders, any supernumeraries, any layabouts. Every agent has a job. That's the traditional way of designing systems. A lot of AI systems are of that sort. But there are other approaches both to AI and more particularly in artificial life which operate just the other way around, they're bottom up. They start with lots of little agentlike things or organism-type things. They let them grow and they build in a lot of variation.

One of the delightful discoveries of this research method is that a whole new space of designs is opened up to analysis. You get something that's profoundly biological and profoundly unartifactual—

designs where multiple functionality is built in everywhere. When human engineers design something, they know that the biggest problem they face is unanticipated side effects. They build this piece here, they build that piece there, and they don't anticipate that these pieces are going to interact and hurt each other in some way. So when human engineers design something—this is particularly true in software design—they compartmentalize, they isolate everything, they give everything just one function, and they work very hard to keep their units from interacting with each other. That's the way they deal with this problem.

Mother Nature—the processes of evolution—has no foresight, so she doesn't have to worry about unforeseen side effects. And as a result, she gets the benefit of unforeseen, serendipitous side effects. So you get multiple functionality. You get items that are not entirely insulated which are playing several roles at once, which is very rare in traditionally designed artifacts. This architectural space, as it is now opening up, is indeed much more biological. As you say, the nervous system looks like a tangled jungle, like an engineer's nightmare. And indeed, it's just about impenetrable to analysis by traditional engineering methods. However, it does not appear to be so impenetrable to these new methods that are working from the bottom up and are beginning to grow very interesting structures that look much more biological and have some nice properties.

GOULD: That's scarcely surprising, since in a sense it's a biologically evolved structure. Evolutionary biologists, of which I'm one, are fond of saying that variation is the only intrinsic reality and that types and means are only the abstractions. But Darwin himself was quite clear on multiple functionality. It's almost a logical need, although there is plenty of empirical evidence in particular cases. Given the mass extinctions and climatic shifts and contingencies of evolution, if you don't have variation and multiple functionalities, you're dead. The hydrodynamically best designed fish in the world dies when the pond dries up, and the pond always dries up in the fullness of time. Lineages that get through do so either because they have massive redundancies or because, by good fortune, structures built for one function through natural construction are co-optable for others.

So with a model like neural Darwinism, though it's analogous to the Darwinian process only on a genetic level, it nonetheless has the same fundamental features as the evolutionary process. Every step of the way there's massive gene duplication, but genes don't duplicate in order to provide flexibility to organisms who will need it 10 million years down the road. Presumably they duplicate for something intrinsic to their own mechanics that probably represents gene selection at its own level. It has nothing to do with the biology of organisms, yet that redundancy is there. How could you ever have evolved anything complex without it?

Take the original fish that has both lungs and gills. The only way it can evolve a swim bladder is that it turns the lung into the swim bladder and keeps breathing through gills. How could you ever get the bones of your inner ear, which are jawbones in a reptile? That's inconceivable. Creationists say it's an inconceivable transition because while the bones were moving from their articulating positions in the reptilian jaw into the mammalian inner ear, you'd have to have an unhinged jaw. But of course you don't. The intermediary forms have a double jaw joint. Once a double jaw joint is established, then the two old bones of the reptilian joint are free to move into the middle ear because functionality is maintained. There's always that massive redundancy. And what that leads to is organic machinery that is vastly nonoptimal by the standards of traditional principles of human design.

**SACHS:** I remembered what I forgot. I think probably another expression of this enormous redundancy or degeneracy is the great neural robustness of identity. You can have a remarkable amount of brain damage, either in specific areas or globally, and the person is still there. It's said that when Henry James was in the terminal delirium of pneumonia, with a temperature of 105 degrees, his utterances were not only Jamesian, they were late James.

But with something like Alzheimer's disease, one sees that even perhaps when people can no longer comprehend or use language, and when their conceptual thinking is much altered, they may still show musical expression or an ability to draw in which their sensibility and idiosyncrasy are clear. I think that if self is lost, it's very late indeed, basically because everything is an expression of self. Every gesture, every movement, every word, every thought, every predilection.

**DENNETT:** But some are more selfy than others. If one had data on the degeneration through Alzheimer's disease of a wide variety of, say, artists, and if we watched their attempts—if they could still make attempts—to produce works of art, one might find that some of them had stylistic habits that were so deeply rooted in their bodies and had so little cognitive mediation that we could still recognize those features, those marks of that person's identity, because they were gestural, let's say. Other artists might have their defined characteristics at a much more cognitive level and they would just disappear completely. And we'd say that artist had gone completely, even though he was no more demented by Alzheimer's than another artist who was still recognizable because what was characteristic of that artist was not so highly mediated by cognition. It's possible.

*May I ask something about Rose, one of the postencephalitic patients? Daniel has said that memory is a process of reinterpretation. Oliver said that it's close to imagination. It's not like a Xerox, it's constantly growing with us. You saw Rose coming out of this sleeping disease land, this nowhere land. And one of your fascinations was that all her memories of the 1920s were still intact. Every song, hundreds of anecdotes. Well, if memory is so close to imagination and constantly transforming, how could all those memories have remained unchanged?*

SACKS: Rose said, "I know it's 1969, but I feel it's 1926." She indicated that Kennedy's assassination, Pearl Harbor, a few things had registered in an isolated way. But she didn't seem to have any coherent memory, no inner chronicle, no inner narrative, and on the whole, no referring of memories to herself for forty-three years. I think she really had not been constructing memories in that time and she hadn't been updated. In some sense she was still in 1926.

*Her memories were frozen.*

SACKS: Yeah, and what one saw was this exuberant surface of someone who is full of gossip, you know. "Yesterday I did this . . . and someone said to me . . . and I went to the concert and, and, gee, I must go do this." . . .

DENNETT: But there's another thing I want to know about Rose and about the others. During this frozen period, did they also not rehearse their own memories of the 1920s? Because we really remember through several earlier recollections, and the freshness of Rose's memory when she was awakened might partly be due to the fact that during that period of time, not only was she not taking in new material, she wasn't even rehearsing the old. Do we know anything about whether during that period they were rehearsing their memories?

SACKS: Well, a little. And I think this is a very crucial point. I describe one patient as rehearsing childhood scenes during this trancelike period. But this didn't seem to be the case with Rose, who mentioned that she had idle, maddening, mechanical activities. On one occasion she said she had been stuck for hours and days and weeks on what she called a "musical quadrangle," which was a mental quadrangle formed of five notes from a Verdi aria. I think she really was not able to rehearse or relive things, and so in some sense one was getting them fresh or raw, which may be very unusual. Normally, of course, we're rehearsing all the time. And no memory ever comes up in the same form again; it's altered by context and fantasy. I need to take back here something I wrote in one of my pieces about two patients with convulsive memories, patients who had temporal lobe seizures and who suddenly apparently had memories from the past. Although I think there was something stereotyped about those memories, they weren't exactly the same. There was equally a quality of construction and reconstruction, which seems to me to be completely against any sort of notion of memory as replica.

*Isn't it strange that our past is constantly rebuilt, transformed? It's not like a film running in the theater. And yet we can talk about robust identity. Isn't that somewhat odd?*

**SACKS:** Memory enlarges us. When Goethe was seventy-five, at his birthday someone made a toast to memory and he got furious. He said he didn't recognize memory in that sense of something isolable. He said that whatever was significant or important was taken into our inmost being, and it enlarges us. There's a very beautiful description of memory and identity as completely interwoven and ongoing all the while. As a neurologist and as a pathologist, I think what I often have to describe are some of the mishaps of this process. For example, the phantom limb is a sort of bizarre fossil memory with a sort of fixity and deadness that no real or living memory has. Maybe neurosis and trauma or other neurological conditions can produce such fossil memories.

**GOULD:** If memories were merely true, there'd be too much of the universally objective about them. I had an experience a couple of years ago which sent me to write an essay about it which gave me some insight into a funny little incident I remembered all my life. In Queens where I grew up, my grandfather and I would buy the *New York Times* every Sunday and then we'd go to some steps and he'd lay out the newspaper—he was a very nattily dressed and formal man—and we'd sit on the steps and have these wonderful conversations. Now the main building in that area was the Forest Hills tennis stadium. And so I was sure that's where it was, that these steps were the back steps of the tennis stadium. All my life I've told that story. Clearly I knew it to be so. A couple of years ago I was in my old neighborhood for the first time in thirty years. I walked down Queens Boulevard and I suddenly realized it couldn't have been the tennis stadium, because that was a mile away and we didn't walk that far. And then I saw this old dilapidated six-story warehouse building, and there were the steps. I had transmogrified the memory onto the more heroic building in that neighborhood. Yet the memory was so clear. Now, if I had been right, it still would have been part of me, but it's so much more a part of me that I had made this mixture.

**TOULMIN:** But this is where the whole question of narrative comes in. As we reconstruct memory, we reconstruct it into a progressively more coherent narrative. So that that extent our personality is the sum of our own construals. I prefer the word "construal" to "construction."

**DENNETT:** And not just our own construals, because we're terribly dependent on the endorsement and the elaboration of those construals by everybody we did it with.

*"Our tales are spun, but for the most part we don't spin them, they spin us," you wrote. "We are in the center of narrative gravity."*

DENNETT: I mean that quite literally. Physicists have the concept of the center of gravity, or center of mass. It's a theoretical abstraction, but it makes for a much more tractable consideration of gravity. Similarly, we organize complex goings-on in our lives around a sort of imaginary point, a center of narrative gravity. And that's what I say a self is. A self is not a little special pearl in the middle of your brain, it's really a theoretical construct that has the same ontological status as the center of gravity. It's that idealized agent who is the author of my speech acts, who is the decider of my intentional actions, who is the recipient of my perceptions, the dreamer of my dreams, the thinker of my thoughts. But however useful that idea is in making sense of a complicated human being, you have to abandon it once you start moving around in the brain. You've got to get away from the idea that there's this place in the brain where all this comes together.

TOULMIN: That's why the relationship between Cartesianism in philosophy and the mechanistic tradition in seventeenth-century physics was an unhappy historical accident. If you take "Cogito ergo sum" to mean "I have an assurance of my identity because I'm the one who has all these experiences," then what you were uttering just now was a very Cartesian thought.

DENNETT: Yes, but neither Descartes nor any of his followers took it that way.

TOULMIN: Oh, I think Descartes did take it that way, at least half the time. I think one can reread the *Meditations* in such a way that he's putting precisely your construal on it. It's only when the thing gets taken up by people who are insisting on building a cosmic picture that it's mechanistic, which Descartes also wanted.

*If I say that language is responsible for forming consciousness, rather than consciousness being a necessary first step in developing language . . .*

TOULMIN: Language is the instrument we use to shape consciousness with.

SACKS: No no no, language is an instrument, but there are all sorts of consciousness and concept formation that must precede language.

DENNETT: I'm going to take a more radical line. Concept formation of a sort precedes language. But the sort of concept formation that precedes language is what some people would call implicit concept formation. Thus a polar bear in one sense has a concept of snow. There are lots of ways you could prove that the polar bear makes discriminations that are appropriate, that show that in a sense a polar bear has a concept of snow, and hence there's concept formation in the polar bear. We could ask to what extent the polar bear has to learn this concept; it might even be in some measure innate. But what the polar bear doesn't have is a *manipulable* concept of snow. The polar bear doesn't wonder about the essence of snow, the polar bear can't think about snow the way even a small child can think about snow. In that stronger sense of concept, the question of whether concept formation can precede language is, I think, not at all an obvious question. For the time being I am defending a radical view, which was a nice fallback, and that is that in fact manipulable concepts—that is, concepts we can think about—really depend on our getting started with language rather than the other way around.

GOULD: I don't think that's necessarily that radical a view. I think a key evolutionary question has to be answered before you can get at it—and it may never be possible to get the information that would allow an answer—which is whether human language evolves in genetic and functional continuity with gestural communication systems. There is no doubt that chimpanzees and other animals are communicating concepts through their grunts and other sounds, and if human language is just that promoted through selection or a large brain, then I think in a sense we have to allow that there may be a fairly strong tie that goes back to other animals. But I think it's just as likely that it's a totally unresolved question.

Chomsky is often misread as an anti-evolutionist, because he keeps talking about the language organ as somehow descending into the mind. But he doesn't mean that it descends in the sense of creation, just that it doesn't evolve in functional and genealogical continuity with the gestural systems of other animals. Rather, it's co-opted at some point from some other property of the brain that evolved for other purposes. And if that's so, it may be that although in animals—certainly in chimpanzees—there are modes of thought that we want in some vernacular sense to call consciousness, they don't include that fundamental capacity for metaphor and abstraction which comes in only with what we call language in humans. And if that comes in somewhat discontinuously, at least through co-opting some other brain system, then there isn't even the continuity. I think that's at least a plausible position.

TOULMIN: This discontinuity, if it exists, is the discontinuity from the pragmatic use of language to the abstract, metaphorical use of language.

GOULD: We know that chimps have that pragmatic sense. But that system is in fact not the genealogical precursor of the linguistic system of humans, which I think is a plausible but unproven position.

**SACKS:** One would certainly think, Dan, that a test of what you were saying, or at least some illumination, might come from looking at intelligent human beings who through some mishap have been denied normal acquisition of language, including sign.

**DENNETT:** The trouble is I don't think there's any very good evidence about nonsigning congenitally deaf people.

**SACKS:** Well, I think there's a fair amount of evidence, though one might want to see it more systematic. Although there is an odd gap between it and the eighteenth-century accounts, like the report of the deaf boy who had no formal schooling until the age of fourteen. He had some deaf siblings, and between them they constructed a so-called home sign, but home sign is really a sort of sempahore rather than language.

**DENNETT:** Do we know they weren't simply underestimated by their observers back then?

**SACKS:** No. William James was interested in this, and had a considerable correspondence in the 1890s with a fine deaf artist who had had no formal language until the age of ten. And recently there's been a fascinating book by Susan Schaller called *A Man without Words*, in which she describes a twenty-seven-year-old deaf man on a remote farm in Mexico, who had had no contact with other deaf people and no schooling. And yet somehow he managed to get on seemingly fairly well with gestures and common sense. She tries to describe his world before and after.

But having said that . . . You know, every footnote I write starts as an inner reservation; many start with "But." "But" seems to me the first sort of cerebral punctuation. I described this boy Joseph, an eleven-year-old deaf boy who had mistakenly been diagnosed as retarded and then as autistic, before it was realized that he was deaf. It seemed to me that Joseph in a way was confined to the here and now, that he had a very concrete perceptual mode of functioning. It was difficult or impossible for him not only to communicate or for others to communicate with him, but for him to think of matters that were remote, out of sight, contingent, hypothetical. So he seemed to me intellectually very, very restricted, although with a very sharp visual intelligence and a sense of humor. It seemed to me that he was wonderingly envious of the rest of us. He seemed to look at our mouths and our hands and he perceived, I think, that we had some sort of remarkable power he couldn't imagine.

In a later edition of *Seeing Voices* I describe another boy, a deaf Italian gypsy boy, who'd got to the age of nine without language. And he didn't seem to me to be disabled or retarded in the same way that Joseph was. He's ten and a half now, and he has subsequently done brilliantly, and not only is fluent in sign and Italian but a very good chess player. He was very richly a member of his own family and community, so that whatever other tools were used to communicate a culture and a feeling of self were not defective. Whereas Joseph had suffered from the stigma of being seen as retarded or autistic, so he had become very isolated socially. But there was something else the matter with Joseph, it wasn't simply that he had no language.

*Freeman, you said to me, "I would like to talk with Oliver Sacks about an autistic child I've known for years."*

**DYSON:** She just happens to be a close friend, and I've been following her life for thirty-five years. This case has a particular interest for me because I'm in the business of searching for alien civilizations. I always felt this child was the closest I'd ever come to an alien civilization. She had plenty of intelligence but looked at the world in a profoundly different way. And I gather you have had even more experience with autism.

**SACKS:** I think the "otherness" that one can see in autistic people and the other ways in which personality and identity can develop are also an immensely rich, important thing to talk about, but at the moment I think the question is how much identity and intelligence in the usual sense can develop without language. Although again it has been said that the difficulty with language, and especially with those pragmatic uses of it, is an essential part of the cognitive and emotional picture of autism. So perhaps they're not unrelated.

**DENNETT:** In Merlin Donald's new book on the origins of the human mind he discusses a very interesting case, the case of Brother John, a French-Canadian monk who has epileptic seizures that render him temporarily aphasic. During those seizures he's not unconscious, but he purportedly not only can't speak but can't even talk to himself. The research is interesting particularly because in this man's communicable phases they were able to instruct him how to turn on a tape recorder, so that as he felt one of these seizures coming on, they'd have some record of what he could actually do and not do during those periods. So they've gathered some pretty good evidence about him, and what he can do is striking. The most striking case, I think, was when he had one of these seizures on a trip. He was in a hotel lobby and the clerk behind the desk and all the people were terribly worried about him. And he has the resourcefulness to come up with some ingenious ways of reassuring them that they should just relax and he'll be all right in a few minutes, even though he's doing this without being able even to talk to himself. But it's also true that this particular patient sheds no light at all on the question of which of his mental competences he could have acquired without language. It may be like barefoot waterskiing—it's amazing that you can do it, but you've got to wear the skis first to get up and going.

**SACKS:** Another very interesting theme is the role of mime, and whether before spoken language there was a whole level of mime in action. Sometimes—in fact, rather frequently—in patients aphasic mimicry may be preserved and can sometimes be formalized. Quite a few of our patients learn a so-called Amerindian gestural code. Some aphasiacs can become incredibly skilled both in understanding and in using mime. I describe this in one of my pieces where a political speech seemed to be seen through because of incongruity between gestures. Inactive representations often seem to be oddly omitted in descriptions of language.

**TOULMIN:** Can I connect back what you just said to what you said a few minutes ago about this Italian gypsy boy, that you thought the very high level of skills he was now able to develop was connected with the fact that he was so closely tied in with the family? This is terribly important, because even in a kind of crude Wittgensteinian way one has to say a language game is a syndrome of types of behavior within which the lexical item is typically learned. The child has to master this particular constellation of behaviors in which the lexical item can be embedded. Now, the fact that you lose the capacity to comprehend or generate the lexical item doesn't necessarily mean you lose the capacity to deal with the situations within which this behavior is evoked. It seems to me that the words eventually become tokens attached to fragmentary life, which may continue comparatively untouched in the absence of the linguistic markers.

**DENNETT:** Indeed, in the jargon of aphasics, after all, you see an amazing parody of this form of life. The aphasic is spouting word salad with all the intonations and the gestural contours, and is apparently oblivious of the fact that this is not successful communication.

*Just in between, Daniel, may I borrow a question from your book* Consciousness Explained: *"Fun has not yet received careful attention from a philosopher. We certainly won't have a complete explanation of consciousness until we have accounted for its role in permitting us, and only us"—I doubt whether that's true—"to have fun." Stephen Jay Gould, any ideas?*

**DENNETT:** Dogs can have fun, Steve. Cats can have fun.

**GOULD:** "Fun" is a hard word. Animals play, and "play" is also a loaded term, but I think there's no doubt that particularly juvenile mammals engage in a lot of purely exploratory behavior. Now, it may be functional in terms of learning, as they tend not to do it after they've become sexually mature, but I don't know what to call it except play.

**DENNETT:** It's interesting that reptiles, amphibians, and birds don't do it.

**GOULD:** There's a whole literature about this. Occasionally adult mammals will play. There's a wonderful story that George Schaller tells in his book on the giant panda. Pandas are the most boring animals in the world, though they are icons because they're so cute. The main reason for their boringness is that they have a carnivore's digestive system, but they eat only bamboo. It's hard enough to just eat bamboo anyway, but with a carnivore's digestive system they have to eat it all the time. The way you track a panda is to follow its trail of feces. They defecate continuously because they can't process this stuff. So that's basically what pandas do, they're very, very dull animals. But Schaller once—once—observed a panda slide down a snowy hill on its stomach, and then it climbed up to the top of the hill and slid down again. You could read that any way you want, I'm not gonna push that too far. Characteristically juvenile mammals play. By the way, virtually all these studies of so-called language in apes are done on juveniles. As soon as chimps become sexually mature, they lose all interest in it.

**DENNETT:** I do think that animals are capable of having fun. Not just of preferring being alive to being dead, but of having fun. It's pretty well restricted to the mammals. Some people think birds can have fun. Some people share my sense that flight is wasted on birds. We would have so much fun if we could fly. They apparently don't really have fun flying. People have a lot of intuitions about fun, and I suspect they line up— maybe even better than any other intuitions—with their moral sensibilities. The worst thing would be to eat an animal that could have fun.

**GOULD:** Intuitions are very historically bound. At the end of *Natural Theology* Paley talks about how God has created katydids with their marvelous capacity for joyous chorusing, which shows that all of nature is involved in endless delight. Self-delight, not delight for us.

*Oliver, why do we have fun?*

**SACKS:** Certainly I think playing is absolutely characteristic, as Steve was saying, of mammals, maybe higher vertebrates, but certainly most mammals in their learning stages. One would imagine that there are rehearsals and perhaps imaginary constructions going on. Play is therefore crucial, and the elimination of play, as Dickens describes in *Hard Times*, would be not only gruesome but intellectually damaging. The thinkers one likes most are very playful. Sea lions are very playful. I think they have fun, but what would their fun be about?

**DENNETT:** Do you think horses and cows can have fun? Colts certainly can. The first thing that comes to my mind when I think of animals having fun is otters scampering up the hill and sliding down on their bellies in the water and doing it again. But notice that we'd have to change only one feature of that and we'd have a completely different sense of it.

**GOULD:** Like the fish at the bottom of the slide?

**DENNETT:** No, if we see them trudging up the hill and sliding down, I think our sense would be: This isn't fun. They're deranged in some way. They're no longer having fun, they're caught in some hypnotic web. It's something about the excess energy expenditure that we think is essential to it's being fun. It they were plodding up the hill . . .

**SHELDRAKE:** What about ski lifts?

**DENNETT:** That's why we have ski lifts, so we can have fun. It wouldn't bc fun if we had to herringbone all the way up the hills all the time.

**SACKS:** Yeah, this may come back also to the notion of spontaneity.

*Freeman and Rupert are listening but not saying very much. Why?*

**DYSON:** I was thinking about baseball. It's probably true that humans evolved mostly by learning to throw rocks, so baseball may have been very essential. That seems to persist in adult life.

*But have you been thinking about baseball these last two hours?*

**DYSON:** No, no. Just now.

**SHELDRAKE:** I have thoughts about what we were talking about earlier, but not so many about fun.

*What is your conclusion, after all that has been discussed the last two hours, for instance about consciousness?*

**SHELDRAKE:** Well, we got into the whole thing about internalization and machine metaphors. My feeling is that we're leaving huge things out of the puzzle. They may or may not be related to this wonder tissue of quantum theory. I like very much what you said about that, Freeman. Dan may not want it in biology, but physicists deal with it all the time. My own feeling is that there are huge areas we don't understand about human and animal behavior, implying forms of interconnection and causal factors, maybe physical principles, that we haven't yet taken on board. And we're just not going to get anywhere solving this like a jigsaw puzzle with several missing pieces. So my approach is to try to find what these areas might be and design experiments where one could find out more about them.

Let me just mention one area in the realm of animal behavior, the homing of pigeons. This is the tip of the iceberg of a much larger range of unsolved biological problems relating to migratory animals and birds. Things like swallows going to South Africa and then coming back to England every year. It's like homing with two homes. Migration and homing are clearly related. Nobody knows how pigeons do it, and every seemingly reasonable hypothesis has been tested to destruction. Now the evidence points to the existence of some unknown means by which they do it, something we haven't taken on board in our models of animal behavior.

**GOULD:** How about the evidence of magnetic particles in the head?

**SHELDRAKE:** Magnetism's been a pabulum for the last twenty years. Magnetic particles may exist in the head. The pigeons may be able to measure the dip of the magnetic displacement. If you displace the north, the compass may dip. But if you move them due east or due west, the dip's exactly the same. The magnet won't help them in the slightest. Even if they've got one.

**GOULD:** How do you know they're working only on dip? Maybe it's a compass.

**SHELDRAKE:** All right. I'll give you a compass and parachute you into some unknown area. Can you get home?

**GOULD:** I'd get close enough to home until I picked up other signals.

**SHELDRAKE:** Can you without a map?

**GOULD:** Oh, I have to know where I am in relation to where I've been.

**SHELDRAKE:** Of course. That's the problem. How do you know where you are in relation to home?

**GOULD:** Because you've migrated there once before. I doubt that you could just take a pigeon in an airplane and drop it randomly somewhere.

**SHELDRAKE:** You can, you can. This was done in World War II. Pigeons were taken routinely on Lancaster bombers. The British Royal Air Force Pigeon Corps supplied these pigeons. The idea was, if the airmen ditched in the North Sea on their way back from a sortie in Germany, the navigator would release the map reference—tie it onto the pigeon's neck and let it go—in case radio contact was broken. Thousands of lives were saved by these pigeons. Some were released in the middle of the night in freezing fog a hundred miles from land and they got home. The really outstanding ones were awarded medals. A record of them can be found in an amazing book called *Pigeons in Two World Wars*, by Colonel Osmond. The meritorious performance list has about five hundred examples of astonishing feats. They were literally dropped out of planes in the middle of the night, sometimes in the middle of the winter in freezing fog. And they got home the next morning.

The reason why pigeon homing is such an interesting problem is that pigeoners in half a million pigeon races in Europe alone routinely race pigeons every weekend. The big races are usually five to seven hundred miles. A pigeon can home from seven hundred miles away in any direction. A compass isn't going to help them. Even if they have a magnetic compass, it'll only tell them where north is, not where home is. Now, the reason the dip was introduced in the magnetic hypothesis was to give a bit more information. If the pigeon could measure the dip of the needle, it could measure north–south displacement. But it won't give it any information on east–west displacement.

DYSON: Suppose you had a very simple strategy—you flip a coin. You fly either due west or due east until you hit land. Half of them then would come west and would arrive at England and the other half would arrive in the Netherlands.

GOULD: You have to record the ones that don't make it in these experiments.

SHELDRAKE: But they do. First of all, they observe the vanishing direction. . . .

DYSON: The point is, the ones that make it get the medals. And the other ones you forget about.

SHELDRAKE: But there've been hundreds of experiments done, you see. Every one of these ideas has been tested by serious researchers over long periods. They've been released on cloudy days. They've been released with their time clock shifted six hours or twelve hours by keeping them in artificially displaced day lengths for weeks. All these pigeons can home. They can home with magnets strapped on their wings or with Helmholtz coils over their heads.

GOULD: With blindfolds on?

SHELDRAKE: Yes! Frosted glass contact lenses. They've been released up to two hundred miles away and they flop down within a quarter of a mile of the loft. Many of them collide with telegraph poles near the loft, but most of them get to the home region.

SACKS: I entirely believe these stories of pigeons and of animals homing. Many years ago we had a dog that my parents decided to sell. It was taken two hundred miles away on a closed train. And it got back to us as fast as fast could get. But I'm sure there must be a variety of intricate but intelligible, highly evolved but quite ordinary mechanisms by which they do it, whereas you seem to me to be looking for some sort of transcendent mechanism.

DENNETT: This is exactly the phenomenon I was asking you for: the phenomenon that defies explanation by all the standard methods.

SHELDRAKE: I've actually been doing research on homing pigeons for years and I have a pigeon loft in Britain. All these theories—they see landmarks and so on—every one of those seemingly reasonable explanations has been ruled out by frosted contact lenses, the cloudy days, the time shift, the magnets on their wings.

**DENNETT:** How about the olfactory senses?

**SHELDRAKE:** Yes, they've had their nostrils blocked up with wax, they get home. They've had confusing smells like turpentine put on their beaks, they get home. And just in case that doesn't work, they've had their olfactory nerves severed. Those get home. To overcome the idea of nonspecific trauma, they've had a local anaesthetic sprayed on their nasal mucosa. Those pigeons home straight off with no delay. It's a fascinating literature. Every seemingly rational theory has been tested and tested and tested. We're in the realm of epicycles now. People are saying it's not any one of those in particular, but knock out two or three and the others somehow take over in an unspecified combination.

Now, my experiment is designed to test their theory to see if there's an unknown factor involved. I think the pigeons are somehow linked to their home. Whereas all previous experiments involved moving the pigeons from their home, my experiment involves moving the home from the pigeons, hence I have a mobile pigeon loft. You can train pigeons to move to a mobile loft. It was done in World War I with the British Pigeon Corps. They had mobile lofts behind the front line. They were converted London buses. I have a fascinating book about the Japanese Pigeon Corps in World War II showing a wonderfully Oriental mobile loft somewhere in Manchuria with sort of pointy ends to it. But if you move their home, you can move it just a hundred yards and the pigeons are totally confused. Even though they can see the loft, they fly around the place where it was for several hours before a brave one goes in. Just as we would, if we went home and found our home had moved a hundred yards down the street.

**DENNETT:** I'd hesitate to walk in, under any circumstances.

**SHELDRAKE:** But after you've done this three or four times, you can get them to home. Now, if you've trained these pigeons up to the point where the loft can be moved four or five miles, you go back, you take them out, put them in a box, you tow the loft away, you go back to the first point. You open the box to release the pigeons, drive back to see when they arrive, and they're sitting on the roof. Well, so far there's no mystery. They could do it by perfectly normal means, fly up in the air and see it.

The crucial experiment, I'm sorry to say, I haven't yet done because the person I was working with has contracted a disease called pigeon lung. It means he can't go in the pigeon loft anymore. And so, I'm sorry to say, this is an unended saga, but here is a perfectly reasonable experiment. I think the chances of its working are only about one in ten, because I think we may need to move more of the home than just the loft. But a floating island or ship would give one the capacity to move more of the home. It's an area potentially open to empirical testing. The budget for this experiment so far has been £500. This is a poor man's sport, so one doesn't need big grants for this kind of work.

But the literature in this area is absolutely fascinating. At every stage people have said, "There must be a rational explanation." But to anyone who actually works in the field, it's completely unsolved. And so we have this pigeon homing, the homing of dogs and cats, the migration of fish, huge tracts of animal behavior which have big implications for the evolution of migratory pathways, which can evolve quite rapidly. And these could have a great deal of relevance to the understanding of faculties of various kinds that we haven't taken into account.

**SACKS:** When you say this is a real mystery, do you mean this is a real problem? A mystery is something that cannot in principle be understood, whereas a problem in principle can be. I mean, the Trinity is a mystery.

**SHELDRAKE:** I mean a problem. I wouldn't be doing research if I didn't think it could be solved.

**DENNETT:** But there is a kind of catch-22 to your research program: it's a good example for your larger theory only so long as nobody's got an explanation of it. As soon as somebody comes up with a traditional mechanistic explanation along the lines that you say have all been discredited, you'll have to drop this phenomenon from your list. Because as near as I can see, you don't have a positive replacement theory. Do you have a positive program for explaining this phenomenon? Or are you simply hostage to this phenomenon until somebody comes along with an explanation?

**SHELDRAKE:** I'll give you another example that's very relevant to the question of internalization. This concerns what you were saying a long time ago, about our minds being out there. I think when you see me, your image of me is a mental construction. We all agree about that, I suppose. Now the usual view, though perhaps not yours, is that your eye produces a pattern of activity in the nervous system which you then subjectively experience as an image of me which you imagine is outside you, while actually it's inside you. The usual view would be that all these images are formed inside the brain. I think your image of me is right where it seems to be: here. And that therefore there's an outward projection of images during perception. Now how the projection works, I'm not sure. It's a field phenomenon of some kind. If this is true, then when you see somebody and you project your image of that person out of you by looking at them, you should be able to affect them. Now, could somebody tell if you were looking at them when they couldn't know by normal means? Could there be such a thing as the sense of being stared at from behind? And as soon as you formulate the question, you see that there's a huge body of folklore and anecdotal evidence that this is the case.

GOULD: And a huge body of attempts to test it, as in the mesmeric experiments of Lavoisier and Franklin, that has disproved it.

SHELDRAKE: Absolutely untrue, Steve. I've gone into this. There are three published papers in the last hundred years on this phenomenon. Even the parapsychologists have ignored this. There's virtually nothing in parapsychological literature.

TOULMIN: I don't think what Dan said need be taken as implying some kind of projection outward. What I was saying is that it has to be inward in order to be genuine at all. The point is that projection is a gratuitous thing to introduce at this point. We can say that the reach of the mind contains all in the world that we can deal with. But this is not to say that my mental capacity to deal with different things in the world means that I'm generating physical influences at these different points of the world. One can talk about construing some situation—for instance, construing the emotion on someone's face at a distance—without having to take that as meaning that you're somehow influencing them.

SHELDRAKE: I'm not saying it has to be taken that way. I'm saying it's an empirical question. You can do experiments to see whether people can tell when they're being looked at or not. I've done thousands of these experiments. Statistically the evidence is very clear. There is some faculty of this kind. How you explain it is another question.

DENNETT: I remain dubious. I wonder if you extend this to other senses as well. There's nothing more normal than for the salesman in the hi-fi shop to say, "You have the speakers here and you project the stereo sound onto this spot right in the middle." Now, if you really mean projection, then presumably that part of the room has actually changed by the fact that you're there listening to the music. To do the right sort of control, we'd have to put something of the same density and elasticity and mass as you in that spot, but not an observer. And then only when there was a real observer there projecting the sound to that intermediate spot, something physical would happen? It's an empirical question, I grant you. Do you also predict that there would be some detectable physical change in that part of the room as a result of the projection of the sound?

SHELDRAKE: Well, I haven't tried to think of an experiment using sound in that way. Perhaps I should, but looking at a thing is a much more direct and clear case. I think the thing about people in the sense of being stared at is that we don't know how this seeming ability works. There's a huge body of anecdotal evidence about this. About 90 percent of a normal population sample believed that this happens. That doesn't tell us that it's true, but the idea of saying that 90 percent of people are wrong in the absence of any experimental evidence one way or the other . . .

**GOULD:** Throughout human history 90 percent of people have been wrong about most things. I'll listen to experimental evidence, but I'm sure as hell not going to put anything to a claim that 90 percent of the people believe in.

**SHELDRAKE:** But the fact is that the anecdotal evidence is natural history. You start with human phenomena. You then try to tighten the thing up.

**DENNETT:** I reject that as evidence. I don't reject it as suggestion that there might be something there.

**SHELDRAKE:** OK, we agree, then. So there's a lot of circumstantial evidence that people think there's something of this kind going on. For me this is simply encouragement that there may be something worth investigating.

**DENNETT:** Suppose I have a person, Jones, standing in one room and there's a mirror between that room and the observer, and then there's another person, Smith, in the room with the observer. The observer looks in the mirror and sees not Jones but Smith. But Smith is, as it were, subjectively located where Jones is in the other room. Now who feels he's being looked at? Smith or Jones?

**SHELDRAKE:** Well, I must admit I hadn't thought it through to such a complicated level.

**DENNETT:** Does this projection go through glass or is it bounced back by the silvering of the glass? You've got to take this question seriously.

**SHELDRAKE:** Oh, absolutely.

*With your approval, I'd like to propose another break for one of Steve's seventh inning stretches.*

■

*Steve Gould, you said to me: "We have this powerful attribute of consciousness and we don't know what to do with it. Basically, we are just evolved apes trying to deal with this powerful mechanism that no species has ever had before." Stephen Toulmin said: "The more I read of history, the less I am convinced that the events of the holocaust were unparalleled." Daniel Dennett said: "If you ask why are fanaticisms so potent, why do they cover people's lives the way they do, I think the answer is in part that we crave simple answers to complicated problems." Freeman Dyson said regarding World War II, "People in the concentration camp bureaucracy were simply taking orders from above, signing papers, writing contracts, getting all the apparatus to work to exterminate the jews. Those were the people who were analogous to myself." Well, if we're talking about consciousness altering the world, what we are doing with it?*

GOULD: It almost takes a paleontologist to realize the magnitude of the issue. Life is three and a half billion years old. It's really only the last few thousand years since we got numerous enough to build cities and establish the technologies that come from home bases and agriculture. In almost every geological situation that's a bedding plane, it's an immeasurably tiny amount of strata. It's remarkable to think how much the surface of the earth has been transformed through the mental activity of one species in this geologically unmeasurable moment.

With respect to our cruelties, I'm not optimistic. Our cruelty has immense power, but I'm not so sure that the overall record in a more statistical sense is really that bad. *Homo sapiens* is in fact a very peaceful species, as species go. I remember something Ed Wilson once said to me which stuck in my mind: that we call a species peaceful if, say, sixty hours of research had been logged on it and only one or two violent acts were noted. If you look at most human beings for sixty hours, you don't see any violent acts. You might see a parent cuff a child or speak harshly to someone, but there are thousands of acts of kindness for every act of nastiness in the genetic and behavioral and mostly cultural program of *Homo sapiens*.

The problem is that the acts of kindness go unrecorded. You can have in a community ten years of work for racial harmony—thousands of meetings and countless thousands of hours. And then there's one random murder across racial lines one day and it's all undone. The point is the newsworthiness of one act of violence overbalances the tens of thousands of unrecorded acts of kindness. With respect to Hitler and the Holocaust, yeah, there are thousands of Hitlers in human history. The only thing that distinguishes this one is that he had a technology that allowed him to do it on such a vast scale. I don't mean that to be read overly optimistically, because you only need one to press the button. But I think it is not a statement about human nature in general.

TOULMIN: I think you've drawn attention to something terribly important and also extremely hopeful, which is that we notice these acts of violence. As I was saying, the things we remember about childhood are the things that almost never happened. For instance, we've been going though this enormous tizzy over terrorism. When you look into the record of the Lebanese terrorists, about half of them belong to one family, the Hamadi brothers. The fact that a significant proportion of the Lebanese terrorists are brothers in a single family reminds us that it's a very limited range of people in these particular communities. They can create an enormous amount of trouble, but even more, they'll get a reputation for being much more pervasive and much more troublesome than they really are.

There was a very interesting item on BBC World Service yesterday. A Serb who had been living in England for a long time got back to Belgrade. He said, "There's a crime wave here in Belgrade now." Why? Because most of the people who were in those Serbian irregular forces who were beating up on Croatia were criminals who'd been allowed out and who'd been recruited to engage in all this mayhem. Now their occupation's gone because the war has moved to Bosnia. Now they're back in Belgrade, returning to their usual occupations. We're always told about the hatred between the Serbs and the Croats. . . . There are clearly enough extremely beastly people who've set their minds on breaking up the situation, but I don't think we have the documentation to allow us to know just how widespread this is.

*You talk about beastly people. Freeman has said it's not about beastly people, it's about common little ordinary people working in the bureaucracy of World War II. The real evil is bureaucracy.*

**DYSON:** There I was speaking specifically about the Holocaust. What goes on in the Balkans is very different. People actually slaughtering each other face to face, which is of course an old pastime, but it's quite different.

*History repeats itself without people learning from each other's mistakes. Is society falling apart again, as though we were living back in the seventeenth century?*

**TOULMIN:** Yes, to the extent that the former Yugoslavs have decided to have their own religious wars. The rest of us whose ancestors lived through the Thirty Years' War have developed the institutions that keep us mindful of what the alternative is if we let religious differences become this kind of object of hostility and mayhem. The tragedy about Yugoslavia is that the Habsburgs and the Turks between them kept them in order, and in the absence of either the Habsburg bureaucracy or the Ottoman bureaucracy and the temporary Serbian domination that there was from 1919 up to 1940, the institutional fabric doesn't exist for restraining these people.

*Oliver, you have said, "We have astonishingly little idea of what basic human nature is like. Clearly the child has to modify or he would become a monster and society would disintegrate."*

**SACKS:** I did?

*Don't you remember?*

**SACKS:** No. Well, first I think the experience of wild children shows that there's really no human nature without culture. There isn't a sort of raw human nature in the sense there is with most other species. I think the most frightening book I ever read was Hannah Arendt's book on totalitarianism. I had an odd dissociation when I was reading it. I thought I was reading the history of a hideous alien species. And then I suddenly thought no, this is us. The coherence of the development from Hobbes to Hitler frightened me. But having said that, I can also believe that this is a relative rarity and that we may biologically be a fairly peaceful, decent species. When I read about the transmission of neurosis from generation to generation, I find there's a sort of melodramatic power there, but I think this is generalizing from pathology. I am much more reassured by talk about good enough mothers and good enough parenting. I think if we have good enough parenting, we're OK. I was part of a sort of generational neurosis myself in that I was one of the 4 million children who were evacuated and taken away from home and put in unpleasant circumstances. And I think this has left its mark on a generation of us. But I think I'm trying to say that on the whole I regard us as a reasonably decent species. Although one that is certainly at risk all the while.

*Rupert, you said, "The present order is doomed. If we have an extrapolation of present trends, we have a kind of apocalyptic scenario within ten, twenty years."*

**SHELDRAKE:** Well, many people think the present order is doomed. The interesting thing about it is the way there's a kind of self-fulfilling quality. It's clear to me that we can't go on doing this forever. We can't base our whole economy on exploiting the capital of the earth. I think the interesting thing is the degree to which the whole of the Western model, both Jewish and Christian and secular, is based on this apocalyptic model of history. In the communist view, it was the withering away of the state as a kind of utopian or millenarian end to history. In the biblical view it involves catastrophic events of destruction. Many of us expect that kind of thing, at least unconsciously. And so the question is: To what extent is it a self-fulfilling prophecy? To a large extent, I think.

**SACKS:** I'm glad I belong to a generation that knew life before Hiroshima. And I feel sort of wistful, as it were, for the few people who grew up before 1914 and who seemed then to have known some sort of security that got shattered forever in 1914. At least the atomic threat has been lifting a bit. But this is why the ecological threats now come to the fore.

**DYSON:** I suppose I'm the only survivor of the 1930s here. I have exactly the opposite feeling. Growing up in the 1930s, the future looked totally black, and I didn't expect civilization would survive. Somehow or other we did survive, and ever since I've taken all this doom and gloom rather lightly.

**Toulmin:** My father had a business association in Germany, so we never had any doubt about Hitler. The day after *Kristallnacht* he gave us a lecture about what it all meant. I remember being terrified by the first searchlight practices, you know, knowing what was coming.

**Dyson:** But hasn't it left you rather cheerful?

**Toulmin:** Comparatively, yes. Saddam Hussein is bad enough, but he's the worst we have to deal with.

*Stephen Gould, you said: "We are doing very badly in moral terms, and that merely illustrates that consciousness didn't arise for reasons for our higher moral development." Should we redefine morality at the end of the twentieth century?*

**Dennett:** I have to redefine some aspects of morality because I think the traditional moralities have simply failed to articulate answers to some of the problems that now face us. If there's one principle of morality which is so obvious that it's trivial, it's the rule of philosophers: ought implies can. If you're unable to do something, you can't be obliged to do it. Now what's happened, really just in this century, is that human competence has exploded. We're now capable of taking action in spheres where before we just couldn't. Now we suddenly have tremendous access to power and we don't know what to do because we suddenly have new obligations that we never had before. And what you see is people casting about desperately to find some way of choosing among all the moral possibilities that are now open to us. Right now we could all decide to pour our energy into Amnesty International or Oxfam or making everybody vegetarians or stopping abortion or stopping capital punishment or feeding the people in Somalia. There's thousands of claims on our moral attention. We cannot respond to them all but nobody has told us what the principles are by which we filter them out. You get people who become moral specialists, who decide they're going to put their energy into one issue. I sympathize tremendously with that move, because it at least removes you from a situation of paralysis. But I don't think that ethical theories, the great systems of morality, have even begun to address that problem.

**Toulmin:** But again I think this idea that ethics should be a matter of great theories is seventeenth-century currency. In the *Nicomachean Ethics*, Aristotle was perfectly clear that ethics isn't basically a matter of theory. Although I would echo a lot of what you say about how our present powers force us to rethink the application of our basic moral perceptions, it doesn't seem to me that the basic moral intuitions have changed all that much. It's the circumstances in which we have to think about them, including the power of standardization and routinization, since, as we said earlier, the essential thing about being human or being an animal is being individual.

**DENNETT:** And this is what's happening now in medicine, for instance. It's going to be the case soon, if it isn't already, that physicians are going to be not just legally obliged but in their own mind morally obliged to avail themselves of a whole array of technologies that will usurp their creative, spontaneous, intelligent diagnostic skills. What's wonderfully and sadly ironic is that it's precisely our morality that puts us in this fix. It's precisely because physicians will feel a moral obligation to avail themselves of the best tools that they will in the process alienate themselves from the task and become operators in a routinized activity.

**TOULMIN:** It's more complicated still. I've worked with doctors who are struggling with precisely these kinds of decisions, and it's extremely hard for any physician the first time they have to make up their minds that it's all right to stop treatment because there's no more good to be done. The moral education consists precisely in helping them to discriminate the cases in which they should refrain from availing themselves of the technology. But I think the argument has got to the point that doctors are no longer unthinkingly multiplying their use of technology. Nowadays there is a much more of a focus on the question of when you stop treatment.

**DENNETT:** I was thinking more of things like expert computer systems in medical diagnosis, where you simply punch in a few facts about the patient's history and do a lot of tests and then it tells you what the treatment is. Very soon it's going to take moral stamina to stand up to that machine, and later a certain sort of madness, because the machine will in fact have such a good track record that you would have to have a sort of hubris to say, "I know better than this machine what the right treatment for this patient is." There's something terribly sad about this, because it's going to remove a certain drama from a certain sort of life.

**GOULD:** But do you all seriously think that individuality was ever pervasively celebrated? Did Peter the Great care when he had his hecatomb of 20,000 people building St. Petersburg? Did generals of the past care when they lined up their soldiers in serried formations to march forward? No, I think that kind of individuality is the particular concern of artists and intellectuals, and should be. And it's in part that our society is much more egalitarian. One of its few decent trends is that we see it as a pervasively greater problem these days. I'm really glad to hear Stephen say that. I've always somehow had a Philistine attitude myself toward morality. Categorical imperatives never much appealed to me because God help us if we pick the wrong one. I don't like hypothetical imperatives. They're messy things. Golden rules. Few things like that. To me individuality is paramount, and your medical example is a very good one indeed. But it does create dilemmas. Every time my mother has a cardiogram it comes out that she's had a heart attack, which she denies, because all these machines of course have to read maximally and there's a little indication of a slight arhythmia that could be interpreted that way and scares her every time she gets one. They have to explain to her: No, this is the way these machines are reading it. When I see my own students walking around with their headphones on, everything coming at them, it does bother me. But I'm not so sure that isn't a hang-up of this intellectual culture of ours. As an evolutionary biologist, I'm committed to diversity above all.

**DENNETT:** Well, let me tell you a personal regret of mine. I love to sail and I learned celestial navigation when I was a boy. I would love to sail across the Atlantic and do my own celestial navigation. And I can't now, because now for a few hundred dollars you can have a Sat-Nav system in your boat, and the insurance company'll cancel your insurance if you don't put it on. You don't have to use it. But in fact I have moral obligations to my family, which means it would be immoral of me, really, to take that trip and not avail myself of that technology.

**DYSON:** You can do your calculations first and then do a spot check with the system.

**TOULMIN:** But notice that then one has to resort to playing games in order to satisfy one's sense of adventure. And I think this is going to happen in medicine and in other areas where people do have tremendous moral obligations to keep people alive. They'll find that to meet these moral obligations, boringly, they will be obliged to avail themselves of routines that are not so life-fulfilling for them as the old-fashioned practices would be. But neither they nor anybody else will stand for them. We wouldn't let a doctor say, "Ha, I'm not going to use X rays. I use seat-of-the-pants diagnosis." We would say that that's an immoral, irresponsible person.

But there's another aspect of it that I took Oliver to be raising, and that has to do with the fact that a lot of this routinization is associated with bureaucratization. The person who really scares me is not Karl Marx but Max Weber. We're at the stage now at which the best we can do is turn the iron cage into an elastic cage, find ways of squeezing between the bars of the iron cage. I see these doctors at work. And the trouble isn't the technology, it's the fact that they work in large, bureaucratically organized hospitals where they can't accept patients of their own because the patients may not have the insurance the hospital administrator is required to insist upon.

**SACKS:** In America the so-called medical burnout is as common as the resentment of patients. And both of these have to do with the attenuation of the relationship between them and the intrusion of technology. It does get more and more difficult for a doctor to use judgment. Twenty years ago I worked in a migraine clinic, and part of the trouble, it seemed to me, was that every patient had seen "my neurosurgeon," "my gynecologist," "my ENT man." None of them had a doctor of their own. None of them had been given any simple commonsensical advice.

There was an interesting social experiment recently in Australia, when a lot of instant medical clinics, the so-called doc-in-a-box or McDoc clinics, were erected everywhere. Some of them had white grand pianos and music round the clock. The notion of having an instant fix for whatever problem one had drew the entire population away from their general practitioners. Then after about two years there was a movement against this, though by that time many general practitioners had sort of gone out of practice. But it was an interesting experiment in trying to replace a personal relationship with a technological fix. For myself, I'm partly shielded from this because I work in an area of medicine which has to do basically with chronic illness and rehabilitation, where every patient has to be recognized as an individual and has to be helped to find his own personal adaptations and pathways to the richest life possible under the circumstances. But this is a sort of backwater, and I'm not under the diagnostic and legal pressures of most of my colleagues. But I'm not quite sure how medicine will survive this. Certainly in the States, there are fewer and fewer medical students. Medicine is no longer seen as fun, is no longer seen as dignified, as decent. And yet obviously one wouldn't want to turn against any of the technology, the expert systems or anything else. We always used to say we must humanize technology before it dehumanizes us. And whether that can be realized I don't know.

**DENNETT:** What if Freeman succeeds in his fondest dream and establishes communication with a civilization on another planet and discovers that the message they're sending us is a heartrending plea for help, together with some suggestions how we might actually help them? Suddenly our moral obligation sphere will grow again. Have you considered whether you want to take on that chance?

**DYSON:** Oh, yes, I think this would do us a hell of a lot of good.

*Daniel, Albert Camus wrote* The Myth of Sisyphus *in 1942, in the middle of the war. Would you read the passage you quote in your book* Consciousness Explained *and then tell us why you put it there?*

**DENNETT:** "And here are trees and I know their gnarled surface; water, and I feel its taste. The scents of grass and stars at night, certain evenings when the heart relaxes—how shall I negate this world whose power and strength I feel? Yet all the knowledge on earth will give me nothing to assure me that this world is mine. You describe it to me and you teach me to classify it. You enumerate its laws and in my thirst for knowledge I admit that they are true. You take apart its mechanism and my hope increases. . . . What need had I of so many efforts? The soft lines of these hills and the hand of evening on this troubled heart teach me much more."

I quoted that because I set that as a challenge to myself in the book. I thought that it very eloquently captured what very many people think of when they think of human consciousness. It captures an attitude, particularly where he says, "You describe it to me and you teach me to classify it. You enumerate its laws and in my thirst for knowledge I admit that they are true," but then he goes on to say in effect there's something else, there's something here missing, if that's all you do. I wanted to acknowledge that challenge and then meet it head-on and say, well, see if we can do justice to what Camus has said here about consciousness. If we don't, then indeed we've left something out. Well, no, we may have left some things in need of explanation, but there may be other things that Camus is suggesting don't need to be explained. It's not so much that we can't explain them as that the very idea that they require explanation is just a mistake.

TOULMIN: Can I encourage you to step that back one stage further? It seems to me that we need to distinguish situations in which explaining is required at all. Roughly speaking, everything can do with explaining. On the other hand, there are lots of situations that do not. You need to recognize whether the situation at hand is one that demands explanation or immediate action. That is surely very often the most important thing to have a feeling for.

SACKS: It seems to me there's been a wave of antiscientific and antirational books in England and elsewhere recently, which see science as a great spoiler of human life and perception—books that the poetic outline of a hill is threatened by any theory of hill formation or whatever. Helmholtz gives a rather nice example when he tells of how he was with some friends in the Alps when a storm blew up. This fascinated him and Helmholtz immediately pulled out paper and pencil and started making some calculations, looking for a theory of storm genesis. One of his friends asked him, "Doesn't this spoil your appreciation of nature?" and he said, "No, it heightens it." Mozart seems to come from heaven, but although one can enjoy Mozart infinitely as a naive listener, being a sophisticated listener it's even better.

DENNETT: And if you knew how Mozart's brain created it, that would be better still. That would make it even more wonderful.

SACKS: I don't think that science or explanation or reason need be felt as a threat. If mystery has a place, it will keep it. Somewhere in the *Four Quartets* Eliot says: "We're not here to inform curiosity or bear report, but to kneel and pray where prayer's been valid," or something like that. Actually, I confess that line annoys me, because in fact I always want to inform curiosity and bear report, even at the very moment that I may want to kneel. It seems to me that respect for the unfathomable whole, plus an actor of investigation of some of the mechanisms are not incompatible.

*Dan, you told me, "I think that science is actually an important component of anything that can be called wisdom. Wisdom in the absence of scientific knowledge seems to me to be a commodity that is vanishing fast. I think it becomes harder and harder to be wise if you are scientifically ignorant."*

**DENNETT:** I think I was probably speaking about my profession, and thinking that those in philosophy who aspire to acquire wisdom in complete ignorance of science are cutting themselves off as much as if they decided they wouldn't learn anything about their neighbors and their friends and their families. They simply are living in an impoverished world. There's a lot out there to know about, and if you know about it, you have a better chance of being wise. I guess I probably wanted to put on the defensive those who have some concept of pretheoretical wisdom which we should all kneel before and not try to understand.

*Freeman, you said that "the idea that we are anywhere close to any sort of ultimate understanding of things is a kind of illusion of grandeur which I don't like. If it should turn out that the whole of physical reality can be described by a finite set of equations, I would be disappointed. I would feel that the creator had been lacking in imagination." Does everybody agree that there is no end to theorizing? Or that in certain fields of science there is an end to theorizing, while others are evolving continually?*

**DYSON:** The great mystery is that we do as well as we do, considering we only just came down from the trees.

**SACKS:** When John Stuart Mill had a depression, probably from too much logic, he found only Wordsworth and music could soothe him, but he then became apprehensive that there was a finite number of melodies and that music was exhaustible. I got a little worried by Stephen Hawking's book, which was partly about the notion of the exhaustibility of science—whether one can have a theory of everything and whether we'll have it all buttoned up in fifty years or so. I think I picked up some of this attitude at CERN when they said, "We've simulated the universe down to ten to the minus thirty seconds of the Big Bang. Another thirty years and we will have got it." I like to think that every solution will reveal a wider horizon and a range of problems one may not even have thought of. I'm sure that's the case in neuropsychology. I'm less sure in physics, but Freeman is the person to meditate on that.

**DYSON:** Well, of course nobody can be sure of anything. I have enormous respect for Stephen Hawking, but I sometimes think he doesn't know the difference between a model and the real thing. That's an occupational disease of theoretical physicists.

**GOULD:** And in many of the natural histories, science is in the details. Melodies may not be formally inexhaustible, but for all conceivable practical purposes there're enough exponents after the ten I write that I'm not going to be worried about them. I feel the same way about natural history. There may be certain theoretical corners that will be adequately resolved, but there are always going to be so many organisms out there with interesting patterns, I don't have the slightest fear that we'll ever get close enough to worry about completion.

**TOULMIN:** In the highest kinds of theoretical physics we succeed better and better in developing comprehensive, abstract systems of ideas which can be used in describing the universe. But the more abstract they are, the more steps have to be put in in order to get back from those to a particular concrete situation.

**DYSON:** Of course, the people at CERN are in the position of a horse wearing blinkers—they're constrained by their machines to look at very narrow questions.

**SACKS:** Luria was very fond of quoting something of Lenin's, although in general he was not a Leninist, the maxim being that science is the ascent to the concrete. This is a very interesting and paradoxical view. We are saying now in a sense we need a science of individuality, a science which allows us to comprehend how each creature, in particular each human creature, sort of makes his own path.

**SHELDRAKE:** I think the antiscience movement is particularly strong in Britain. Science is extremely low in public esteem now, science funds are cut year after year by the government. The scientific community is extremely demoralized. No one wants to be a scientist. Science seems responsible for pollution, nuclear disasters, and so forth. No doubt there are many reasons for this, but I think one of them is the habit of scientific popularizers of the triumphalist kind who keep saying, "This is nothing but this," you know, "the human being is nothing but a machine." All these nothing-but-eries have sickened a lot of people, including myself, I must say.

**GOULD:** You're not going to seriously link the decline of science in Britain to a few journalistic meliorists, are you? It's a much deeper and more problematical issue.

**SHELDRAKE:** Well, I think the public alienation from science is caused partly by the feeling that it takes away the mystery of life and partly by the sense that it's responsible for the ecological catastrophe. There's a whole series of reasons related to that which throw science, at least in Britain, into a kind of crisis.

GOULD: I'd be a little bit more optimistic when people say how terrible public knowledge of science is. Of course, I'm not going to claim it's great. In the United States it's certainly true that public knowledge of academic science is very poor indeed. But start adding up this enormous fund of knowledge that is truly scientific, that is inherent in institutions that we don't usually put in that category. I'll just give you a few obvious ones: amateur astronomers; amateur paleontologists; women's garden clubs, they have enormous horticultural knowledge. The biggest sport in America? Horse racing. A lot of people go there and know a lot about the probability calculus and bet intelligently. Sure, there are people who bet on a horse who's named after their granddaughter, but there is a lot of real probability knowledge. If you add all that up, it's not nearly as hopeless as it seems.

*Oliver, you once wrote, "In science and in scientific life there can be some regaining of an imaged idyllic sort of purity and transparency of childhood."*

SACKS: I did?

*Yes.*

SACKS: I'm not quite sure what I meant by that. Although I think for myself, and perhaps this is so for all of us, the roots of scientific wonder go back to childhood wonder to some extent. Perhaps I had something like that in mind.

> *When I took forth at dawning, pool,*
> *Field, flock and lonely tree*
> *All seemed to gaze at me*
> *like chastened children sitting silent in a school.*
> *Upon them stirs in lippings mere,*
> *As if once clear in call,*
> *But now scarce breathed at all,*
> *We wonder, ever wonder why we find us here.*

*Can you remember why you quoted that?*

GOULD: Because that's one of Hardy's many poems in which he argues that scientific knowledge of the kind gained in the nineteenth century has taken away that sense of wonder we once had. That's a very common perception of what the Darwinian revolution had done. I remember doing an article on the paintings of Frederick Church, America's greatest mid-nineteenth-century landscape painter, for whom the notion that he was painting God's illuminating and harmonious landscape was vital. One of the main reasons why he stopped painting after 1860 was that he could no longer see his beloved landscapes like that again. In the Hardy poem you just quoted, he conjures up this image of the beasts and the plants, saying, "We used to know what the meaning of our lives was and its harmonious order, but now Darwin has come along and we wonder, ever wonder why we find us here." But that was a false psychological hope that was deeply rooted in Western culture. Darwin's basic answer was—you quoted it earlier—that nature, if invested with moral properties and therefore seen as the source of our answers for solace, is not going to return very good answers to us. As Darwin saw, the source of morality is not to be found in the factual products of nature. The source of moral instruction is within us, which I think is an optimistic answer.

**SACKS:** At the beginning of the nineteenth century there were a lot of people who were objecting to Newton. Goethe is interesting in that regard because he's somehow much more constructive than perhaps Blake. Some of Goethe's color theory started when he fiddled with a prism and saw some colored shadows and things and said, "Newton is wrong." Basically I think Goethe's studies on color can almost be seen as studies in neuropsychology and aesthetics. He is restoring subjectivity to color, so that it's not merely differently refrangible rays. One is much richer for knowing Newton *and* Goethe. They're not opposed.

*What are the first books everybody can remember?*

**GOULD:** *Lucky to Be a Yankee*, by Joe DiMaggio.

**DENNETT:** I recalled just a week or two ago a book I loved in my childhood, called *Paddle to the Sea*, which had these wonderful drawings in it. It was about an Indian boy who made a little birchbark canoe, and on the bottom he put a little brass plate which said, "If you find me, put me back in the water, I'm on my way to the sea." He was up at the end of Lake Superior and the boat gets blown by the wind through the Great Lakes and eventually gets out through the St. Lawrence to the sea. The illustrations were brilliant and the story completely captured my imagination as a sort of wonderful quest. It didn't turn me into either a geologist or a marine biologist, but it turned me into a canoe paddler.

**SACKS:** I'd like to say *Alice in Wonderland*. I think for all of us the Alice books were crucially important. There was a series of books about a doctor Doolittle in his house in Puddle-by-on-the-Marsh, and all the animals. I also loved Kipling's *Just So Stories* and *Jungle Book*. My middle name is Wolf, and I think there was some part of me which liked to identify with the wolf boy. Somehow this was seen as sort of cleaner and better and nicer than being human, though of course, coming back to language and consciousness, one of the things that Kipling does is to endow the animals with language. And so he has it both ways.

*Do they speak to each other, the animals?*

**SACKS:** Oh, they do, yes indeed.

*In the book, but in your fantasy?*

**SACKS:** I found it difficult and disillusioning to realize that animals didn't speak to one another. Another early book my mother was fond of reading to me was *Flatland*.

*Do you remember your mother's voice reading to you?*

**SACKS:** It either comes back to me totally or I can't remember it at all.

**GOULD:** I was remembering my mother's voice. Yes, I can remember it.

*What kind of a voice was it?*

**GOULD:** Good strong New York accent, just like me. Warm, loving, and comforting. Not very dramatic.

*And the books?*

**GOULD:** *The Little Engine That Could, Lucky to Be a Yankee*. I spent my childhood on the New York streets playing stickball. This notion that all adult intellectuals somehow had glasses and played chess when they were five is really not right.

*So these are the first books that played an important role in your life?*

**GOULD:** I didn't mean to be facetious. *Lucky to Be a Yankee* is the story of Joe DiMaggio, a great American baseball player, who was and still is my hero. It actually is a fairly inspirational story. It's the story of a man driven, absolutely maniacally, to excellence. *The Little Engine That Could* is the same kind of story, maybe a little bit overly heroic, but they both are inspirational.

*OK, Rupert. You're the youngest here.*

**SHELDRAKE:** Well, two things come to mind. One is, in England there's a series of stories called *Rupert Bear*. Rupert is a little bear who has all sorts of adventures, he goes underground into caves, he flies through the air. I recognize these as shamanic themes, and it's full of talking animals, of course. I love those books and I read them to my own children now. So I've recently started getting a new dose of Rupert Bear. I suppose I liked them partly because, being called Rupert, I identified strongly with the central character. And quite early in my life, my father, who was an amateur naturalist, gave me a copy of Fabre's *Social Life in the Insect World*. Those stories of the different insects gave me a tremendous interest in these alien worlds of scarab beetles and spiders and so on.

**TOULMIN:** The first book that made an extraordinary impact on me was *Greek Mythology Told to Children*. In particular "Theseus and the Minotaur." The image of Ariadne and Ariadne's thread became deeply embedded in me. The task of finding one's way back down Ariadne's thread is something which has really stayed with me. It has played a large part in the fact that for me all these intellectual inquiries cluster around the question of how much one can rediscover about the things that have always seemed important to us. How much of this is finding one's way back into one's own ways of thinking and retracing the origins of the things that seem important? I can still take out a piece of paper and draw the picture of Theseus and Ariadne and the entrance into the Minotaur's lair.

*I've heard beautiful answers and beautiful questions from all of you over the last couple of months. The most beautiful question I can think of is one that Steve raised in one of his books: "Why does a bamboo flower every 120 years, and how does it count the years passing?" Would you give the answer?*

**GOULD:** I don't know the answer.

**DENNETT:** Is it exactly a hundred and twenty?

**GOULD:** Different species have different cycles, there is one that did it every hundred something years. Nobody knows how they count because the species flower simultaneously.

*Other beautiful questions?*

**GOULD:** Why did you think that my question was beautiful? I don't know why it was beautiful.

**TOULMIN:** I tried to ask a question earlier which seems to me to be a beautiful one. And that is one I hoped Oliver might say more about, which has to do with how people who use sign language talk to themselves or think to themselves. I feel at first glance that to know what it's like to be a signer talking to oneself is a bit like knowing what it is to be a bat. It's so distant from my own experience that I rather resent not having learned signing and being able to do this for myself.

**SACKS:** A gifted deaf woman I know who is an anthropologist has said that even though she's also very fluent in English and an excellent writer, she sometimes feels as if she comes from another species when she's among hearing people. Certainly there's a very intense sense of unity and identity among signers. There are very strong old traditions among deaf people. There are itinerant poets and bards, storytellers. There's no written form of sign language, or rather, there have been attempts at it, but they have never found favor with deaf people. Basically the books of the deaf are videotapes. One deaf poet I know sort of feels the lines forming on his fingers. Finally, I think there's some sort of inner speech which Vygotsky has described with this extraordinary phrase of his, "Words die as they give up their meaning." He sees inner speech as thinking in pure meanings. Now, I don't know what that means.

*Isn't that "Words die when they are translated into meaning"?*

**TOULMIN:** No, he wants to say that the entire meaning of a thought is condensed into a little drop. He has this analysis of what he calls the compression of speech. Wittgenstein always used to laugh at people who thought there was a problem about how you could think about anything in an instant when the sentence you would have to utter in order to say it took so much longer. This is what has been a standing question which we learn to study developmentally, that indeed there is a strong case for saying that we get better and better at condensing our thought, until at the end there seems to be nothing but a single meaning, like a drop of water, which you capture as a whole, even though to utter it you would have to unwrap it again and put it back into the words which have originally been condensed.

**SACKS:** Again this E. M. Forster thing of "I don't know what I think until I see what I say" becomes "I don't know what I think until I feel what I sign."

**TOULMIN:** I remember seeing a wonderful film of two signers signing together in what was described as a joint poem, which was halfway to being a ballet. I was told by a signer that some of the beauty of two people signing together in a jointly conceived poem was that it clearly became something that was halfway for us between poetry and ballet.

**SACKS:** Absolutely. One cannot really quite have a language ballet: either you talk or you dance. You'd spoil either if you did them together, but certainly one can have intermediate or joint forms with signing and dancing.

One of the things that fascinated me when I went to Gallaudet, this great university of the deaf, was to see philosophy and chemistry and mathematics lectures in sign. Whatever you can write or speak you can sign.

**GOULD:** My best experience speaking at Gallaudet was the bimodality of laughter, because the audience was partially hearing and I would get two laughs for every comment I made, once when people heard it and the second time when the signer got to it. Good for the ego. But surely you can say anything, because a word that's so abstract it doesn't have a sign is spelled out.

**DENNETT:** I've been thinking about Wim's question. So often for me a beautiful question is when you take a big question and replace it with two little questions. And they don't look impressive unless you've already been puzzling about the big question. And then you can think, "Ah, beautiful, I've made some progress here. I've replaced a real stumper with some questions I know how to deal with at least a little bit." But the beauty is more in the process than in the particular question itself.

*"We are such stuff as dreams are made on, and our little lives are rounded with a sleep." I quoted that for each of you. Oliver, you said immediately, "We dream all the while until we come to the sleep at the end." Rupert said, "It's dream before, dream after, and a sort of dream in between." But that I could have expected.*

**SACKS:** This might seem like just a sort of poetic conceit, but there's some physiological evidence for the fact that waking consciousness is not that different from dreaming consciousness, except by being constrained by the outer world and by the senses. Both the creative and the fantastic invest waking consciousness. There doesn't seem to me to be some clear, purely rational part of the mind with dreams below. I think there's something of the quality of dreams all the while. Perhaps one feels this most intensely when one is in love, or in some sort of enthusiasm or rapture, when the inner stimuli are so intense. I think at best some of the qualities of fairyland and dreamland are about us all the while, and that our creativity and our depth as people are rooted in this, and that if we divorce ourselves from the dream stratum, we're in big trouble.

*"The mind is as real as the illusions it produces."*

**DENNETT:** That's what I've said. I was trying to be oracular on that occasion, wasn't I? As I put it in my book, "the mind is the brain's user illusion of itself." And this looks like a trick with mirrors, but I don't think it is. I think that one can understand how there can be consciousness if one understands how this particular variety of hominid brain that we have has invented ways of making its own operations visible to itself. When you draw a picture in the sand and look at it, you're actually rendering some of your thought processes visible. You can use these wonderful pattern-recognition devices, your eyes and the visual system, to see what you're doing. For me, the task is to show how this brain has developed ways of rendering its own activities perceptible to itself. In the process, it creates a center of narrative gravity, and a whole set of user illusions to go with it. If that seems circular, I just haven't succeeded in explaining it well enough.

**TOULMIN:** But there's one whole area where I do think we should have said more, and that has to do with the room that there is for differences between different people within this general pattern that Dan's talking about. I'm struck by the fact that different people's everyday mental lives proceed in different modalities. For myself, when I'm not doing anything else, I usually have music running through my head. My wife has a very strong spatial imagination, and the free play of her mind is with colors. This is what the Greeks call *phantasia*, the free play of the imagination. I remember going to talk to David Green, who is basically a classical scholar, and discovering, I suppose not really to my surprise, that when he's not doing anything else, great chunks of Sophocles or Shakespeare are playing themselves out in his mind. The continual rehearsal of understanding for him is essentially a literary thing. That illuminated something I could never otherwise understand, which was that during the times that he spent in Chicago, he would live in a run-down hotel apartment with neither a hi-fi nor any pictures on the wall, because the substance of his inner life was basically literary, and he got all the deep satisfactions he needed out of this. I would have been lost without some source of music in that situation. So I don't think we're all the same. We have these alternative modalities, and different people do make different kinds of use of all these resources that we have. So it isn't the mind, it's how each of us makes of him- or herself what our natural bents turn us toward. I'm sure you find, Oliver, that different people's talents result in their having quite different kinds of free-play imaginations.

There's a very nice example that Gerald Holton has written about, which has to do with the effect that Einstein had on patterns of explanation in theoretical physics, which there is some reason for connecting up with the fact that he was never very good at handling language. He really seems to have had this direct apprehension of spatial relations. There was an emphasis on symmetry when we were children, isn't that true, Freeman? The emphasis on symmetries, which seems to me to have become a standard part of physical theory, was something quite new and essentially associated with Einstein rather than other physicists.

**GOULD:** If you want to talk about interior dialogues, of course we're all different. But I would have thought for most us, in most of our lives, the vast majority of interior images are sexual. Most of the time you have to push them away to do other things.

**SACKS:** Yes, and that may lead to the highest motivations. Gerald Edelman always says he want to lift the skirts of nature, to see what's underneath.

**DENNETT:** I thought of a question I was asked recently. I'm not sure it's a beautiful question, but it fascinated me. Somebody said, "Which would you prefer, to write something that was so right and so clear that everybody thereafter just accepted it, took it for granted, and as a result in twenty years nobody would ever bother mentioning your name again, because it had entered into culture? Or would you rather be like Kant and write a book which was so obscure that you'd be immortal because it would be studied and studied and studied for centuries?" One has to face the fact that the cost of the first course is oblivion, however honorable. My answer, but only after a little soul-searching, was that I would prefer the former.

**GOULD:** But, Dan, you could steer it in such a way that you gain an eponym out of it, so it becomes Dennett's Law.

**DENNETT:** You hope for that. Philosophers never get that sort of glory, though.

*Well, what kind of day has it been, this little meeting? Disappointing? Fascinating? Illuminating?*

**SACKS:** I feel we've only just started. But perhaps that's a feeling one needs to have in life, that one has just started.

**TOULMIN:** I just came from some very exciting meetings in the last four days, and I was thinking, first of all, that the people there were mostly young. And a lot of them were women. This was somehow lacking here.

*What would the situation have been like if there had been women here?*

**DYSON:** I think we would have had livelier talk.

**SACKS:** I had a day of reading yesterday. I had a big packet of all of your books, and it gave me, amongst other things, a perhaps needed sense, which I don't too often have, of contemporaries. But when I was reading, and again today, I suddenly got this feeling of us as contemporaries sort of encountering the end of the twentieth century in our different ways. All of us in our different ways. All of us in our different ways have some sense that the end of modernity or modernism is in sight, and perhaps we feel some need to reach back to before Galilio or to the pre-Socratics or whatever. We're probably all in a sense solitary people with solo lives. So it's been rather exciting and unusual having the sense of contemporaneity and parallelism.

**TOULMIN:** But it's difficult in this situation to feel as unbuttoned as all of us presumably did in the solo phase of the operation. Each of us was then free to range off and ramble after anything, but inevitably there's a certain minimal professional constraint involved in having to say things in front of colleagues who have their own good reasons, quite different from one's own, to want to leap in and qualify what you've said.

**SHELDRAKE:** I think it was very nice to have the space and the time, the whole day, abstracted artificially from the rest of one's normal concerns, just to talk. I don't usually sit around a table all day just talking, with an endless supply of food and drink. It's a real symposium in that sense, and I've really enjoyed it.

**GOULD:** When Wim came and interviewed me, I accused him of being a hopeless romantic. I would reinforce that accusation. In a sense your hope was that by getting a group of people together who are, in false modesty, reasonably competent or at least noticed in what we do, the meaning of life or something deep and profound would emerge. I'm not sure it has. But then, that's what conversation is. It has been a wonderful conversation.

**DENNETT:** And tonight as we lie in our beds, the conversations will get better and better.

**GOULD:** Yeah, they're remembered in retrospect. Think of the history of quotation, for example. Almost no major pithy quotation is true. The great deathbed quotes were never said. The great battlefield quotes were never said in quite that way. They're all improved later. It's the same when you remember the snippets of a conversation.

*What I'm afraid of is that once we sit down for dinner in a restaurant around here, then the real thing will happen.*

**GOULD:** Wim, you're a romantic. This *is* the real thing.